FURTHER PRAISE FOR *FAULT LINES*

"In their new book, *Fault Lines*, [Kevin M.] Kruse and [Julian E.] Zelizer do an admirable job of creating a narrative out of the chaotic events of the recent past according to the themes of crisis, consolidation, and polarization. Using the post-Vietnam crisis of legitimacy as their jumping-off point, the authors trace the country's current divisive state through various periods of cultural fragmentation. . . . Kruse and Zelizer have composed the standard work for those teaching courses on the recent American past and the forces of polarization that have produced our contemporary divided public."

—L. Benjamin Rolsky, *Los Angeles Review of Books*

"*Fault Lines* is an excellent history of U.S. political dysfunction. . . . A sharp summation of how we moved from post–New Deal liberalism to an increasingly hard-right philosophy, culminating with Donald Trump. . . . If *Fault Lines* doesn't provide easy answers to our current dilemma, its clear-eyed, pin-sharp overview is a necessary map of how we got here."

—Michaelangelo Matos, *Rolling Stone*

"Kevin M. Kruse and Julian E. Zelizer's *Fault Lines* grafts a geologic metaphor onto three divisive threats to our democracy as suggested by Barack Obama in his January 2017 farewell address—economic, racial and political—while adding a fourth, gender and sexuality. . . . Kruse and Zelizer argue for Americans to build bridges 'that can bring us closer together' . . . they are also refreshingly frank."

—Eric Wakin, *New York Times Book Review*

"*Fault Lines* is a brilliantly written and urgently needed account of the last half century of American history, decades during which, as Kruse and Zelizer argue, Americans abandoned a search for common ground in favor of a political culture of endless, vicious, and—very often—mindless division. A gripping and troubling account of the origins of our turbulent, desperate times."

—Jill Lepore, author of *These Truths: A History of the United States*

"Kevin M. Kruse and Julian E. Zelizer's *Fault Lines* is a brilliant primer for understanding the troubling precedents for today's mass American political dysfunction. Both historians are deeply informed and surefooted thinkers. A must-read foundational work for our time!"

—Douglas Brinkley, history commentator for CNN, contributing editor to *Vanity Fair* and *American Heritage*, and author of *Cronkite*

"*Fault Lines* is a stunning work of the history of our present. An antidote to fake news and historical propaganda. In the age of Trump, Kruse and Zelizer's book sets the record straight. Every major cultural and political division over the past four decades comes to life in these pages, and in the telling we are confronted with the country we have been and the country we might become."

—Khalil Gibran Muhammad, professor of history, race, and public policy at Harvard Kennedy School and author of *The Condemnation of Blackness: Race, Crime, and the Making of Modern Urban America*

"*Fault Lines* is a must-read. Kruse and Zelizer have taken the fragmented histories of a polarized, divided nation and masterfully woven those threads into a tapestry that allows us to see not only what divides but what unites, and that the choice is ours."   —Carol Anderson, Charles Howard Candler professor of African American Studies at Emory University and author of *White Rage* and *One Person, No Vote*

"A forcefully argued analysis of the rifts that divide us and a lively, wide-ranging chronicle of the nation's odyssey from Nixon to Trump."

—Bruce J. Schulman, William E. Huntington Professor of History at Boston University and author of *The Seventies: The Great Shift in American Culture, Society, and Politics*

"For Kevin M. Kruse and Julian E. Zelizer, Donald Trump is not some singular figure. He is 'the result of trends decades in the making.' Sober, clearly written, and profoundly insightful. This is a must read for anyone who wants to understand the forces of the last half century that have brought the country to the brink of disaster."

—Eddie S. Glaude Jr., James S. McDonnell Distinguished University Professor at Princeton University and author of *Democracy in Black: How Race Still Enslaves the American Soul*

"With commanding knowledge and an eye for the telling detail, Kruse and Zelizer address the pressing historical question of how we arrived in today's polarized America. The answer, they show, is not simple, but they explain its various dimensions in a cogent and fair-minded fashion. A splendid book."

—Fredrik Logevall, professor of history and international affairs at Harvard University and author of *Embers of War: The Fall of an Empire and the Making of America's Vietnam*

"*Fault Lines* is Kruse and Zelizer at their very best, deftly guiding us through four decades of polarized politics, economic disruption, and cultural transformation in a lively and moving historical narrative. An indispensable resource for understanding America's recent past, contextualizing its fractious present, and healing its divisions in the future."

—Margaret O'Mara, professor of history at University of
Washington and author of *Pivotal Tuesdays: Four Elections
That Shaped the Twentieth Century*

"In this sweeping, readable account of America's recent past, Kruse and Zelizer powerfully connect politicized evangelicalism to the seemingly endless culture wars, the rise of deregulation and free-market economics to deepening inequality, and the corrosive effects of the 24-7 news cycle and the internet to partisan, religious, racial, and sexual divisions to show how we have become a bitterly polarized nation. This is an indispensable history of our time."

—Thomas J. Sugrue, professor of social and cultural analysis and
history at New York University and author of *Sweet Land of Liberty:
The Forgotten Struggle for Civil Rights in the North*

"*Fault Lines* provides a crisply written and insightful history of the political twists and turns of recent American history. Kruse and Zelizer chart the profound transformations in media, culture, and the economy, providing readers with a critical framework for thinking about the present dilemmas the country faces." —Kim Phillips-Fein, associate professor in the Gallatin School
at New York University and author of *Fear City: New York's
Fiscal Crisis and the Rise of Austerity Politics*

"A concise, riveting, and carefully argued chronicle of the last four decades of American history. . . . This highly readable, compelling book should be required reading for all Americans of voting age." —*Library Journal*, starred review

"[Kruse and Zelizer's] study showcases innovative approaches to the major—mostly domestic—events of the recent American past, while providing ample historical grounding for comprehending the nation's current state of division and despair. . . . [They] write their eminently readable book in a single, clear voice. . . . Its timeliness and valuable insights will ensure that it will receive a wide readership outside of upper-level college history courses."

—Zachary J. Lechner, *PopMatters*

"[*Fault Lines*] is a readable, well-paced history that depicts in chronological order major events of the [last] four decades, including the AIDS epidemic, the Iran-Contra affair, the rise of the Tea Party, and the passage of the Affordable Care Act. . . . [Kruse and Zelizer's] analysis is thoughtful and credible."   —*Publishers Weekly*

"This is a book for those who wonder, to quote new wave pioneers, the Talking Heads, 'Well, how did I get here?' . . . A valuable road map for readers seeking to understand why the U.S. is the way it is and ends with the hopeful message that the wear-and-tear inflicted on the country has inspired new institutions before and may do so again."   —*Booklist*

"[Written] in a clear, lively style. . . . [A] readable, comprehensive history of the political and cultural trends that continue to erode any sense of American national unity."   —*Kirkus Reviews*

"*Fault Lines* gives brilliant context to help us understand how Americans have become so fragmented and rigid in our beliefs."
                                                            —Deborah Mason, *BookPage*

"[Kruse and Zelizer] skillfully navigate the recent American past, explaining the developments that have polarized our citizenry. . . . This is a smart history geared to wide audiences. . . . *Fault Lines* tells a lively story with fairness and insight, providing some order amidst our chaos. It's a perspective we need."
                                        —Aram Goudsouzian of University of Memphis, *Chapter 16*

"[Kruse and Zelizer] go where many other historians have feared to tread, presenting a multileveled view of contemporary America starting in 1974. . . . Hats off to these adventuresome historians who have fashioned a rip-roaring account of our divided nation."
                                        —Frederic and Mary Ann Brussat, *Spirituality and Practice*

FAULT LINES

BOOKS BY KEVIN M. KRUSE

ONE NATION UNDER GOD:
HOW CORPORATE AMERICA INVENTED CHRISTIAN AMERICA

WHITE FLIGHT:
ATLANTA AND THE MAKING OF MODERN CONSERVATISM

BOOKS BY JULIAN E. ZELIZER

THE FIERCE URGENCY OF NOW:
LYNDON JOHNSON, CONGRESS, AND THE
BATTLE FOR THE GREAT SOCIETY

ARSENAL OF DEMOCRACY:
THE POLITICS OF NATIONAL SECURITY FROM
WORLD WAR II TO THE WAR ON TERRORISM

Fault Lines

A HISTORY OF THE UNITED STATES SINCE 1974

Kevin M. Kruse and
Julian E. Zelizer

W. W. NORTON & COMPANY
Independent Publishers Since 1923

For information about permission to reproduce selections from this book, write to
Permissions, W. W. Norton & Company, Inc., 500 Fifth Avenue, New York, NY 10110

For information about special discounts for bulk purchases, please contact
W. W. Norton Special Sales at specialsales@wwnorton.com or 800-233-4830

Manufacturing by LSC Communications, Harrisonburg
Book design by Lovedog Studio
Production manager: Julia Druskin

Library of Congress Cataloging-in-Publication Data

Names: Kruse, Kevin Michael, 1972– author. | Zelizer, Julian E., author.
Title: Fault lines : a history of the United States since 1974 / Kevin M. Kruse and
  Julian E. Zelizer.
Description: First edition. | New York : W. W. Norton & Company, [2019] | Includes
  bibliographical references and index.
Identifiers: LCCN 2018035645 | ISBN 9780393088663 (hardcover)
Subjects: LCSH: United States—History—1969– | United States—Politics and
  government—1945–1989. | United States—Politics and government—1989– |
  United States—Social conditions—1980– | Polarization (Social sciences)—United
  States—History. | Social change—United States—History. | Social conflict—
  United States—History.
Classification: LCC E839 .K78 2019 | DDC 973.92—dc23
LC record available at https://lccn.loc.gov/2018035645

ISBN 978-0-393-35770-7 pbk.

W. W. Norton & Company, Inc., 500 Fifth Avenue, New York, N.Y. 10110
www.wwnorton.com

W. W. Norton & Company Ltd., 15 Carlisle Street, London W1D 3BS

1 2 3 4 5 6 7 8 9 0

To our families
for all their support, encouragement, and love

CONTENTS

Fault Lines

Introduction

WHEN PRESIDENT BARACK OBAMA DELIVERED HIS FARE-
well address to the nation in January 2017, much of the country still
seemed in shock over the election two months before. In one of the
most surprising results in American political history, former secretary
of state Hillary Clinton, an experienced public servant with a lengthy
resume, had lost the presidential race to real estate developer and reality television star Donald J. Trump. Defying the polls and the pundits, the political novice had pulled off a stunning upset. In a sign of
the unlikely nature of his win, Trump pieced together an improbable
patchwork of states to secure his victory in the electoral college, even
though he lost the popular vote by a margin of nearly three million ballots nationwide.

To many observers, Trump's stunning victory revealed a nation deeply
divided. More troubling, the president-elect had come to power largely by
widening those divisions. In a bruising bare-knuckle campaign, he had
thrown aside the traditional niceties of American politics and repeatedly
taunted both his own party rivals in the race for the Republican nomination and then his general election opponent as well. Most ominously,
Trump had singled out large segments of American society for attack.
He characterized Mexican immigrants as rapists and murderers and proposed barring Muslims from entering the country; he mocked a disabled
reporter in a campaign appearance and was even caught on tape brag-
ging about sexually assaulting women. Aside from the standard election-
night rhetoric about uniting the nation, the incoming president showed
little inclination to bring the country together. With control of the White
House, both houses of Congress, and thirty-three state governor's man-
sions, the Republican Party now had the most dominant presence in

American politics since just before the Great Depression. As a result, the president-elect and his allies saw little need to reach out to the opposition party in any effort to find common ground.

Accordingly, in his farewell address, President Obama felt forced to address the tension himself. In keeping with past practices, the departing chief executive spoke about the many accomplishments of his administration. Refusing to abandon the hopes that he had expressed in his famous keynote speech to the 2004 Democratic National Convention, Obama listed the many ways in which the basic foundation of the country remained strong and, in areas like the overall economy, stronger than it had been before.

Yet, Obama warned, America's democracy faced a number of serious threats. The first, he noted, was the growing economic inequality that separated the rich from the poor and left the middle class in a state of insecure anxiety. He pointed in particular to "the laid off factory worker, the waitress or health care worker who's just barely getting by and struggling to pay the bills. Convinced that the game is fixed against them, that their government only serves the interests of the powerful. That's a recipe for more cynicism and polarization in our politics."

The second threat to democracy, racial division, was more difficult for Obama to address. His election as the first African American president had initially raised hopes about the dawn of a "postracial America." Obama's ascendancy, one observer insisted, had been "a seismic event" that sent the troubled history of race relations "crashing into apparent obsolescence." But racial divisions—broadly defined and deeply rooted in the nation's history—had never really gone away. Racial minorities still lived in a country in which many key institutions didn't afford the same benefits to them that they did to whites. The criminal justice system, in particular, seemed to have pronounced biases. Even though the previous years had seen a steady stream of videos showing unarmed African Americans being killed by police officers in suspect circumstances, much of the nation still refused to recognize the problem, much less show a willingness to confront it.[1]

The third threat to democracy, Obama noted, was political. The deep degree of partisan polarization had been painstakingly clear throughout the 2016 presidential election. The distance between the two major parties—between an imagined Republican "red America" and a Democratic "blue America"—had grown so pronounced that it consumed most talk among the nation's pundits and scholars. Polarization, the hardening of partisan loyalties and the refusal to compromise, not only damaged the health of the polity, the departing president warned, but also prevented the government from handling pressing issues like climate change.

Obama's farewell address touched on trends that had been long in the making, not just through his presidency, but for decades before him. In many ways, these three basic "fault lines" of division—the economic, racial, and political lines Obama outlined, plus a fourth line on gender and sexuality—had always been part of the national experience. For much of the twentieth century, however, strong centripetal forces pushed back against these traditional sources of discord and tension. A robust federal government, a thriving middle-class economy, and a powerful union movement had each, in its own significant way, ameliorated these sources of division. But the turbulent decade of the 1960s caused the common ground of the mid-twentieth century to crumble beneath Americans' feet. Rather than seek to find new sources of agreement, the nation reconstituted itself in the 1970s and the decades that followed in ways that augmented and institutionalized these lines of division. Believing consensus was beyond reach, Americans sought to guarantee that different voices could be heard and divergent views could be seen. Abandoning the search for common ground in political and economic life, they increasingly valued competition and even conflict. From the 1970s on, the United States would seem less and less united with each passing decade.

WHILE THESE FAULT LINES in America were important, so too were the lines Americans were fed about who was at fault. The media became increasingly fractured during these decades, changing from a fairly rigid industry dominated by three television networks and a handful of prominent newspapers to a more cluttered, chaotic landscape. The realm of what might be counted as "media" was soon populated by practitioners who ranged from professional reporters to a growing rank of partisan pundits and, with the rise of the internet, ordinary Americans who used platforms like Facebook and Twitter to break (or fake) news of their own. The somewhat forced "consensus" of the postwar era gave way to chaos, in which virtually every slice of the American populace found an outlet that was willing to reflect and refract the news in ways that confirmed and deepened their own existing biases.

Americans received Obama's farewell address, for instance, over separate channels. Most did not hear it live and direct, as they would have in the heyday of network television, but digested it through sensational headlines and selected online clips. They received the speech not as it was intended, but according to their own intent, on their own terms and on their own time. Like all other news in their lives, it was translated through their preferred partisan outlets and transmitted directly to their own personal devices. In the new era, messengers mattered as much as the message, if not more.

For liberals, coverage of the Democrat's departure was sentimental and celebratory. On Twitter, for instance, those who "followed" the president's official account first saw him preview the speech, noting his plans to discuss "the remarkable progress that you made possible these past 8 years." Hours before the address, the left-leaning cable news channel MSNBC featured a countdown clock in the corner, ticking off the seconds until the speech with an image of a grinning Obama in the corner. Liberal outlets online, such as the *Huffington Post*, covered the speech itself uncritically, noting that the president had offered the nation a "heartfelt farewell." More than that, several posts on the site humanized the drama, noting how "Obama teared up as he spoke about his 'best friend,' first lady Michelle Obama." The site ran a series of lighthearted tweets insisting that even *animals* were in mourning over his departure: "No One Is Sadder About Barack Obama Leaving Office Than These Pets."[2]

Those on the right, however, framed the speech in a rather different way. At the conservative media giant Fox News, for instance, the network's star host Sean Hannity said that Obama's address "can't hide a disastrous legacy," while contributor Laura Ingraham placed blame for all the divisions Obama described directly at the president's own feet. "He has laid waste to our productivity, to this idea of a vibrant economy, to a foreign policy that has some semblance of pragmatism. He's laid waste to all of that. We have more racial division in the country." (Even the emotion Obama showed, the two asserted, was little more than contrived "crocodile tears.") Meanwhile, the Alt Right web-site Breitbart.com, whose publisher Steve Bannon led the Trump cam-paign to its triumph, offered similar criticisms of "Obama's Farewell Campaign Speech": "Obama admitted during his speech that the idea of 'post racial America' was never realistic," one piece noted, "but said that race relations were better than they were 10, 20, 30 years ago— conveniently leaving out the eight years of his presidency." (They, too, mocked the president's tears, with the Breitbart Daily News satellite radio program deriding the "hour-long, self-congratulatory, snooze fest" from the "Commander-in-Handkerchief.")[3]

HOW DID WE COME to this? How did the United States fall into such a state of division and discord? While some observers try to pin-point "the" single source of division in America today, we find that there were multiple forces transforming the nation in these decades. That is the story of this book.

The sources of division are not entirely obvious. Indeed, as we will show, during the past four decades, the country actually seemed to be coming together in some significant ways. In the marketplace, in the spread of social norms and in the propagation of popular culture, dispa-rate parts of the nation were becoming less and less dissimilar. For all the talk of a deeply divided nation, pollsters found that many issues that were contentious in the political arena, such as LGBTQ rights and women's rights, were much less so outside of the confines of Washington, DC.

That said, the forces of division were persistent and powerful, often rooted in institutional forces that moved the nation in destructive direc-tions. The rebellions and discord of the 1960s led to widespread disillu-sionment and cynicism about the viability, or even the value, of national consensus and unity. As the country moved on from the tumultuous decade, national leaders rebuilt institutions that privileged division, competing views, and fragmentation.[4] Shifts in the national economy resulted in the steady disappearance of the kinds of jobs and security that many working-class and middle-class Americans had come to take for granted. The failure to enact public policy that addressed institu-tional racism and ethnic pluralism ensured that the social tensions that persisted even after the civil rights movement of the 1960s only became more aggravated. Fundamental changes in the political process combined with an aggressive new conservative movement that pushed the GOP sharply to the right to erode the political center in Washington. The victories of the conservative movement were often incomplete. The ideas and institutions of liberalism proved to be more durable than the Right imagined. Fueled by what they had gained but frustrated by how much further they had to go, conservatives in politics and media drove themselves, and the nation, into an ongoing and ever-expanding partisan clash. The decline and demise of the Cold War removed one of the last sources of consensus in American life, allowing for polarization and partisanship to reach new depths. The fracturing of our politics was amplified by a fragmented partisan media, to be sure, but its power was also bolstered by an increasingly polarized population.

With a wide-angle lens, this book traces the political, economic, racial, and sexual divisions in modern America, but also the cultural and technological changes that confronted and contorted the country along the way. Following these fault lines, in both senses of the term, we examine the history of our divided America.

CHAPTER 1

A Crisis of Legitimacy

TRUST IN GOVERNMENT WAS THE FIRST THING TO GO.

Washington had loomed large in the previous decades, guiding the nation through crises like the Great Depression, World War II, and the early decades of the Cold War too. Its vision of a unifying "American way of life" offered a powerful countervailing force to other lines of division—race, religion, region, inequality, and gender—that might otherwise have torn the country apart.

But over the course of the chaotic 1960s, the basic political consensus that had held Americans together started to come undone as those fault lines continued to fracture. Grassroots social movements, especially the struggles for civil rights and feminism, had exposed racial and gender inequalities at the very foundations of American government at home. The growing movement against the war in Vietnam, meanwhile, shattered the so-called "Cold War consensus," the notion that the spread of Communism must be challenged all around the globe, which had forged a united front in foreign affairs. During the 1970s, in the wake of Vietnam and Watergate, the soundness of "the establishment" suddenly seemed in doubt. President Lyndon Johnson had left the White House with his credibility shattered by the war abroad, and then President Richard Nixon resigned in disgrace over scandal at home. In the aftermath, Americans wondered if the entire nation was following its presidents to ruin.

Watergate

Initially, the scandal seemed to involve little more than a bungled burglary at the Watergate Complex in Washington, DC. But the June 1972 break-in at the Democratic National Committee's headquarters proved to be just the beginning. Two local reporters for the *Washington Post*, Bob Woodward and Carl Bernstein, dug into the story, soon discovering that the five burglars had surprisingly deep connections to both Nixon's Committee to Re-Elect the President (CREEP) and the Central Intelligence Agency (CIA). During their trial before the US District Court, James McCord, one of the burglars and chief of security for CREEP, sent a letter to Judge John J. Sirica, indicating that other high-ranking officials in the Nixon campaign had been involved too. As the burglars' trials concluded in March 1973, Judge Sirica surmised that there must have been serious connections between the burglars and the presidential campaign. Over the next months, investigations into those ties only intensified. In May 1973, Attorney General Elliot Richardson appointed a special prosecutor, Archibald Cox, to investigate the president's men, while a new Senate select committee began holding its own televised hearings in Congress.

Over the summer of 1973, the various investigations revealed that President Nixon had abused his executive authority in alarming ways. While it was initially unclear what role the president played personally in the break-in, White House aide Alexander Butterfield revealed in July 1973 that the president had tape-recorded all Oval Office conversations. As the press and the public called for the release of the tapes, Nixon refused, insisting that presidents had the right to withhold information under certain circumstances. Undeterred, the special prosecutor pressed on. In October 1973, the president lashed out, demanding that the attorney general fire Cox. Richardson not only refused; he resigned in protest. When the deputy attorney general refused the presidential order as well, he too was pushed out. Solicitor General Robert Bork, third in line at Justice, finally did the president's bidding. For all the drama, the bloodletting of the so-called "Saturday Night Massacre" did nothing to stop the release of the tapes. In July 1974, in the aptly titled case of *The United States v. Richard Nixon*, the Supreme Court ruled that "executive privilege"—the doctrine that Nixon claimed protected the tapes from public release—did not apply in the investigation of criminal matters like the Watergate break-in. The president had to release the recordings. While the tapes provided some answers, they ultimately raised many more questions. Some had some suspicious erasures, including an eighteen-and-a-half-minute gap in a recording made on a key day in the crisis. Even with that part erased, there was still more than enough evidence to prove convincingly that the president had attempted to obstruct justice in the Watergate investigation.

As the details of the scandal came to light, Americans watched in shock. The televised hearings before Congress, conducted with equal measures of prosecutorial professionalism and folksy charm by North Carolina's Democratic senator Sam Ervin Jr., brought the drama directly into their living rooms. The nightly news and morning papers, building on each other's reporting and amplifying their findings, combined to form a single voice. Day after day, in a steady drumbeat of dramatic headlines, they revealed the secrets of what the president and his men had done behind closed doors, all in the pursuit of power. The nation was stunned to hear all manner of criminal activity—bribery, burglary, wiretapping, intimidation, etc.—casually discussed as business-as-usual inside the Oval Office. Among other things, Americans learned that White House operatives had broken into the office of a private psychiatrist, hoping to discredit Daniel Ellsberg, a former national security staffer who had released the "Pentagon Papers," secret documents that chronicled the flawed origins and poor planning of the Vietnam War. As the incriminating evidence mounted, the House Judiciary Committee moved to impeach Nixon. When his last remaining allies made it clear that the rest of the full House would follow suit in impeaching the president and the Senate would then vote to convict, the president finally resigned in disgrace on August 9, 1974.

Stunning as it was, the resignation of the president initially seemed to resolve the crisis. Vice President Gerald Ford called the decision a "selfless and courageous act" that would allow the nation to focus on the real problems it faced. *New York Times* columnist Anthony Lewis claimed the episode proved the political system worked, noting that the outcome of the impeachment process demonstrated to Americans that a president "may not turn the regular course of justice aside for the sake of his friends or his own political interest. Nor may he use his great power to violate the constitutional rights of individuals—by invading their privacy without legal cause, for example, or by punishing them for their politics." Writing for the *Washington Post*, columnist Joseph Kraft said that Nixon had actually brought the country together "in relief at the resignation of the leader who betrayed every value and every friend in a desperate effort to save his own skin." After outlining the many accomplishments of Nixon's presidency, Kraft wrote of a leader who tragically lost his way: "Out of pride and sycophancy there was born a monstrous fraud. Contempt for others festered the belief that lies and tricks would work even as mounting evidence showed the truth would out. In the end, Mr. Nixon was alone, divorced from friends and reality in a psychic bunker of his own making." The public, it seemed, agreed with the politicians and the press that Nixon had been sufficiently humbled. According to polls taken soon after his resignation, 79 percent of Americans thought the president had done the right thing by stepping down; a majority believed that there was now no need for further criminal investigations.[1]

Distrusting Government

If there was a moment when elected officials hoped that Nixon's resignation might restore trust in government, it vanished quickly. Never elected to national office, President Gerald Ford had ridden a wave of resignations to the top. In October 1973, Vice President Spiro Agnew, long dogged by charges of extortion, bribery, and conspiracy, pleaded no contest to lesser charges of tax evasion and resigned in disgrace. Two months later, the Senate confirmed Ford, a congressman from Grand Rapids, Michigan, who served as House minority leader, to be the new vice president. Only eight months after that, Ford found himself promoted again, to the presidency. The nation Ford now sought to govern was reeling from not just the resignations of both the president and vice president in less than a year's time, but the resulting revelations about the depths of corruption throughout the executive branch.

After Watergate, both parties agreed: the nation needed to heal. "Our long national nightmare is over," Ford promised in his first words as president. He urged his countrymen to put the past behind them and move forward with confidence: "As we bind up the internal wounds of Watergate, more painful and more poisonous than those of foreign wars, let us restore the golden rule to our political process, and let brotherly love purge our hearts of suspicion and hate." But Ford believed that true healing would require more than words. And so, on September 8, 1974, precisely a month after Nixon announced his decision to resign, Ford announced on television that he was issuing a blanket pardon to him for any crimes he might have committed while in office. Speculating about the impact of further investigations, the new president imagined the worst. "During this long period of delay and potential litigation," he surmised, "ugly passions would again be aroused, our people would again be polarized in their opinions, and the credibility of our free institutions of government would again be challenged at home and abroad." Ford pardoned Nixon, he said, to spare the nation.[2]

Ford hoped his announcement would bring calm to the country, but it had the opposite effect. No longer seen as an accidental president who could serve as a caretaker and guide the nation to recovery, Ford now seemed implicated in the crimes and their cover-up. Some Americans speculated openly that Ford's pardon had been the result of a corrupt bargain: that he had been offered the vice presidency on the condition that he would pardon Nixon if the time ever came. Ford quickly became a target of popular outrage. Protesters stood outside the White House holding a long sheet with the words "PROMISE ME PARDON AND I'LL MAKE YOU PRESIDENT," while one even made it into a presidential appearance in Pittsburgh to shout "Jail Ford! Jail Ford!"[3] Newspaper columnists and television reporters joined the chorus denouncing him. "He said he was 'healing the country,'" wrote one *Washington Post* columnist. "What he was doing was a favor to an old friend while simultaneously trying to sink a nasty situation well before his own re-election campaign."[4] The editors of *The New Yorker* agreed. "The pardon may be the final blow to [Americans'] faith in America. After the cheering revival of the public's spirits in the first month of the Ford Administration, there is suddenly gloom everywhere—a compound of shattered hopes, cynicism, despair about the future, and helplessness."[5] Support for the new president evaporated, with his approval ratings plummeting from an impressive 71 percent after taking office in August 1974 down to just 42 percent by the end of the year, and still falling. In the end, Ford would experience the steepest drop in presidential approval since Gallup started keeping track.[6]

Not all Americans were incensed at Ford's pardon, however. While polls showed that many Republicans had reluctantly come to accept that Nixon had in fact committed crimes in office and deserved his fate, some conservatives saw the Watergate scandal through a different lens. They thought Nixon was far from perfect, but believed the Watergate scandal was simply part of an ongoing series of partisan attacks against the Republican Party that emanated from several corners of the so-called "liberal establishment," especially the universities, the media, and Congress, which was controlled by the Democratic Party. According to one of his colleagues, Dick Cheney, then the deputy chief of staff for Ford, argued that the entire Watergate scandal was "just a political ploy by the president's enemies."[7] Already suspicious, such conservatives believed that the Democratic reaction to the presidential pardon proved that their political opponents had little interest in rebuilding national unity.

As the nation reacted to Watergate and the pardon controversy, other scandals accelerated Americans' loss of confidence in Washington. On October 7, 1974, for instance, the Washington Park Police stopped House Ways and Means Committee Chairman Wilbur Mills's speeding car near the Tidal Basin. One of the most powerful figures in Washington, the Arkansas Democrat had shaped national tax policy for decades and designed the Medicare and Medicaid programs of 1965. When the police pulled over the chairman's car, Annabelle Battistella, a stripper who performed locally as "Fanne Fox, the Argentine Firecracker," jumped out and began to splash around in the basin. Unfortunately for the chairman, a cameraman who was on the scene captured it all on film. The media soon reported not only that Battistella and the long-married Mills were having an affair but also that the chairman—publicly known for abstaining from the DC cocktail party circuit—was actually an alcoholic who was addicted to prescription pain pills.

Many politicians hoped that Watergate and Wilbur Mills were aberrations, idiosyncratic problems that could be waved away rather than signs of a serious, systemic crisis in American politics. In the midst of Watergate, proponents of electoral reforms had pushed forward legislation that aimed to diminish the power of money in politics and thereby remove a root cause of corruption. Accordingly, Congress passed legislation that set limits on campaign contributions and spending, established public financing for presidential elections (though not congressional races), and created an independent body called the Federal Election Commission to monitor campaigns. President Ford, still reeling from the public outrage over the pardon, reluctantly signed the bill on October 15, after being warned that refusing to do so would show he had "misread the lessons of Watergate." "There are certain periods in our nation's history," he said upon signing the measure, "when it becomes necessary to face up to certain unpleasant truths. We have passed through one of those periods. The unpleasant truth is that big money influence has come to play an unseemly role in our electoral process. . . . This bill will help to right that wrong."[8]

But campaign finance reform was not enough. In the wake of Watergate, the demands for a thorough overhaul of the federal government grew steadily stronger. While promises to "throw the bums out" have been a perennial of American politics, the new crusade for government reform ran much deeper than ever before. Riding the backlash over Nixon's resignation and Ford's pardon to the 1974 midterm elections, a new generation of Democrats ran confidently on a promise to clean up government. Candidates like Henry Waxman of California and Gary Hart of Colorado assured voters that they would pursue new ethics and transparency laws to open up the workings of government and subject politicians to more restrictions than ever before. On their watch, they promised, another Watergate would never happen. That fall, Democrats had major successes at the polls. They increased their majority in the House by 43 seats, for a total of 291, and their majority in the Senate by 3 more, for a total of 60.

The "Watergate Babies," as the new class of Democrats were known, entered office in January 1975 determined to change the status quo. "There is a mood of reform in the air on Capitol Hill," the watchdog organization Common Cause noted, and the new arrivals seemed intent on seizing the moment. A large number had won races in traditionally Republican districts and states where frustration with Watergate had created at least a temporary backlash against the GOP. They immediately shook up the status quo, enacting rules changes that made the political process more open and codified ethical principles for political behavior.[9] They gave special attention to the role of congressional committee chairmen, who had long enjoyed incredible power and independence, and succeeded in deposing several of them. Meanwhile, they strengthened the tools that could be used by congressional leaders to strip committee chairs of the autonomy they had enjoyed for so long.

While there were some small glimmers of hope in domestic politics, they were overshadowed by the dismal state of foreign affairs. For a brief moment in 1972 and 1973 it had seemed that Richard Nixon was on the cusp of introducing a new paradigm in foreign policy: détente. According to its supporters, détente had the potential to rebuild America's relationship to the world in the wake of Vietnam and create a new consensus for the United States that could bring together a sizable number of Democrats and Republicans. By signing the Strategic Arms Limitation Treaty (SALT) in 1972 and opening relations with China that same year, Nixon and National Security Advisor Henry Kissinger sought to ease tensions between the United States and the Communist superpowers, while still preserving America's hegemonic power. But the hopes for détente had been severely diminished, first when tensions in the Middle East sparked an oil embargo by Arab states in 1973, and then with Nixon's downfall. While détente retained support in the Ford administration, where Kissinger continued to serve, its potential to transform US foreign relations seemed much more precarious with Nixon gone.

Meanwhile, there was the ongoing turmoil in Southeast Asia. As the Vietnam War entered its death throes, Americans took stock of the incredible toll it had taken. More than 58,000 US soldiers had been killed in the decade-long conflict, with another 270,000 badly wounded, many of them permanently. The losses extended well beyond the death and disabling of soldiers, however, with America's economic strength and national unity suffering considerably, and its overall confidence crushed by its inability to exact a clear victory in Vietnam. The United States had begun orchestrating its gradual withdrawal from the conflict in 1973, but the final stages still came as a shock. In late April 1975, the last Americans left the country, and the South Vietnamese capital of Saigon swiftly fell to the nationalist forces of the North. In the final episodes of the "television war," Americans watched with horror as crowded helicopters scrambled to evacuate the last remaining military and civilian personnel in a panicked, frantic withdrawal.[10]

The embarrassments over American military power abroad coincided with a growing distrust of the nation's intelligence agencies at home. In 1975 and 1976, Democratic senator Frank Church of Idaho chaired hearings on the operations of the national security state that revealed the types of activities that the CIA had supported in its fight against Communism. With the media breathlessly relaying lurid details to a nation riveted by the televised proceedings, the Church Committee revealed assassination attempts against foreign politicians and incidents of spying on individuals living in the United States. In response, Congress passed new regulations that placed constraints on what national security officials could do and imposed more "sunshine" requirements that required disclosure and open hearings on formerly covert government agencies. Even with the new reforms, revelations from the hearings had further shaken Americans' confidence that government officials could be trusted to do the right thing on their own.

At the local level, meanwhile, countless examples reinforced the growing belief that public officials were ineffective across the board. In 1975, reports from New York described a city on the brink. An eleven-day wildcat strike by sanitation workers in early July had left streets overflowing with 70,000 tons of garbage piled on the sidewalks. As the city edged to the brink of bankruptcy, other municipal employees skipped work too. Cars gridlocked as traffic cops stayed home; basic health services for seniors and children shut down without workers. A reporter for the *Times* filed a bleak account: "With mounted policemen's horses tied up to park railings, trash piling up in plastic bags and gray barricades blocking off demonstrators from the surrounding park, the exterior of City Hall these days has a besieged air—almost a modern-day equivalent of Mont St. Michel during the Middle Ages."[11] In the popular imagination, New York was no longer a city of dreams, but a devastated landscape of rampant crime and corruption, crippling poverty, and urban decay. Its dystopian image was best illustrated in the popular film *Taxi Driver* (1976), which told the story of Travis Bickle, a mentally unstable Vietnam veteran driven to violent acts by the decadence and decay of the city around him. "All the animals come out at night," he narrates: "whores, skunk pussies, buggers, queens, fairies, dopers, junkies; sick, venal. Someday a real rain will come and wash all this scum off the streets."

As the financial crisis mounted, New York's governor Hugh Carey warned federal officials that New York City could end up defaulting on its debt. The governor struggled to obtain federal assistance from both the Democratic Congress and the Republican president. Ford, who was focused on attacking congressional spending and tackling rising inflation, informed New York officials that they needed to take stringent measures to get their house in order. Proposals included cutting the salaries of city workers and charging tuition at the city college, which had historically offered a free path for the city's residents to obtain a first-class education. "The people of this country will not be stampeded," Ford scolded. "They will not panic when a few desperate New York City officials and bankers try to scare New York's mortgage payments out of them."[12] The front page of the *New York Daily News* broadcast the response in a blunt headline, "Ford to City: Drop Dead."[13] Congress proved more receptive to the city's plight, however, and ultimately offered to provide some funds. The government of New York took drastic action itself, imposing severe budget cuts that curtailed government services and creating the Municipal Assistance Corporation, which allowed the city to lend money to itself to avert total catastrophe.

The city reached a crisis point on July 13, 1977, when New Yorkers suffered a massive blackout. When the city went dark on a scorching summer night at the start of a heat wave, chaos quickly ensued. More than a thousand acts of arson broke out across the five boroughs, and another 1,600 stores were looted. "We've seen our citizens subjected to violence, vandalism, theft and discomfort," the mayor reported. "The blackout has threatened our safety and has seriously impacted our economy. We've been needlessly subjected to a night of terror in many communities that have been wantonly looted and burned." After months of complaints about layoffs and pay freezes, the police showed little interest in going to work. The situation was worse in impoverished African American and Latino communities that were suffering upwards of 80 percent unemployment.[14] Even the "looters were being mugged," according to the *New York Post*.[15] To many, New York City increasingly seemed like a lost cause. It was now commonplace for popular films to depict the city's future as desolate. *The Warriors* (1979) showed the city's landscape ruled by ruthless teenage gangs, while *Escape from New York* (1981) predicted that the entire island of Manhattan would be handed over to criminals and become a godforsaken federal prison.

The dystopian image of New York in the 1970s reflected a growing regional division between the booming states of the South and Southwest—collectively known as "the Sunbelt"—and the rusting economies of the industrial Midwest and Northeast. States located between Michigan and New York, which had long been the heart of the national economy as well as the core of the Democratic coalition, suffered greatly as the industries that had sustained the region crumbled. Businesses moved to southern and western states, or even to other countries altogether, seeking places where unions did not exist and labor was therefore cheap. The firms remaining behind in the "Rust Belt" found they simply could not meet their bottom line and soon learned the federal government would not save them. "Like blacks, Hispanics, women and homosexuals, Northeasterners are an oppressed minority," one New Yorker complained. "We are only beginning to realize how badly the federal government discriminates against us."[16]

With the federal government seemingly unable to handle national or local problems, polls showed that public confidence in political institutions had plummeted. Trust in government fell from about 55 percent of those polled in 1972 to slightly over 30 percent in 1978.[17] The widespread sense of dissatisfaction was captured in Robert Altman's film *Nashville* (1975), which featured a never-seen presidential candidate, Hal Phillip Walker, only heard speaking angrily through a loudspeaker. His platform is largely a list of things he opposes. "In keeping with the country's dark mood," one reviewer noted, "he has little to say about what he is for." The leaders of government stand at the top of his hit list. "Who do you think is running Congress?" he blares through the loudspeaker in one scene. "Farmers? Engineers? Teachers? Businessmen? No, my friends. Congress is run by lawyers. A lawyer is trained for two things and two things only. To clarify—that's one. And to confuse—that's the other."[18]

Making matters even worse, the efforts to reform government were halting and difficult, and sometimes even reversed. The Supreme Court shocked supporters of campaign finance reform when it overturned a key component of the post-Watergate wave of reform legislation in the landmark case of *Buckley v. Valeo*. The court had taken a conservative turn in the early 1970s, with four new Nixon appointees signaling a stark change in direction from the liberal era of the Warren court. In its January 1976 ruling, the new court, now led by Chief Justice Warren Burger, asserted that congressional limits on campaign spending represented an unconstitutional violation of free speech. While the court said that it was legitimate for the government to require spending limits of presidential candidates who accepted federal funds, anything beyond that basic step violated the First Amendment. Notably, the decision also knocked down spending limits on wealthy individuals who paid for their own campaigns. The conservative editors of the *Wall Street Journal*, pleased with the decision, noted that "The United States Supreme Court has administered a semi-fatal blow to that malformed product of 'post-Watergate morality,' the 1974 Federal Election Campaign Act. . . . [T]he court was absolutely right in overthrowing the keystone of the law, a blatantly unconstitutional limit on campaign expenditures." Still, the editors were unhappy that so much of the law remained, fearing that "the remains of the law will probably act like the Frankenstein's monster it truly is. It will be awfully hard to kill, and the more you wound it, the more havoc it will wreak."[19]

There were, indeed, two significant results of the *Buckley* decision. First, since the ruling upheld many restrictions on campaign contributions from outsiders but struck down all restrictions on how much of his or her own money a political candidate could spend, it created a political climate in which very wealthy candidates would have a tremendous advantage over candidates without a personal fortune. Second, because the ruling allowed independent expenditures from groups unaffiliated with a candidate's campaign, it encouraged business leaders to take an active and direct role in politics themselves.

In the wake of the decision, businesses significantly increased their involvement in American politics. First, corporations expanded the number of lobbyists they employed to make their case to Congress. Between 1971 and 1982, the number of individual businesses with full-time registered lobbyists in Washington skyrocketed from 175 to 2,445. Meanwhile, individual industries and companies overcame their narrow interests and banded together in powerful umbrella lobbies, such as the Business Roundtable. Second, business leaders took on a more active role in Washington by forming their own political action committees, or PACs. The first PAC had been a creation of the labor movement in the 1940s and, for decades thereafter, PACs had been a key to the influence of labor unions in American politics while businesses shied away from them. In 1974, for instance, there were 201 labor PACs and just 89 business PACs. But with the *Buckley* decision, and its insistence on unlimited outside spending, business PACs boomed. In 1976, there were 433 business PACs. In 1978, there were 784; in 1980, there were 1,204. That year, the new business PACs contributed some $19 million to probusiness politicians.[20]

For some observers, the changes wrought by *Buckley* weren't simply a return to the days before Watergate; they instead heralded something even more troubling. As they saw it, the new rules that privileged wealthy candidates threatened democracy itself. "The combination of this law, this decision, and very expensive campaigns predictably provides an enormous electoral advantage to candidates of great personal wealth who can avoid the angst of fund-raising by their check writing skills," worried Mark Green in the *New York Times*. "Then does a House of Representatives become a House of Lords, as heirs and businessmen predominantly end up writing the laws that affect the rest of us."[21]

Pack Journalism

In the wake of Watergate, reporters continued to unearth stories of political corruption and incompetence. Importantly, the scandal and its coverage had helped launch a new era of investigative journalism. The previously unknown reporters Bob Woodward and Carl Bernstein had become overnight stars at the young ages of thirty-one and thirty, respectively. Their status as full-fledged celebrities only increased when their best-selling account of the scandal, *All the President's Men*, was made into a major film. Robert Redford and Dustin Hoffman, two of the most popular actors of the day, portrayed the pair and elevated them in the process. The reporters vainly tried to draw a line between their reality and the Hollywood version of their story. "We hope all the attention will be transferred to them," Bernstein said of the actors. "Let them do the dog and pony show. We're reporters." But the film, which was nominated for eight Academy Awards and won four, only served to build up the mythology around the celebrity reporters.[22]

The model set by Woodward and Bernstein revolutionized the world of reporting. "Suddenly, it's become glamorous, romantic, chic, respectable, even, to be a reporter," a longtime journalist marveled. "The two young men who broke the Watergate story have glorified the image of reporters and probably inspired legions of bright, honest people to enter" the field. And indeed, evidence showed a new surge of interest in reporting, especially from younger Americans who took Woodward and Bernstein as role models. "Applications to journalism schools are at an alltime high," *Time* noted in a cover story in the summer of 1974, "and many of the youngsters say that they want to be investigative reporters." Established journalists welcomed the attention and prestige that Woodward and Bernstein had brought to the profession, but many resented a new generation of writers who seemed more focused on fame and fortune than the painstaking drudgery of real reporting. "Editors' inboxes are filled with resumes and clippings from determined graduates looking for jobs," an editor at the *Los Angeles Times* complained. "It seems sometimes that the search is more for glamor than excellence and that the business of plain hard work gets lost somewhere among all the dreams and dreamers."[23]

Whatever the motivations of the new generation of investigative journalists, they soon made their presence felt. The path to becoming the next Woodward or Bernstein, many reporters assumed, lay in uncovering the next Watergate. In a sign of the original scandal's lingering impact on the profession, the "-gate" suffix quickly became a mainstay of political reporting. Only a month after Nixon's resignation, conservative *New York Times* columnist and former Nixon speechwriter William Safire wrote about the "Vietgate Solution," a rumored call for blanket amnesty for Watergate conspirators and Vietnam War draft dodgers. Newspapers that winter spread stories of a French scandal involving fraudulent bottles of Bordeaux under the name "Winegate," while a more serious influence-peddling scandal in 1976 involving the South Korean government and several members of Congress came to be known as "Koreagate." As such scandals with their echoes of Watergate continued to reverberate through the media, they served to deepen the sense that the original scandal was not an isolated incident, but rather the start of a new series that might never end.[24]

Despite the momentum behind investigative journalism, or perhaps because of it, the new trend quickly reached a crisis point. In the summer of 1976, Don Bolles, a reporter for the *Arizona Republic* who was probing political corruption and organized crime in the state, was killed in a car bomb explosion. A few months later, a team of journalists from twenty different newspapers banded together under the banner of a new organization called Investigative Reporters and Editors to continue Bolles's investigation. In a new development, this disparate group of journalists agreed to research, write, and publish their findings as a collective force, producing a series of fifty articles on Arizona corruption that were published in newspapers across the country. Notably, the most prestigious newspapers of the era—the *Washington Post,* the *New York Times,* the *Los Angeles Times,* and the *San Francisco Chronicle*—refused to take part in the project and then sharply criticized the results. "It is a venture in pack journalism," the *Post*'s ombudsman Charles Seib complained, "with overtones of revenge, subsidization and an unhealthy abandonment of competition." Defenders of the new trend pushed back, noting that smaller papers' pooling their resources on one occasion didn't suggest a lack of competition; the overwhelming influence of a few major papers like the *Post* did.[25]

For smaller newspapers and upstart magazines, investigative journalism represented a way to break through the monopoly held by the major newspapers. *New Times,* a magazine founded in 1972, originally showcased the stars of what Tom Wolfe called "new journalism," a style of reporting that abandoned old standards of objectivity for more subjective perspectives and dramatic literary styles. Tapping into the public's renewed interest in investigative journalism, *New Times* reached new heights of popularity, with circulation peaking at 350,000 within a few years. But the same scandal-driven coverage that initially drew readers in soon served to drive them away. Subscriptions plummeted, and the increasingly unpopular magazine announced in 1978 that it was shutting down for good. "We bore readers the bad news," one *New Times* editor reflected, "and they slew the messenger." Others in the media drew lessons from the publication's rise and fall. "It is true that on some days the sins, crimes and lapses of man are too much to read about," columnist Colman McCarthy noted in the *Washington Post*. "The news is so heavy that picking up the paper is risking a hernia of the mind. If Ford's Pintos or Firestone's radials don't get us, cancer-causing hamburgers or saccharin will. If it isn't another congressman convicted of bribery, it's another corporation."[26]

While the topics of investigative journalism weighed it down, so too did the tempo of newspapers. Concern for getting a story right still took precedence over getting a story first, and as a result newspapers worked at a slow, methodical pace. Editors and publishers retained tight control over stories that appeared in their pages, especially when they involved politically explosive topics that might generate lawsuits from powerful individuals or even backlash from readers. Accordingly, each piece had to be vetted several times, with one source willing to go on the record to supplement any anonymous ones in the background. In television, the pace was much quicker, though still measured. Typically, the news day at TV networks began with the producers of the nightly news programs, which aired for a half hour in the dinner hour, planning out possible stories with their bureau chiefs. Over the course of the day, bureaus across America and overseas would then work up their stories, returning together for a meeting in the afternoon. (In the meantime, politicians and policy makers had a chance to react to the pending news and prepare themselves for the public revelations to come.) When the producers and anchormen decided on the main stories for the evening, staffs went to work polishing the final script and video before going on air live that evening. The vetting process still occurred, but the usual weeks and months that took place in print journalism had now been compressed to days, if not hours.

The news business was compressed on television in another sense as well, as the three major television networks—ABC, NBC, and CBS—held an effective monopoly that was much more powerful and persuasive than anything the major-market newspapers had ever enjoyed. Unlike the print world, where there was theoretically a chance for competition from new upstarts, television networks had a built-in advantage in terms of basic infrastructure. The networks sent their signal to local affiliate stations through underground landlines controlled by the telephone giant AT&T, which by arrangement worked to keep barriers for new networks impossibly high as to limit competition. Corporate control of the television networks, critics complained, affected not just the reach of television news but also its content. "We have a Big Three in New York just as we have a Big Three in Detroit," argued *Rolling Stone* editor Jann Wenner in December 1976. "And what has happened to news is no different from what has happened to cars: We are offered products that are essentially similar, inefficient, and unresponsive to the public interest." Because the three major networks were all seeking "the same audience," he continued, they drove their reporting to the middle and neglected to represent "the diversity of views and competition for ideas" that represented a wider range of opinions in the general public. "We should have a half dozen, or a dozen networks," he proposed, "in which there will be aggressive competition for news, on which the interests, ideological and otherwise, of smaller population groups—such as young people, old people, black people, women, conservatives, the intelligentsia, etc., are reflected."[27]

The call for more networks beyond the "Big Three" was widely shared, with rumors of a possible "fourth network" continually cropping up across the decade. In 1975, Reese Schonfeld, who had previously run a TV news service for United Press International (UPI), launched the Independent Television News Association. Funded by the conservative beer magnate Joseph Coors and advised by former Nixon aide Roger Ailes, the news service offered independent stations pooled coverage and a nightly newscast.[28] In early 1977, three more plans emerged to challenge the hegemony of the television networks. In "Operation Primetime," or "OPT," twenty-one independent stations banded together with Universal Studios productions to create a six-hour miniseries that they hoped might compete with the networks' hit shows. Meanwhile, "Metronet," a venture between five independent stations and the ad agency Ogilvy & Mather, hoped to create just a half-hour of weeknight programming for its affiliates. Likewise, another ad agency, Benton & Bowles, sought to make family-friendly specials for independent stations to show on Sunday nights. But ultimately, the upstarts simply couldn't compete. With "no central organization, no national hook-up, no news division, and no apparatus for continuing service," a report noted, these independent forces paled in comparison. That said, the simple fact that there was some competition struck some as a positive sign. "If we're not the fourth network, we are at least a counterbalance to the networks as a new force in the market," an OPT official said. "The networks won't change their system unless something goes up against them."[29]

While a fourth network never took off in fact, it did in fiction. In 1976, the hit film *Network* offered a scathing critique of the ways in which corporate control of the network news had shifted its priorities to profit-seeking and sensationalism. The film revolved around a fictitious fourth network, the Union Broadcasting System (UBS), and its failing news program. Informed that he will soon be fired for low ratings, the venerable news anchor Howard Beale (played by Peter Finch) calmly informs viewers that he will commit suicide, on air, the following night. Talked out of it by the UBS network news president, Beale instead launches into an angry televised rant that tapped into the real nation's growing anxieties. "I don't have to tell you things are bad. Everybody knows things are bad," he begins. "Everybody's out of work or scared of losing their job. The dollar buys a nickel's worth, banks are going bust, shopkeepers keep a gun under the counter. Punks are running wild in the street and there's nobody anywhere who seems to know what to do, and there's no end to it. We know the air is unfit to breathe and our food is unfit to eat, and we sit watching our TVs while some local news-caster tells us that today we had fifteen homicides and sixty-three violent crimes, as if that's the way it's supposed to be. We know things are bad—worse than bad. They're crazy. It's like everything everywhere is going crazy, so we don't go out anymore. We sit in the house, and slowly the world we're living in is getting smaller, and all we say is, 'Please, at least leave us alone in our living rooms. Let me have my toaster and my TV and my steel-belted radials and I won't say anything. Just leave us alone.' Well, I'm not gonna leave you alone. I want you to get mad!" At this, Beale urges viewers to walk to their windows, lean out and scream into the night sky: "I'M AS MAD AS HELL, AND I'M NOT GOING TO TAKE THIS ANYMORE!" Thousands do as they're told.[30]

With Beale suddenly a ratings hit, the corporate leaders at the net-work decide to keep him on the air, promoting him as "the mad prophet of the airwaves." Through the character's increasingly angry rants, director Sidney Lumet and screenwriter Paddy Chayefsky offer sharp criticisms of the real television news. "The only truth you know is what you get over this tube," Beale chides his viewers at one point. "Well, television isn't the 'truth'! It's a goddamn amusement park! A circus! A carnival! We're in the boredom killing business. You're never going to get any truth from us; we'll tell you whatever you want to hear!" The rants initially draw ratings, but audiences increasingly find Beale's bleak pronouncements too depressing, and the show's ratings once again begin to slide. Seeking to get him off the air and provide a short-term boost in the ratings once more, the network has Beale assassinated, on live television. "This was the story of Howard Beale," the narrator notes in conclusion, "the first known instance of a man who was killed because he had lousy ratings."[31]

Network proved to be a popular film and a critical success. In March 1977, the film won four Academy Awards, including best actor for Peter Finch and best original screenplay for Paddy Chayefsky. (Meanwhile, the Oscar for the best adapted screenplay went to *All the President's Men*.) Leaders at the real television networks recoiled from the movie's satirical depiction, especially its claim that news programs were becoming little more than entertainment. "There'll never be that kind of show-biz approach to the news," ABC anchorwoman Barbara Walters insisted. "The entertainment side of television is more respectful of the news side now than at any time in the past." Still, Chayefsky insisted the criticism was rooted in real truth. Networks were focused on ad revenue, and therefore on ratings above all else, even in the news divisions. "Television is democracy at its ugliest," he noted quietly in an interview. "Give the people what they want."[32]

By the late 1970s, the damage from Watergate and its various aftershocks was readily apparent. The scandal itself had shattered the nation's faith in its government, and what little reform legislation had been tried in an attempt to repair the trust had itself been weakened or undone. The media forces that had uncovered the truth, meanwhile, first seemed to flourish in the aftermath of the scandal, but steadily succumbed to problems of their own as they moved from embracing prophets like the real Woodward and Bernstein, or the fictional Beale, to chasing profits instead. Despite Gerald Ford's assurances that the "long national nightmare" was over, for too many Americans it seemed that it had only just begun.

CHAPTER 2

A Crisis of Confidence

As Americans lost faith in government, their confidence in the economy shattered, too.

Perhaps even more so than the federal government, the industrial economy of the postwar era had served as a pillar of American prosperity. Steadied by the economic restructuring of the New Deal and spurred to new levels of production by the military mobilization of World War II, the nation's manufacturing-based economy boomed during the postwar decades. As the United States entered a new era of profit and production, ordinary Americans basked in the consumer culture of a new "affluent society" characterized by high wages, high standards of living, and high hopes for the future. The growth of unions offered economic protection to workers who could count on steady wages and good jobs. Poverty remained an intractable problem throughout the nation, most notably in rural areas and inner cities, yet the steady growth of the suburban middle class greatly diminished the kinds of inequality that routinely take form in capitalist economies.

But much like trust in government, Americans' trust in the Cold War economy began to falter in the 1960s. Deindustrialization began to weaken the manufacturing sector and worries about inflation and unemployment swept through the electorate. As the 1970s wore on, Americans' faith in capitalism wore thin.

Stagflation

The decades after World War II, in the words of historian James Patterson, had been an era of "Grand Expectations," a time of remarkable economic growth in which the possibilities for progress and profit in America seemed limitless for many white middle-class families. Upward mobility defined the national character, as incomes kept rising and more and more Americans found their way into the middle class. Homeownership rates, buoyed by government mortgage plans, jumped from over 40 percent in 1940 to almost 64 percent by 1965. Harsh discriminatory practices such as red-lining prohibited many parts of the population, such as African Americans, from enjoying these changes, but for a significant portion of the country the gains were stunning. By 1955 one out of every twenty-two homes had air conditioning, and one out of ten in the South, a development that allowed for massive growth in residential population in booming Sunbelt cities like Houston and Atlanta. Access to higher education, retirement benefits, and health care continued to expand as well. Productivity also showed huge gains, with key sectors of American industry, such as automobiles, dominating international markets. Inflation, meanwhile, remained extremely low by historical standards, averaging 2.2 percent between 1950 and the mid-1960s. Unemployment rates remained low as well, still under 4 percent at the end of the 1960s.[1]

These economic conditions changed dramatically during the next decade, as the era of growth and grand expectations gave way to a period of diminished hopes and decline. The economic crisis of the 1970s stemmed from a number of factors, none of which bore sole responsibility. Inflation, triggered by high levels of government spending on the Vietnam War in the late 1960s, proved difficult to contain. President Lyndon B. Johnson, fearing the political repercussions, had refused to raise taxes to fund the war until it was much too late and, as he delayed, an inflationary spiral began. In the private sector, meanwhile, poor managerial decisions downplayed long-term investment in pursuit of short-term profits, preventing major companies from innovating new products, such as fuel-efficient cars that foreign competitors would soon use to dominate the auto market. In the long run, the 1970s turned out to be a transition period, when newer sources of economic vitality emerged, such as the service sector and computing industry; but at the time, these developments remained on the margins of the economy, distant bright spots on the horizon that could not compensate for the massive problems plaguing the older manufacturing sector.

Of all the problems confronting the economy, none equaled the energy crisis, in which America's dependence on foreign sources of oil was exposed as a major liability. In 1973, the Organization of Petroleum Exporting Countries (OPEC) imposed an oil embargo on Western nations in response to America's support for Israel in the Yom Kippur War. The embargo had major ripple effects throughout the country, reminding Americans of their economic woes on a daily basis. The oil shortages were felt most powerfully on the East Coast, where dependence on foreign oil was greatest.[2] The price of heating homes in the Northeast skyrocketed, leaving some residents struggling to survive the frigid winter of 1974. As gas supplies dwindled, frustration and desperation set in. Most service stations abided by voluntary "Gasless Sundays" to conserve, but owners worried about the cuts. "Our stations' December allotments have been cut from 10 to 20 percent," lamented the head of the Long Island Gasoline Retailers Association.[3] Drivers were forced to wait in long lines to purchase ever-dwindling amounts of gasoline, leading to short tempers and violent outbursts. In Maryland, for instance, a group of angry drivers grabbed a man from his car after he tried to cut in line, dragged him away and beat him mercilessly, leaving him bruised and bleeding by the road. In Connecticut, one gasoline dealer reported that a woman had offered to sleep with him in exchange for two dollars' worth of fuel.[4] With all of these stories, the news constantly reminded audiences that the once omnipotent United States was being held hostage by a small group of countries that did not possess anything near America's military power.

As the energy crisis revealed the limits imposed on the American economy from abroad, the new environmental movement demonstrated a growing awareness among Americans that they might need to place limits on themselves as well. The postwar economy, with its emphasis on industrial growth and consumer abundance, led to ecological consequences that were, by the 1960s, impossible to ignore. Rachel Carson's *Silent Spring*, published in 1962, had awakened an entire generation to the kind of immense damage that commercial practices such as the use of pesticides inflicted on the ecosystem. "Only within the moment of time represented by the present century has one species—man— acquired significant power to alter the nature of his world," she wrote.[5] The rapid growth of middle-class suburbia had spread political support for focusing on the "quality of life" and not simply economic goals.[6] Meanwhile, ecological disasters focused the nation's attention on the costs of their economy. A massive oil spill off the coast of Santa Barbara, California, in January 1969 resulted in millions of gallons of oil polluting the ocean, fouling beaches, and killing thousands of birds. Six months later, in June 1969, the Cuyahoga River outside Cleveland—a waterway so polluted *Time* magazine said it "oozes rather than flows"— actually caught fire. Such incidents, coupled with more commonplace concerns like the near-constant "smog alerts" of poor air quality in Los Angeles, prompted action. New laws like the Clean Air Act of 1970 and Clean Water Act of 1972, and new government offices like the Environmental Protection Agency, created in 1970, signaled an end to an era of unfettered industrial output and unquestioned consumer activities. The environmental movement had pushed forward a new set of values in thinking about the overall economy, where the importance of protecting the Earth took precedence over profits and productivity. For many political leaders, however, economic concerns still came first. If there were ever "a flat choice between jobs and smoke," Nixon told his chief domestic advisor, the nation would always choose jobs.[7]

Indeed, despite the new limits on energy use imposed on them from both home and abroad, many ordinary Americans angrily resisted cutting back on their own consumption. In 1974, the federal government installed new guidelines that encouraged the adoption of 55 mph speed limits across the nation as a means of conserving energy. Though the new limits succeeded in reducing oil imports (and reducing the rates of auto fatalities as well), many resisted the restrictions on their car-centered lifestyle. A midwestern trucker spoke for many when he denounced the speed limit as "a noose around the neck of this nation's economy" and vowed to ignore it. Sales of radar detectors soared as more and more Americans sought ways to skirt the law and avoid a speeding ticket.[8] Notably, in 1977, one of the biggest songs on both the country and pop music charts was C. W. McCall's "Convoy," an antiauthority song about eighteen-wheel trucks speeding down the highways despite the complaints of environmentalists and the enforcement efforts of the police. The hit song by McCall—a fictional character played by an advertising executive named Bill Fries—sold over two million copies and was even made into a feature film, by the acclaimed director Sam Peckinpah.[9]

Another problem that weighed heavily on the economy, connected to the rising prices in oil, was the toxic combination of inflation and unemployment known as "stagflation." In direct contradiction to the economic orthodoxy of the New Deal era, which stipulated that a country could suffer from either inflation or unemployment, but never both at the same time, Americans experienced a double pinch throughout the decade. Inflation, which had started to accelerate in the mid-1960s, doubled between 1969 and 1974, and then increased, albeit at a slower rate, over the remainder of the decade. As the cost of living soared, unionized jobs became scarcer. Unemployment rose from 4.7 percent in 1973 to 7.5 percent two years later.[10] Squeezed between soaring prices and a tanking job market, Americans began to experience the most significant economic crisis since the Great Depression.

The American auto sector, which for much of the twentieth century had symbolized the nation's economic power, now found itself outpaced by upstarts from Japan and West Germany. The cars that these foreign competitors produced proved to be better built and more fuel-efficient, attributes that, in an era of high maintenance costs and gas shortages, were more attractive to consumers. As a result, the US share of world exports had fallen from 15.9 percent in 1960 down to just 12.2 percent by 1975.[11] The sea change had been augured by the 1972 introduction of the Japanese Datsun, with a simple and effective pitch: "Datsun Saves." The company touted the fact that their cars averaged 37.9 miles per gallon compared to the much lower average for American cars—13.5 miles per gallon.[12] By the end of the decade, the number of Japanese cars sold in the United States had climbed from 4 million to 12 million.[13] Meanwhile, German corporations introduced an attractive line of cars as well that were equally competitive. In 1975, they exported the Volkswagen Golf, a small hatchback style car that was also more fuel-efficient than most of the American competition. The United Auto Workers launched "Buy American" campaigns to persuade, or intimidate, consumers into spending their money only on American goods. The campaigns, laced with anti-Japanese sentiment, were not very effective. Appeals to patriotism were unable to trump superior products.

The auto sector was not the only pillar of the old unionized economy to crumble. The New England textile industry, for instance, suffered crippling downturns as more and more companies closed their doors and moved south or abroad for cheaper labor. In March 1975, the Chicopee Manufacturing Company in Manchester, New Hampshire—one of the last standing survivors—finally closed its doors. "People don't say very much when they're leaving," one of the factory workers noted, watching as his friends left jobs that generations of family members had enjoyed. "They're very sad, and a lot of them cry. It's a bad thing when there are no jobs to be had."[14] In New Bedford, Massachusetts, another quintessential textile town, unemployment reached over 12 percent that same year. "We're in terrible shape," lamented Arnold Dublin, a local labor organizer, "absolutely horrendous."[15]

Likewise, the steel industry was suffering. In 1977, *Fortune* published a report on the ravaged Rust Belt titled "Hard Times Come to Steeltown." The piece profiled places like Youngstown, Ohio, and Conshohocken, Pennsylvania, to capture in dark detail what happened when "Steeltown, USA" saw the mills close down due to foreign competition. "Steeltown has been shaken literally to its foundations," author Lee Smith noted. "Steeltown is in danger of losing its reason for being, much as the New England textile mills lost theirs when their mills began to move south. Steeltown seems to be left with only two alternatives: turn to some other useful enterprise, or die." The images accompanying the piece provided stark illustrations of the steelworkers' plight. In one, photographer Stephen Shore captured a thirty-two-year-old steelworker from Bethlehem Steel's Lackawanna Mill, staring numbly at a bottle of beer in Curly's Bar after being laid off from a job he'd had since high school. In another photo, a protesting ex-worker held up a sign that demanded "Don't Write Off Youngstown. Fight For Every Job!"[16]

These difficult economic conditions generated high levels of insecurity and anxiety. The bleak outlook was captured by a new generation of filmmakers in the 1970s, who painted a dark portrait of the national mood. In movies such as *Taxi Driver, Chinatown,* and *The Exorcist,* social decline was prevalent. Martin Scorsese, director of the gritty drama *Mean Streets* (1973), argued that his films reflected the realities of urban decay and dysfunction. "It's pretty tough stuff," he insisted. "It's not like some movie where everybody's singing and dancing and drinking bottles of Chianti."[17] The film's dark portrayal of New Yorkers driven to desperate measures was repeatedly echoed in other major movies of the decade, such as *Death Wish* (1974), *Dog Day Afternoon*

(1975), and *Saturday Night Fever* (1977). More broadly, films now regularly turned their attention to working-class subjects, highlighting their struggles to survive in an increasingly stagnant economy. *Blue Collar* (1978), starring Richard Pryor, Harvey Keitel, and Yaphet Kotto, covered the complaints Detroit autoworkers had with the leaders of their company and their union. Likewise, *Norma Rae* (1979) told the story of union organizing at a textile mill in North Carolina, resulting in an Oscar win for best actress for its lead Sally Field. In the same vein, the Oscar-winning documentary *Harlan County U.S.A.* (1976) chronicled a coal miners' strike in rural Kentucky.

Meanwhile, television shows increasingly shifted their attention from the happy, thriving suburban families that had dominated the programming of the 1950s and 1960s, to struggling working-class subjects. Norman Lear's hit sitcom *All in the Family* (1971–1979) set the pace, with its portrayal of a blue-collar family in Queens, New York. Fresh from that success, Lear followed up with other programs that put the spotlight on a variety of working-class families: *Sanford and Son* (1972–1977), about an African American junk dealer in the Watts section of L.A.; *One Day at a Time* (1975–1984), about a divorced suburbanite who moved with her daughters to Indianapolis to look for work; and, most notably, *Good Times* (1974–1979), about a working-class African American family living in a housing project in Chicago. Similar sitcoms followed suit: *Chico and the Man* (1974–1978) was set in a run-down garage in an East L.A. barrio, while *Alice* (1976–1985) centered on a widowed mom who found work at a roadside diner outside Phoenix, and *Taxi* (1978–1983) showcased the employees at a dingy cab company in New York. Though a few sitcoms in the 1970s showed paths of upward mobility—most notably in Lear's hit *All in the Family* spinoff, *The Jeffersons* (1975–1985)—more often than not these shows portrayed families treading water. As always, the uneasy portrayals reflected the popular mood. According to public opinion polls, for the first time in a generation Americans doubted whether it was possible for individuals to move up the economic ladder.[18] Indeed, according to a 1975 Gallup Poll, 87 percent of Americans expected the unemployment crisis to continue to get worse, not better.[19]

As complaints about the economy grew louder, many business leaders began to worry that the very idea of "free enterprise" was under attack.

In 1971, Lewis Powell, a corporate lawyer who would soon become a Supreme Court justice, sent an important memo to the head of the US Chamber of Commerce. "There always have been some who opposed the American system," Powell wrote. But unlike in the past, when such dissent was confined to a few extremists, "We are not dealing with sporadic or isolated attacks. . . . Rather, the assault on the enterprise system is broadly based and consistently pursued." Powell encouraged the Chamber and its corporate allies to respond to these complaints with an enormous public relations campaign that would promote the idea of free enterprise. The Chamber, for instance, sent "Economics for Young Americans" kits to 12,000 schools across the country, while Goodyear Tire and Rubber Company employed a traveling representative to visit local teachers and discuss the content of their curricula. Many universities responded by establishing business schools in the 1970s, and by the end of the decade, business had become the fastest-growing major for undergrads.[20] Ironically, corporate leaders' worries about the public image of big business came at a time when their private fortunes were soaring. As average after-tax earnings declined for most wage earners by 13 percent in the 1970s and 1980s, CEOs saw their after-tax compensation grow by almost 400 percent during these same decades, fueling a trend of growing inequality and a shrinking middle class that would characterize the coming decades in American life.[21]

President Ford struggled to deal with the economic crisis, but found little success. Aside from a tax cut passed by Congress in 1975, Ford's major initiative was a public relations campaign called "Whip Inflation Now." The program encouraged Americans to purchase less fuel, drive fewer miles, and do more to conserve basic items like food. Ford hoped to persuade families to participate in this voluntary program and work together to achieve common goals. He understood that government was needed but, as a true midwestern conservative, was not interested in expanding the power of Washington. His middle way approach failed, as the public proved uninterested. The three television networks only broadcast Ford's speech announcing the plan after considerable pressure from the White House. Hoping to drum up public support, the administration had a Madison Avenue public relations firm design special "WIN" pins and then distributed fifteen million of them to spread the word. Arnold Palmer, the champion golfer, supported the effort by brandishing a pin of his own. "This button, it's not a joke," he insisted. "I put it on because I believe in it."[22] Despite his support, the pin did become a source of ridicule, a symbol of an administration that had no concrete solutions to the crisis. Turning the pins upside down, some of Ford's detractors interpreted them as "NIM": "No Immediate Miracles." The cover of *New York Magazine* featured a photograph of a clown, dressed in a suit with a "WIN" button, standing at a presidential podium. Over the image ran the title of Richard Reeves's cover story: "Ladies and Gentlemen, The President of the United States."[23]

In another symbolic gesture, the Ford administration hoped to unite the nation with the bicentennial celebration in 1976. At a state dinner marking the two hundredth anniversary of the Declaration of Independence, the president welcomed Queen Elizabeth II with a gracious toast. Nearly a hundred historic "tall ships" traveled from New York City to the ports of Boston in a spectacular flotilla. Across America, local and state governments organized events of their own, with residents painting mailboxes red, white, and blue and hanging flags from their porches. At Disneyland, the popular Main Street Electrical Parade was rechristened "America on Parade." For many, the bicentennial celebrations promised to wipe clean the troubles and turmoil of the last decade, whether for good or for bad. "Nixon, Watergate, Patty Hearst, the Bicentennial," complained a San Francisco resident, "the Media got bored with 1967, so they zapped it . . . . I mean, what's left? There's not a single fucking place where it's still 1967."[24]

In the end, though, the bicentennial celebrations did little to bind the nation's wounds. Polls showed that the segment of Americans who trusted government institutions continued to plummet over the decade, falling from a historic high of 80 percent of all Americans in 1966 to roughly 25 percent in 1981.[25]

Jimmy Carter:
A President for the Times

The politician who best responded to the bleak mood of the bicentennial year was Jimmy Carter. Through a skillful campaign that played to the feelings of distrust after Vietnam and Watergate, as well as the economic desperation that so many people felt, the former governor of Georgia showed that in 1976, at least, he had his finger on the pulse of the nation.

As the election began, Carter made it clear that he understood the impact Watergate had made on national politics. While his rivals for the Democratic nomination emphasized their collective decades of experience in Washington, Carter played up his status as an outsider and emphasized it repeatedly on the campaign trail. Insisting that voters could trust him in office, the former Georgia governor pointedly contrasted himself with not just Richard Nixon, but all Washington insiders who had let the nation down. Promising a new start, Carter refused to embrace the policy orthodoxies to which most Democrats subscribed and promised to challenge the entrenched interests in Washington.

Despite his image as an outsider, however, Carter ran a campaign that demonstrated deep knowledge of the inner workings of politics. His team shrewdly recognized the impact of important changes in the presidential selection process that had resulted from reform efforts inside the Democratic Party in the early 1970s. The old bosses, who had held sway at the Democratic National Convention for decades, suddenly found their sources of power drained. In their place, new segments of the electorate—especially African Americans, Latinos, and women— were empowered by new party rules. Even the convention itself was diminished in importance, as primaries and caucuses became the main arena for the selection of presidential candidates. Carter grasped that local political organizations would be the key to securing delegates for the convention, and also recognized that the media would be invaluable in turning success in a single state's primary or caucus into a larger sense of momentum. Accordingly, while the other contenders largely ignored the Iowa Caucuses, as politicians had traditionally done, Carter poured his energies into them. In the end, the Georgia governor won Iowa handily, securing twice as many votes as his nearest competitor.

Moreover, Carter used his victory there to propel himself into the national spotlight and thereby create the perception that he was the frontrunner in the race. Television ads proved to be the key here. While presidential campaign spots had been a mainstay of elections since the Eisenhower era, they had nevertheless played a fairly small role in political outreach. (The amount spent on televised political ads at all levels of politics in 1972 was less than 3 percent of what would be spent forty years later.) Carter suspected the medium could play a much more significant role, however, particularly in letting candidates craft images and create arguments to contrast their "character" with their opponents', an important issue in the wake of Watergate. Carter's TV ads were largely positive, using a cinema verité style to show interviews with people who knew him and insisted he could fix the government. "In the beginning," one ad explained, "Jimmy Carter's campaign was a lonely one. But through the months, more and more people recognized him as a new leader, a man who would change the way this country was run. A competent man, who can make our government open and efficient. But above all, an understanding man, who can make ours a government of the people again."[26]

This outsider spirit thrived in the Republican Party as well. Although the GOP had an incumbent president seeking another term, Ford soon found himself facing a strong challenge from within the party. Former California governor Ronald Reagan ran against him from the right, seeking to harness the enthusiasm of a new conservative movement. Over the previous decade, a new set of grassroots activists, intellectuals, and policy entrepreneurs had built a dense institutional network with the objective of pushing politics to the right. Believing that Republican leaders had compromised with Democrats too often and were complicit in Washington's sins, these conservatives urged a thorough rejection of the status quo. Tapping into this discontent, Reagan argued that, on foreign policy, President Ford had moved too far to the center by embracing détente and, on domestic policy, he had likewise made peace with the welfare state and accepted too large of a government presence in national life. Ford was ultimately able to beat back Reagan's challenge, but the new contender made it clear that he had successfully mobilized conservatives in a new movement.

Though he held off Reagan in the primaries, Ford's general election campaign never gained steam. His failure to restore trust in government and stabilize the economy constantly held him back. Moreover, while his own efforts at inspirational symbolism and imagery had largely failed, Ford found himself caricatured and ridiculed by the media. A former college football star at Michigan who had been recruited by several NFL teams, Ford was perhaps the most athletic man ever to serve as president. But after tripping on the stairs to Air Force One and other small mishaps, he found himself portrayed on *Saturday Night Live*—a new comedy program launched in October 1975—as a bumbling idiot who staggered from one crisis to the next. "No one who knew the president ever quite understood Chevy Chase's *Saturday Night Live* impersonation of him as a genial dolt who stumbled over doorsteps and big words," Republican operative James Baker later recalled. "Unfortunately, the caricature—particularly the physical humor—took on a life of its own."[27]

As the 1976 presidential campaign began, the themes of reform and trust dominated. Running against the incumbent administration, Carter appealed both to the core of his party and to independents who did not want continued Republican rule. His campaign, however, was far from smooth. Carter struggled throughout the fall, including in an interview with *Playboy* magazine where the born-again Christian confessed to the interviewer that he had "committed adultery in my heart" over women other than his wife.[28] When speaking at a campaign stop in Indiana, Carter angered many African American Democrats by saying that the federal government should not try to alter the "ethnic purity" of neighborhoods, a comment that seemed a direct attack on the initiatives to bus African American students into better-off white schools.[29]

Despite such problems, the Carter campaign outpaced his rival's. Ford made a terrible gaffe during a televised presidential debate when he stated that "there is no Soviet domination of Eastern Europe, and there never will be under a Ford administration." Though he meant that Eastern Europeans did not feel as if they were under the political domain of the Soviets despite their territorial control—a response meant to placate conservative critics of détente—the statement seemed to suggest the president was unaware of basic facts. The impact of the moment on the campaign reflected the larger influence of television. Politicians now had to make their pitch to voters in "sound bites" that were then roughly forty-five seconds long, but which would grow steadily shorter as the years wore on. For all the depth and drudgery of a political campaign, Ford's mistake showed how a single minute of televised time could transform a race suddenly.[30]

In the end, Carter won the election by the slimmest margin, with his 50.1 percent share of the popular vote serving as another reminder of the deep divisions in the nation. Meanwhile, Democrats retained control of both chambers of Congress with sizable majorities, offering the party a brief moment of optimism. This mood of hope continued at the new president's inauguration. Seeking to distance himself from the "Imperial Presidency" of the Nixon era, Carter left his limousine and walked the streets of Washington with his family, seeking to meet and greet the people. As he did so, Carter thought that the happy crowd before him presented a sharp contrast with the "angry demonstrators who had habitually confronted recent Presidents and Vice Presidents, furious over the Vietnam War and later the revelations of Watergate."[31] The press reports were equally positive. Finally, it seemed, there was someone in the White House who might signal a fresh start.

Despite this initial optimism, the sour mood of the 1970s remained. Though the economic crisis had helped put him into office, President Carter proved to have as little success in that realm as his predecessor had, no matter what he tried. In his first year, the president persuaded Congress to pass a watered-down economic stimulus bill that ultimately did little to boost depressed industries. Then, after 1978, he turned to anti-inflationary measures, including spending cuts, but they too had little impact. Carter proposed a sweeping new energy program, but the bruising battle in Congress only produced weak legislation that failed to lower dependence on foreign oil. Ultimately, his most consequential move in economic terms proved to be his appointment of Paul Volcker as chairman of the Federal Reserve Board in 1979. Volcker was committed to fighting inflation, even at the expense of aggravating unemployment. In the short term, his policies meant a double-dip recession. But in the long run they were successful in turning the economy around, even if the positive impact of his policies at the Federal Reserve would not really be felt until the early 1980s when a Republican was in the White House.

The latter half of the 1970s was not entirely characterized by decline and downturn, however. Beneath the surface of industrial decay, there were early signs of new growth. Indeed, one of the reasons that the manufacturing sector lost so many jobs during the decade was that there was a larger shift taking place in the economy toward expanding segments of the service sector: banking, health care, department stores, food, entertainment, and travel. During the 1970s, these service and retail trade sectors constituted 70 percent of all the jobs that were created in the private sector. While these service sector openings offered some hope, these new jobs, located in industries with less of a union presence, had less reward and less reliability than the older manufacturing positions they replaced. They were, on balance, marked by lower wages, fewer benefits, and shorter and less predictable working hours.[32]

Three events toward the end of the decade best symbolized the fragility of the economy. First, the promise of nuclear power as a replacement for oil was quickly dashed when the nation experienced the worst commercial nuclear accident in its history. The nuclear industry had long promised that its plants were virtually failsafe, but on March 28, 1979, the nuclear plant at Three Mile Island, near Harrisburg, Pennsylvania, experienced a partial meltdown that released radioactive gases into the air. Governor Richard Thornburgh ordered the evacuation of high-risk groups—pregnant women and preschoolers, for instance—from a five-mile radius around the disabled nuclear plant, but the confusion between politicians and plant officials only caused residents to panic. In an odd coincidence, the Three Mile Island accident happened at the same time a hit thriller about a nuclear meltdown, *The China Syndrome*, was playing in theaters. The convergence of the accident and the movie stirred a fierce backlash against the construction of new nuclear power plants and left many in the country feeling that there was no cure to the nation's economic blues.[33]

The second major shock to the economy was another energy embargo that occurred in 1979, following a revolution in Iran that toppled the Western-friendly regime of the shah and placed Islamic fundamentalists in power. Cutoffs in the supply of oil from Iran, combined with a renewed round of price increases from OPEC, pushed the United States into another energy crisis. With memories still fresh from the first, the panic was even more pronounced as the nation rushed for supplies, leading to huge spikes in the cost of heating homes and long lines at gas stations. Across the country, local TV news programs brought the crisis home, interviewing gas station owners and operators about the shortage. In Cleveland, the ABC affiliate reminded viewers that the shortage meant "we're all going to pay, because this country runs primarily on oil." Likewise, in Knoxville, the local NBC station described gas stations running out of supplies and closing early, showing images of pumps with handwritten signs scrawled with "OUT."[34]

"Anger and bewilderment are growing," the MacNeil-Lehrer Report noted on PBS, "as more and more Americans cope with gasoline lines and empty pumps."[35] The lines were so bad that, according to one estimate, drivers were burning through 150,000 barrels of oil a day solely in their efforts to get more gas.[36] Drivers purchased locks for their gas tanks and siphon hand pumps in huge numbers, reflecting the sense of desperation that many felt. In the Bay Ridge section of Brooklyn, a man was shot dead by another motorist for trying to cut into the shorter of two lines at a gas station selling fuel for a discounted 98.9 cents a gallon.[37] Elsewhere in Brooklyn, a group of angry residents formed the American Gas Party and alleged that the oil companies were manipulating prices at the expense of consumers. They even planned to dump mock barrels of gas into the water to express their frustration.[38] The oil industry understood the depths of public outrage. One day the chairman of Exxon, Clifton Garvin, was waiting in the back of a gas line in Greenwich, Connecticut. The station manager recognized Garvin from his regular appearances in the media promoting the industry and asked if he wanted to move up to the front. "How are you going to explain that to everyone else in the line?" Garvin asked. The dealer responded, "Why I'll tell them who you are." Stunned by the naïve comment, the chairman replied, "I'm sitting right here."[39]

Seeking to calm the situation, President Carter scheduled a major speech for July 15, 1979. In the address, the president focused on the psychological and cultural causes of America's pattern of overconsumption. "In a nation that was proud of hard work, strong families, close-knit communities and our faith in God," Carter said, "too many of us now tend to worship self-indulgence and consumption. Human identity is no longer defined by what one does but by what one owns." In echoes of Ford's failed WIN campaign, Carter called on the nation to take steps to conserve fuel. Not surprisingly, the speech fell flat, as many Americans wanted concrete solutions to the crisis rather than a cerebral lecture about its causes.

Conservatives saw the situation differently and readily pounced on Carter's address. They dismissed it as "the malaise speech," and even though the president never used that word, the label stuck. Some critics went beyond mocking Carter's failure to solve the energy crisis and actively blamed him for it, claiming that the gas shortage was actually a fraud perpetrated by supporters of the administration's energy program.[40] If the government really wanted to take steps to protect the interests of consumers, the editors of the *Wall Street Journal* argued, "it is only necessary to remove the mind-boggling federal array of price ceilings, price tiers, incremental prices, fuel use restrictions, fuel allocations, fuel use barriers, crude oil entitlements, drilling restrictions and other entanglements that result in so much of the human energy of the energy industry being immobilized and wasted by regulation."[41]

The third major event that captured the state of the economy was the near collapse of the Chrysler Corporation. The once thriving auto firm had in recent years been known as the "sick man of Detroit," but now its disease looked terminal. While all American automakers were struggling, Chrysler seemed especially doomed. As a result of poor managerial decisions and difficulty keeping up with new environmental regulations, the company reported losses of $207.1 million in the second quarter of the fiscal year. The larger cars it produced, like the Dodge St. Regis, were not selling at all. Meanwhile, two of its major products— the Dodge Aspen and the Plymouth Volare—were frequently subjected to recalls due to poor designs. "This company is in the saddest shape," a former auto executive remarked after reviewing the numbers.[42] Soon, Chrysler laid off workers, shutting down plants and canceling stock dividends. In company towns like Hamtramck, Michigan, a Polish working-class city that had revolved around its Dodge Main plant for over seventy-five years, the impact was devastating. The factory there had employed 20,000 people in 1959, but its workforce had dwindled to only 8,000 people in 1978 and then just 2,600 in 1979.[43]

As the third biggest automobile manufacturer and the tenth largest firm in the nation, Chrysler represented a major pillar of the American economy. With 250,000 employees and another 500,000 or so whose livelihoods indirectly depended on the company, its failure would have far-reaching impacts. "We couldn't go belly up," Chrysler executive John Riccardo worried. "We'd take down banks, towns and even some countries. It would be fantastic."[44] Going into an election year, the political ramifications were clear. "Letting the company fold," Louisiana senator and Democratic leader Russell Long told reporters, "would cost us a lot of revenue, a lot of jobs."[45]

As the company struggled, the Board of Directors hired Lee Iacocca to take over as CEO in 1978. Upon his arrival, Iacocca implemented drastic steps to cut costs, such as selling off the corporation's European wing. But in the end, none of the steps was sufficient to save the company. In a dramatic moment, Iacocca went to the White House and Congress in September 1979 to ask for help. He blamed new environmental regulations and consumer safety requirements (like the airbag) as the source of the company's huge costs, and sought over $1 billion in special tax credits to alleviate the impact. But his proposals ran into fierce resistance. Many in the business community insisted that the company should be forced to fend for itself. One manufacturer in Long Beach, California, said "the right solution is to let the natural forces take place. In general, I don't think the government should underwrite private enterprise's failures. If we do that we aren't going to have private enterprise."[46] Labor leaders, however, were supportive. When United Auto Workers (UAW) leader Douglas Fraser heard that Thomas Murphy, chairman of General Motors, was "firmly opposed" to the plan, he lashed out, "If the shoe were on the other foot and GM were in trouble, Mr. Murphy would become a flaming socialist."[47]

Despite labor's enthusiasm for the proposals, many on the left resisted Iacocca's plan. "Mismanagement at the company has been incredible," complained consumer advocate Ralph Nader, so "why should a subsidy solve Chrysler's problems? Let it go bankrupt."[48] On the right, meanwhile, Texas representative Ron Paul agreed. "In a nation that is sinking in a sea of debt," he warned, "it is irresponsible for this Congress to be considering a measure that would add billions to that debt."[49] Despite warnings from legislators like Paul, Congress grudgingly provided most of the loans. Unions suffered a major blow from the deal. In exchange for $1.5 billion in guaranteed loans, Chrysler was required to reach a deal with the UAW to implement a wage freeze along with other major concessions, and then to wage cuts the following year under the supervision of the Loan Guarantee Board established by the law. Rank-and-file union members, furious at the deal, grew angrier with their union leaders, and the Democratic politicians aligned with them.

Critics warned that the move sent a bad message to American industry. "There is a strong case," said *Time* magazine, "that such help rewards failure and penalizes success, puts a dull edge on competition, is unfair to an ailing company's competitors and their shareholders, and inexorably leads the Government deeper into private business. . . . Where should the government draw the line?"[50] The Business Round-table, a powerful lobbying organization, soon announced that "whatever the hardships of failure may be for particular companies and individuals, the broad social and economic interests of the nation are best served by allowing this system to operate as freely and fully as possible . . . now is the time to reaffirm the principle of no federal bail-outs." In response, Chrysler withdrew from the organization.[51]

As the decade drew to a close, there seemed little cause for optimism. Experts routinely discussed American economic decline, unsure if the nation could recover. Most of the major economic indicators continued to be unfavorable. Unions watched as their once-strong position in the postwar era steadily crumbled. The federal government was struggling to respond, usually with halfmeasures such as the Chrysler bailout, but officials lacked any coherent plan for revitalizing economic growth. Conservative Republicans were gaining steam in opposition to the failures of the Carter administration and the Democratic Congress, yet their plans remained vague as well. The leaders of the nation's private sector were likewise scrambling to offer plans of their own, though many industries still clung to outdated products that were no longer economically competitive. The future seemed dire.

Stagflation and turmoil overseas only deepened the division and discord within the electorate. The actual strength and vitality of the economy had severely weakened, leaving many fearful about how the nation could ever recover. *Time* magazine predicted in 1981 that there would be "Gloom and Doom" for America's workers in the years to come.[52] With basic economic indicators in horrible shape, few Americans could rekindle the kind of optimism that had existed in the 1950s and 1960s. An era of grand expectations had given way to a decade of disillusionment.

CHAPTER 3

A Crisis
of Identity

As THE POLITICAL AND ECONOMIC FOUNDATIONS OF THE postwar decades cracked apart in the 1970s, that era's racial order crumbled as well.

While Americans had watched the decline of government and industry in this era with a growing sense of despair, most welcomed the dismantling of the old structures of racial segregation and immigration restriction. The liberalism of the Great Society era, it seemed, had succeeded in addressing long-standing problems of racial division and discord. Most notably, the Civil Rights Act of 1964 and the Voting Rights Act of 1965 tore down institutional barriers that had served to oppress racial minorities within the nation across the twentieth century, while the Immigration and Nationality Act of 1965 dismantled the walls of immigration restriction constructed during an earlier era of nativism and racism.

White liberals celebrated the passage of these measures as a sign of the ultimate triumph of racial integration and assimilation. "Our beautiful America was built by a nation of strangers," President Lyndon B. Johnson announced when he signed the new immigration law on Liberty Island in New York harbor. "From a hundred different places or more they have poured forth into an empty land, joining and blending in one mighty and irresistible tide." Such comments ignored the original presence of indigenous peoples, of course, but they also spoke to the popular belief that Americans had forged a single national identity from a wide array of sources, a belief as old as the nation's original motto of *E Pluribus Unum*.[1]

Ultimately, however, the optimism of that moment would not be fulfilled. The civil rights and immigration reforms of the mid-1960s succeeded in tearing down old walls of division, but in the rubble that remained it became increasingly difficult to discern anything that resembled a coherent or cohesive "American" identity. Rather than adopt the mainstream values of the white majority and adapt to its culture, racial and ethnic minorities increasingly sorted themselves into communities they made on their own terms and in their own images. The influx of new immigrants, meanwhile, contributed to a broad remaking of the population as well. As the nation moved to embrace a sense of diversity, it came to accept that a new fault line came along with that development.

The Struggle for Black Equality

In the 1960s, the modern civil rights movement consumed the American imagination. Grassroots protest campaigns, coordinated by organizations like Martin Luther King Jr.'s Southern Christian Leadership Conference (SCLC) and the Student Non-Violent Coordinating Committee (SNCC), focused national attention on the segregated South. Employing strategies of nonviolent direct action, protesters exposed the inherent inequalities of the so-called "separate-but-equal" society of the region. Local campaigns cropped up all across the South, from the seemingly civilized "All-American City" of Greensboro, North Carolina, to the isolated rural areas of backwoods Mississippi. Shrewdly drawing in the attention of the national media, civil rights activists succeeded in forcing the nation to confront the raw ugliness of American apartheid. In 1963, for instance, the front pages of major newspapers carried photos of black children in Birmingham, Alabama, besieged by attack dogs and high-pressure fire hoses. Two years later, the ABC network interrupted the broadcast of its Sunday Night Movie—*Judgement at Nuremberg*, the story of Nazis on trial for genocidal atrocities against European Jews—to show film of another racial minority being savagely beaten by lawmen on the Edmund Pettus Bridge outside Selma, Alabama.[2]

Through such confrontations, the civil rights movement dispelled the fictions that had propped up the old racial order. Nonviolent direct action, King had once predicted, would awaken "the conscience of the great decent majority who through blindness, fear, pride, or irrationality have allowed their consciences to sleep." Forced to confront the ugliness and unfairness that had lain for too long in the foundation of their nation, Americans moved in the mid-1960s to uproot the legal structures of racial segregation and discrimination. Two landmark laws stand out. The Civil Rights Act of 1964 outlawed discrimination based on race, color, religion, sex, or national origin, and sparked the end of legal racial segregation in schools, workplaces, restaurants, hotels, and similar "public accommodations." The Voting Rights Act of 1965 then committed the federal government to ensuring that there was no racial discrimination in the electoral process. Setting down clear rights for all Americans and establishing a new federal role for enforcement when those rights were violated, these landmark laws set new standards for greater social and political equality.[3]

Despite such significant successes, it soon became clear that the civil rights movement had not ended racial inequality. Indeed, just days after the Voting Rights Act was signed into law, the black working-class community of Watts in Los Angeles exploded in violence. A neighborhood of single-family homes, Watts seemed to have little in common with more congested urban neighborhoods, but it shared the same problems: poor schools, high unemployment, high crime, and growing reports of police brutality. Sparked by rumors of a violent arrest, the Watts riots lasted for six days, resulting in thirty-four people killed, a thousand injured, and more than three thousand more in jail, as well as two hundred fifty buildings burnt down. Watts merely marked the beginning of a new wave of urban riots that spoke to the persistence of economic inequality and police brutality in the inner cities. In the summer of 1966, there were forty-three riots across America; in 1967, there were fifty-five. In response to the violence, Lyndon Johnson appointed a presidential commission to seek out the root causes and report back to the nation.

The findings of the Kerner Commission, as it was known, ultimately cut to the heart of black people's frustrations over the many problems arrayed against them and, just as importantly, to white ignorance of those same problems. "What white Americans have never fully understood—but what the Negro can never forget—is that white society is deeply implicated in the ghetto," it concluded. "White institutions created it, white institutions maintain it, and white society condones it." The Kerner Report offered a stark warning: "To continue present policies is to make permanent the division of our country into two societies; one, largely Negro and poor, located in the central cities; the other, predominantly white and affluent, located in the suburbs and in outlying areas." Despite the clarion call to address these lingering inequalities, there ultimately proved to be little political will to act. The report came as political winds in Washington shifted strongly to the right. President Lyndon Johnson, then in his final months in office, lacked the ability to act on the recommendations. Instead, Johnson approved legislation that vastly expanded federal power over local law enforcement, helping to militarize the police in what he called the "war on crime."[4] Johnson's successor Richard Nixon, meanwhile, ran as a "law and order" candidate who promised to bring calm to cities not with new programs of government aid but a renewed commitment to harsher policing.[5]

The urban riots revealed the limitations of liberal change and gave room to those who challenged the movement for integration. Black nationalism, a more radical philosophy grounded in an ideology of economic self-sufficiency and political separation, had been picking up strength for decades. It took on new urgency in the late 1960s. Under the leadership of chairman Stokely Carmichael, SNCC turned increasingly away from the old principles of interracialism and nonviolence and to a new rallying cry of "Black Power!" As older organizations like SNCC changed course, new ones like the Black Panther Party for Self-Defense emerged to set the pace for radical black activism. Seeking to combat police brutality in Oakland, California, the Panthers famously advocated armed revolution and openly displayed firearms. But in a larger sense, they worked to call attention to the manifestations of institutional racism, the ways in which racial inequality was embedded in the political, social, and cultural structures of American life. Accordingly, the Panthers sought to solve systemic problems in their community, initiating free breakfast programs for schoolchildren and setting up free health clinics. The media, however, focused solely on their clashes with police and political leaders, serving to marginalize them in the mind of the white majority as a problem, not a solution.[6]

Traditional civil rights leaders increasingly turned their attention to economic inequality as well. In his final presidential address to the

SCLC in August 1967, for instance, Martin Luther King Jr. pointed out that 40 million people still lived in poverty in America. It was their responsibility as Christians and citizens not simply to take care of the poor, he insisted, but to challenge the capitalist system that allowed them to be poor. "We've got to begin to ask questions about the whole society," he asserted. "We are called upon to help the discouraged beggars in life's marketplace. But one day we must come to see that an edifice which produces beggars needs restructuring." Soon after his address, King organized the Poor People's Campaign with plans to craft an interracial coalition that would wage a massive protest in Washington, DC. Much of his remaining time was devoted to promoting union causes across the country, including the sanitation workers' strike that would bring him to Memphis, and to his murder, the following spring. In the aftermath of his assassination in April 1968, the nation's cities erupted, once again, in destructive riots.[7]

As the 1970s began, the civil rights movement seemed adrift. The SCLC limped along under the leadership of Ralph Abernathy, a loyal King aide who seemed unable to live up to the icon's standards. Meanwhile, as SNCC turned to black nationalism, embracing racial separatism and making sharper critiques of institutional racism, it lost the support of white liberal funders and attracted the hostility of state and federal law enforcement. Most of SNCC's chapters closed down, before the organization itself finally went under in 1976. The Congress of Racial Equality (CORE) likewise saw its membership hemorrhage as its embrace of black self-determination led it to whipsaw across the political spectrum, first moving to radical separatist politics aligned with Black Power advocates and then into a promotion of black capitalism in alliance with the Nixon administration. Even the oldest integrationist organization, the National Association for the Advancement of Colored People (NAACP), faced plummeting membership numbers and barely avoided bankruptcy by the end of the decade. Black Power organizations fared no better. Torn apart by internal struggles and police infiltration, most chapters of the Black Panther Party had closed down by the dawn of the 1970s. Increasingly isolated, the organization's remaining leaders retreated to Oakland, seeking to shore up a base of support there.[8]

As the organizations that shaped civil rights activism in the 1960s lost strength, the struggle for black equality entered a new chapter. "The marching has stopped," a collection of essays by intellectuals and activists announced with authority in 1973. "In less than a decade, America has deaccelerated from a March on Washington, where hopes for the future were as high as the brilliant August sun that bathed black and white alike, to the shadows of the '70s and the depths of despair, where the bright dreams of yesterday strangled on the bitter gall of rising indifference toward efforts to solve America's racial dilemma." Though the era of mass protests had accomplished much, much more still was left undone. "Untouched by the civil rights movement," two officials with the Urban League observed, "are millions of blacks whose days begin and end with one goal—Survival!"[9]

In hopes of addressing the unfinished agenda of the civil rights era, black leaders increasingly spoke of the ongoing transition "from protest to politics." Civil rights strategist Bayard Rustin used that phrase as the title of a 1965 manifesto and, in short order, the promise for securing black political power within the existing system seemed at hand. In 1966 and 1967, for instance, black mayors were elected in sizable midwestern cities including Flint, Michigan; Gary, Indiana; and, most notably, Cleveland, Ohio. By 1970, black mayors had won control of localities ranging from northern industrial cities like Newark and East Orange, New Jersey, to smaller southern towns like Chapel Hill, North Carolina. During the same period, African American representation in Congress grew rapidly. The number of black representatives in the House tripled over the course of the 1960s, from four to twelve; meanwhile, in 1966 Republican Edward Brooke of Massachusetts became the first African American popularly elected to the Senate. Black officials at the local and national level saw themselves working in common cause. In a 1971 address to the Cleveland Urban League, for instance, Charles Evers—a former NAACP field director who had won election as the first black mayor in Mississippi—pointed to African American representative Louis Stokes of Cleveland: "He's my congressman, too." Thinking of themselves increasingly as champions of not just their individual districts but black America as a whole, the thirteen African Americans in Congress formally banded together to form the Congressional Black Caucus later that year.[10]

The rising power of black politics was displayed in all its diversity at the National Black Political Convention, held in Gary, Indiana, in

March 1972. Over four thousand delegates from forty-seven states responded to the formal call to the convention, which set the stakes for black America in the bleakest terms: "Our cities are crime-haunted dying grounds. Huge sectors of our youth—and countless others—face permanent unemployment. Those of us who work find our paychecks able to purchase less and less. Neither the courts nor the prisons contribute anything resembling justice or reformation. The schools are unable—or unwilling—to educate our children for the real world of our struggles." Despite the dire tones of the call, the convention itself signaled empowerment for its ideologically diverse set of participants, who ranged from Marxists to members of the Nixon administration. Gary's own African American mayor Richard Hatcher set the mood with his keynote address. "As we look out over this vast and expectant assemblage," he enthused, "we can imagine how Moses and the People of Israel thrilled when they witnessed the parting of the Red Sea!" Others were equally excited. Jesse Jackson, a former King associate who left SCLC to found his own group, People United to Save Humanity (PUSH), applauded Hatcher and echoed his optimism in a speech whose rallying cry insisted it was finally "Nation Time!" Blending the traditions of civil rights integrationism and black separatism—even in his physical appearance, sporting a gigantic Afro and a medallion with Martin Luther King's image—Jackson offered an optimistic path forward.[11]

That path lay in politics. Participants left the convention with a bold blueprint for activism in hand, a program for social, economic, and institutional change grandly titled the National Black Political Agenda. But as a series of compromises, it ultimately satisfied no one completely and was even rejected outright by key organizations like the NAACP. Still, if the Gary Convention failed to secure a unified agenda for all African Americans, it confirmed a general course. "Political action," Hatcher insisted in his keynote, "is an essential part of our ultimate liberation." The potentials drawn from political engagement seemed to be increasing with every passing moment. The year of the convention, black politicians won elections to be mayors of cities like Cincinnati and Tallahassee; the next year, African Americans took over city halls in Atlanta, Detroit, Los Angeles, and Raleigh. Throughout this era, the total number of black elected officials in the nation rose at an impressive rate—from 193 in 1965, to 764 in 1970, all the way to 1,909 in 1980, a tenfold increase in a decade and a half.[12]

In obvious ways, the rise in black political representation was a result of the success of the civil rights movement, particularly the substantial changes wrought by the Voting Rights Act. But black political power also stemmed in no small part from an unintended consequence of the civil rights era. Even as the movement toppled many of the structures of state-sanctioned segregation and some of the nation's institutional discrimination, other forms of racial separatism persisted and, in many ways, actually intensified. For when courts ordered American cities and towns to tear down formal systems of segregation, large numbers of white citizens simply refused to take part. Rather than share desegregated urban public spaces such as public parks and pools, public transportation or public schools with racial minorities, such whites retreated from them entirely, opting for private versions instead: country clubs and private pools, private forms of transportation, and, most notably, a new crop of private, all-white schools that were commonly known in the South as "segregation academies." Meanwhile, as the sociologists Douglas Massey and Nancy Denton chronicled in the aptly named *American Apartheid*, residential segregation in most major cities actually intensified over the course of the 1960s and 1970s. "Desegregation," the 1970s soon made clear, did not mean the same thing as "integration."[13]

This growing racial polarization mapped itself with increasing clarity on the larger landscape of America. Responding to desegregation as well as the deindustrialization and decay of older downtowns, more and more white residents fled from cities entirely, opting for lily-white suburbs instead. The phenomenon of "white flight" happened across the nation, with central cities in US metropolitan areas experiencing an almost 10 percent drop in their white populations over the course of the 1960s. In the North, however, the pattern was even more pronounced, with rates nearly twice the national average. Detroit, for instance, lost 350,000 whites over the decade. The inner cities that had been left behind, marked by what demographers awkwardly termed "minority-majority" populations, then selected black officials to represent them in city hall and Congress. In such ways, the successful integration of African Americans into the political system partly stemmed from the failures of integration in society at large.[14]

Cultural Nationalism

White withdrawal wasn't the only reason the promises of integration were unfulfilled. Increasingly, African Americans and other racial minorities expressed growing reservations about a process of integration that seemed to unfold solely on terms established by whites. A notable element of black nationalism was an insistence that African Americans should not adopt the icons or ideals of a "WASP" (White, Anglo-Saxon, Protestant) mainstream culture but instead reaffirm heroes and histories of their own. As Malcolm X put it, just as a tree severed from its roots soon died, "a people without history or cultural roots also becomes a dead people."[15]

Accordingly, African Americans advanced a new form of cultural nationalism in the 1960s and 1970s that championed distinctive styles of black expression and celebrated accomplishments of prominent African American artists, intellectuals, and entertainers. Academics and athletes alike set models for cultural expressions of black power, as soul and funk musicians broadly popularized the theme. James Brown captured the mood in his 1968 hit, "Say It Loud: I'm Black and I'm Proud!" Television, as always, both echoed and amplified the growing trend, most noticeably with ABC's *Roots*, an eight-part serialization of Alex Haley's best-selling family history. Broadcast over eight nights in January 1977, the series attracted the single largest audience in television history, with network officials estimating that 130 million Americans watched all or part of the program. Indeed, *Roots* was a national phenomenon. "It's [the] Super Bowl every night," marveled the Associated Press. "People are bringing TV sets to work, watching in airports and bars, leaving meetings early and emptying movie theaters and restaurants to get home in time for the nightly episode." Hundreds of colleges and high schools used the broadcast in courses to expose students to black history. These explorations of black identity and expressions of black pride, well received across the country, fueled in African American communities a growing sense of black distinctiveness and, in a political sense, black separatism.[16]

In a similar fashion, Mexican Americans likewise came to question the wisdom of political and cultural integration. The most visible activists of the 1960s, labor leaders Cesar Chavez and Dolores Huerta, had succeeded in securing change through existing channels of liberal reform. Using nonviolent protests and boycott campaigns, they publicized the plight of migrant farmworkers in the Southwest and secured recognition for their union with an empowering motto of "Sí, se puede!" ("Yes, we can!") But while their labor activism succeeded, other Mexican American leaders increasingly grew disillusioned with the limits of integrationist action. In 1966, Rodolfo "Corky" Gonzales, a former boxer and Democratic Party operative, founded the Crusade for Justice in Denver to secure better housing, improved economic conditions, and judicial reforms. Increasingly drawn to separatist politics, he embraced a dream of reclaiming the American Southwest as a distinct nation of "Aztlan." For his part, Gonzales saw a peaceful path forward for the nationalist agenda, suggesting at one point that a United Nations plebiscite might settle the question whether *la raza* (the race) should formally secede from the United States. Others took more direct approaches. Reies López Tijerina, leader of the militant Alianza Federal de Mercedes (Federal Alliance of Land Grants), occupied the Kit Carson National Forest in New Mexico in 1966; a year later, he went to prison after a shootout with local deputies, and the Alianza withered away.[17]

While campaigns for a geographically distinct nation never did accomplish their goal, increasingly more Mexican Americans embraced a cultural nationalism of their own. Rejecting the in-between label of "Mexican American," they called themselves "Chicano" instead. This new identity represented a rejection of "gringo" civilization and a reclamation of their own. "The North American culture is not worth copying," declared Armando Rendón in his 1971 *Chicano Manifesto*; "it is destructive of personal dignity; it is callous, vindictive, arrogant, militaristic, self-deceiving, and greedy; . . . it is an $80 billion defense budget and $75 a month welfare; it is a cultural cesspool and a social and spiritual vacuum for the Chicano." Historian Rodolfo Acuña, a pioneer scholar in the field of Chicano Studies, likewise declared in 1972 that the previous decade had dispelled any illusions Chicanos had about their place in American society. "Many Chicanos participated actively in the political life of the nation, during which they took a hard look at their assigned role in the United States, evaluated it, and then decided that they had had enough," he observed, "and so they bid good-bye to America."[18]

Chicanos declared "good-bye to America" only in a cultural sense; they still sought to use the political process to protect and empower their communities. Initially, activists pinned their hopes on a distinct political party. La Raza Unida, founded in 1970, launched electoral campaigns across the Southwest but found itself unable to gain traction and folded by 1978. Returning to the Democratic Party, Chicanos found greater success, not just by working in its broader coalition but also by embracing broader identities as "Hispanic" or "Latino," moving beyond their Mexican American roots to encompass a much wider range of peoples who spoke Spanish or descended from Latin America, respectively. In 1976, for instance, the Carter campaign highlighted Hispanic outreach while five Democratic members of the House of Representatives—three of Mexican descent and two Puerto Ricans—united to form the Congressional Hispanic Caucus. Likewise, the National Council for La Raza, which began in 1968 as a nonprofit organization advocating for Mexican Americans in the Southwest, relocated to Washington, DC, in 1973 to increase its national influence and then broadened its reach to represent all Latinos. By 1978, Council president Raul Yzaguirre could claim "a national constituency-based organization with over 100 affiliated community organizations representing over a million Latinos." At the local level, meanwhile, Latino politicians began to win races in major metropolitan areas as well: Henry Cisneros in San Antonio in 1981, Federico Peña in Denver in 1983.[19]

As these Americans embraced varied new identities as Chicanos, Hispanics, or Latinos, Japanese and Chinese Americans aligned in an innovative identity of their own: "Asian Americans." Despite their different experiences as immigrant communities across the late nineteenth and early twentieth centuries, the two populations had increasingly been blurred together in the eyes of white legal and political authorities. By the 1960s, the undifferentiated "Oriental" was routinely held up by white liberal reformers as the "model minority," a population that had experienced unquestioned racial discrimination and yet still managed to thrive economically. Though white authorities often set them apart from—and indeed against—other racial minorities, Japanese and Chinese Americans came to feel a kinship with other nonwhites. In the late 1960s and 1970s, activists embraced a new, pan-ethnic "Asian American" identity and rejected their previously privileged status as a "model minority." In a 1969 manifesto titled "The Emergence of Yellow Power in America," Amy Uyematsu argued that Japanese and Chinese Americans had lost "self identity" by adopting the values of the white middle class. They had been complicit in the old racial order, "allow[ing] white America to hold up the 'successful' Oriental image before other minority groups as the model to emulate. White America justifies the blacks' position by showing that other non-whites—yellow people—have been able to 'adapt' to the system." Asian Americans needed to reject that status, she said, and instead engage in "yellow political power."[20]

As African Americans, Mexican Americans, and Asian Americans recoiled from accepting any notion of a mainstream culture, so too did significant numbers of whites themselves. During the late 1960s and 1970s, white ethnics—descendants of late nineteenth- and early twentieth-century immigrants from countries like Ireland, Italy, Poland, and Greece who had arrived as outsiders to the nativist culture of America but gradually won acceptance as "white" themselves—reclaimed their own distinct identities as well. While earlier generations of immigrants had worked hard to shed their ethnic identities and adopt the civic and cultural traditions defined by a Protestant America, their heirs in the 1970s moved in the opposite direction, recovering older identities. Notably, the expressions of ethnic pride had self-conscious echoes of the cultural nationalism of racial minorities, with slogans like "Polish Power" and "Italian Pride." Much as black nationalism was voiced in *Roots*, films like *The Godfather* (1972), *The Godfather II* (1974), and *Rocky* (1976)— which all won Oscars for Best Picture—emphasized the cultural roots and distinct communities of their white ethnic protagonists. As critics noted, however, there was an important distinction: white ethnics who made such claims could, and often did, alternate at will between an "ethnic" identity and a safer "white" one that afforded majoritarian privilege and protection. Even so, the claim to an ethnic identity, however lightly it was made, represented an important development. "The new ethnic politics is a direct challenge to the WASP conception of America," the Slovak American intellectual Michael Novak noted in his 1972 book, *The Rise of the Unmeltable Ethnics*. "It asserts that *groups* can structure the rules and goals and procedures of American life. It asserts that individuals, if they do not wish to, do not have to 'melt.'"[21]

As the nation's racial and ethnic minorities came to think of themselves as distinct and disparate groups, increasingly untethered to any standard "American" identity, the country found its population transformed by a major new wave of immigration. The Immigration and Nationality Act of 1965, one of the most important changes of the Great Society era, abolished the old national-origins quota system that had severely restricted immigration into the country for four decades. The National Origins Act of 1924, passed at the peak of nativist panic in what historian John Higham called "the Tribal Twenties," was intended as a way to reverse the rising tides of immigration in the early twentieth century.[22] Horrified at new waves of Italians, Greeks, Poles, and Russian Jews, the authors of the law sought to restore the population to an "older stock." The legislation established quotas for immigration from various nations, manipulating census data to guarantee that 85 percent of new arrivals would come from northern and western Europe. In a gratuitous insult, the act also barred entry to "all aliens ineligible for citizenship," a clause that, in light of recent Supreme Court decisions, banned all Asians. Such measures were slightly relaxed in the ensuing decades, but restriction remained the rule for the middle swath of the twentieth century.[23]

The Immigration and Nationality Act of 1965 abolished the old system and ushered in a revolutionary new era of migration to America. While the previous law had privileged immigrants from northern and western Europe, the new structure, with its preferences for individuals who worked in white-collar jobs or who had family ties in the United States, encouraged massive migration from Latin America and Asia. Mexico remained the most significant source of the new wave of immigration from Latin America, but Hispanic nations such as the Dominican Republic, El Salvador, Peru, and Ecuador witnessed a striking surge in emigration to the United States, as did, to a lesser degree, Costa Rica, Guatemala, Honduras, and Panama. The increase from Asian nations was even more pronounced; by the early 1980s, roughly half of all immigrants to the United States arrived from Asia. The new Asian immigrants came most notably from China, India, Pakistan, South Korea, Vietnam, and the Philippines, but also Cambodia, Laos,

Thailand, Indonesia, Burma, Sri Lanka, Singapore, Taiwan, Malaysia, and Bangladesh. During the 1970s, the overall US population increased by 11 percent, but the subset of the Asian American population grew 141 percent. The sheer size and internal diversity of the new waves of Asian and Latin American immigration contributed to both the growth and the breadth of larger cultural identities such as "Asian American," "Hispanic," and "Latino" within the United States.[24]

As these new immigrants took their place in a nation that was increasingly sorting itself into distinct racial and ethnic groups, they did the same. The new arrivals gravitated in significant numbers to major metropolitan areas like New York City, Los Angeles, San Francisco, Miami, Houston, San Diego, Chicago, and Washington, DC. Inside such cities, immigrants often grouped together. Where applicable, established ethnic enclaves like the Chinatowns and Little Tokyos, common in many cities, stood ready to welcome them, but in new settings these immigrants forged their own communities. Nicaraguans, Salvadorans, and Guatemalans flocked to San Francisco and Los Angeles. Dominicans migrated en masse to New York City, soon rivaling the older Puerto Rican concentration there. Cubans steadily expanded their presence in Miami. The Hmong from Laos and South Koreans set down roots in Los Angeles, as Indians and Pakistanis forged a thriving new "South Asian" or "desi" community of their own in Houston. Settling down in their own neighborhoods with their cultural ties intact, these new immigrants made worlds for themselves that resembled those already made by their fellow Americans.[25]

The influx of immigrants, however, did not sit well with sizable portions of the public who feared that the nation had already changed too much in the previous decade. The media began to cover the changes in immigration as a challenge to the national character, drawing special attention to new waves of undocumented arrivals, styled as "illegal aliens." For instance, U.S. News and World Report, one of the most popular news magazines of the era, treated readers to headlines such as "How Millions of Illegal Aliens Sneak into the U.S." and "Border Crisis: Illegal Aliens out of Control."[26] The use of metaphors like "crisis" or "invasion" to describe Mexican immigration, barely in use when Congress passed immigration reform in 1965, steadily increased during the 1970s.[27]

Diversity and Divisions

As Americans, old and new alike, sorted themselves into disparate and distinct communities, the political and judicial system responded in kind. Most notably, the Supreme Court, which had once seemed so receptive to the arguments made by civil rights activists, increasingly set limits on how far it, and the nation, would change in the movement for racial integration. Over the course of the 1970s, a new emphasis on divisions and diversity took hold.

The legal campaign for school desegregation, for instance, stalled as the focus shifted from central cities into the suburbs. Originally, the promise of metropolitan programs of desegregation seemed bright. In 1971, the Supreme Court had given its approval to the use of busing plans—programs which moved children in largely minority neighborhoods to largely white schools, and vice versa—in the landmark case of *Swann v. Charlotte-Mecklenburg Board of Education*. The decision proved starkly unpopular with suburban whites, many of whom had fled cities over the previous decade to avoid the growing pattern of what many derided as "forced integration." Indeed, for the remainder of the decade, busing stood as *the* top political issue for white suburbanites. A Gallup Poll in October 1971, shortly after *Swann*, showed that whites opposed busing by a margin of 3–1. While previous stages of the civil rights movement faced opposition largely in the South, national polls showed that hostility to busing was common among whites across the country. Eighty-two percent of white southerners opposed busing, while the percentages in the Northeast, Midwest, and West were not far behind, ranging from 71 percent to 77 percent.[28]

The controversy over busing, and the larger conflicts between cities and suburbs, came to a head in Detroit. In the 1960s, Detroit had emerged as a prime example of the twin processes of urban decay and suburban white flight. The city had witnessed one of the worst riots of the late 1960s, leading more than one-third of a million whites to leave the city over the course of the decade. By 1970, Detroit had become 44 percent black, while the suburbs around it were almost completely white. In Warren, only 132 people out of a total of 179,000 were black; in Dearborn, only 13 out of 104,000. The segregation of Detroit and its suburbs was even starker in its schools. Although blacks and whites lived in roughly equal numbers inside the city, Detroit's neighborhoods were starkly segregated by race. The vast majority of census tracts were more than 90 percent black or 90 percent white, and schools in those neighborhoods followed suit. More than 70 percent of the city's schools were either all-white or all-black.[29]

Because of the obvious segregation in Detroit's metropolitan area, the NAACP initiated what would become the Supreme Court case of *Milliken v. Bradley*. Local courts reviewed the overwhelming evidence provided by the NAACP and ruled in 1972 that Detroit's schools had been intentionally segregated. The judge ordered a "multi-district" remedy that would require the busing of 310,000 students across district lines to new schools. White children would ride from the suburbs to the inner city to attend school, while black children would ride out to the suburbs to attend suburban schools that had been all-white. The ruling represented an escalation of the *Swann* decision. In that case, the busing in the Charlotte area had all taken place within a single district—a very large district that encompassed both the city and suburbs, but still, only one district. The lower court ruling in *Milliken*, however, encompassed fifty-three districts. If upheld, it would set a precedent that would mean the effective integration of countless cities and suburbs across the country. Indeed, if the Supreme Court upheld the ruling, the NAACP planned to follow up with similar challenges to integrate suburbs around Chicago, Cleveland, Kansas City, St. Louis, Philadelphia, Boston, and other areas with largely black city schools and lily-white suburbs.[30]

By the time the *Milliken* case reached the Supreme Court, however, it had been transformed by the appointments of Richard Nixon, with the busing issue specifically in mind. What Nixon cared about most in his judicial nominations was protecting the white suburbs from "forced integration" with the cities. When Nixon outlined his requirements for court nominees with his attorney general, the president was explicit. He wanted conservatives and, he said, "within the definition of conservative, he must be against busing and against forced housing integration. Beyond that, he can do what he pleases." Nixon soon got his wish. His four appointees, plus Potter Stewart, an Eisenhower holdover, formed a new conservative majority on the court that did everything in its power to protect the white suburbs from the people and the problems of the inner city.[31]

The *Milliken* case proved to be the keystone to the court's new approach. Writing for a slim 5–4 majority, Chief Justice Warren Burger claimed that only the city of Detroit had engaged in *de jure* discrimination and segregation, and that the suburbs were innocent of any wrongdoing. Ignoring the massive role that the federal government had played in the creation of suburbia and, more importantly, the installation and perpetuation of segregation there, Burger ruled that suburban segregation had unfolded unintentionally, by private custom, not public act. (Legal scholars would soon describe the difference as *de facto* segregation, as opposed to *de jure*.) Because the government had not created the problem, Burger said, the Supreme Court had no right to correct it. The city of Detroit could use busing within its city limits, but the white suburbs had to be excluded from any program of integration. The four dissenters had never been on the losing side of a school segregation decision. Justice Thurgood Marshall, a former NAACP attorney, wrote a scathing dissent on their behalf. In an unusual move, he read portions of his opinion from the bench, his tone both sad and scornful as he rebutted Burger's decision point by point. "Today's holding," he said in conclusion, "is more a reflection of a perceived public mood that we have gone far enough in enforcing the Constitution's guarantee of equal justice than it is the product of neutral principles of law. In the short run, it may seem to be the easier course to allow our great metropolitan areas to be divided up each into two cities—one white, the other black—but it is a course, I predict, our people will ultimately regret."[32]

Even in the short run, tempers flared. The court's decision only ruled out busing across district lines; within districts, it could still be used. The distinction sparked resistance and riots inside cities where busing was employed. Boston emerged as the most visible battleground. In December 1974, antibusing protesters clashed with police in South Boston and trapped 125 transferred African American students inside a local school. As they threw rocks at school buses and flipped over police cruisers, the white mob became menacing. "Bus them back to Africa" yelled one of the protesters.[33] The violent confrontation forced the city to shut down the school for over a month, while the national press portrayed the events as indicative of a brewing race war. Dem-

ocratic politicians soon became the focus of protesters' attacks, with
Senator Ted Kennedy chased by an angry crowd into the Federal Building downtown. Of all the shocking images of violence to come from
the city's busing crisis, none outdid a famous photograph by the *Boston Herald-American* photographer Stanley Forman. Titled "The Soiling
of Old Glory," the Pulitzer Prize–winning photo showed a black civil
rights lawyer about to be stabbed by a white teen brandishing a pole
with the American flag. As the nation watched such images in horror,
the White House seemed unable or unwilling to act. In a press conference, President Ford called the confrontations "most unfortunate" but
voiced sympathy for the whites who were, in his mind, the real victims
of "forced busing." Boston's mayor Kevin White pled with the president
to send in federal marshals to keep the peace. Ford refused.[34]

The growing tensions on civil rights—on the court and in the nation
at large—were also seen in the debate over affirmative action. Like busing, affirmative action was an extension of civil rights strategies born in
the 1960s. Presidents Kennedy and Johnson had embraced the term as
a necessary remedy for past injustices, and civil rights leaders readily
agreed. In his last book, *Where Do We Go from Here?*, Martin Luther
King Jr. acknowledged that "special treatment" for African Americans
might seem to conflict with his previously professed ideal of opportunity based on individual merit. But, King continued, "a society that has
done something special *against* the Negro for hundreds of years must
now do something special *for* him." However, critics charged that affirmative action programs often focused on aspects of society—college
admissions, employment, and promotions—where there were a finite
number of beneficiaries. Opportunities given to individuals in those
spaces would necessarily come at the expense of others. In their view,
affirmative action thus represented a "zero sum game" in which gains
for one group meant a loss for another. Affirmative action, they argued,
was essentially "reverse discrimination" against whites.[35]

In 1978, the Supreme Court addressed the matter directly for the
first time in the landmark case of *Regents of the University of California
v. Bakke*. The plaintiff Allan Bakke had graduated from the University
of Minnesota in 1962 with an engineering degree, served in Vietnam
from 1963 to 1967, and then got a Master's degree in engineering from
Stanford. At the age of 33, however, Bakke decided he would rather

be a doctor. In 1973, he applied to a dozen medical schools, but was rejected by all of them. While Bakke had fine grades and very good MCAT scores, most of the schools pointed to his weak performance in interviews as grounds for his rejection. However, Bakke seized on the fact that one of the twelve schools that rejected him, the University of California, Davis, had a special admissions program that reserved sixteen of one hundred places in its entering class for minority students. He sued the university, charging that it had violated his rights guaranteed by the 1964 Civil Rights Act and the equal protection clause of the Fourteenth Amendment. With the case before the court, a national conversation unfolded on its merits, one that took place on the pages of major newspapers and the campuses of countless colleges across the country.[36]

As in *Milliken,* the Supreme Court split into two distinct factions, each of which was completely unwilling to compromise. Four liberal justices—Marshall, Blackmun, Brennan, and White—argued that the quota system used by the UC Davis medical school was completely acceptable. The Constitution had never been "color blind," they pointed out, so it was perfectly fine to use group-based quotas as a remedy for past discrimination. Meanwhile, four conservatives—Burger, Rehnquist, Stewart, and Stevens—argued that not only was the quota system used by UC Davis unconstitutional, but *any* form of affirmative action, whether it be in the form of specific quotas or general goals, was an unconstitutional form of bias. With the court split into two camps of four men each, it was left to the ninth justice, Lewis Powell, to come up with a compromise. It took him eight months to come up with the "judgment of the court" in *Regents v. Bakke.* In the end, he essentially produced two decisions in one.

In the first half of Powell's decision, he sided with the four who opposed all forms of affirmative action. Together, they struck down the UC Davis quota system, ruling that it established a "classification based on race and ethnic background" and was therefore unconstitutional. In the second half of Powell's decision, however, he sided with the other four who wanted to uphold all forms of affirmative action. He claimed that "race or ethnic background may be deemed a 'plus' in a particular applicant's file," to be weighed along with grades, test scores, and interviews. The decision, in essence, sanctioned the overall policy of affirmative action while striking down the specific practice of race-based quotas. In a sign of how contentious the issue had become, though, only Powell agreed with all parts of the court's so-called "majority" opinion. The result was an awkward truce on the issue that left all sides uneasy. "It was a landmark occasion," a leading law professor noted, "but the court failed to produce a landmark decision."[37]

Still, *Bakke* made an important mark. In his decision, Justice Powell defended race-conscious admissions programs with an assertion that diversity represented a compelling state interest. The defense of diversity would, in many ways, keep affirmative action programs alive in the coming decades, but it did so with considerable cost. "With the emergence of the diversity rationale," sociologist John Skrentny noted, "affirmative action has become separated from *discrimination*." No longer giving weight to the plight of disadvantaged racial or economic minorities, as individuals or groups, courts would think more about the advantages that the mere presence of people from different backgrounds might have on the larger polity.[38]

The new directive of diversity spread across the courts' handling of issues of race and ethnicity during the 1970s. In the 1974 case of *Lau v. Nichols*, for instance, the Supreme Court established important new guidelines for bilingual and bicultural education. Sweeping away immersion courses that sought to improve the skills of students with limited English proficiency (LEP) and thereby integrate them into the standard school curriculum, the court now mandated native-language instruction for younger students who spoke languages other than English at home. Instead of promoting cultural integration, these "Lau remedies" aimed to preserve the unique cultural traditions of non-English speakers. Practically speaking, the change would largely impact Hispanics, who accounted for some 80 percent of all LEP students in the late 1970s. But its importance was more widely felt. In 1979, the Department of Education considered new regulations that would have mandated massive staffing changes to support bilingual education. In response, Chicago's public schools complained the rules would obligate them to hire certified bilingual instructors for 90,000 students who would then need to be taught in 139 different languages. The proposed federal regulations were ultimately abandoned, but the underlying emphasis on bilingual instruction and multicultural education continued to thrive.[39]

The legal and political changes on busing, affirmative action, and bilingual instruction reflected a much larger transformation across American society. "The ideological shift to diversity led to a reconception of the very nature of America," historian Bruce Schulman noted, "to see the nation not as a melting pot where many different peoples and cultures contributed to one common stew, but as discrete peoples and cultures sharing the same places—a tapestry, salad bowl, or rainbow." While such changes did much to preserve and protect the individual cultures of different groups, they effectively eroded any sense of national community along the way and established one of the deepest of the new fault lines. Instead of a coherent and cohesive identity, Americans now had diversity and division.[40]

CHAPTER 4

A Crisis
of Equality

As Americans underwent a significant transformation in their thinking about the fault lines of race, ethnicity, and national identity in the 1970s, they reckoned with an equally important revolution on essential notions of gender, sexuality, and the family.

Much like the government and the corporation, the "nuclear family" stood as a fundamental pillar of American life in the decades after World War II. This new norm for American life—understood as a married couple with children—became the basic building block of postwar society, a microcosm of the larger nation. More than that, the nuclear family set expectations for the roles that individuals played within its boundaries. Men, typically, served as the breadwinner, working outside the home and providing for their dependents; women, in most cases, were confined to the homes where they focused on their roles as wives and mothers, responsible for raising children and creating a nurturing environment. The two came together, in this understanding, in a supposedly natural relationship, rooted in heterosexual attraction to each other, manifested in a "traditional" marriage, and devoted to having and raising children.[1]

All these assumptions, which seemed so steadfast in the early years of the postwar period, steadily crumbled. For many Americans, they had been unrealistic from the start. In African American and immigrant communities, as well as in much of the white working class, the male breadwinner model had never reflected realities on the ground. But as the 1960s dawned, even more affluent whites began to cast off the old model as unrealistic. White feminists, for instance, rejected the subordinate roles to which women had long been restricted and advocated instead for an autonomous identity of their own, and of their own making. Meanwhile, as feminists questioned reigning notions of "proper" gender relations, gay and lesbian activists made similar challenges to a postwar system that had defined them as "deviants" who deserved, at best, second-class citizenship. In their public forms, the movements for feminism and gay and lesbian rights simply sought equal treatment before the law. But those invested in the old order saw these grassroots movements as an existential threat to the nuclear family and, thus, a threat to the nation itself. Conservatives, presenting themselves as the defenders of "family values," launched a massive counterattack that prompted the "culture wars" of the coming decades.

Feminism

The changes in women's roles were rooted, in important ways, in the larger changes of American political and economic life.

Many Americans assume that feminism inspired more women to move into the workforce, but in truth the reverse was true. It was the movement of women into the workplace, where they confronted chronic gender discrimination and widespread sexual harassment, that fueled feminism. Working-class women, organized in unions, had been at the forefront of the campaign for government protection since the 1930s. As deindustrialization dismantled the postwar economy in the 1970s, the blue-collar union jobs that had long provided working-class men with steady wages and good benefits became harder to find. Some of these displaced workers found jobs in the new service sector, but positions there generally paid less than the ones they had theoretically replaced. Significantly, by 1976, only 40 percent of the nation's jobs paid enough to support a family on their own. As the average take-home pay for most families dwindled, rising rates of inflation sent their cost of living skyrocketing. Taken together, these changes meant the end of an era in which male breadwinners were the norm. The movement of married women into the workforce, a trend under way for decades, significantly accelerated. At the same time, as the divorce rate in America doubled between 1966 and 1976, a greater number of newly single mothers found themselves forced into full-time jobs as well, having to support themselves and their children. The rise of working mothers was unmistakable: in 1970, 30 percent of women with preschool children held a paid job; in 1976, 43 percent; in 1985, 50 percent.[2]

The movement of mothers into the paid labor force was part of a larger trend of women at work. In 1970, 43 percent of American women over the age of sixteen held jobs outside the home; in 1980, 52 percent did. As these 45 million women went to work, they traversed an economic landscape with decidedly uneven terrain. On the surface, women seemingly benefited from the fact that the booming business sectors of the 1970s were in fields that had traditionally been regarded as "women's work." As the manufacturing sector declined, the service economy began to soar. Between 1973 and 1980, 40 percent of all new private jobs were service sector positions focused on food, health care, and business support. Employers in those fields often preferred to hire women, but usually in part-time positions with low wages and little or no union protections. Even women who were able to secure full-time work, however, faced persistent patterns of unequal pay. In fact, despite their growing presence in the workplace, women's average wages lagged further behind men's with each passing year. In 1956, the median income for a woman who worked a full-time job was 63 percent of that of a man who had the same position; by 1964, it had dropped to 59 percent; and by 1974, down to just 57 percent. At service sector jobs, women fared even worse: in sales, for instance, women on average earned only 44 percent of what men did.[3]

As women faced gender discrimination on the job, they found the federal government unable or unwilling to help. The Civil Rights Act of 1964 had a tangled legislative history when it came to gender. The law outlawed employment discrimination on the basis of sex, but the origins of that clause severely undercut its impact. Seeking to sabotage the bill, Congressman Howard Smith, a conservative Virginia segregationist, had inserted "sex" into the list of categories for which discrimination was banned. Liberal representatives might be willing to back equality for racial minorities, he assumed, but they would likely draw the line at equality for the sexes. And indeed, when Smith suggested the idea, the men in the House treated it as laughable. (Liberal Democrat Emanuel Celler, for instance, joked that in arguments with his wife, he always got in the last words: "Yes, dear.") Despite the derision of their colleagues, the few women in the House took the idea seriously and shamed their colleagues who did not. "If there had been any necessity to have pointed out that women were a second-class sex," Representative Martha Griffiths of Michigan noted, "the laughter would have proved it." With her backing, the Civil Rights Act passed with the ban against gender discrimination intact.[4]

But the law meant little on its own. The Equal Employment Opportunity Commission (EEOC), the agency Congress tasked with implementing the legislation, simply refused to enforce the ban on gender discrimination. Between 1964 and 1966, women filed more than 4,000 complaints with the EEOC, but the agency dismissed every single one as frivolous. When the commission did take action, it often made matters worse. In August 1965, for instance, the EEOC ruled that sex-segregated want ads did not violate the law. The *Wall Street Journal*, suggesting that the very idea of gender-neutral job advertisements was ludicrous, dared readers to imagine "a 'matronly vice president' gleefully participating in an old office sport by chasing a male secretary around a big leather-topped desk" or a "black-jacketed truck driver skillfully maneuvering a giant rig into a dime-sized dock space—and then checking her lipstick in the rear-view mirror." Such prospects might seem "ridiculous," the paper reported, but some women were actually arguing for just such a right. Businesses remained bewildered at the very idea. An airline personnel officer wondered, "What are we going to do now when a gal walks into our office, demands a job as an airline pilot and has the credentials to qualify?"[5]

Realizing that the political and business establishment would not end the persistent problems of gender discrimination, women activists resolved to do it themselves. In late 1966, leaders including author Betty Friedan and Representative Griffiths banded together in a new feminist civil rights organization, which they called the National Organization for Women (NOW). Its founding statement of purpose called for "a true partnership between the sexes" that demanded "a different concept of marriage, an equitable sharing of the responsibilities of home and children, and of the economic burdens of their support." NOW initially focused on the last item in that list, targeting sex-segregated want ads in its first major campaign. Picketing the offices of the *New York Times* and dumping piles of newspapers outside local EEOC offices across the country, the new organization convinced the EEOC to reverse course and outlaw gender-specific job ads in August 1968. At the same time, NOW targeted gender discrimination in individual industries. Most notably, it succeeded in getting airlines to end their traditional rule that required stewardesses, as they were then called, to resign as soon as they married or turned thirty-two. This practice had previously allowed the airlines to showcase stewardesses who were young, attractive, and presumably sexually available to their largely male passengers. More significantly, it let companies avoid granting these women raises, pensions, or Social Security payments, thereby inflating profit margins at their employees' expense. In such ways, NOW's first president Betty Friedan observed, "sex discrimination *was* big business."[6]

While feminists found some successes with this piecemeal approach based on grassroots pressure and protest, the leaders of NOW sought to secure broader protections for women in federal policy. To do so, they turned their attention to the campaign for the Equal Rights Amendment (ERA), a longtime goal of the feminist movement. The ERA had been idling before Congress since the 1920s, but in the early 1970s it finally secured passage. The amendment seemed straightforward, a simple assertion that "equality of rights under the law shall not be denied or abridged by the United States or any state on account of sex" with enabling clauses that allowed Congress to enforce it. In a testament to the newfound clout of feminist organizations like NOW, politicians from across the spectrum readily endorsed the amendment. Leading liberals like Ted Kennedy and George McGovern embraced it, but so did prominent conservatives like Richard Nixon, George Wallace, and Strom Thurmond. In March 1972, the ERA passed Congress easily—in the House, the margin was 354–23; in the Senate, 84–8—and seemed sure to win swift ratification by the required three-fourths majority of the states. Hawaii ratified the amendment the very same day it was sent to the states by Congress; over the next two days, Delaware, Nebraska, New Hampshire, Idaho, and Iowa did too. "Ratification by mid-1973 looks probable, but not easy," noted the editors of the feminist *Ms.* magazine.[7]

The forces of reaction, however, proved strong. Despite the promising start, the campaign for the ERA's ratification soon slowed and stalled. Opponents of the amendment were able to draw on much more support at the state and local level than they had in the halls of Congress. In October 1972, conservative Catholic activist Phyllis Schlafly founded STOP ERA to make the case that the Equal Rights Amendment would reduce women's rights rather than expand them. (Pointedly, "STOP" stood for "Stop Taking Our Privileges.") An accomplished attorney and a force in the Republican Party, Schlafly nevertheless described herself as "just a housewife" who was seeking to preserve traditional protections for mothers and homemakers, including married women's rights to conjugal support, the obligations of alimony and child support in cases of divorce, and the tendency for women to get custody of children almost automatically when a marriage dissolved. "What about the rights of a woman who doesn't want to be treated like a man?" she asked in one tract. In 1977, Schlafly made her strongest case against the amendment in her book *The Power of the Positive Woman*. "The Positive Woman opposes ERA," she argued, "because it would be hurtful to women, to men, to children, to the family, to local self-government, and to society as a whole."[8]

As Schlafly helped mobilize opposition to the Equal Rights Amendment, she shrewdly transformed the terms of the debate. While proponents of the amendment claimed to be fighting for the rights of women, Schlafly insisted that she was working to protect the entire family—women, men, and children, too. Claiming the term "pro-family" for the opponents of the amendment, she marginalized its supporters as radicals who "hate men and children." Her STOP ERA chapters led the fight against ratification in the states, but other conservative women created organizations of their own. Following Schlafly's lead, these opponents of the ERA emphasized traditional gender roles, as seen in organizational names like Happiness of Motherhood Eternal (HOME), Mississippians for God, Family and Country, and the Texas-based Women Who Want to be Women. In intensive lobbying campaigns at state legislatures, these women likewise played up their identities as housewives and mothers. In Illinois and New York, for instance, they hand-delivered homemade baked goods to state legislators, with a simple rhyme attached: "My heart and hands went into this dough. For the sake of the family, please say no."[9]

While such appeals to traditional gender norms targeted male politicians, they had deep resonances for many women as well. In an article for *Redbook*, Vivian Cadden reported that the cause of "women's liberation" had little appeal "to the wives of truck drivers and farmers and salesmen and auto workers and struggling small businessmen and beginning lawyers" who believed their lives as homemakers compared favorably to the long hours and grueling demands of their husbands' jobs. Simply put, they didn't want to be liberated. "I *like* what I'm doing," insisted one young housewife. Even those who worked full-time and would have benefited from equal protection on the job still worried about the ERA's impact off the clock. The amendment, they feared, would have horrible cultural consequences. "This whole Women's Liberation thing is a crock of you-know-what," complained a female factory worker at a General Electric plant in Ohio. "Next thing you know it'll be my turn to drive by and toot the horn and pick him up on Saturday night. Before you know it, it'll be my turn to pay."[10]

These defenses of traditional gender identities were especially compelling for evangelical and fundamentalist Christians who believed such roles had been divinely determined. From their perspective, God had purposefully given men and women different abilities, in both body and mind, when he created them. Women had a duty to serve their husbands as "helpmeets" (a version of the term *helpmate*, derived from the Bible) and were bound by their wedding vows to submit to them at all times. In popular books published over the decade, evangelical authors asserted that submission to their husbands actually elevated women. For instance, in her 1973 best seller *The Total Woman*, Marabel Morgan argued that "it is only when a woman surrenders her life to her husband, reveres and worships him, and is willing to serve him, that she becomes really beautiful to him. She becomes a priceless jewel, the glory of femininity, his queen!" Not surprisingly, conservative Christians with such attitudes played a pivotal role in the state-level campaigns against the ERA's ratification. In midwestern states like Illinois, the opposition was predominantly Catholic; in Mountain West states like Utah, Nevada, and Arizona, Mormons dominated; in the South, STOP ERA chapters were overwhelmingly staffed by the Churches of Christ and Southern Baptists. In Texas, for instance, 98 percent of the women who testified against ratification belonged to a church, with 66 percent describing themselves as "fundamentalist Protestants."[11]

This conservative opposition effectively killed the Equal Rights

Amendment. Even though the amendment had secured ratification in 35 of the needed 38 states by 1977, the countermovement stopped it in its tracks. Its supporters on Capitol Hill did everything in their power to get it moving again, with Congress extending the deadline for ratification to 1982. No more states signed on; indeed, several moved to rescind their earlier ratifications. In the end, the Equal Rights Amendment died. But its demise, its opponents still insisted, was actually a triumph for women. "The defeat of the Equal Rights Amendment is the greatest victory for women's rights since the women's suffrage amendment of 1920," Schlafly proudly announced, but the battle had only begun. "We must renew our efforts and develop the quality of perseverance so that we win in the battle for God, family and country."[12]

And, to be sure, the struggle over the status of women in 1970s America was far from over. While feminists failed to secure ratification of the ERA, they succeeded in obtaining some smaller but still significant legal changes throughout the decade. An early notable victory came in Title IX of the 1972 Higher Education Act amendments, a measure that banned gender discrimination at all colleges and universities that received federal funding. Linking funding to institutions that adhered to certain social regulations had been integral to the success of the Civil Rights Act of 1964, and supporters of women's rights hoped once again to use the leverage of money to ensure change. Democratic Senator Birch Bayh of Indiana emerged as the chief champion of the proposal. "We are all familiar with the stereotype of women as pretty things who go to college to find a husband, go on to graduate school because they want a more interesting husband, and finally marry, have children and never work again," he told his colleagues in the Senate. "The desire of many schools not to waste a 'man's place' on a woman stems from such stereotyped notions. But the facts absolutely contradict these myths about the 'weaker sex.'" Title IX, Bayh argued, would help women secure "an equal chance to attend the schools of their choice, to develop the skills that they want, and to apply those skills with the knowledge that they will have a fair chance to secure the jobs of their choice with equal pay for equal work." After passing both houses of Congress by large margins, the measure was signed into law by President Nixon in June 1972.[13]

Title IX represented a significant milestone in equal education for women, but even before its measures went into effect, the revolution in higher education was already apparent. In 1975, a *U.S. News and World Report* article titled "The American Woman: On the Move, But Where?" informed readers that the numbers of women in professional schools had already dramatically risen. Between 1960 and 1974, the percentage of female students in dentistry schools increased from 1 percent to 7 percent; in medical schools, from 6 percent to 18 percent; in law schools, from 4 percent to 19 percent; in pharmacy schools, from 12 percent to 32 percent. As programs that served as gateways to white-collar careers shed their sexism, so too did the professions they served. In 1971, women represented only 4 percent of all lawyers and judges, 9 percent of doctors, and 10 percent of PhD recipients; by 1981, they counted for 14 percent of lawyers and judges, 22 percent of doctors, and 30 percent of PhDs. Undergraduate education was likewise transformed. Notably, Ivy League schools, which, except for Cornell, had been sex-segregated since their founding, began admitting women over the course of the decade. Yale and Princeton sparked the modern trend in the late 1960s; Dartmouth, Penn, Brown, and Harvard followed suit in the early 1970s; and Columbia, the last holdout, finally admitted women in 1983. Meanwhile, when it went into effect in 1978, Title IX had an immediate impact on education across the board. An unforeseen consequence of the measure was a significant boost to women's athletics, now that funding could no longer be used solely on men's sports. In the early 1970s, there were fewer than 30,000 female college athletes on NCAA teams; only one out of 27 women played in high school sports in 1972, with games that were usually relegated to secondary events for the student body.[14] By the end of the 1970s, girls' participation in high school athletics was nearly five times greater than it had been at the decade's start.[15]

In many ways, the fight to secure access to the world of athletics symbolized the larger struggles of feminism in the 1970s. To achieve their goals, feminists were determined to remake the world of culture and social relations where ideas of gender were forged in the popular psyche. As much as any other segment of society, sports had long been considered "a man's world," and the rise to fame of female athletes signaled important cultural changes in the country. No one better represented the trend than tennis star Billie Jean King. In 1972, after winning three major titles, she became the first woman ever to be honored as *Sports Illustrated*'s "Sportsman of the Year." (The achievement was slightly lessened by the fact that the magazine decided to split the title, for the first time in its history, making King share the honor with UCLA men's basketball coach John Wooden.) One of the tennis titles King won that year was the US Open. In keeping with the unequal pay of the era, the prize money for the women's championship was $15,000 less than that for the men's. King shocked the sports world when she announced that, unless the prizes were equalized, she would not return to defend her title at the 1973 tournament. Afraid of losing a star attraction, the US Open changed its policies and became the first tournament to offer equal money for men and women. From that victory, King went on to launch the Women's Tennis Association and its tour, the Virginia Slims Championship. In many ways, the tour's cigarette sponsor seemed to be the perfect symbol of the era, as its slogan blended feminist accomplishment with male chauvinist patronizing: "You've Come a Long Way, Baby."[16]

Despite her many accomplishments, Billie Jean King's biggest moment in the national spotlight came in what had originally seemed just a public relations stunt, the so-called "Battle of the Sexes" match. The idea came from Bobby Riggs, an aging Wimbledon champion who believed that women did not deserve equal prize money and bragged that, even at 55 years old, he could still beat any of the top female players.[17] King accepted the challenge. Their September 20, 1973, contest at the Houston Astrodome became a media circus, with ABC broadcasting the contest on its popular "Wide World of Sports" program to an international audience of nearly 90 million, a record for tennis that would last for another three decades. The stakes were clear: both Riggs and King were guaranteed $100,000 for the appearance, with the winner getting another $100,000. (This meant that, if King won, she would nearly double her annual earnings as the world's top female tennis player.) An inveterate gambler, Riggs promoted the contest as the "battle of the sexes. Man against woman; sex against sex. Husbands argue with wives, bosses with secretaries. Everybody wants to bet." Las Vegas put him as a 5–2 favorite. Despite the long odds, King dominated from the start and swept Riggs in three straight sets. Even the curmudgeonly announcer Howard Cosell was impressed with her performance, yelling out "Equality for women!" when King won it all.[18]

In many ways, the ABC "Battle of the Sexes" broadcast fit well with new trends elsewhere in television news. For decades, TV news programs had only featured women in minor roles, mostly as "weather girls." Slowly, however, women began to find new roles in the male-dominated world of sports journalism. Jane Chastain, for instance, had a twelve-year background in local sports reporting before being signed by CBS to do sideline reports in NFL games in 1974. The next year, former Miss America Phyllis George also joined CBS as a sportscaster; a year later, she became part of the NFL Today team, working alongside Brent Musberger and Jimmy "the Greek" Snyder. In 1978, Jayne Kennedy (a former model and actress) replaced George and became the first African American female host on a network sports program. Such milestones were notable, but in some ways the highest-profile hires—a former Miss America, a future Playboy cover girl—were still in keeping with the old practices in which women were hired with their physical attractiveness in mind, rather than their expertise. Complaints came from all sides, as feminists resented the objectification of such women and male chauvinists complained about their lack of qualifications.[19]

Meanwhile, in the world of hard news, women made clearer gains. Since the start of television news, few women had been allowed to serve as reporters, while anchoring was entirely reserved for men. "I have the strong feeling," NBC News president Reuven Frank noted in 1971, "that audiences are less prepared to accept news from a woman's voice than from a man's." That attitude quickly changed. In 1972, Jean Enersen became the first female anchor of a local evening news program, at KING-TV in Seattle. Soon, other women, many of whom would go on to become prominent figures in national news, followed suit as local anchors: Judy Woodruff in Atlanta, Jane Pauley in Indianapolis, and Connie Chung in Los Angeles. Women increasingly took on prominent roles at the networks, too. On NBC, Nancy Dickerson anchored the daily political program Inside Washington from 1971 to 1974. Then, in 1976, Barbara Walters at ABC became the first female coanchor of a network evening news show. In her first one-hour broadcast, she featured a profile on Jimmy Carter and his wife Rosalynn as well as a piece on the singer Barbara Streisand and her partner John Peters. The first show blew away the competing networks, exciting ABC executives who instantly sensed they had a hit on their hands. In such ways, women's voices were increasingly heard not just in the delivery of news, but in the shaping of its stories as well.[20]

Meanwhile, women increasingly took top billing in network sitcoms and dramas. *The Mary Tyler Moore Show* (1970–1977), notably, chronicled the life of an unmarried woman working as a reporter at a Minneapolis television station. (The show's theme song assured its single-woman star and its similarly situated viewers: "You're going to make it after all!") The sitcom was such a hit, it led to eponymous spinoffs for the star's two supporting characters, Mary's neighbor *Rhoda* (1974–1978) and her widowed landlady *Phyllis* (1975–1977). Meanwhile, Norman Lear's hit *All in the Family* featured an outspoken feminist and launched a spinoff of its own, *Maude* (1972–1978), in which star Bea Arthur frankly tackled feminist topics including sexism and even abortion. *One Day at a Time* (1975–1984) and *Alice* (1976–1985) featured working mothers who were divorced and widowed, respectively. Even action shows, long dominated by male leads, increasingly placed women at the center, as seen in prime-time hits like *Police Woman* (1974–1978), *Wonder Woman* (1975–1979), and *The Bionic Woman* (1976–1978). More controversially, *Charlie's Angels* (1976–1981) featured three female leads as private detectives, but in portrayals that reinforced sexist stereotypes. "The only good thing I can say about it is that three seasons ago it would have been three young men," noted Norma Connolly, head of the women's conference committee of the Screen Actors Guild. "The women take orders from a male voice; they're little idiot cheerleaders."[21]

While television proved to be a bit problematic, print media offered new opportunities for feminists to make their case on their own terms. In 1972, journalist Gloria Steinem founded *Ms.* magazine. (The title itself signaled a new attitude, a demand on the part of feminists that women not be designated as a "Miss" or a "Mrs."—terms that hinged on marital status—but rather by a more broadly drawn term of "Ms." that let a woman stand on her own.) The magazine championed a proudly aggressive feminism, modeled after its first cover image, which depicted the superhero Wonder Woman. It repeatedly broke new ground. In 1975, the black radical Angela Davis authored a piece about a black inmate who was tried for murder after killing a prison guard who sexually assaulted her; in 1976, the magazine ran a cover story on the still-taboo topic of domestic violence titled "The Truth About Battered Wives." In 1977, Ms. broke ground with a story about sexual harassment in the workplace and, a year later, sparked a national debate when Steinem wondered what federal policies would look like if "men could menstruate."[22]

Outside the world of media, women notched several substantial milestones. The ranks of the clergy, long reserved for men, slowly began to open. In 1972, the Jewish Reform seminary in Cincinnati, Hebrew Union College, ordained the first female rabbi in America. The Episcopal Church formally approved its first female deacons in 1970 and its first female priests in 1976. In academia, women achieved several breakthroughs, including selection of the first female Rhodes Scholar in 1976. Meanwhile, in the political realm, Ella Grasso won the Connecticut governor's race in 1974, becoming the first woman who was neither the wife nor the widow of a former male governor to serve in such a role. The Democratic National Committee appointed its first female head in 1972; the Republicans followed suit in 1974. During the Ford and Carter administrations, four more federal departments were led by their first female cabinet secretaries. By the decade's end, major cities such as Chicago, San Francisco, Phoenix, and San Antonio had all elected a woman as mayor.[23]

As professional opportunities such as these increased, younger women adjusted their private lives to meet their broader obligations. Getting married and having children right after school were no longer top priorities for many women, a development that alarmed conservatives who looked back on the Cold War norms of the suburban nuclear family with nostalgia. The marriage rate, which had increased over the 1960s, now reversed course and reached a new low in 1976. Birth rates declined as well, dropping precipitously from 18.4 births per 1,000 women in 1970 down to a rate of just 14.8 five years later. Some speculated that the plummeting birth rate was solely a result of the hard economic times, but in truth the starkest drops took place among the upper classes. The changes were a choice about values and aspirations, not simply a response to need. An alumnae survey conducted by the elite Bryn Mawr College in 1971 reported that the previous five classes had gone on to have some seventy babies after graduation; when the college repeated its survey five years later, it discovered that the women from the next five graduating classes had only combined to give birth to three babies among them. At the US Census Bureau, nervous officials openly worried that the new generation of women had not simply decided to delay having children, but that they might in fact remain childless forever.[24]

The newfound control women had over their reproductive lives represented a major breakthrough in the decade. In 1972, the Supreme Court ruled that unmarried women (and men) had the right to use contraception. The following year, in the landmark decision of *Roe v. Wade*, the court extended that logic to establish a constitutional right to abortion as well. The ruling reflected an ongoing revolution in American attitudes about abortion. While most states had outlawed the practice in the nineteenth century, public opinion rapidly changed in the late 1960s and early 1970s. A series of Gallup Polls, for instance, showed that the percentage of Americans who believed a woman should be allowed to terminate a pregnancy in the first three months sharply increased from 40 percent to 64 percent between December 1969 and June 1972. Reacting to these changes in public attitudes, states across the country moved to liberalize their abortion laws. In 1967, Colorado, Oregon, and North Carolina led the way with significant reforms of their abortion restrictions; that same year Governor Ronald Reagan signed legislation that liberalized California's abortion laws as well. All told, a third of the states enacted such reforms between 1967 and 1973.[25]

The case of *Roe v. Wade* took place against this still-shifting legal landscape. The plaintiff, listed as "Jane Roe," was actually an unemployed carnival worker from Texas named Norma McCorvey. She had given birth to two children before she turned twenty, placing them in the care of others because she lacked means to support them. In 1969, discovering she was pregnant for the third time, she looked into getting an abortion. In her home state, the procedure was still banned by an 1854 law that outlawed all abortions unless the pregnancy posed a significant risk to the mother's life. McCorvey knew other states had begun to do away with similar laws, but she lacked the money to travel to one of them. Her doctor refused to discuss even the possibility of an abortion, or refer her to a physician who would. But in investigating the realities of abortion restrictions in Texas, McCorvey came across two young feminist lawyers, Linda Coffee and Sarah Weddington, who were looking for a plaintiff to challenge the statute. By this time, McCorvey was too far along in her pregnancy to have an abortion herself, but she nevertheless agreed to serve as a plaintiff on behalf of other Texas women, as long as she could be given anonymity as "Jane Roe."[26]

On January 22, 1973, the Supreme Court delivered its ruling in *Roe v. Wade*. By a vote of 7–2, the justices held that women had a constitutional right to abortion. Justice Harry Blackmun, a Nixon appointee, wrote the majority opinion, building on earlier rulings in which the court held that a broad right to privacy shielded individuals from having the state meddle in their sexual and reproductive lives. "The right of personal privacy includes the abortion decision," he announced. But he immediately added that "this right is not unqualified, and must be considered against important state interests in regulation." Blackmun asserted that as a fetus grew to viability—to an ability to live outside the womb—the state had a legitimate interest in protecting it. Therefore, he divided pregnancy into three trimesters: during the first, states could not interfere with a woman's decision; during the second, they could regulate the procedure; and during the final trimester, they could outlaw it entirely. The right to abortion now existed, but as Blackmun cautioned, their decision had not established "an unlimited right to do with one's body as one pleases." The initial reaction to *Roe* was fairly restrained, but in the coming years and decades Americans would enter into fierce arguments about the proper limits, or lack thereof, on the constitutional right to an abortion.[27]

As the Supreme Court considered the rest of women's rights, it showed much of the same approach: a general willingness to strike down measures that seemed to discriminate against women, though often with a note of hesitation. Such rulings placed weight on ambiguities in the laws themselves and encouraged legislators and lawyers to advance alternative measures in their stead. Most notably, in the 1976 case of *Craig v. Boren*, Justice William Brennan declared that the Supreme Court would now take a closer look at laws that made distinctions between the sexes. Speaking for a 7–2 majority, Brennan announced that the court would not adopt the same "strict scrutiny" standard they used to review laws that laid down different rules for different races, but would instead employ an approach of "intermediate scrutiny." Following the *Boren* decision, feminist attorneys brought successful challenges against many of the discriminatory barriers women faced in the realm of employment and education. "The ERA was defeated," conservative writer David Frum later complained, "but the federal courts proceeded to decide cases as if it had won."[28]

Gay Rights

As feminists struggled for their rights as full citizens under the law, gays and lesbians began to fight for simple recognition as such.

Before the 1970s, being gay or lesbian was regarded as a form of insanity. This classification began in World War II, when US Army psychiatrists started to identify gays and lesbians as a personality type unfit for service. In keeping with the new policy, thousands of gay soldiers and sailors were discharged from the military as "psychopathic undesirables," a designation that would haunt them in their civilian lives. This attitude spread through the federal government during the "lavender scare" of the 1950s, when gays and lesbians were officially banned from all government positions through an executive order. The Federal Bureau of Investigation increased its formal surveillance of gays and lesbians, while local police departments followed suit with campaigns designed to harass and humiliate them. Arrests soon grew to substantial numbers. In Washington, DC, they topped a thousand a year; in Philadelphia, more than a hundred a month. Newspaper editors promoted these "morals" crusades, often printing the names, addresses, and places of employment of those arrested.[29]

As the rights revolution unfolded, gays and lesbians began to push back. Gay and lesbian activists had laid a foundation for a new movement in the early 1950s, founding "homophile" networks such as the Mattachine Society and the Daughters of Bilitis. While these organizations worked to connect gays and lesbians to each other and to reconnect them to their rights as citizens, they were necessarily secretive, as most gays and lesbians in the postwar climate of repression kept their sexual identities "in the closet." But as they gained inspiration and experience from the civil rights and feminist movements, they began to stage more direct challenges to the discrimination and harassment they faced.

The most famous incident came unexpectedly. On the night of June 27, 1969, the New York Police Department staged a raid of the Stonewall Inn, a popular bar in Greenwich Village. The NYPD assumed this would be yet another routine raid of a gay establishment, but the working-class patrons put up a surprisingly strong resistance. Transgender women of color, including several self-identified "drag queens"—the most marginal members of a marginalized community—led the way. Screaming and cursing as they were led to the paddy wagons, they quickly drew a crowd of onlookers, whose initial curiosity soon turned to rage and resistance. As cobblestones and coins rained down on the policemen, they were forced to retreat into the Stonewall until they could be rescued by reinforcements. When the NYPD beat a hasty retreat, the crowd celebrated. In Christopher Park, a group of young transgender protesters sang and danced in a defiant, triumphant kick line: "We are the Stonewall Girls! We wear our hair in curls!"[30]

After Stonewall, the movement for what would later be termed LGBT rights accelerated with incredible speed. Hundreds of gay and lesbian periodicals sprang up in the next few years, spreading a philosophy patterned on the self-pride program advanced by Black Power groups. While part of the movement revolved around securing rights for gays and lesbians, another important dimension focused on helping them to feel safe and comfortable enough to declare their identity in public. To underline the message that "gay is good," groups like the Gay Liberation Front (GLF) urged gays and lesbians to "come out of the closet" and no longer hide their identities in shame. In doing so, they hoped to transform what had formerly been a private act of acknowledgment to oneself and close friends into a public, political act that represented a rejection of the stigma attached to homosexuality. It was a difficult case to make to a community whose members had been stigmatized and persecuted for decades. "Other minorities have everything to gain by demanding their rights," worried a closeted oil company executive. "We have everything to lose." But organizations like the GLF persuasively argued that "coming out" was a crucial step for gays and lesbians, one that was both a sign of personal liberation and public resistance against society. Moreover, it would also help create a stronger and more vibrant movement that could then return to the fight for gay rights, pushing for policy changes and challenging unjust laws. The banner for a GLF newspaper in New York put it simply but powerfully. "Come Out For Freedom!" it urged readers. "Come Out of the Closet Before the Door is Nailed Shut!"[31]

Consumer culture began to change in response to a new source of demand. As gays and lesbians came out of the closet, countless private entities sprouted to meet the needs of a newly identified clientele: bars and restaurants, law firms and travel agencies, churches and synagogues, and on and on. In some cities, the breadth of personal and professional services that catered to gay and lesbian customers was such that a gay man in New York City joked he could now "do anything and never see a straight person again." As consumer options spread, gays and lesbians became a more visible presence in the business and professional world as well. A *Time* cover story in 1975 titled "Gays on the March" breathlessly reported the "spread of unabashed homosexuality, once thought to be confined to the worlds of theater, dance, fashion." Pushing aside such stereotypes, gays and lesbians soon formed their own caucuses within major professions like teaching, health care, and banking. By the end of the decade, there were several thousand gay and lesbian organizations in America, with new groups mirroring virtually every type of straight organization. One reporter informed readers about a gay Nazi group and the lesbian Jewish organization that had formed to fight it.[32]

As gays and lesbians came out and claimed their place in society, they forced heterosexuals to reconsider their own attitudes and actions. In a significant step, the American Psychiatric Association removed homosexuality from its official list of mental disorders in 1974, taking away a foundation of homophobia. The following year, the Pentagon issued the first security clearance for an openly gay individual, while the US Civil Service Commission ended the policy that barred gays and lesbians from working for the federal government. The United Church of Christ decried "the use of scripture to generate hatred and the violation of the civil rights of gay and lesbian persons" in 1977 and, two years later, the United Methodist Church announced that gays could be ordained as ministers in the denomination. During this period, gays and lesbians made their mark in the political realm as well. In 1972, two gay and lesbian delegates were invited to address the Democratic National Convention; in 1980, the party formally adopted a gay rights plank to its platform. Over the course of the decade, sodomy laws were removed from the books in twenty-two states. Meanwhile, several dozen cities—including major metropolises like Boston, Detroit, Houston, Los Angeles, San Francisco, and Washington, DC—added sexual orientation to the list of categories protected from discrimination by their civil rights ordinances.[33]

Despite the changes in the political world, popular culture only haltingly began to discuss gay and lesbian issues. On TV dramas, gay characters often appeared in a negative light, especially early in the decade. Police dramas like *The Streets of San Francisco* (1972–1977) portrayed gays and lesbians as deviant criminals, while medical shows like *Marcus Welby, M.D.* (1969–1976) advanced an image of gays as sexual psychopaths and child molesters. In sharp contrast, gay and lesbian characters found more positive portrayals on sitcoms, but still only infrequently, in supporting roles or on single episodes. Still, some progress was made, as hit shows like *All in the Family, Maude,* and *Barney Miller* (1975–1982) had multiple episodes that featured both sympathetic portrayals of gay and lesbian characters and mockery of homophobic ones. Later in the decade, the comedy *Soap* (1977–1981), a spoof of daytime soap operas, included Billy Crystal in its cast, playing an openly gay character. Not all Americans welcomed such changes, of course. Just as with feminism, the new public profile of gays and lesbians prompted a backlash. Companies whose ads appeared in the broadcast for *Soap*, for instance, found themselves subjected to a letter-writing campaign that threatened a boycott before its September 1977 debut. (Notably, the complaints centered not just on the show's portrayal of an out-of-the-closet gay man but also its larger themes of heterosexual promiscuity as well.) As a result, several ABC affiliates announced they would refuse to air the show entirely. The controversy, of course, only drew attention to the program, which premiered as the fourth-highest-rated show in the country and continued to run for four years.[34]

In the realm of politics, the backlash against gay rights was more prolonged and pronounced. After commissioners in Dade County, Florida, voted to extend civil rights protections to gays and lesbians in their jurisdiction—which included much of metropolitan Miami—conservatives mounted a major protest. Anita Bryant, a devout Southern Baptist who then served as the spokeswoman for the Florida Citrus Commission, believed that county officials had given the government's formal approval to gays and lesbians, whom she regarded as "human garbage." She soon founded an organization called Save Our Children, Inc., to organize conservative opposition to the ordinance and to place a repeal measure on the next ballot. Portraying "homosexuals" as a threat to heterosexual families, Bryant warned Floridians that gays and lesbians were literally coming to take their kids away from them, because they could not biologically bear their own. "They can only recruit children, and this is what they want to do," she told terrified parents. "Some of the stories I could tell you of child recruitment and child abuse by homosexuals would turn your stomach." Duly alarmed, residents voted to repeal the ordinance by an overwhelming margin of 71 percent to 29 percent. "The people of Dade County—the normal majority—have said 'Enough! Enough! Enough!'" Bryant cheered in celebration. "They have voted to repeal an obnoxious assault on our moral values." Basking in the national spotlight, she promised to launch a massive effort "to repeal similar laws . . . which attempt to legitimize a life-style that is both perverse and dangerous."[35]

The defeat of the Dade County ordinance marked a turning point in the struggle over gay rights. The Miami measure had attracted national attention, and in its wake conservatives launched successful campaigns to defeat similar gay rights measures in cities like St. Paul, Minnesota; Wichita, Kansas; and Eugene, Oregon. The most significant campaign against gay rights came with the Briggs Initiative, a 1978 proposal to ban gays and lesbians from teaching in the public schools of California. Its sponsor, Republican state senator John Briggs, had taken part in the Dade County campaign and sought to replicate it in his home state. Like Bryant, he argued that "homosexual rights" represented a direct threat to heterosexual family life. "In San Francisco," he repeatedly claimed, "they actually require that they teach a life-style class about homosexuality as an alternative to family life." The local school board repeatedly denied that such a class actually existed, but Briggs nevertheless repeated the rumor to crowds that ran, in his estimation, to "hundreds of thousands" of people. Though he won significant support for the measure, some conservatives believed the initiative went too far. Notably, former governor Ronald Reagan came out against it, stating that its intrusion on the "basic rights of privacy" ultimately had "the potential for real mischief." In the end, the Briggs Initiative failed at the polls by a margin of a million votes.[36]

In San Francisco, the fight over the proposition inflamed all sides. A week after Briggs announced his plan at San Francisco's City Hall in June 1977, the city's streets erupted in violence as gay activists and conservative opponents clashed. Robert Hillsborough, a gay man, was stabbed fifteen times by four straight men who screamed "Faggot! Faggot!" and "Here's one for Anita!" His murder prompted the largest gay rights demonstration yet that summer; that fall, Harvey Milk won election as San Francisco's first openly gay city supervisor. Milk proved an able activist for the cause, convincing his colleagues to pass one of the country's strongest municipal measures for gay rights by a margin of 10–1 in early 1978. He then turned his attention to rallying opposition to the Briggs Initiative, helping to turn public opinion around and securing its defeat in November 1978. Just a few weeks later, however, tragedy struck San Francisco again. Dan White, a conservative former police officer and the lone commissioner to vote against the city's ordinance, resolved to use bullets where ballots had failed. On November 27, he assassinated Harvey Milk and Mayor George Moscone in their offices at City Hall.[37]

The aftermath of the assassinations showed how far the cause of gay rights had come, and how much further it had to go. As the first "avowed homosexual" to win election to a major political position, Milk had drawn a great deal of hate mail. He understood he might well be the victim of violence, but hoped such a moment could lead to some good. "If a bullet should enter my brain," he said in a recording before his death, "let that bullet destroy every closet door." A massive candlelight vigil of gays, lesbians, and sympathetic straights seemed to suggest that it had. "Several people, right that following week, came out of the closet because they had been there," a friend later reflected. Changes in the legal landscape, wrought by Milk and others, had encouraged a new spirit of openness. "That's what Harvey stood for," his friend continued, "and it took his death for them to realize it. They just came out. No one would fire them from their jobs because it's against the law, and . . .

that part of our society that's very closed could open." The trial that followed, however, showed that much of society was still very much closed to gay equality. White had confessed to the two murders soon after the fact, but his attorneys argued that he had been driven temporarily insane due to excess consumption of junk food. On the basis of this so-called "Twinkie defense," White received a light sentence of just over seven years for the two assassinations, with the possibility of early parole. The verdict stunned the gay community and sparked a night of violent rioting across San Francisco. "Dan White's getting off is just one of a million things that happen in our lives: the beatings, the murders, the people driven to suicide by the hostility of the straights," one rioter explained. "Dan White's straight justice is just the last straw."[38]

Faced with such setbacks, gay and lesbian activists redoubled their efforts to defend their rights. In March 1977, the first delegation of gay and lesbian leaders was welcomed to the White House for a meeting. "This is the first time in the history of this country," noted Jean O'Leary of the National Gay Task Force, "that a president has seen fit to acknowledge the rights and needs of some 28 million Americans." President Carter did not attend the meeting, sending an aide in his place, but he soon made his sympathies clear. Though he was a devout Southern Baptist who had reservations about gays and lesbians, the president noted that he did not share the larger concerns of many of his fellow religionists. "I don't see homosexuality as a threat to the family," he said in a Father's Day interview in 1977. "I don't feel that society, through its laws, ought to abuse or harass the homosexual." Hoping to make that attitude more commonplace, gay rights advocates—again taking a page from the playbooks of civil rights and women's rights campaigns—worked to build up an organizational capacity in Washington, DC, that would match the energy at the grass roots. In 1978, they placed their first full-time lobbyist in the Capitol to stand guard against legislation that might affect their interests. In 1980, more than three dozen gays and lesbians served as delegates to the Democratic National Convention; even the Republican National Convention had two. As O'Leary put it, "We're taking advantage of the most powerful closet we have: the voting booth."[39]

The feminist and gay rights movements radically transformed American society in the 1970s. For individual straight women, lesbians, and gay men, the social and legal changes brought about by such movements were nothing short of revolutionary: a new world of openness and opportunities that transformed their lives in countless ways. But those who seemed outside the movements were likewise impacted. In the eyes of some, yet another traditional institution from the Cold War era—the nuclear family—had been significantly transformed and weakened, just as the government and economy had been before them. As a result, some Americans grew increasingly disturbed by a new set of fault lines, unfolding before them in ways that resembled the new fracturing of society along lines of race and immigration. As their sense of a "traditional America" slipped away from them, they resolved to act.

CHAPTER 5

Turning Right

AS THE OLD INSTITUTIONS OF THE POSTWAR DECADES crumbled in the 1970s, new opportunities arose for the Right.

The movements for feminism and gay rights had disrupted the nation's norms on gender and sexuality, but in doing so they also helped inspire an intense countermovement. Religious conservatism, once deemed so far outside the mainstream that even conservative Christians themselves thought they had no role to play in national politics, made a strong resurgence in the form of the modern "Religious Right." At the same time, a "New Right" likewise made inroads in politics, taking positions that had been dismissed as too extreme just a decade before and marketing them anew for the mainstream. Business conservatives made the case for deregulating large swaths of the economy and lowering tax rates, seeking to roll back the massive expansion of the federal government of the previous half-century. Despite their different agendas, social conservatives and capitalist libertarians joined together in a remade Republican Party, where they forged a common cause against the liberal state.

In the new coalition on the right, these forces overcame the traditional fault lines that had long divided them—the doctrinal divisions that had kept the many varieties of religious conservatives from working with one another, for instance, and the ideological differences that had prevented libertarians and social conservatives from making common cause. But patching up those differences was merely the prelude to a larger project in which they singled out new enemies at home—gays and lesbians, feminists, liberals writ large—and drew new lines of division between themselves and their opponents.

To do so, these conservatives forged new ways to circumvent the mainstream media that had, in their eyes, long frustrated their efforts to get their message out. Co-opting old outlets like radio for their own use and innovating new techniques like direct mail, the architects of the New Right and Religious Right advanced an aggressive message together, with the man they called the Great Communicator in the lead: Ronald Reagan.

The Religious Right

For many conservative Christians, the campaigns for feminism and gay rights in the 1970s had represented a direct threat to what they understood as the "traditional" heterosexual nuclear family. Initially, religious conservatives largely reacted to liberal proposals with targeted counter-measures of their own, like Phyllis Schlafly's lobbying campaign against the Equal Rights Amendment or Anita Bryant's drive to repeal municipal gay rights ordinances. But as the decade wore on, conservative Christians began to coalesce into larger, longer-lasting coalitions that set their own agendas.

The Religious Right as we understand it, however, was not created overnight. Though conservative Christians shared a common revulsion to the advances of feminism and gay rights, they had long been divided by theological disagreements and denominational rivalries that kept them from finding common political ground. For instance, while opposition to abortion rights would soon become a key issue in the mobilization of conservatives across the religious spectrum, the immediate reaction to Roe showed a more complicated picture. At the start of the 1970s, evangelical and fundamentalist Christians still regarded opposition to birth control and abortion as "Catholic issues" and kept their distance. "In general, I would disagree with [the Catholic stance]," the evangelist Billy Graham announced in 1968. "I believe in planned parenthood." Southern Baptist leaders shared this perspective. In 1970, an internal survey of ministers and lay leaders in the denomination revealed widespread support for the liberalization of abortion laws. In cases where the woman's health was threatened by a pregnancy, nearly 70 percent of Baptist pastors and nearly 80 percent of Sunday

School teachers supported abortion access; in cases of rape or incest, 70 percent and 77 percent, respectively; and in cases of fetal deformity, 64 percent and 76 percent. Even W. A. Criswell, a fundamentalist firebrand from Dallas who later led the conservative takeover of the Southern Baptist Convention, initially expressed a fairly liberal stance on abortion. "I have always felt that it was only after a child was born and had life separate from its mother . . . that it became an individual person," he noted a month after *Roe*; "it has always, therefore, seemed to me that what is best for the mother and for the future should be allowed."[1]

For fundamentalists and evangelical Protestants, this long-standing belief that abortion was a "Catholic issue" was difficult to shake. Harold O. J. Brown, a prominent evangelical theologian, later recalled that many Protestants had the attitude that "'If the Catholics are for it, we should be against it.'" Some worked to change that attitude. In a 1976 editorial titled "Is Abortion a Catholic Issue?" the editors of *Christianity Today* dismissed the question as a "smokescreen" and urged evangelicals to stop worrying about Catholic political influence and start worrying about "the most fundamental of human rights, the right to life." Likewise, Dr. C. Everett Koop and Francis Schaeffer advanced the evangelical case against abortion in a best-selling book that was later made into a five-part film series distributed widely by Gospel Films: *Whatever Happened to the Human Race?* Schaeffer took the show on the road, speaking to large audiences on an eighteen-city tour across the country in 1977.[2] Meanwhile, Robert Holbrook, a prominent Southern Baptist minister, won election to the National Right to Life Committee, which had until then largely been a creation of Catholics. Other evangelicals formed parallel pro-life organizations, such as Baptists for Life and the Christian Action Council.[3]

As religious conservatives put aside their denominational differences and rallied around the common cause of opposing abortion, they found themselves able to force a shift in both policy and politics. In 1976, Congress adopted a measure that Republican congressman Henry Hyde of Illinois had introduced to ban the use of all federal Medicaid funds for abortion. Because Medicaid provided the only real access to medical care for low-income families, the Hyde Amendment significantly undercut access to abortion for the working poor. For its supporters, the measure represented a significant triumph. Before its passage, roughly 30 percent of all legal abortions had been financed with Medicaid money; but when that source of funding stopped, so too did roughly 300,000 abortions a year. Meanwhile, in electoral politics, the new National Pro-Life Political Action Committee (NPLPAC) and related pro-life groups worked to make abortion an important campaign issue. Their strategy was to focus narrowly on people who felt most passionately about the issue, mobilizing local citizens to campaign and producing extensive public relations material focused exclusively on abortion. Seeking to deliver a small slice of the electorate in a small number of races—3 to 5 percent of the vote in several dozen congressional elections—they hoped to transform the national debate.[4] And indeed, conservatives soon found themselves facing a pro-life litmus test, while liberals were targeted for past support for abortion rights. These efforts found quick success, as pro-life activists succeeded in defeating the incumbent Iowa senator Dick Clark, a pro-choice Democrat, in the 1978 midterms. Two years later, they would help end the political careers of leading Senate liberals like George McGovern of South Dakota, Frank Church of Idaho, and Birch Bayh of Indiana, the champion of Title IX.[5]

As conservative Christians came together in opposition to abortion, feminism, and homosexuality, they created a new movement for social conservatism that served as a visible counterpoint to the nascent movements for feminism and gay rights. Notably, in 1977, the two sides simultaneously staged rival rallies in Houston that dramatized their differences and inflamed passions on all sides. Two years earlier, the United Nations had proclaimed International Women's Year (IWY), prompting a bipartisan group of feminists to secure $5 million in funding for a massive conference on the status of women in the United States. Held in November 1977, the IWY National Women's Conference attracted nearly 20,000 women, including Betty Friedan, Gloria Steinem, Margaret Mead, Coretta Scott King, and three First Ladies, whose presence garnered a great amount of media attention for the event. ("I never seen so many women in one place in my life," a Houston cabbie marveled. "How come their husbands let them come?") In the end, the delegates passed a strongly progressive platform that endorsed reproductive rights, federal child care programs, state ratification of the ERA, and civil rights protections for gays and lesbians. The support for gay and lesbian rights in particular represented a significant turning point in the course of feminism. Prominent leaders of women's rights organizations like Friedan had long shied away from such steps, but in Houston, she threw her support to the proposed plank and helped it win passage. When it did, excited lesbian activists shouted out: "Thank you, sisters!"[6]

Not everyone, of course, was thrilled with the National Women's Conference. Phyllis Schlafly denounced it as "a front for radicals and lesbians" and helped stage a counterdemonstration held in Houston at the exact same time. Pointedly titled the "Pro-Family Rally," the event drew in a conservative crowd that equaled the one at the liberal conference in both numbers and energy. "They came with their Bibles, their flags and their signs," a journalist noted. "They came to show their disgust for the lesbians, the perverts and the baby-killers meeting across town." When another reporter asked an attendee about a button she wore that read "God's Way," she explained it meant "that homosexuality is a sin, that God meant for a woman to take care of the family, and that every child that was conceived was a life that could not be taken." Not surprisingly, the Pro-Family Rally passed a set of resolutions that opposed virtually all of the recommendations made by the National Women's Conference across town. "The issues that divide the two groups are important," reported a *Time* bureau chief, "but the thing that binds them is their commitment to militant action. Houston taught all women that the world can be compelled to watch."[7]

The Pro-Family Rally in Houston signaled the rise of a new wave of activists who would advance social conservatism with the attractive frame of "family values." In 1977, Dr. James Dobson founded his Focus on the Family organization in the suburbs of Los Angeles. A devout evangelical and noted child psychologist, Dobson led the charge against sex education in local public schools and, through his popular radio program, rallied statewide opposition to gay and lesbian rights as well. Meanwhile, Beverly LaHaye, the wife of a fundamentalist minister in the San Diego suburbs and author of *The Spirit-Controlled Woman*, founded Concerned Women for America (CWA) in 1979. Although CWA never received as much popular attention as its liberal counterpart, the National Organization for Women, it consistently boasted of both a larger membership and a bigger budget.[8]

The media emerged as a key target of the new "family values" crusade, sparking several new activist organizations of social conservatives. In 1977, Rev. Donald Wildmon of Mississippi launched the National Federation for Decency, later rebranded as the American Family Association. The group established itself as a media watchdog, standing on guard against gratuitous displays of sexuality and positive portrayals of homosexuality. The organization gained national attention between 1977 and 1981, as it amassed millions to lobby local stations and threaten national television and advertising executives through boycotts. Focusing on programs that celebrated promiscuity or homosexuality, such as *Soap* and *Three's Company* (1976–1984), Wildmon's group singled out major advertisers like Sears, prompting them to drop advertisements from the shows.[9]

At the same time, religious conservatives advanced alternative programming of their own. Rev. Pat Robertson, the politically savvy son of a former US senator and a Southern Baptist minister, led the way. In 1961, he began by airing religious programs over a small UHF channel in coastal Virginia. Then, in 1977, Robertson purchased a local leased-access channel and rebranded it as the Christian Broadcasting Network (CBN). Robertson himself became the face of the network, hosting *The 700 Club*, aptly described by one reviewer as a "soft-sell program, which offers penetrating interviews, fervent prayers for 1.25 million callers annually and an upbeat 'Top 40' in gospel tunes." With personal religious testimony from celebrities ranging from former Black Panther Eldridge Cleaver to Dallas Cowboys coach Tom Landry, the program offered a friendly face for evangelical Christianity. Though Robertson often recoiled from the term himself, he created a powerful new form of religious broadcasting—"televangelism"—that rapidly transformed the world of broadcast media. Countless others followed his example. Jim and Tammy Faye Bakker, who started on CBN, soon launched a satellite network of their own, the Trinity Broadcasting Network (TBN), which likewise brought conservative religious programs like their *Praise the Lord* show to the masses in digestible form.[10]

The most significant "pro-family" development on the right, however, was the creation of the Moral Majority. Founded in 1979, this new coalition of religious conservatives was led by Rev. Jerry Falwell, a Baptist minister from Lynchburg, Virginia. Like many conservative Christians, Falwell had long argued that religious leaders should play no role in national politics. But the social revolution wrought by feminism and the gay rights movement persuaded him—and many like him— that they could no longer stand idly by. In 1978, for instance, Falwell delivered his first sermon against abortion, which he began decrying as "America's national sin." Feminism, which he blamed for a wide range of problems, also stood at the root of the abortion crisis, he insisted, because most of the women who sought them had "been caught up in the ERA movement and want to terminate their pregnancy because it limits their freedom and their job opportunities." The ERA, he charged, was a "delusion" and a "definite violation of Holy Scripture." At the same time, Falwell emerged as an outspoken opponent of gay rights. In 1978, for instance, he campaigned for the Briggs Initiative in California and later proclaimed that the murders of Milk and Moscone were simply God's judgment against homosexuals.[11]

Having made connections with like-minded Christian conservative leaders, Falwell resolved to bring them together in a national coalition. In May 1979, they founded the Moral Majority, which they described as a "pro-life, pro-family, pro-moral and pro-American" organization. In doing so, they sought to strengthen not only the political clout of religious conservatives but also their self-image as a representation of the majority's will. Repeatedly, these leaders insisted that their entry into politics was a defensive reaction to the state's meddling in matters of faith. "We believe the government has intruded into areas of morals," explained Rev. Tim LaHaye, "and if we don't speak out on moral issues, the government will conclude by our silence that we won't care how immoral they get." Waving away the traditional reluctance that ministers had about political matters, Falwell now said that preachers had three obligations to their flocks: "Get 'em baptized, get 'em saved, and get 'em registered to vote." Speaking to a thousand ministers at a Florida church rally during the 1980 election, the leader of the Moral Majority insisted there was nothing they could not accomplish together if they worked hard enough. "What can you do from the pulpit?" he asked rhetorically. "You can register people to vote. You can explain the issues to them. And you can endorse candidates, right there in church on Sunday morning."[12]

As the 1980 election season began, another new organization—the Religious Roundtable—led a campaign to "coordinate Christian leaders from around the nation who are willing to fight in the political arena for pro-God, pro-family, pro-America causes." They connected the organizational structure of their movement to the grassroots activists and leaders who would be central in mobilizing the final vote. In seminars and workshops, the Religious Roundtable taught ministers how to mobilize their congregations on behalf of conservative causes and candidates. The most significant of these gatherings, the National Affairs Briefing, brought over ten thousand ministers together in Dallas in August 1980. Rev. James Robison, head of the Roundtable, estimated that between the ministers' own congregations and the wider audiences on their many radio and television programs, the conference's message would likely reach between 50 and 60 million voters in all. The event featured a number of prominent religious conservatives, including Jerry Falwell, Pat Robertson, Phyllis Schlafly, and the head of the National Right to Life Committee. But Ronald Reagan stole the show, winning over the audience with a line that had been scripted specifically for him by his hosts. "I know this is non-partisan, so you can't endorse me," the Republican nominee noted, "but I want you to know that I endorse you."[13]

While the union of the Religious Right and the 1980 Reagan campaign was a significant development, the larger arrival of religious conservatives to the national political scene was even more so. Believing that the movements for feminism and gay rights had willfully distorted the natural order of life and the national order of politics, these conservative Christians argued that they were merely responding in kind to set things right once more. In their eyes, they were simply protecting tradition from dangerous new changes. "I am sick and tired of hearing about all the radicals and the perverts and the liberals and the leftists and the communists coming out of the closet," James Robison thundered at the National Affairs Briefing. "It's time for God's people to come out of the closet!" Conservative Christians were convinced not only that they should fight against the liberal forces they saw arrayed against them, but that they would win in the end. "We have enough votes to run the country," boasted Pat Robertson. "And when the people say, 'We've had enough,' we're going to take over the country."[14]

The New Right

As the Religious Right gained ground, they found ready allies in a more secular movement that styled itself as "the New Right." In the words of former Nixon strategist Kevin Phillips, the Old Right had been an elitist establishment aligned with "high church religion" and opposed to mass culture or the concerns of the common man. The New Right, he argued, was more aligned with a populist agenda that "puts principal emphasis on domestic social issues—on public anger over busing, welfare spending, environmental extremism, soft criminology, media bias and power, warped education, twisted textbooks, racial quotas, various guidelines and an ever-expanding bureaucracy."[15]

While the New Right distinguished itself with distinct themes, its innovative tactics were even more important. Conservative activist Richard Viguerie, for instance, helped pioneer a new form of grassroots mobilization known as the direct-mail campaign. Using the millions of names he'd acquired from people who had sent in donations to the presidential campaigns of Barry Goldwater and George Wallace, Viguerie compiled a massive list of conservative voters across the country. He put the information, then stored on punch cards, into a giant computerized database, sorted according to the various concerns and complaints of these voters. He could then send direct-mail solicitations to these voters, solicitations that were tailor-made to their concerns. This revolutionary approach enabled conservative activists to reach out to their core supporters, mobilize their anger with focused appeals, and receive financial contributions in return. Direct-mail appeals were provocative and to the point. As one Republican operative put it, "the shriller you are" in these appeals, "the easier it is to raise money." They reframed political debates in stark terms and presented socially conservative issues in ways that politicians would've been scared to do from the campaign trail. For instance, one direct-mail appeal urged recipients to "stop the baby killers! These anti-life baby killers are already organizing and raising money to re-elect pro-abortionists. Abortion means killing a live baby." Recipients were urged to send their donations and their votes to the conservative candidate in order to stop it all.[16]

Another key organizer of the New Right was Paul Weyrich, whose main contribution was the creation of new conservative foundations and think tanks. He established close relationships with a number of wealthy conservatives, such as Joseph Coors, head of the Coors beer empire, and Richard Mellon Scaife, the heir to the vast Carnegie-Mellon fortune. Drawing on their funding, Weyrich established the Heritage Foundation in 1973. Coors donated a quarter-million dollars to start the foundation, and in the following years, it received generous funding from the founders of the Amway Corporation and conservative philanthropists at the Bradley, Olin and Scaife foundations. Heritage quickly emerged as one of the leading conservative think tanks of the modern era. It led the way in popularizing conservative thought, publishing various materials and sponsoring conferences to advance its probusiness and antigovernment policies. Heritage was also directly involved in the legislative battles on Capitol Hill, where it provided advice and assistance to conservative legislators on a wide variety of issues. While traditional think tanks produced thick policy papers, the Heritage Foundation pioneered the practice of coming up with short, slick, and direct publications called "Heritage Backgrounders" that could be read by politicians on the go. Unlike earlier think tank papers, which were laden with academic-style analysis, Heritage's output resembled op-ed essays in newspapers, meant to make an easily digestible point. Other foundations—most notably the American Enterprise Institute, the Hoover Institution, and the Cato Institute—also moved forward aggressively to pressure congressional figures to join the New Right and, more broadly, to popularize the arguments of conservative and libertarian intellectuals.[17]

Business interests made their presence increasingly felt in Washington, too. Hoping to discard the New Deal infrastructure of the 1930s and angry over the vast expansion of workplace and environmental regulations put into place in the 1960s and 1970s, corporations converged on the capital to set up sophisticated congressional lobbying operations. Washington's K Street soon filled with firms representing individual business as well as particular sectors of industry that were eager to remove as much of the government burden that they faced as possible. These businesses relied on the intellectual firepower of libertarian authors and foundations, but they also used the power of the purse. Notably, spending by corporate political action committees (PACs) on congressional races increased fivefold between the late 1970s and the 1980s.[18]

As with the Religious Right, the most effective messenger for the New Right was Ronald Reagan. After barely losing in the Republican primaries in 1976 to President Ford, Reagan had continued to hone his political skills through the radio. The medium had become the home to many conservative talk show hosts like Bob Grant in New York, who took to the airwaves to hammer away at progressive taxes, welfare, Communists, and illegal immigration. Reagan followed suit, taking a similar hard line but in smoother tones. In daily syndicated radio addresses, he reached somewhere between 20 and 30 million people on over three hundred stations.[19] Like many conservatives of the decade, Reagan used this medium both to express his arguments and expand his constituency, circumventing the seeming liberal dominance of the mainstream press and presenting the country with a political perspective that contrasted sharply with the Democratic dominance in Washington. Reagan took pride in developing the addresses himself, writing and revising repeatedly, carefully crafting every sentence and adjusting each word so that it would have maximum impact. In particular, he railed against taxation and Communism, rejecting the notion that most Americans agreed with liberal values and refuting any claim that persons living under Communism actually liked the system they experienced. "Maybe we should drop a few million typical mail order catalogues on Minsk & Pinsk & Moscow to whet their appetites," he said in one broadcast.[20]

During the Carter era, Reagan emerged as one of the president's fiercest critics, targeting his foreign and domestic policies in equal measure. He believed Carter's foreign policy, like those of Nixon and Ford before him, had endangered the nation with its commitment to the policies of détente. The Soviets, he argued, were rapidly expanding their military arsenal, while the Democratic Congress systematically cut defense spending. After Vietnam, defense spending declined to approximately 4.8 percent of the GNP in 1978. At the height of World War II, defense spending had reached a whopping 41 percent of GNP, before dropping down to roughly 10 percent, where it remained for the decades that followed. The 1970s had brought a sharp drop. More than a matter of money, Reagan believed Carter's priorities were entirely wrong.

The Democrat, he thought, was overly focused on achieving diplomatic breakthroughs with the nation's enemies while ignoring the threats they still posed and neglecting the military might he thought necessary to oppose them. America not only needed to be strong again, he argued, but also had to make it clear to the world that it would be willing to use that strength in the post-Vietnam era. "It doesn't make any difference if you have all the arms you need," Reagan asserted, "if the other fellow is convinced you won't fight."[21]

The Middle East quickly became the focal point of the growing debate over American foreign policy. For his part, President Carter had focused his time and energy on the long-standing problem of finding peace in the Middle East. After twelve days of intense negotiations between Israeli prime minister Menachem Begin and Egyptian president Anwar Sadat in September 1978, Carter proudly unveiled the Camp David Accords, which led to peace between the two longtime enemies and to the Nobel Peace Prize for Begin and Sadat. Carter was widely praised for the breakthrough, with Capitol Hill celebrating in what one congressman called "bipartisan euphoria." But the feeling was fleeting, as events in Iran quickly eclipsed the Israeli-Egyptian agreements. In January 1979, followers of the exiled radical Ayatollah Ruhollah Khomeini overthrew Iran's ruler, Shah Mohammed Reza Pahlavi, and forced him to flee into exile. A month later, extremists in the Iranian revolution stormed the US embassy in Tehran and, after a two-hour gun battle, took 102 Americans who were stationed there hostage, including the ambassador. The new Iranian regime forced their release, but the damage to American prestige had been done. "I'm beginning to wonder," Reagan said after their release, "if the symbol of the United States pretty soon isn't going to be an ambassador with a flag under his arm, climbing into the escape helicopter."[22]

And, indeed, that soon became America's image, as the situation in Iran spiraled out of control. In October, Carter allowed the shah, critically ill with cancer, to come to New York City for much-needed surgery. Two weeks later, a mob of Iranians overran the US embassy again and took sixty-six Americans hostage; unlike the first time, the Iranian regime now refused to intercede. The revolutionaries demanded that America apologize for aiding the shah and turn both the dying man and his vast personal wealth over to them. Carter refused, and at first, the country rallied around the president. But as the Iranian hostage crisis stretched on, the stalemate increasingly suggested a state of American paralysis and powerlessness. The media became consumed by the drama. ABC launched a nightly news program, titled "The Iran Crisis: America Held Hostage," that kept the hostage situation at the forefront of viewers' minds and crowded out all other news. Purporting to provide daily updates on a crisis in which there was truly little breaking news, the program instead became an outlet for American frustration. "Viewers sometimes see [anchorman Frank] Reynolds almost trembling with rage over the occupation of the embassy," one TV critic noted, "and using language that might call his objectivity into question." Meanwhile, CBS news anchor Walter Cronkite began closing his nightly news broadcast with a reminder of the ongoing hostage crisis. "And that's the way it is," he said somberly, announcing the date and then noting that it marked "the _____ day of captivity for the American hostages in Iran."[23]

Reagan pointed to the Iranian hostage crisis as the perfect illustration of Carter's failures in foreign affairs. Just weeks into the stalemate, the front-runner for the Republican presidential nomination blamed the "vacillation, the weakness of the foreign policy" of the Democratic administration for the embassy's seizure. Reagan was "as mad and frustrated" as the American people, he said, insisting that the country needed to take a tougher line against the "rabble" that had seized its embassy. As the crisis continued, with daily reminders of the stalemate in the media, Reagan intensified his rhetoric. In March 1980, for instance, he charged that the Carter administration had "dillied and dallied for five months now, trying various diplomatic maneuvers" with nothing to show for it all but more failure. "And now apparently he's just sitting, waiting for a miracle and hoping that miracle will happen just shortly before the November election."[24]

Instead of miracles, however, the months before the election only brought more misery for Carter and the Democrats. Over the course of the campaign season, the public learned the details of an elaborate FBI operation known as "ABSCAM." For two years, undercover agents posing as representatives of a fictional Arab sheik had bribed a range of elected officials at the local, state, and federal level, purportedly to help Middle Eastern elites secure casino deals in Atlantic City and special legislation. (According to investigators, "ABSCAM" simply stood for "Arab Scam.") In late August 1980, Democratic congressman Michael "Ozzie" Myers, a former longshoreman from Philadelphia, was convicted of taking $50,000 in exchange for promises to help foreign elites with their immigration issues. Weeks later, the House of Representatives voted to expel Myers, the first time Congress had expelled a member since the start of the Civil War. Myers's conviction would merely be the first, as the ABSCAM scandal soon led to the conviction of five more congressmen, a senator, the mayor of Camden, New Jersey, and three city council members in Philadelphia. All of the politicians convicted in the scandal were Democrats, except for a lone Republican congressman.[25]

Even more so than Watergate, the lurid details of ABSCAM unfolded on television. In mid-October, soon after Myers's conviction and removal from Congress, the Supreme Court ruled that tapes of the FBI's undercover recordings could be released to the public and, in a first for evidence in a criminal case, broadcast on television as well. The networks rushed to get the tapes on the air that same night, with five-minute segments on the nightly news shows and then full half-hour specials later that night on ABC and CBS. The tapes, viewed by millions, showed Congressman Myers meeting with undercover agents, taking envelopes filled with cash and assuring them that he would now be "100 per cent" on their side. "You're going about this the right way," the representative assured them. "Money talks in this business and bullshit walks." The crass corruption revealed in the tapes only seemed seedier thanks to the low-quality nature of the recordings. "It had the photographic quality of a porno reel from the '50s," columnist Tom Shales noted in the *Washington Post*, "and one felt a similarly naughty voyeuristic fascination watching it. Fuzzy, grainy and black and white though it was, it was changing the face of television and maybe of our legal system."[26]

As the Democrats' standing on foreign policy crumbled thanks to ABSCAM and the Iranian hostage crisis, Republicans made a strong attack on domestic issues too. The combination of a weak job market, inflation, and excessive government regulatory interference had produced disastrous economic conditions, Reagan said. Although the weak economy had its roots in a mixture of public and private mistakes made largely in the late 1960s and early 1970s, Reagan placed the blame squarely on Carter's shoulders, and government more broadly. "When we talk of these problems all of us seem to do so in the context of what should government do about them," he noted in April 1979. "May I suggest that government has already done too much about them and that's why we have the problems."[27] While the Democratic president had begun the process of deregulation in key sectors like aviation and trucking, Reagan argued that much more needed to be done. Rejecting entirely the New Deal institutions that Democrats had insisted were essential to ensuring the economic security of Americans, Reagan claimed that even greater deregulation and massive tax cuts were the only way to restore robust economic growth.

For Reagan, the political promise of the new tax revolt was crystal clear, as the movement had begun back in his old home state of California. Property taxes there had risen dramatically in the late 1960s and early 1970s, largely due to new assessments and rising land costs. In general, the steepest increases hit middle-class homeowners in the booming suburbs. The wealthy could afford the increases with little sacrifice, while the poor usually rented and therefore did not directly pay property taxes themselves. But middle-class homeowners found themselves faced with huge tax increases that imposed a real hardship on their family budgets. For some on the right, criticizing and challenging the tax system was a way to assault a much more significant issue: the welfare state. Within California, notably, the blasts against the skyrocketing property taxes were often more about the progressive social services paid for with that money.[28]

There had long been a number of antitax groups in California, such as the United Organization of Taxpayers (UOT). Before the middle-class outrage of the mid-1970s, however, these groups found little broad support for their cause. But with suburbanites reacting in unison to the higher taxes, UOT suddenly discovered a committed constituency. The result of their outrage was a revolutionary measure known as Proposition 13. Placed on the ballot by antitax activists Howard Jarvis and Paul Gann, it called for a massive decrease in property taxes across the board. It would slash property taxes by 57 percent, roll back tax rates, and ensure that unless a house was sold, the rates would rise by no more than 2 percent a year. Finally, Proposition 13 would amend the state constitution as well, establishing a new requirement that the state legislature had to secure a two-thirds vote before it could ever increase state taxes. Proposition 13 had supporters across the state, but its strongest backers were middle-class suburbanites. Although these were not people normally thought of in populist terms, the leaders of the tax revolt did. "You are the people," Jarvis told supporters at one suburban rally, "and you will have to take control of the government again, or else it is going to control you." In June 1978, Proposition 13 passed by a huge two-to-one margin.[29]

After the passage of Proposition 13, the tax revolt took on a national scope. The victory in California quickly inspired successful crusades against property taxes in thirty-seven states and against state income taxes in twenty-eight states. Observers of American politics realized that a fundamentally important issue had emerged on the national scene. Reagan argued that the passage of Proposition 13 "triggered hope in the breasts of the people that something could be done. It was a little bit like dumping those cases of tea off the boat in Boston Harbor." Likewise, in the words of the *New York Times*, the tax revolt signaled nothing less than a "primal scream by the People against Big Government." Indeed, the protest represented the dawn of a new era in American politics. It helped create a coalition against the liberal welfare state, gave the New Right a unifying issue, shaped a growing antigovernment ethic, and generally generated more dissatisfaction with the Democratic Party. It also further cemented the growing links between ideological conservatives, business leaders, and the Republican Party. As a Democratic pollster said, "This isn't just a tax revolt. It's a revolution against government."[30]

The political power of the tax revolt became even clearer in the 1978 elections. After Proposition 13's triumph, Michael Barone noted in the *Wall Street Journal,* "the major question on taxes became not whether they should be held down, but how." During the fall campaign, many Republican candidates ran on a tax-cut plan proposed by Representative Jack Kemp of New York and Senator William Roth of Delaware. In essence, the Kemp-Roth Plan called for the reduction of all federal income taxes by 30 percent across the board. It took the arguments of the tax revolt, escalated them to the national stage, and reduced them to a simple, appealing argument. Voters were still a little wary of the idea, with polling showing the public opposed by a margin of 47 to 34 percent. As a result, Republicans made only small gains in the midterms, winning eleven seats in the House and three in the Senate. Though the new class of Republican freshmen was small, it proved to be powerful; among its ranks were several who would soon become leaders in the GOP, including future Speaker of the House Newt Gingrich and future Vice President Dick Cheney. Their election proved to be a harbinger of things to come. Two years later, with the stagflation crisis of the late 1970s reaching a fever pitch, Republicans would make even greater gains.[31]

After a decade of work laying the foundations for change, the conservative constellations that had come to be known as the New Right and the Religious Right coalesced in Ronald Reagan's 1980 presidential campaign. The GOP convention made it clear that Reagan, long loved by the party's Goldwater libertarians, had been warmly embraced by the forces of religious conservatism too. "There is no formal Christian caucus at the Republican National Convention," a reporter marveled. "None is needed. Overlap between the Reagan campaign and evangelical Christians is substantial." Reagan's acceptance speech showed a skillful blend of the New Right and Religious Right movements, with lengthy passages on the need to lighten the "tax burden" capped off by a dramatic call for a silent prayer at the end of his address. Despite their different agendas, the two conservative camps were held together by a simple promise that Reagan had made repeatedly on the campaign trail, a claim that as president he would work to "get the government off the backs of the people."[32]

After the widespread distrust and disillusionment of the 1970s, that simple message proved enormously popular with the electorate. Moving beyond the ranks of the Republicans, Reagan made such strong inroads with white working-class voters who had long been a cornerstone of the New Deal coalition that a new term would soon be coined for the phenomenon: "Reagan Democrats." The sweep of Reagan's victory was clear early on election night, as the colored maps on network news steadily turned blue, the color assigned to Republicans that year. Shortly after 8pm eastern, NBC News anchor David Brinkley marveled that the map was "beginning to look like a suburban swimming pool"; soon after, the network called the election for Reagan. In some ways, the broad blue maps of the network news exaggerated the size and scope of Reagan's victory: he had racked up a staggering 489-to-49 margin in the electoral college, but barely cleared 50 percent in the popular vote in an election that had the lowest turnout in one-third of a century. Nevertheless, Reagan had won the White House and, equally important, had shown strong enough coattails to enable Republicans to take control of the Senate as well.[33]

Taking stock of the election returns that weekend, the *Washington Post*'s Haynes Johnson noted the new conventional wisdom in town: "it was clear to all the wise men in Washington what historic shift had occurred. A Reagan Revolution . . . had altered the American political landscape with profound implications for the nation and the world." Johnson cautioned readers against reading too much into the results, noting that the president's victory held no signs of an "ideological mandate," but the revolutionaries in Reagan's camp proved undeterred.[34] Nevertheless, the president seemed to have brought a new mood and a new attitude to Washington, one best reflected in an Iranian announcement on the day of his inauguration, that the American hostages were being set free, after 444 days in captivity. Seemingly, with a new president in office, the paralysis and pessimism of the previous decade had disappeared, if only for a moment.

The Reagan Revolution

The confident attitude of the new president and his administration was, at heart, a tried and true political strategy. As governor of California in the late 1960s and early 1970s, Reagan had learned how a Democratic legislature could force the chief executive to compromise. With Democrats dug in at the House, White House aides invoked the "Reagan Revolution" to claim a mandate. The president wanted to build a sense of momentum for his policies by presenting the election in the most favorable light.[35]

Reagan assembled a skilled team of advisors, such as Deputy Chief of Staff Michael Deaver and Director of the Communications Office David Gergen, who worked diligently to influence news coverage of the White House. Their operating premise, as presidential pollster Richard Wirthlin said, was that "There's no question that how the press reports [on] the President influences how people feel about the President. People make up their minds on the basis of what they see and hear about him, and the press is the conduit through which they get a lot of their information." Accordingly, Deaver and Gergen started each morning with a "line of the day" meeting during which they settled on a single theme around which all major events, presidential proclamations, and even visual backdrops for the next ten to twelve hours would be coordinated. Gergen was the mastermind behind this innovation. According to campaign strategist Ed Rollins, "Gergen really understood sound bites. He understood how to pick a story, how to get a story that somebody was working on and change it, how to get the reporters to call the people you wanted them to call and make the story come out how you wanted. He understood that you had to be proactive about it, as opposed to just letting your guys do your job and just reading about it in the paper the next day."[36] Every morning Gergen delivered the line to the cabinet, launching their common point of discussion for the day. "We had to think like a television producer," White House spokesman Larry Speakes explained, which meant they had a "minute and thirty seconds of pictures to tell the story, and a good solid sound bite."[37] An experienced actor, President Reagan understood the process well and gladly played his part. Every single hour of the president's daily schedule was structured around the "line of the day," with speeches designed to yield the right sound bite and public appearances deliberately staged to deliver the perfect photograph. The events themselves were carefully thought through down to the detail of the lighting and physical position of the president.[38]

Reagan's first major policy move focused on securing substantive tax cuts, which he had long believed were the best form of economic policy. Tax cuts offered a way to bridge grassroots activists who saw tax cuts as a symbolic strike on the state and business organizations that were throwing their support behind the new GOP. Like anti-Communism, the administration saw taxes as a unifying issue that would attract the support of almost every faction in Reagan's coalition and from parts of the Democratic Party as well. Practically speaking, the president was less concerned about the impact of federal deficits and more focused on "freeing" individuals and corporations alike from their tax burden.

Relief from taxes, he argued, would enable them to pour that money into investments that would then stimulate overall economic growth. This "supply-side theory" of economics—derided by critics as the "trickle down theory"—rested on a premise that helping wealthier Americans would eventually bring benefits to those who stood lower on the income ladder. Its adherents, Reagan among them, rejected the conventional wisdom of Keynesian economists who had been arguing since the 1930s that tax cuts should be targeted to middle-class Americans who would immediately spend the money on consumer goods.

The challenge for Reagan was that there were still a decent number of prominent Republicans and conservative Democrats who ranked balancing the budget as the most important of all political objectives. Even Reagan's own vice president, George H. W. Bush, had originally mocked the supply-side theory as a nonsensical form of "voodoo economics" when he was Reagan's rival in the 1980 primaries. Fiscal conservatives like Bush warned that enacting sizable tax cuts, without making corresponding reductions in domestic spending, would instantly produce larger deficits and thus destabilize investment. Reagan pushed back, advancing the theory that short-term deficits were economically tolerable. He believed that the tax cuts would stimulate growth, that growth would increase overall income, and, in the end, that the government would actually take in more tax revenue than it had before.[39]

Reagan's views on the centrality of tax cuts to economic growth had gained intellectual support through conservative economists who gave academic rationales for his political positions. According to key proponents of supply-side economics like the economist Norman Ture, the Keynesians, who had shaped economic policy since the New Deal, had erroneously focused on manipulating demand, which conservatives said would not cure the threat of inflation and unemployment. They pointed to the 1970s phenomenon of "stagflation"—that seemingly inexplicable rise of inflation in a stagnant economy—as the clearest evidence that the Keynesian policies had failed. Instead, conservative economists argued, the government needed to focus on the "supply side" of the economy by cutting business taxes, lowering the burden on wealthy Americans who could put their money in the market, and creating more incentives for research and investment, in addition to dismantling regulations.[40]

Conservatives had long believed in unfettered capitalism, but during the 1970s their traditional faith in free markets took a turn into fundamentalism. Within the universities, changes in the field of economics were part of a broader intellectual shift that was taking place in the world of ideas and scholarship. Increasingly, cutting-edge thinkers in different fields of study were giving less weight to the role of power structures, society, history, and institutions, and placing more emphasis on a world shaped by free-floating, rational individuals and free choice. In economics, a growing number of scholars were concluding that government efforts to sway consumer and business behavior by managing the economy through taxes and spending, the way that proponents of Keynesian economics had advocated since the 1930s, stifled productive decisions by market actors. The markets, they concluded, had to be left on their own.[41]

Public intellectuals helped to bridge the new research in economics departments with the world of politics. The University of Chicago economist Milton Friedman led the way with pioneering works like *Capitalism and Freedom* (1962), a best-selling book that characterized government policies as inefficient and ineffective and championed free-market alternatives instead. Friedman's influence became increasingly felt during the coming years, not just within academic circles but in larger political and popular debates as well. When he was awarded the Nobel Prize for Economics in 1976, Friedman used the moment to lambast old orthodoxies, arguing that only the laws of supply and demand could provide economic equilibrium and that all forms of government interference in the economy—from campaigns for full employment to social welfare programs—invariably made matters worse. The marketplace would solve most problems, he insisted, if only the government would get out of the way.[42]

Friedman's faith in free markets was shared by other enterprising economists such as Arthur Laffer, who proved instrumental in popularizing the new supply-side theory. While teaching at the University of Southern California, Laffer had played a prominent role in the 1978 campaign to pass Proposition 13. Upon entering the White House, Reagan appointed Laffer to his Economic Advisory Board, where he made the case for massive new tax cuts. The "Laffer Curve," as he called it, showed the tradeoff between tax rates and tax revenues, with high tax rates creating a disincentive to earn. Keynesianism, Laffer argued, had failed. "If there was one clear economics lesson from the 1970s," Laffer wrote, "it is that economics focusing on consumer demand, and which attempt to redistribute income, do not work."[43] Laffer's ideas had strong support in Congress from Republicans such as Jack Kemp and conservative media outlets like the editorial board of the *Wall Street Journal*.

Others helped spread the word. The *Journal's* Jude Wanniski was so taken with supply-side theory that he secured a year-long position as the first-ever research journalist at the American Enterprise Institute to write an entire book about it. The result, *The Way The World Works* (1978), popularized supply-side economics for a general audience. Promoting the book, Wanniski argued that tax cuts would solve a host of problems, helping America win the Cold War abroad and even fight the problems of drug abuse and divorce at home. "Instead of a society smothered, crushed by disincentives, with all its tensions, there would be light, air and hope," he promised in one op-ed. "We will once again feel confident about ourselves as a nation." The sudden surge of support for supply-side economics astounded even its most ardent fans. "In the short period of five years," marveled Paul Craig Roberts, an associate editor for the *Journal* who joined Reagan's Treasury Department, "supply-side economics has progressed from 'voodoo economics' to presidential policy—a remarkable success story."[44]

Tax cuts were also attractive to Reagan because they offered a way to create pressure for reducing the size of government in an era when directly attacking government spending was difficult. Budget Director David Stockman, who led the drive for tax cuts in 1981, understood that, contrary to the claims of supply siders that tax cuts would eventually lead to greater government revenues, the enactment of rate cuts would actually diminish the amount of tax revenue that Congress had available to fund domestic programs. As deficits inevitably rose, legislators would find themselves under pressure to cut domestic spending rather than take the unpopular step of raising taxes to the pre-cut rates. Stockman called this the "starve the beast" strategy. "The beast is big government," he explained in a 1981 interview. "You starve it by cutting taxes and reducing revenues, so the programs must be cut back."[45]

In February 1981, Reagan proposed a sweeping package of tax cuts to a joint session of Congress. In addition to over $40 billion in cuts to domestic spending and a sharp increase in the defense budget, the president called for 30 percent across-the-board tax rate cuts over the coming three years. "Marching in lockstep with the whole program of reductions in spending is the equally important program of reduced tax rates. Both are essential if we're to have economic recovery," Reagan said. "It's time to create new jobs, to build and rebuild industry, and to give the American people room to do what they do best. And that can only be done with a tax program which provides incentive to increase productivity for both workers and industry."[46]

Initially, the proposal received a lukewarm response. Americans had found Reagan's antigovernment campaign rhetoric appealing in theory, but they were much less enthusiastic when the cuts to specific programs were outlined. While ordinary Americans would be most affected by the broad rollback in government programs, the majority of tax relief would be directed to the wealthiest. Members of Congress soon heard from constituents about the types of hardships the reductions would cause in their daily life, a concern that was soon reflected in the opinion polls. In mid-March 1981, Gallup revealed that only 59 percent approved of Reagan's performance so far (compared to Carter's 75 percent approval at a similar point in his presidency), while his disapproval rating was 24 percent (nearly double the norm for presidents in the "honeymoon" period).[47] The president's agenda seemed to be stalled in the first hundred days.

An assassination attempt saved Reagan's political standing. On March 30, 1981, John Hinckley Jr. shot the president outside a Washington hotel, apparently seeking to impress the actress Jodie Foster by re-creating a scene from her 1976 movie *Taxi Driver*. Of the six bullets fired, one bounced off the president's car and into his body; another struck James Brady, Reagan's press secretary, in the head, causing permanent brain damage. Caught on camera, the shooting was replayed endlessly in the media. One *New York Times* reporter recounted: "Within minutes, Americans were witnessing for the second time in a generation television pictures of a chief executive being struck by gunfire during what appeared to be a routine public appearance. For the second time in less than 20 years, too, they watched as the nation's leaders scrambled to meet one of the sternest tests of the democratic system."[48]

Reagan not only survived the assassination attempt, but found that his political standing had been considerably strengthened as a result of the ordeal. His lighthearted response to the shooting helped change public perceptions of him and his programs. Reportedly, he had joked with his surgeons: "Please tell me you're Republicans." After he was released from the hospital, his popularity rose, with his approval ratings increasing by seven points. The president immediately turned his attention back to the tax cut, daring Democrats to take him on. His opponents in Congress were suddenly reluctant to strike out at a president who had almost been struck down. "Because of the attempted assassination," Democratic Speaker of the House Tip O'Neill acknowledged, "the President has become a hero. We can't argue with a man as popular as he is."[49]

The administration conducted an aggressive campaign to sell the tax bill, especially as it became clear that proposed spending cuts would never come to pass. Combined with his own proposals to increase the military budget significantly, the president understood he was pushing a bill that would vastly expand the deficit. He blitzed the airwaves, promising Americans that the tax cuts would have a dramatic impact on economic conditions. Although tax reduction would provide the greatest benefits to wealthier Americans, Reagan depicted the legislation as a populist measure that would help average wage earners recover from the devastation of the 1970s. The president urged voters to write their representatives in Congress to let them know how much they wanted a cut. Meanwhile, allied conservative organizations ranging from business lobbies to religious groups likewise pressured legislators to act. Republican leaders in Congress, who were not always comfortable with the far Right in their party, were brought into line with an aggressive whip operation. "Our fundamental position must not change," House Minority Leader Robert Michel told them. "We must continue to strive for multi-year, across the board tax rate reductions this year. We must not accept anything less. We can compromise, but we must not capitulate."[50]

House Democrats, realizing that many conservative members in their caucus would cross the aisle, abandoned any effort to kill the bill. Instead, they pursued additional tax breaks to benefit middle- and working-class Americans. The result was what some called a "Christmas Tree," with members of both parties adding ornaments to the final package. Despite Democrats' provisions, the tax cuts remained highly regressive overall, giving the largest benefits to those in the upper income brackets. On August 13, 1981, Reagan signed the measure, then known as the Economic Recovery Tax Act. It cut deeply into the revenue capacity of the federal government and created a fiscal straight-jacket for policy makers who would have to confront ballooning deficits.

But that reckoning still lay ahead. The new president's tax cut was heralded in the national press as nothing less than "triumphant." Reagan had not simply delivered on a signature promise made to the conservative base; he had also provided a sense of bipartisanship by bringing in large numbers of Democrats. Most important, he had shown that Washington might actually work after all.[51]

CHAPTER 6

Fighting Right

CONSERVATIVE CELEBRATIONS OVER REAGAN'S INITIAL
successes did not last long.

While it represented a significant triumph for the Republican Party,
the 1981 tax cut also proved to be a powerful warning for the opposition. Democrats realized that the president's legislative victory would
give the GOP momentum for further policy gains, while the practical
impact of the reduction in federal funding would leave other domestic
programs in a weaker position across the board. As Reagan entered his
second year, the opposition recovered its footing. Refusing to believe
there had been a "Reagan Revolution" at all, Democrats argued that the
1980 election did not represent a permanent shift in political power and
resolved to take Washington back.

Frustrated on domestic affairs, the new president made greater headway in foreign policies in his first term. Ramping up military spending and encouraging a more confrontational attitude across the globe,
the Reagan administration sought to dispel any lingering enthusiasm
for détente and to restore American military might and patriotic confidence. In its drive to renew American confidence, however, the new
administration also sparked widespread fears—at home and abroad—
that the renewed Cold War conflict of the 1980s might well lead to a
nuclear holocaust. Reagan's fights with his enemies, foreign and domestic, came to a dramatic head in the election campaign of 1984.

Democratic Resurgence

Whatever his powers of persuasion, Reagan alone could not remake the political landscape. The new movements of the late 1970s had created a powerful base for conservatism, but liberalism remained a force in national politics. For all its fracturing in the 1970s, the New Deal state still dominated. Policies that had seemed radical when they were introduced decades earlier—from labor protections to welfare state measures—had come to be not only widely accepted but deeply entrenched as well. Institutional defenses had grown up around these policies and programs over the decades and, more important, voters had come to rely upon them and resist calls for their removal. One election would not change that.

Liberalism's staying power became clear as early as 1981, during the showdown over Social Security. One of the most popular domestic programs of the New Deal, Social Security provided retired workers a monthly pension financed through a payroll tax on current workers. Conservatives had long resented the program, but had found it impossible to end. In 1964, Republican presidential candidate Barry Goldwater talked on the campaign trail about the possibility of privatizing Social Security, only to find voters recoiling from him as a result.[1] As a key supporter of Goldwater's, Reagan understood the political risks of challenging Social Security, but still hoped to tackle it. In 1976, in his primary race against President Ford, Reagan suggested that Americans who had sufficient money for retirement should be able to opt out of the program.[2] Now, as president, he was optimistic that the political climate had shifted enough to make change possible. In May 1981, the administration proposed lowering Social Security benefits for some early retirees, claiming that the program was in danger of failing. "The crisis is inescapable," argued Secretary of Health and Human Services Richard Schweiker. "It is here. It is now. It is serious. And it must be faced."[3]

While the White House focused on the nation's finances, millions of retirees who depended on Social Security worried about their own. For three-fifths of the beneficiaries in 1981, Social Security accounted for 50 percent or more of their total income. Gregory Kaplan, a former painter from Brooklyn who had retired to West Palm Beach, Florida, argued that each Social Security check was essential. "I never expected to live this long," he told a reporter. "I really didn't figure on living on just my Social Security." But now he was. For others, the current benefits didn't go far enough. Gladys Curtis, an 81-year-old retiree in the District of Columbia, noted that her $229 monthly check was already insufficient to cover the rent for her small apartment. She worried about it being reduced further.[4]

When the president circulated his proposal to reduce early retirement benefits, Speaker Tip O'Neill made it clear the Democrats would resist the move. This was, he recognized, the first step in a much bigger plan to eliminate the nation's premier social insurance program. An ardent New Deal and Great Society Democrat, O'Neill had little sympathy for the new conservatism. "I will be fighting this every inch of the way," he promised. Though he was in his late 70s at the time, O'Neill answered the Social Security proposal with uncharacteristic energy. He had long avoided the media, routinely turning down invitations to the networks' Sunday morning shows so he could relax at his home in Cape Cod. But now the Speaker took to the airwaves, showing how congressional leaders could use television to push back against the bully pulpit of the presidency.[5] The Boston politician used dramatic rhetoric, warning voters that Reagan sought to destroy the entire Social Security program and leave elderly Americans without the support that they expected and, indeed, deserved. "It is a rotten thing to do," he said. "[It was] nothing but a sneak attack on Social Security."[6]

As Democrats renewed their sense of purpose, they found support outside Capitol Hill. Organizations representing the elderly, such as the American Association of Retired Persons (AARP), conducted a fierce campaign to kill the proposal. They united 100 groups through the Save Our Security coalition, headed by Wilbur Cohen, former secretary of health, education, and welfare, and Robert Ball, former Social Security commissioner. Pushing back against the proposed cuts, the coalition denounced the "despicable plan" aimed at the disadvantaged. Jack Ossofsky of the National Council on Aging said that "the President's safety net is under water, and old people are being thrown to the sharks." More pointedly, critics noted that cuts to Social Security would only be needed to offset proposals for increased government spending in other areas, most notably on national defense. Douglas Fraser, the president of the United Auto Workers, declared it was simply "wrong to wring tens of billions of dollars out of retiree benefits so that they may be applied to other parts of the federal budget."[7]

Under intense fire from the public and politicians alike, Reagan reluctantly shelved the plan in September 1981. The president, David Gergen told the press, needed some "breathing space" to sell the idea. Buying time, Reagan appointed a fifteen-member panel to spend the next two years studying the issue. While the president was chastened, Democrats emerged from the fight emboldened and determined to defend liberal legacies. The New Deal programs, they now realized, were more popular than the "Reagan Revolution" triumphalism had originally led pundits to believe. "Social Security is the third rail of American politics," Democratic staffer Kirk O'Donnell joked, comparing it to the electricity-laden rail of a subway system. "Touch it, you're dead."[8] Ultimately, the battle signaled to all sides on Capitol Hill and outside Washington that rumors of liberalism's death had been greatly exaggerated.

Reagan, for his part, was well aware of the limits he faced. Despite his roots in the conservative movement and his ideological commitment to the Right, he had learned in his years as California's governor that entrenched Democratic opposition could rule out a lot of options for a Republican. Accordingly, to the frustration of social conservatives, Reagan ignored much of the Religious Right's agenda during his first term. But the president's belief that there wasn't much political support for proposals prohibiting abortion or regulating the airwaves only led right-wing activists to press them with greater passion. As a result, social conservatives found their alliance with the new administration fraying.

This disconnect was clear from the very first days of Reagan's term, with the politics of abortion deepening the lines of division. On January 23, 1981, the eighth anniversary of *Roe v. Wade*, 50,000 antiabortion activists marched from the White House to Congress, chanting, "We want life, yes we do; we want life, how about you?" North Carolina's Republican senator Jesse Helms, a darling of the Religious Right, promised the crowd he would introduce a constitutional amendment to guarantee the right to life from the moment of conception. Despite his previous claims of kinship with social conservatives, Reagan did not attend the rally in person, rejecting an invitation to address them.[9] Then, in the summer of 1981, Reagan angered social conservatives again by appointing Sandra Day O'Connor to the Supreme Court. As a state legislator in Arizona, O'Connor had supported the Equal Rights Amendment and sided against the pro-life movement on at least one occasion. Accordingly, the National Right to Life Committee, the Moral Majority, and other groups in the Religious Right announced their firm opposition. Jerry Falwell went so far as to say that Christians should unite to "turn their backs" on Reagan in response to the insulting nomination. Reagan stood fast, though, and O'Connor soon became the first female justice on the Supreme Court.[10]

Sometimes Reagan distanced himself from social conservatives in less obvious ways. In September 1982, for instance, the Senate considered legislation introduced by Helms to prohibit federal funding of abortions on a permanent basis, for the first time. Reagan supported the legislation, but the White House stayed at arm's length. Without its full backing, the measure went down to defeat. Behind the scenes, the administration rationalized that Reagan's focus on economic and political change meant that social issues simply had to be sidelined. "For better than a year," acknowledged Elizabeth Dole, an administration official charged with political outreach, "the President has marshaled the forces of his conservative supporters behind his efforts to revitalize the economy and restructure government which, in turn, relegated the conservative social agenda to the back burner."[11]

The president also encountered growing criticism from fiscal conservatives who warned that deficits were skyrocketing. The combination of cutting taxes and increasing defense spending, while maintaining the spending status quo on domestic programs, they noted, meant that the federal government's books were growing deeply imbalanced. The federal deficit, which had reached $80 billion under Carter, now surged to $200 billion. Private grumbling became public in December 1981, when *The Atlantic* published "The Education of David Stockman." A true believer in supply-side economics, the budget director had allowed the journalist William Greider to follow him around to demonstrate that Reagan's administration was full of serious ideas and advisors. But the piece proved the opposite. On the record, Stockman admitted that he waved away worries about growing deficits by using a "magic asterisk" that promised future budget savings from unnamed sources. "None of us really understands what's going on with all these numbers," he later confessed.[12]

The growing concerns over the Reagan budget prompted a showdown within the Republican Party. Figures from the New Right urged Reagan to stay the course. The economist Norman Ture insisted that "the deficits aren't the mischief makers. History shows they have no relation to interest rates, inflation or capital formation."[13] Congressman Newt Gingrich, meanwhile, mocked Democrats for worrying about deficits at all. "Think about it—liberal Democrats concerned about deficits. It is as confusing to me as if we were back in the 1920s and whisky dealers came out in favor of prohibition."[14] Such voices, however, were in the minority. Leading Republicans pushed back and called on the president to reverse course. Kansas senator Bob Dole, the fiscally conservative chairman of the Senate Finance Committee and a supply-side skeptic, fought off critics and championed the Tax Equity and Fiscal Responsibility Act of 1982. Recognizing the shortcomings of his original tax plans, Reagan signed the measure into law that September. Along with higher excise taxes on items like tobacco and alcohol, the 1982 tax hike reversed some of the 1981 income tax cut as well.

Reagan's promise to rebuild American strength seemed shattered by the deepening recession of 1982. Unemployment, which had hovered under 6 percent during the last year of Carter's term, steadily rose during the first two years of Reagan's administration, largely due to Paul Volcker's strategy for beating back inflation. Over the course of 1982 alone, the unemployment rate soared from 8.6 percent in January to 10.8 percent in November, the highest rate since the Great Depression. All told, nearly twelve million people were out of work. Unemployment hit certain parts of the nation harder than others: northern manufacturing states, which saw jobs moving to other parts of the country, suffered the worst of it. With 20.9 percent of its workforce unemployed in October 1982, Youngstown, Ohio, had the highest rate in the country, with several towns across Illinois, Wisconsin, and Michigan not far behind.[15] The ranks of the unemployed extended beyond industrial workers, though. As reporters soon discovered, Ronald Reagan Jr., was unemployed, too, after his dance company suffered layoffs. "Everybody's collecting unemployment," the president's son told CBS News with a shrug. "I'm no different."[16]

The worsening recession set the stage for the 1982 midterms. Senator Ted Kennedy called soaring unemployment figures "a national tragedy," prompting President Reagan to denounce critics "who would try to make a political football" out of the jobless rate.[17] But Reagan, of course, had done exactly that during the 1980 election, claiming that the incumbent president deserved all blame for the recession. Voters had agreed with his argument then, and to his dismay, they still agreed two years later. Polls showed that 54 percent of Americans believed that Reagan's policies had made their own financial situation worse, not better. Accordingly, Speaker O'Neill worked to nationalize the campaign on economic issues. Democrats focused on the "Reagan Recession," calling for renewed attention to "fairness" in domestic policy and attacking the administration for having made conditions even worse than they had been under Carter. The recession, said O'Neill, was a "deliberate and conscious policy" of the Reagan administration. "The economic fate of the greatest democracy in the history of the world," he said, "depends on a novel, unproven theory called 'supply side' economics."[18] Reagan's advisors fretted as they saw his approval ratings plummet down to 40 percent. It was, officials at Gallup noted, the worst midterm rating of any president in thirty years.[19]

Midterm elections usually go poorly for the president's party, and this one was no different. Democrats gained twenty-six seats in the House and one in the Senate. Though neither chamber of Congress changed hands, Democrats strengthened their hold over the House to an impressively large margin: 269–166. Liberal members of the Democratic caucus fared well, while the ranks of conservatives who'd been willing to work with Republicans on certain issues had been thinned. More numerous and more liberal, House Democrats could now more easily check major conservative advances. Many reporters interpreted this as a significant blow to Reagan's agenda. Surveying the results, the journalist Tom Wicker declared: "There is no Reagan Revolution."[20]

After this rough start, the economy finally began to recover in 1983, as unemployment started to decline and the major economic indicators pointed to the nation moving in the right direction. Economists disagreed on the cause of the revival, though most credited the policies of Federal Reserve Chairman Paul Volcker. (In contrast, Reagan officials pointedly credited the 1981 tax cuts while ignoring the 1982 reversal.) The revived economy allowed the administration to project a sunnier mood of optimism, one that was soon reflected in public opinion polls that showed renewed confidence in the administration and the economy. A closer look at the polls, however, showed that the electorate was deeply divided along lines of race and class. African Americans had been particularly hard hit in the "Reagan recession," seeing their unemployment rate spike to nearly 19 percent—almost twice the national average. As a result, they remained more cynical about the recovery than whites. An April 1983 poll showed that 46 percent of whites believed the economy was recovering, but only 17 percent of blacks did. Likewise, the same poll showed that wealthier Americans were more optimistic than working-class ones. Among those earning more than $40,000 a year, 62 percent agreed that the economy was recovering; for those making less than $20,000, only 34 percent did.[21]

As the economic mood lightened for some Americans, Reagan turned to other domestic issues, looking for proposals that already had bipartisan support. Notably, in 1983, Reagan returned to Social Security. The bipartisan commission he appointed in 1981 now reported that the program faced a severe financial shortfall and proposed raising payroll taxes and containing costs to restore the program's strength. No longer aiming to destroy the social safety net, Reagan now positioned himself as its savior and sought to shore it up. The president formed a coalition with fiscal conservatives in the GOP and House Democrats to pass the Social Security Amendments of 1983, which raised payroll taxes and made small cuts to benefits, all of which corrected the short-term financial crisis of the program. "This bill demonstrates for all time our nation's ironclad commitment to Social Security," President Reagan said, sounding much different than he had as the Republican candidate in 1980.[22]

While old New Deal programs proved to be difficult to dismantle in Congress, Reagan found ways to undermine them on the executive front. Pointedly, the president staffed key government roles with appointees who were strongly opposed to the stated mission of their agencies. His first head of the Occupational Safety and Health Administration (OSHA) was Florida businessman Thorne Auchter, whose construction firm had repeatedly been fined by OSHA in the past. Believing that businesses would take care of their workers if not faced with government regulation, Auchter drastically reduced the number of fines issued by OSHA and tamped down on enforcement. "We have slots for only 1,200 inspectors," he noted. "They were supposed to cover more than three million workplaces. Of course, that was ridiculous." Accordingly, he reduced the total number of inspections by 21 percent. Labor leaders were furious with what they saw as an executive end-run. "He's ripping the entrails out of the act creating OSHA, without even going to Congress to do it," the AFL-CIO's safety and health expert complained. "OSHA is not enforcing its standards. They're downgrading the seriousness of many violations and they're settling out of court with slap-on-the-wrist penalties."[23]

Reagan took the same approach with environmental regulations, seeking to undermine the significant reforms undertaken in the 1970s. The administration did little to enforce existing laws and had no interest in giving support to environmentalists who called on the government to do more to combat issues such as pollution, acid rain, or toxic waste. The Conservation Foundation—known as the "Vatican of the Environmental Movement"—had avoided taking political stances in its thirty-four years of existence, but warned in its "State of the Environment 1982" report that Reagan officials had "broken" the "bipartisan consensus that supported federal protection of the environment for more than a decade."[24] Chief among these officials was Secretary of the Interior James Watt, who strongly supported the development of public lands by private interests. Like Auchter at OSHA, Watt cut the department's budget and severely curtailed its regulatory efforts. An outspoken social conservative, he caused a minor sensation in the summer of 1983 when he banned the Beach Boys from a Fourth of July concert on the National Mall on the grounds that they encouraged "drug abuse and alcoholism." (Watt replaced them with Las Vegas crooner Wayne Newton.) A few months later, he caused a more significant crisis for the administration when he made flippant comments about the diversity of a coal advisory committee. "We have every kind of mixture you can have," he bragged. "I have a black, I have a woman, two Jews and a cripple. And we have talent." A lightning rod for critics, Watt finally resigned in October 1983.[25] Meanwhile, Anne Gorsuch Burford, the first female head of the Environmental Protection Agency, believed it regulated businesses too aggressively and worked to ease its impact. "The entire organization is suffering from a paralysis from the top down," noted a Carter holdover at EPA. "The appalling insensitivity of these appointments," said William Turnage of the Wilderness Society, "the egregious conflicts of interest, the groveling to regulated industry is truly without parallel in the history of our great nation."[26]

In the same vein, Reagan administration appointees at the Equal Employment Opportunity Commission (EEOC) worked to make sure that its reach was limited as well. A creation of the Civil Rights Act of 1964, the EEOC had led the fight against racial and gender discrimination in private sector employment for nearly a decade and a half. Clarence Thomas, the 34-year-old African American head of Reagan's EEOC, argued in July 1982 that the commission had previously been too aggressive in its work. "We are simply in the habit of saying that, if a company has not hired minorities in numbers commensurate with their presence in the population, then discrimination has taken place. But discrimination does not account for all of the differential," he told a journalist. "Employment is typically based on skills. To become a news reporter, you must be able to write. Simple as that." It was wrong for the EEOC to stand up for all of those left out of an industry. "To say we are protecting their rights, when in fact they are unqualified, is to create a false hope," Thomas argued. "It's like protecting my right to become a concert pianist when I cannot play the piano."[27] Ultimately, the change in leadership at executive branch agencies like the EEOC, OSHA, and the EPA showed that the institutional stickiness of liberal policies was not as strong as Democrats might have assumed. The New Deal and Great Society might not be eradicated, but their impact could be limited considerably.

Reagan the Hawk

The early years of the Reagan presidency were more amenable to the conservative movement when it came to national security. During the first term, the administration amplified the tensions with the Soviet Union as the Cold War heated up to dangerous levels. Though Reagan ultimately wanted the elimination of nuclear weapons, he believed the means to that end was a massive military buildup and an adversarial stand against the Soviet Union. "Peace through strength," he said, was the only way to obtain freedom from nuclear war. "If history teaches us anything," the president said, "it is that a strong defense is a prerequisite to a lasting peace, the only credible deterrent against aggression."[28]

During his first four years, Reagan handled national security issues as a hawk. Although he secretly authorized contact with the Soviet leadership to see if there was any possibility for peace, Reagan publicly made a number of moves that signaled to the American people, and the world, that he was serious about confronting the Soviet Union. In a 1983 speech to religious leaders, Reagan famously denounced the USSR as an "evil empire." "There is sin and evil in the world," Reagan said, "and we're enjoined by Scripture and the Lord Jesus to oppose it with all our might."[29] Reagan's defiant tone was shared by his national security team. Many of his key appointments, including those who were responsible for negotiations, were ardent conservatives who had long been outspoken critics of détente. The neoconservative Democrat Richard Perle, who had been a staffer for hawkish Washington senator Henry "Scoop" Jackson, became assistant secretary of defense for international security policy. Perle, according to one policy maker, had an "unshakable belief that the Soviets had always managed to bend arms control agreements to their advantage and always would." Negotiating, he believed, was simply naïve.[30]

To solidify its militaristic stance against the Soviet Union, the White House proposed a vast expansion of the defense budget. Working with allies in Congress, Reagan steadily increased how much the nation spent on its military, reversing a sharp decline in spending initiated by Democratic Congresses after Vietnam. Secretary of Defense Caspar Weinberger, who ironically had been known as "Cap the Knife" for his budget-cutting fervor when he worked for President Nixon as director of the Office of Management and Budget, now ushered in a spending spree on the military.[31] His mission, he said, was to "rearm America." "If we value our freedom," Weinberger insisted, "we must be able to defend ourselves in wars of any size and shape and in any region where we have vital interests."[32] Democrats, worried about being tagged as weak on defense, were reluctant to resist calls to fund the military. As a result, defense spending increased by over 40 percent between 1980 and 1987.[33]

In keeping with Weinberger's promise to fight Communism in all corners of the world, the White House instituted an aggressive new policy of interventionism through proxy wars. In Central America, the administration provided support to anti-Communist forces in Nicaragua and El Salvador. When Congress passed a series of amendments to prohibit such direct assistance in 1982 and 1984, measures known as the Boland Amendments (after their sponsor, Massachusetts Democratic congressman Edward Boland), Reagan's advisors pressed on. Without public knowledge and in direct defiance of the law, they continued to fund the authoritarian government of El Salvador in its fight against Communist insurgents, and the Nicaraguan Contras in their battle to overthrow the left-wing Sandinista government.

One of the most daunting obstacles Reagan faced in the realm of foreign policy was the nuclear freeze movement. In June 1982, almost 700,000 people gathered in New York's Central Park to insist Congress place limitations on the production of nuclear weapons. "Reagan is a Bomb—Both Should be Banned," read one placard. Coretta Scott King, the widow of slain civil rights leader Martin Luther King Jr., praised those in attendance: "We have come here in numbers so large that the message must get through to the White House and Capitol Hill." A protester from upstate New York told reporters, "There's no way the leaders can ignore this now. It's not just hippies and crazies anymore. It's everybody."[34] The Reagan administration certainly took note. "We took it as a serious movement that could undermine Congressional support for the [nuclear] modernization program," National Security Advisor Robert McFarlane recalled, "and . . . a serious partisan political threat that could affect the election in '84."[35] According to one internal administration poll conducted in 1982, "The American public is concerned about the possibility of the U.S. and the Soviet Union stumbling into a nuclear war. Only about 30 percent are confident that a nuclear war between the superpowers will not occur within the next decade."[36]

While the administration fretted about the domestic impact of the nuclear freeze movement, it also had to worry about its ramifications on foreign relations. Reagan enraged Europeans when he authorized the deployment of 572 intermediate-range nuclear missiles, a product of a NATO agreement from 1979, in response to the Soviet deployment of SS-20 intermediate-range missiles. The announcement, which moved the NATO member states closer to a direct military conflict, sparked massive protests throughout Western Europe. On October 22, 1983, over a million demonstrators marched to voice their opposition. In Rome, for instance, almost 100,000 people lay down on the ground in John Lateran Square as part of a "die-in" to remind the world of the impact of a nuclear war. In Bonn, West Germany, 300,000 people applauded when former chancellor Willy Brandt said, "More than 70 percent of West Germans, and this is a good thing, do not want Germany being crammed with this devilish nuclear stuff."[37]

Fears over the growing likelihood of nuclear war wound their way into popular culture, where the threat became a significant topic. The German band Nena, for instance, had a hit song "99 Luftballons," about nuclear war being accidentally triggered by children's balloons. Most notably, *The Day After* (1983) depicted in graphic detail the impact of a nuclear strike in Kansas. Nearly 100 million Americans watched the movie, making it the third-most-watched program in network history. ABC produced an eight-page viewer guide for discussions in schools and civic organizations. "Developmentally, the show could be frightening for children," warned one psychologist. "The sense of loss suffered by the families on the screen may provoke profound fears about children's separation from parents."[38] Nuclear freeze organizations believed the show would help their cause. "ABC was doing a $7 million advertising job for our issue," marveled the Campaign Against Nuclear War. Representative Edward Markey, a leading proponent of the nuclear freeze resolution in the House, concluded that it was "the most powerful television program in history."[39]

Cold War tensions continued to escalate in Reagan's first term. On September 1, 1983, Soviet military leaders mistook a Korean airliner that had strayed into the USSR's airspace for an American reconnaissance plane and ordered it shot down into the Sea of Japan.[40] Sixty-one Americans were on board, including Congressman Larry McDonald, a conservative Democrat from Georgia. President Reagan said that he felt "revulsion" over what was a "horrifying act of violence," abruptly ending a trip to California to return to Washington and meet with the National Security Council.[41] Seeing the incident through the lens of the Cold War, congressional conservatives demanded retribution. The "deliberate murder of 269 human beings," said Newt Gingrich, should "remind all of us of the nature of Soviet dictatorship."[42] In an unexpected move, however, Reagan decided to take a different approach. He resisted the calls for military intervention, fearing that such action would only weaken the international outrage toward the Soviets.

But the tragedy fueled concern that the superpowers were entering a new stage of conflict, a growing sense of dread that only seemed to deepen. In November 1983, NATO launched a military training exercise called Able Archer 83. With troops from member nations spanning territory from Turkey to Britain, NATO simulated the transition from a conventional to a nuclear war. Mistaking the exercise for an actual mobilization, the Soviet leadership became convinced a nuclear attack was imminent. The Kremlin placed Soviet troops on high alert and prepared their nuclear weapons for launch.[43] As Defense official Robert Gates noted in his memoirs, "they really felt a NATO attack was at least possible and they took a number of measures to enhance their military readiness short of mobilization . . . I don't think the Soviets were crying wolf . . . they did seem to believe that the situation was very dangerous."[44]

As Cold War tensions escalated at home and abroad, Reagan sought to allay Americans' concerns. The president announced that he was in complete agreement with the goals of the nuclear freeze movement, but differed in his approach. "A nuclear war cannot be won and must never be fought," he announced. "So, to those who protest against nuclear war, I can only say 'I'm with you.'"[45] In March 1983, he announced a new plan, the Strategic Defense Initiative, to build a "missile shield" (using X-rays and other technology) that would theoretically protect the United States from incoming missile attack. "Wouldn't it be better to save lives than to avenge them?" the president asked.[46] Most scientists and engineers, however, dismissed the proposal as a fantasy, labeling it "Star Wars" after the popular science-fiction film franchise. (Reagan officials didn't mind their opponents using the term, rationalizing that the film had been a smash hit.) Critics, however, warned that if the program *did* work, it would significantly undermine the stability of international relations. For decades, both the Soviet Union and the United States had depended on the grim realities of "Mutually Assured Destruction," the realization that each side was capable of annihilating the other in a nuclear war that therefore reduced the incentive for either side to start one. But if one side could defend against the other, as SDI proposed to do, then there would be no barrier to that side launching an attack. Ironically, the measure that Reagan proposed to calm nuclear tensions only increased them.[47]

If "Star Wars" failed to dazzle, the Summer Olympics did. The administration transformed the games in Los Angeles into an advertisement for the greatness of America and, by extension, the greatness of the American president. Their effort was made all the easier by the fact that the Soviet Union boycotted the games, essentially forfeiting the competition to their rival. Reagan called the Soviets "losers" for boycotting, even though the United States had done the same four years earlier in response to the Soviet invasion of Afghanistan. In sharp contrast, the host nation presented itself as a country of winners. Under the direction of businessman Peter Ueberroth, the Los Angeles Games stood as the first Olympics not funded by a government.[48] Corporate sponsors and television deals paid for the events, prompting even more comparisons with the market-friendly Republican administration. Reagan was more than happy to encourage such connections. During an interview at the opening games, he told ABC anchorman Peter Jennings, "there is a great patriotic feeling that is sweeping this country and which bodes well for our future."[49]

Some, however, worried the Olympics portrayed Americans as sore winners. Events were choreographed with endless celebrations of the host nation's athletes; fans chanting "U-S-A, U-S-A" often drowned out the rest of the arena. "Oh, what we've done to the Olympics," wrote sports columnist Frank Deford. "God only knows what the 2.5 billion people around the globe who are watching the games will think of a vain America, so bountiful and strong, with every advantage, including the home court, reveling in the role of Goliath, gracelessly trumpeting its own good fortune while rudely dismissing its guests."[50]

But the fact that America finally had good fortune eclipsed everything else. When the Los Angeles games were over, the host nation stood far ahead of the rest of the world in terms of the medal count. The USA won 83 gold medals, 61 silver, and 30 bronze, for a total of 174 in all. (The next best country, for comparison's sake, was Romania with less than a third of that: 20 gold, 16 silver, and 17 bronze, or 53 in all.) America may have been a sore winner, but it was a winner all the same.

Morning in America

In many ways, the 1984 election replayed the themes of that year's
Summer Olympics. In keeping with Reagan's skills at stagecraft, the
Republicans ran a campaign that stressed an optimistic, patriotic
theme of "Morning in America." The campaign's one-minute centerpiece was a gauzy advertisement: "Prouder, Stronger, Better." Produced
by a group of the brightest advertisers, working out of a suite in Radio
City Music Hall, the ad struck a chord.[51] With sentimental music playing in the background, the ad showed paperboys riding their bicycles
and families walking out onto well-manicured lawns of their suburban
homes and cheerfully heading to work. "It's morning again in America," the narrator said in a calm, soothing voice. "Today more men and
women will go to work than ever before in our country's history. With
interest rates about half the record highs of 1980, nearly 2,000 families today will buy new homes, more than at any time in the past four
years. . . . It's morning again in America, and under the leadership of
President Reagan, our country is prouder and stronger and better. Why
would we ever want to return to where we were less than four short
years ago?"[52]

The threat that America might slip back to the late 1970s seemed
possible, as Democrats nominated Carter's vice president, Walter Mondale. Mondale had secured the nomination after surviving an unexpectedly strong challenge from Colorado senator Gary Hart and civil rights
activist Jesse Jackson. While Mondale stressed a return to an older style
of Great Society–era liberalism, each of these challengers offered a different path for the Democratic Party.

In many ways, a forward-looking identity stood at the core of Gary
Hart. First elected to Congress as part of the "Watergate Babies" class
of 1974, he had quickly emerged as a leader of an emerging "neoliberal-
ism" that sought to achieve traditional liberal goals through free-market
means. (Self-consciously styling themselves as hip, forward-looking
visionaries, neoliberals like Hart were known as "Atari Democrats,"
named after the pioneer in home video games.) With his entrance to
the Democratic primaries, Hart dismissed Mondale as a champion of a
tired old liberalism. Beholden to "special interests" like labor, Mondale

was nothing but a candidate from "the establishment past . . . brokered by backroom politics and confirmed by a collective sense of resignation." Hart proved to be a surprisingly strong challenger, upsetting the favorite in the New Hampshire primary and then racking up major wins in Ohio and California. Mondale challenged Hart's platform of "New Ideas" as lacking any real substance. In a televised debate, Mondale likened Hart's platform to the target mocked in a popular TV commercial for Wendy's Hamburgers: "When I hear your new ideas, I'm reminded of the ad: Where's the beef?" The attack caught Hart off guard and resonated with voters. Mondale slowly pulled away in the remaining primaries and wrapped up the nomination.[53]

The other challenger, Jesse Jackson, did not pose as much of an immediate threat to Mondale, but represented a promising path forward in the future. Jackson, who had worked closely with Martin Luther King in the 1960s, continued to rely on grassroots mobilization to protect the legacy of the civil rights movement and challenge the conservative movement. After running Operation PUSH for a decade, in 1984 Jackson took over the "Rainbow Coalition," an umbrella organization working for progressive causes such as federal health care, housing assistance, and fuller employment. The name testified to Jackson's roots in the urban political tradition that had served as a pathway for black political success. In 1983, African American congressman Harold Washington had engineered an upset over Chicago's incumbent mayor Jane Byrne, largely thanks to a new Democratic coalition—dubbed "the Rainbow Coalition"—that included African Americans, Hispanics, labor, and white liberals.[54]

Despite his origins in the black politics of Chicago, Jackson made it clear that he sought to represent all Americans, including marginalized groups from a variety of backgrounds. "This candidacy is not for blacks only," he said when he announced his campaign. "This is a national campaign growing out of the black experience and seen through the eyes of a black perspective—which is the experience and the perspective of the rejected. Because of this experience, I can empathize with the plight of Appalachia because I have known poverty. I know the pain of anti-Semitism because I have felt the humiliation of discrimination. I know firsthand the shame of bread lines and the horror of hopelessness and despair."[55] Though he never had a clear path to the nomination, Jackson nevertheless won millions of votes and thereby demonstrated the power of a multiracial liberal coalition. At the convention, Jackson delivered a thunderous address in which he promised delegates their work would be rewarded. "In the end, faith will not disappoint. Our time has come. Our faith, hope and dreams will prevail. Our time has come. Weeping has endured for nights, but now joy cometh in the morning."[56]

Despite their disagreements, the Democrats came together in their belief that the "Reagan Revolution" was meaningless. Mondale's campaign redoubled the party's emphasis on traditional policies and constituencies. Most notably, in an effort to rally women to the Democratic Party, he selected as his running mate the first woman to appear on a major party's presidential ticket, Representative Geraldine Ferraro of New York. He coupled this forward-looking attitude on gender equality with a more traditional approach to New Deal–era economics. Yes, Mondale admitted, the nation was doing better on the whole, but Reagan had instituted a two-track economy in which the rich enjoyed the rewards of economic growth while the middle and working classes continued to struggle. The divide between rich and poor, he noted correctly, was steadily growing. During his acceptance speech, Mondale said: "Four years ago, many of you voted for Mr. Reagan because he promised you'd be better off. And today, the rich are better off. But working Americans are worse off, and the middle class is standing on a trap door."[57] Mondale warned that these economic changes were just a harbinger of things to come, and the middle class would steadily wither away. Specifically, he pointed to the plight of unions. In the New Deal era, they had long been an important means of accessing middle-class success, but their membership had declined from a high of more than one-third of the workforce in the 1950s to about one-fifth in the 1980s. Reagan had made challenging unions' strength a central theme of his first term, most famously when he fired more than 11,000 striking aircraft controllers in an August 1981 showdown. As unions became endangered institutions, Mondale warned, the middle class became threatened too.[58]

Reagan countered by arguing that Mondale was a tired throwback. "The central economic issue in this campaign is growth," he noted in an October radio address. "Will we have policies that give each of you opportunities to climb higher and push America to challenge the limits of growth . . . or will we go back to those failed policies of the Carter-Mondale administration that inflicted unprecedented hardship on people?"[59] In sharp contrast, his campaign advanced images of an America on the rise, especially when it came to global affairs. The patriotic imagery of the Los Angeles Olympics replayed across the country and even the world. In June 1984, Reagan had delivered a carefully staged speech at Normandy, celebrating the World War II generation and reminding the world of the noble ends American military might had previously achieved. "These are the men who took the cliffs," Reagan said, invoking their valor. "These are the champions who helped free a continent. These are the heroes who helped end a war. . . . You all knew that some things are worth dying for. One's country is worth dying for, and democracy is worth dying for, because it's the most deeply honorable form of government ever devised by man."[60] Reagan proved to be a brilliant marketer of patriotism. He even co-opted Bruce Springsteen's "Born in the USA," a devastating antiwar anthem about the travails of Vietnam veterans, and played it at campaign rallies as a patriotic mantra. His crowds caught the chorus, he knew, without listening to the rest of the lyrics.

Reagan's campaign of optimism ultimately trumped the doom and gloom of the Democrats. The Republican ticket took 58.8 percent of the popular vote, but its margin in the electoral college was even more lopsided. Winning every single place except for Mondale's home state of Minnesota and overwhelmingly Democratic Washington, DC, Reagan won a staggering 525 electoral votes out of a possible 538. Democrats found a slight silver lining by retaining control of the House, but the election proved to be a major victory for the GOP. The Reagan Revolution, it seemed at last, had claimed control of the country. When Reagan walked into the Century Plaza Hotel to find a raucous crowd of supporters chanting "Four More Years," he flashed a grin and joked, "I think that's just been arranged." "You know, so many people act as if this election means the end of something . . . To each one of you I say, tonight is the end of nothing, it's the beginning of everything."[61]

From the perspective of conservatives, Reagan's election and reelection had represented nothing less than a revolution that toppled the old order. The president had brought together the various factions of the conservative movement and, together, they had pushed political debate sharply to the right. In some areas of domestic policy, such as passing tax cuts or weakening federal agencies, Reagan had scored some important successes that reversed the momentum of politics for the first time since the New Deal. But in other areas, it quickly became clear that Reagan's presidency had not represented a revolution at all. Despite his promises to dismantle the welfare system and the regulatory state, by the end of his two terms both largely remained intact. And though he had announced his intention to cut federal spending and federal payrolls, both actually increased dramatically on his watch. Some of the hike in federal spending was linked to the ballooning military budget, but a significant portion came from interest payments on all the debt piled up in Reagan's deficits.

The halfway revolution of the Reagan years ultimately revealed that Americans were still ambivalent in their political leanings. In principle, many agreed with the arguments advanced by the Great Communicator about the need to reduce the role of government in their lives; but in practice, Americans had grown accustomed to the programs and policies the president sought to end. Even as they voted for him, many of his supporters continued to send Democrats to the House and Senate. If anything, Reagan's rhetorical assault on the role of government had energized many liberals who had long been searching for a sense of direction and a common opponent.

Accordingly, Reagan's second term began with a new focus on smaller pieces of legislation and bipartisan deals that could make it through the increasingly liberal House. In 1985, for instance, Congress passed the Gramm-Rudman-Hollings Balanced Budget and Emergency Deficit Control Act, which technically mandated a balanced budget. The following year, Reagan worked with Democrats to enact the Tax Reform Act of 1986, which lowered the rate structure in exchange for closing a number of loopholes that had long favored powerful interests. He also worked with Congress to pass the Immigration Reform Act of 1986, cosponsored by Wyoming Republican Alan Simpson and Kentucky Democrat Romano Mazzoli, which allowed undocumented immigrants who had been in the United States since 1982 to obtain temporary legal status. The Census Bureau reported that there were somewhere between three and five million undocumented immigrants in the United States. If they were able to learn English, they would be eligible for green cards after eighteen more months in the country. The law imposed stronger surveillance technology at the border with Mexico and implemented new federal sanctions on businesses that hired undocumented workers, but enforcement was toothless; the bill continued to allow for the massive influx of migrants from other countries. "The bill is a gamble," said New York Democratic representative Charles Schumer, "a riverboat gamble. There is no guarantee that employer sanctions will work or that amnesty will work. We are headed into uncharted waters."[62]

As the country set off on that gamble, other bets came up short. From the start, the biggest winners of the age of Reaganomics had been wealthier Americans who benefited from regressive tax cuts that brought down their rates dramatically. The income of the top 20 percent of families grew by about $10,000 a year; the income of the lower 20 percent steadily declined. As the decade wore on, the promises of the supply-siders—that tax cuts for the wealthiest would trickle down to benefit Americans across the economic spectrum—simply failed to come true. "Supply-side economics was supposed to promote savings, investment, and entrepreneurial creativity," historian Garry Wills noted. "It failed at all three." Indeed, those at the bottom and middle levels of the economy actually found themselves struggling more and more. Working-class Americans without a high school degree saw a 6 percent drop in an average week of earnings between 1980 and 1990. Median family incomes, adjusted for inflation, had grown from the late 1940s to the mid-1970s, but now proceeded to fall. Economic insecurity increasingly became commonplace. Just in 1985, over 12 percent of the country had suffered through an economic loss severe enough to categorize them as being financially at risk. At the end of the decade, Kevin Phillips, the Republican strategist who had helped usher in Nixon's Silent Majority, offered a cold reckoning for Reaganomics in a study titled *The Politics of Rich and Poor*. The "capitalist blowout" policies of the Republicans, Phillips concluded, had ushered in "a second Gilded Age," one in which "many Americans made and spent money abundantly" but far too many more were left behind. "By several measurements," he noted, "the United States in the late twentieth century led all other major industrial countries in the gap dividing the upper fifth of the population from the lower—in the disparity between top and bottom."[63]

Even many of the apparent winners of Reaganomics came tumbling down over Reagan's second term. The financial and business sectors had moved into high-risk investments as old regulations were weakened and new opportunities arose. A new generation of financial stars dominated the news. Investment bankers like Michael Milken at Drexel Burnham Lambert made millions in high-yield "junk bonds," while Ivan Boesky gained fame through a series of aggressive corporate takeovers. The high-stakes speculative spirit of the era was captured well in Oliver Stone's film *Wall Street* (1987), where the slick villain Gordon Gekko— in a speech inspired by real comments by Boesky—proudly proclaimed that "greed, for lack of a better word, is good." Soon, however, these financial stars fell from grace; by decade's end both Boesky and Milken had been sentenced to jail for insider trading schemes.[64] Meanwhile, the stock market as a whole lost much of its earlier allure. On October 19, 1987, a global market crash—known as "Black Monday"—hit Wall Street with the worst single-day losses since the Depression.

Despite the Reagan Revolution's promises to cast off the tired old rules of a rigid federal government and unleash the innovation and energy of the private sector, the revolution—like all revolutions—had inspired as much chaos as it had creativity. The economic initiatives of the Reagan era had sparked uncertainty and, in the case of the insider traders, illegality, and led even the revolutionaries themselves to roll back their initial efforts and undo much of the original tax cut. The campaign to curtail the federal government had a similarly mixed record of success, with administration appointees succeeding in limiting the reach of some agencies but other programs, like Social Security, emerging from the struggle even stronger than before. The Reagan Revolution, it seemed, was a halfway revolution, but its influence wasn't over yet.

CHAPTER 7

Changing Channels

WHILE CONSERVATIVES STRUGGLED TO PROMOTE THEIR values and their vision of America, powerful commercial and cultural forces were transforming the country in ways that dwarfed even the Reagan Revolution. New developments in technology and telecommunications signaled massive revolutions in media that promised both to bring Americans together and, paradoxically, drive them further apart.

The late 1970s and 1980s had witnessed the dawn of a new era in telecommunications, one that fundamentally changed the ways in which Americans interacted, consumed popular culture, and even conducted their politics. Over most of the twentieth century, the trend had been toward consolidation of communications outlets. At the start of the 1970s, the institutions of American mass media had long been centralized into a small, insular establishment. Three major networks dominated television; a small number of movie studios controlled the film industry; a handful of major cities' papers shaped the national news. Personal communication, meanwhile, still took place through the mail, largely the US postal system that had been established in the eighteenth century, as well as through landline telephones that were dominated by a single provider, AT&T.

This all changed with the rise of cable television, personal computers, and the internet. While ownership continued its path toward consolidation, the variety of media options and outlets available to consumers rapidly proliferated. The new technology simultaneously reshaped the experience of all Americans, diminishing the regional differences in the lives of people who all depended on similar modes of interaction, while also fragmenting life by offering more individual choices and a variety of targeted cultural content. Ultimately, the emerging media created a new common public square, but one that was internally divided, rapidly changing, and ultimately uncontrollable. Cable TV and computers brought more Americans into a shared media ecosystem, but that development only served to speed the growing divisions in politics, economics, society, and culture because that shared space was in fact deeply fractured.

Multiple Channels

Cable television provided a stark example of these changes. From the 1950s through the 1970s, the "big three" broadcast networks—ABC, NBC, and CBS—ran television as an oligopoly. Local stations relied on expensive landlines to broadcast their shows; those landlines, in turn, were controlled by the telephone monopoly AT&T. The phone giant cooperated with the three networks to maintain their mutual advantages, giving them significant discounts on landline prices, such that smaller companies could never afford to enter the market as competitors. Public policy also supported the dominance of the television networks, as regulators at the Federal Communications Commission (FCC) maintained anticompetitive policies that protected them. AT&T pressured legislators and the White House, wielding influence through campaign contributions, to prevent the use of satellites that would serve as a cheaper way of disseminating programming.

Over the course of the 1970s, however, the foundations of this monopoly steadily eroded. First, the deregulation movement built political support for changing these kinds of practices. Conservative free-market economists allied with liberal consumer advocates like Ralph Nader to push back against federal regulations that had, in this instance, actually benefited the regulated entities and stifled consumer choice. Congress responded by loosening the restrictions on competition. During the Nixon administration, the White House Office of Science and Technology promoted these changes, and the FCC responded by lowering the barriers to the market. As the industry opened, Western Union and RCA jumped into the competition in 1974 and 1975. The new satellites they purchased could transmit shows to televisions without the landlines owned by AT&T; as a result, independent stations could use them to transmit programming.

As more stations used satellites to get on the air, cable television flourished. Originally, cable had been a system to deliver television to remote rural areas which were unable to receive a standard broadcast television signal. Cable offered an alternative to these communities in the 1960s. In Huntsville, Alabama, an advertisement promised that "TV Cable" would bring viewers "Clear, Snow-Free TV" without "unsightly antennas, costs, and repairs" so that they could see the three major networks.[1] To deliver on that promise, enterprising individuals in isolated communities placed an antenna in a high area and then literally ran a cable through neighborhoods to provide coverage in individual homes. In northwestern Oregon, for instance, radio engineer Ed Parsons started experimenting with the technology when he couldn't receive a signal for the television set he bought his wife in their home in Astoria, over a hundred miles from Seattle. His solution was to put a huge antenna up high on a mountain and run a coaxial cable to their home. "People would drive for hundreds of miles to see television," he recalled.[2] Others went to even greater lengths. In Williamsport, Pennsylvania, for instance, Robert Genzlinger hooked up over 11,000 televisions to a cable system. John Walson Jr., an appliance store owner in nearby Mahanoy City, soon started his own cable television company, charging local residents $100 for installation and then $2 a month for the service.[3]

By the late 1970s, cable television was no longer simply a means for reaching rural residents. In 1979, cable systems were located in over 4,000 communities nationwide, with one-fifth of the national television audience, a little over 14 million homes, receiving programming through them. Initially owned by individual operators, many of these systems were purchased in the early 1980s by major companies like the American Television and Communications, Inc., a subsidiary of Time, Inc., as well as Times Mirror, Westinghouse, Warner-Amex, and more. With corporate control, cable's reach across America rapidly expanded. By 1981, 30 percent of US households had cable, with roughly 250,000 new subscribers every month. By 1987, cable covered 48 percent of all television households, 42 million subscribers in all. Cable was earning $12 billion, up from $2.6 billion seven years earlier.[4]

Cable systems represented a distinctly new and decidedly differ-ent kind of television. They brought together a number of independent channels that provided subscribers with a variety of programs previ-ously unseen on the networks. Most systems in the early 1980s had a dozen channels, while some had three times as many. In an important innovation, these channels were offered to consumers in combination packages that allowed individual subscribers to tailor television to their own personal tastes. Religious broadcasting, such as Pat Robertson's Christian Broadcasting Network (CBN), emerged as a popular early genre. Premier stations, meanwhile, could be purchased separately. Home Box Office (HBO) was an early pioneer. At a time when few executives believed that viewers would ever pay for television, the sta-tion hoped to capitalize on its unique ability to present feature films or special sporting events free from commercial interruptions.[5] It worked. By 1981, after nine years of operation, HBO had roughly six million subscribers nationwide.[6]

One of the first stations to take advantage of the new cable tech-nology was the Entertainment and Sports Programming Network, Inc. (ESPN). William Rasmussen, the communications director for the New England Whalers pro hockey team, had been searching for a way to broadcast the team's games across the state of Connecticut. He looked into a number of local options, but in 1978 he discovered he could actu-ally create a national network for the same price. The newly launched RCA satellite, he learned, had been largely ignored by major broadcast-ers and desperate officials at RCA "would talk to anybody" to fill the unused transponders. Rasmussen secured an early license from the FCC and, with that edge, landed $10 million in funding from Getty Oil. Signing contracts with NCAA teams and the LPGA, the fledgling ESPN announced bold plans to launch a channel devoted entirely to sports broadcasts. "I know it's a bold, kooky, wild approach," Rasmussen told a reporter, "but it's a logical vehicle. There's a stock market chan-nel. So why not all sports?" ESPN debuted in September 1979, with an estimated four million subscribers. The network began small, but had its sights set high. "The potential is enormous," enthused ESPN pres-ident Chester R. Simmons. "I can foresee the day when we'll be out-bidding networks for things like NFL football and other sports. It's not impossible. Not at all."[7]

Another early pioneer was the Cable News Network (CNN). This channel was the product of Atlanta entrepreneur Robert "Ted" Turner III, the son of a prominent billboard businessman who entered the family business after a career sailing yachts around the globe. In 1970, Turner invested in WTCG-TV, a small television station in Atlanta that operated on the Ultra High Frequency (UHF) used to broadcast non-network channels in urban areas. In his new role, he quickly grasped the potential opportunities that satellite technology offered smaller television stations to reach broader audiences and stand alongside more established channels as an apparent equal. Accordingly, he reinvented his station, rebranding it as WTBS and using it to broadcast games of the Atlanta Braves to national audiences. Turner owned the team as well, having bought it for the bargain price of $10 million after a disappointing 1975 season dropped attendance to new lows. The Braves offered Turner cheap programming for 162 days out of the year; he broadcast games live each night for three or four hours and then replayed them the following morning. As profits from the new "Superstation" grew, Turner bought the Atlanta Hawks basketball team, airing their games as well. Despite the odd mix of sports and old sitcoms, WTBS quickly carved out a national audience. Within six years, the new cable station reached 26 million homes.[8]

As he sought to start a second cable network, Turner looked for unmet markets. "There are only four things that television does," he told a potential partner in the fall of 1978. "There's movies—and HBO has that. There's sports—and now ESPN's got that, unfortunately. There's the regular series kinda stuff—and the networks do that. All that's left is news." Hoping to pioneer a new direction in cable news, Turner joined forces with Reese Schonfeld, who had made early forays in the field through his work at the Independent Television News Association. Hearing Turner's initial ideas, Schonfeld found himself impressed by his daring. "For anyone to take a shot at this represents a commitment beyond all reason," he later told a reporter. "It's an act of faith—and an act of genius."[9]

At first, Turner and Schonfeld tried to pressure AT&T into lowering its rates so that they could broadcast through the same landlines as the networks, but the telephone monopoly sided with its biggest customers. Instead, Turner and Schonfeld purchased space on RCA's satellite, following the path taken by ESPN. Alternately describing their plans as replicating an old-fashioned newspaper or all-news radio stations like 1010 WINS in New York, CNN's ultimate goal was to beat the networks in terms of the speed and depth of its coverage. It aimed both to break news before the "big three" but also to handle a broader range of stories, from human-interest tales to coverage of weather catastrophes. They believed doing so would offer a product that was fundamentally different from the short nightly newscasts of the networks. "We have to let 'em know we're here," Schonfeld explained as he formulated the programming plan. "We're gonna match 'em and then we're gonna go beyond—to show ourselves to be something."[10]

CNN debuted at 6:00 p.m. on June 1, 1980. With modest resources, it had only six domestic bureaus and a few foreign correspondents. Two hundred of Turner's guests were invited to watch the start of this channel, which its founder promised would continue to broadcast "until the world ends." Turner dedicated the channel, on air, with a speech about his commitment to improving the world through knowledge, followed by the national anthem. Anchors David Walker and Lois Hart, a married couple, then began the first broadcast. The rest of the original on-air talent featured veteran journalists like Daniel Schorr, formerly of CBS News, as well as a host of established figures, ranging from political pundits like Rowland Evans and Robert Novak to popular personalities like pop psychologist Dr. Joyce Brothers. But behind the scenes, CNN's small headquarters in Atlanta had a production staff filled with young 20- and 30-year-olds who had little experience in the industry.[11]

To compensate for its meager resources, the network purchased footage from reporters at independent local stations, a strategy that let CNN keep its staff small. Due to these limitations, CNN's original format was fairly straightforward. The daily schedule was divided into segments that covered a variety of topics, including entertainment, politics, business, sports, and more. In addition, there was a two-hour evening news show, an expansive format that contrasted with the half-hour network news programs. Meanwhile, thanks to its twenty-four-hour format, CNN was able to go to live breaking news at a moment's notice, unlike the networks, which were reluctant to break into their regularly scheduled programming except in extreme circumstances.

CNN quickly demonstrated the advantage the twenty-four-hour news channel provided when it was the only network live-broadcasting Ronald Reagan during the event at the Washington Hilton that culminated with John Hinckley's assassination attempt in March 1981. As CNN took news into directions previously unseen in print or network television, its subscriber base rose considerably, from 2 million to 4.3 million in its first year.[12]

The networks immediately saw the threat posed by CNN. "It's only the broadcasting establishment that doesn't like me," Turner said. "They're pea-green with envy."[13] And indeed, the networks soon sought to imitate Turner's model. They launched one- or two-hour "news magazine" shows that focused on crime, crises, and scandals, expanding on the successful models of *Nightline* and *60 Minutes*. But they tried to compete with CNN on cable, too. Within a year of CNN's launch, ABC and Westinghouse started a new Satellite News Channel of their own in June 1981. The station, funded by advertising, broadcast eighteen-minute shows, with another five minutes of each half hour devoted to regional news stories. In January 1982, Turner responded by introducing CNN-2, later restyled "Headline News," an offshoot that provided thirty-minute news blocks throughout the day. Importantly, it was offered free of charge to subscribers of the original CNN. Unable to compete, ABC shut down its operation, selling Turner the rights for $25 million.[14] With no real competitors on cable, CNN quickly became the major source of breaking news for many people around the nation. Within two years the station reached about 13.9 million homes and attracted over 200 advertisers. In short order, it fundamentally restructured the American news cycle, making it ongoing and instantaneous.[15]

The growing competition from televised news stimulated changes in the print industry, which struggled to keep up. On September 15, 1982, the Gannett Company launched a new national newspaper called *USA Today*. With color print, attractive visual graphics, and shorter, punchier articles, the newspaper sought to capture readers who would otherwise turn on the tube for their news. In response to criticism that the press only covered scandal and tragedy, the editors self-consciously sought to put more "good news" into stories. The front page of the first issue included traditional stories about politics and a plane crash in

Minnesota (though the paper distinguished itself with a color photograph of the burning airplane). But it also carried softer stories, such as a piece called "Your Kid REALLY may be sick of school" and another on the death of Princess Grace in Monaco, which the editors selected instead of a piece on the assassination of the president-elect of Lebanon.[16] Other newspapers would eventually follow USA Today's lead, including the esteemed New York Times, which instituted weekly special sections on issues such as science and "living" and, finally, in 1997, started using color photographs as well.[17]

As CNN reshaped the news world, another innovation in cable—Music Television (MTV)—did the same for entertainment. The idea came from Robert Pittman, a former NBC official who had produced a music video show for the network in the 1970s. Believing the show could be expanded to a full channel, Pittman forged a partnership between Warner Communications, which sought to be on the cutting edge in technology and entertainment, and American Express, the credit card company that saw cable and computers as its next great markets. The Warner Amex Satellite Entertainment Company set up the operation and got it running. On August 1, 1981 at 12:01 a.m., cable viewers saw the image of astronaut Buzz Aldrin from the 1969 Apollo 11 moon landing, with the MTV logo superimposed on the American flag. "Ladies and gentlemen," an announcer intoned, "rock and roll." The first video aired on the network, by the rock band the Buggles, was aptly titled: "Video Killed the Radio Star." "In my mind and in my car, we can't rewind, we've gone too far," the band sang. "Pictures came and broke my heart."[18]

Playing music videos all day long, MTV pioneered a faster, provocative format for entertainment, one that was visually splashy and rapid-fire. The videos, according to one of the best studies on the channel, distinguished themselves with "aggressive directorship, contemporary editing and FX, sexuality, vivid colors, urgent movement, nonsensical juxtapositions, provocation, frolic, all combined for maximum impact on a small screen." Older musicians were surprised by the new style. Billy Gibbons, one of the guitarists from the rock band ZZ Top, first thought he'd stumbled onto the broadcast of a concert. "Twelve hours later, we were still glued to the TV," he recalled. "Finally, somebody said, 'No, it's this twenty-four-hour music channel.' I said, 'Whaaat?'

MTV appeared suddenly—unheralded, unannounced, un-anything."[19] The innovative form elevated new bands as varied as the synthesized British duo the Eurythmics and the L.A. glam metal band Mötley Crüe, acts that learned how to adapt and exploit the new format well. Some older bands, meanwhile, adjusted themselves too. ZZ Top became a popular fixture on the channel, pairing their old style with new videos that highlighted fast cars and attractive women. Dire Straits, another established rock band, found the greatest success of its career with a 1985 album fueled by slick videos. Notably, the video for "Money for Nothing" featured cutting-edge computer animation and guest vocals by Sting, lead singer of the Police, who offered the cable network's slogan as the song's refrain: "I want my, I want my, I want my MTV!" The song, intended as a tongue-in-cheek critique of MTV, nevertheless became a hit on the channel.[20]

MTV followed a strategy from radio advertising, known as "narrow casting." In contrast to the "broad casting" approach of traditional television networks, which sought to build large audiences, MTV targeted smaller specialized markets.[21] "Rock music is not just a form of entertainment," Pittman explained. "It also represents a lifestyle, a value system, to that age group. If you're 50 years old, you might ask a new acquaintance what church they go to. But if you're 30, you'd ask what kind of music they like."[22] Accordingly, MTV's programming revolved around video jockeys ("VJs") introducing blocks of three-to-four-minute videos, much as a radio DJ would. The station was only available in a few cities when it started, but the phenomenon quickly caught on. "The buzz in this town for MTV is incredible," a radio station manager in Tulsa, Oklahoma, told *Billboard*. "We added two records [to our rotation] due to MTV airplay." As the VJs toured America to meet with cable operators and sell their product, their influence became clear. "Within six months," VJ Mark Goodman recalled, "we started getting these stories back from small towns in the Midwest and in the South where people were going into record stores and asking for the Buggles, who had been off the shelves for about three years by 1981. I also remember doing an appearance in Cheyenne, Wyoming at a record store where thousands of people showed up. I said, 'What's going on?' They said, 'You.' I was completely blown away, and I said, 'Okay, it's working.'"[23]

While successful, MTV's narrowcasting approach was soon criticized as being a bit *too* narrow. In a live interview on the network in 1983, icon David Bowie noted that MTV has "a lot going for it. I'm just floored by the fact that there are so few black artists featured on it. Why is that?" When Mark Goodman defensively noted that "the company is thinking in terms of narrow-casting," Bowie responded coolly: "That's evident. It's evident in the fact that the only few black artists that one does see are on about 2:30 in the morning to around 6. Very few are featured predominantly during the day." Chastened by the criticism, the network soon began broadening its lineup to feature more popular black artists. Michael Jackson's "Billie Jean" video, which debuted on March 10, 1983, opened the door to black performers on a station whose primary audience had been middle-class white kids. The video, along with two others from the smash album *Thriller*, weakened the race barrier and brought the still-struggling channel what it had long sought: ratings and profits. MTV now reached 24 million homes and, more importantly, a quarter of teens who watched television daily. Notably, when MTV held its first annual Video Music Awards in 1984, the biggest winners were both African Americans. Keyboardist Herbie Hancock won five awards; Jackson took home three. (Bowie, meanwhile, won Best Male Video.)[24]

MTV's narrowcasting model was replicated in larger cable systems. The goal was to develop stations that appealed to distinct portions of the viewership that would focus on their favorite channels. "Cable has not so much won its audience as broadened to meet it," one reporter explained. "In part this makes the absurd little competitive duels on commercial TV . . . seems quite quaint. Because it is all-inclusive, the cable systems must, it is true, cater to different tastes and here you will find a practically continuous obbligato of nowhere Clint Eastwood shoot-'em-ups, of religious barkers exhorting me to send $15 a month to some missionary in Elyria, Ohio, of reruns of 'Get Smart' and 'Petticoat Junction' or worse." With each channel seeking small segments of the market, there was no need for a commons anymore.[25]

Technology Splitting

The fragmentation of consumer culture was also fueled by the spread of the videocassette recorder (VCR). The technology had been around for decades but only started to reach a significant market share during the early 1980s. With several Japanese-based companies such as Sony, Toshiba, and JVC pioneering new products, the VCR market grew from representing 10 percent of homes in 1982 to over 30 percent by 1985.[26] Initially, there were two rival formats for videocassettes: Betamax and VHS. Though Betamax was the more sophisticated form of technology, VHS won out. The pornography industry was one of the first to capitalize on the technology and become a leading force in home entertainment; executives there decided to produce films solely for VHS. While the VCR revolution allowed Americans to watch movies of all kinds at home, they soon found that they could record television programs as well. In a landmark decision in 1984, *Sony v. Universal City Studios*, the Supreme Court ruled that as long as the tapes were not resold for profit, home recordings of network broadcasts did not violate existing copyright laws. The decision was a huge victory for those who produced the machines, which would greatly enhance the ability of viewers to control when they watched certain shows and to gain access to movies and programming that were not being aired on the networks.[27]

That same year, the telephone monopoly AT&T also fell. The Department of Justice had initiated an antitrust suit in 1974 and, after eight years of litigation, the company reached a settlement in January 1982. Under the landmark agreement, AT&T promised to divest its local companies. Starting on January 1, 1984, the communications giant was divided into seven independent companies—Regional Bell Operating Companies, or "Baby Bells"—that worked on their own. For many consumers, the adjustment to the new fragmented telecommunications landscape was initially confusing. "When there was one [AT&T] account group handling us and we had a problem, we could turn the whole thing over to them," noted a frustrated executive at Xerox. "Ma Bell's end-to-end responsibility no longer exists." But the breakup also spurred competition. The new freedoms of deregulation, noted the chairman of one Baby Bell, means "we're fleeter afoot." Most significantly, the new marketplace led to breakthroughs in phone technology as competitors sought to gain advantages with improvements on the traditional landline.[28]

The cellular phone was one of the first of these innovations to hit the market. The FCC had loosened the regulations that served as barriers to this kind of innovation back in the 1960s, but it took time for the technology to develop. Following FCC approval for carriers to develop cellular machines in 1982, Motorola finished work on the DynaTAC 8000X phone, the first major cell phone available for consumer purchase. When it debuted in March 1984, the phone sold for almost $4,000, lasted for only half an hour of talking time, and weighed nearly two pounds. Despite its costs, "the Brick" became a huge success. "We didn't design them for teenagers—well, unless it was a teenager with $4,000," one executive explained, "but we couldn't build them fast enough. Businesses started taking them on and it became something else, a part of business—not a convenience, but a necessity."[29] The technology for carrying calls steadily improved, and the size and price dropped too. By 1987, there were almost a million cell phone subscribers nationwide.

The greatest technological innovation of the decade, however, came with the arrival of personal computers. Although computers had become a fixture of life in postwar America, their considerable size, complexity, and cost meant that they were largely confined to the workplace. In August 1981, industry leader IBM introduced its first desktop computer designed for home use. IBM had benefitted from a partnership it launched in 1980 with the upstart computer software company Microsoft, which had been founded five years earlier by Bill Gates and Paul Allen. As ordinary consumers rushed to buy the new machines, many predicted that personal computing would revolutionize the way people lived. In January 1983, *Time* ran a cover story on "The Computer: Machine of the Year." "By the millions," the article began, "it is beeping its way into offices, schools and homes. . . . A personal computer . . . can send letters at the speed of light, diagnose a sick poodle, custom-tailor an insurance program in minutes, test recipes for beer."[30]

Although IBM led the way, it faced competition from an upstart. Since the mid-1970s, Steve Jobs's Apple Computers had been working to make computers cheaper and easier to use. Jobs, a college dropout who had been taught to fix cars, radios, and televisions by his stepfather, had become interested in computing at a young age and quickly found friends who shared his new hobby. While computing had previously been reserved for massive institutions like the federal government or large corporations, Jobs's generation set its sights on creating a truly "personal computer," a machine that was small, compact, and

On September 8, 1974, in a televised address, President Gerald Ford, seeking to heal the nation from Watergate, pardoned Richard Nixon, former president, for whatever crimes he might have committed. *(Photo: Gerald Ford Presidential Library)*

After the Nixon pardon, the nation erupted in outrage. Sign-carrying protesters gathered outside the White House, as distrust in government worsened across the country. *(Photo: Bill Pierce/ LIFE Magazine/ Getty Images)*

Tensions over race relations intensified in the early 1970s. Here, a white woman from North Boston angrily gestures to black students being bused to a white school as part of the new court-ordered busing system to desegregate the public schools, to "go home and stay home" in September 1974. *(Photo: Charles Dixon/The Boston Globe/ Getty Images)*

The fall of South Vietnam constituted a devastating defeat for US Cold War policy. Crowds of Vietnamese and Western evacuees wait around the swimming pool inside the American Embassy compound in Saigon, hoping to escape Vietnam via helicopter before the arrival of North Vietnamese troops. Nearly all were left behind as the evacuation stopped at nightfall, and the following day, April 30, 1975, NVA tanks rolled into Saigon and the Vietnam War officially ended. (*Photo: Nik Wheeler/Getty Images*)

New York subway cars, covered in graffiti, served as a visible reminder of the urban crisis, which symbolized the broken state of the national economy in the 1970s. New York City was widely perceived to be in a state of decay, losing nearly 800,000 residents between 1970 and 1980. (*Photo: Erik Calonius/Library of Congress*)

President Ford stumbled in his debates against Georgia governor Jimmy Carter, including when he seemed to say to a stunned national audience that there was no Soviet domination of Eastern Europe. (*Photo: Gerald Ford Presidential Library*)

The only slight sign of economic hope came from California, where numerous entrepreneurs were developing a personal computer. American businessmen and engineers Steve Jobs (left) and Steve Wozniak, cofounders of Apple Computer Inc., at the first West Coast Computer Faire. The Apple II computer debuted there, in Brooks Hall, San Francisco, California, April 1977. (*Photo: Tom Munnecke/Getty Images*)

The conservative movement offered a compelling response to Americans who were losing faith in national institutions. Phyllis Schlafly (center), demonstrating in front of the White House against the Equal Rights Amendment in 1977. (*Photo: Getty Images*)

Liberal Democrats such as Senator Ted Kennedy (left), meeting with the president in the Oval Office, continually urged Carter to defend the traditions of the Democratic Party. Frustrated that the president moved too far to the center, Kennedy would unsuccessfully challenge Carter for the 1980 Democratic nomination. *(Photo: White House/ National Archives)*

An anti-Iranian protest in Washington, DC. The hostage crisis in Iran that started in November 1979 crippled President Carter's administration and added to the frustration, which grew out of Vietnam, about American power overseas. *(Photo: Marion S. Tikosko/U.S. News & World Report/ Library of Congress)*

The energy crisis caused turmoil throughout the country and dampened confidence that policy makers would be able to do anything about the economic malaise. Cars lining up for fuel at a gas station in Maryland in June 1979. *(Photo: Warren K. Leffler/National Archives)*

An unemployed man looking for work in Denver, Colorado, in June 1980. (*Photo: Ernie Leyba/The Denver Post/Getty Images*)

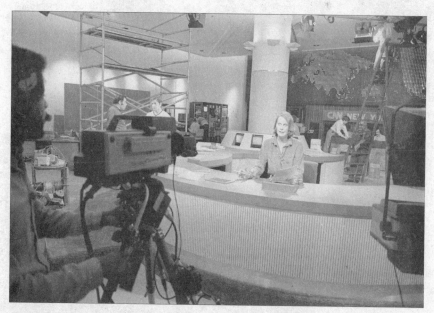

The rapid expansion of cable television transformed the media landscape, including the news cycle. Anchorwoman Mary Alice Williams broadcasts from new cable TV news network CNN's studio during its first weeks, when the station went on the air in the summer of 1980. (*Photo: Allan Tannenbaum/Getty Images*)

Ronald Reagan's victory in the 1980 presidential election was a triumph for conservatism. Reagan (right), here voting with his wife, Nancy, in the historic election, promised to bring the ideas of conservatism to the halls of power in Washington. (*Photo: Ronald Reagan Presidential Library*)

Supreme Court justice nominee Sandra Day O'Connor, with President Ronald Reagan at the White House, July 1981. Many of the president's fellow conservatives, who considered O'Connor to be far too liberal on social issues, grew angry with Reagan when he took steps that did not fit with his campaign promises to the Right. (*Photo: Ronald Reagan Presidential Library/ National Archives*)

Another technological breakthrough came with the introduction of the videocassette recorder, which was mass-marketed in the early 1980s. The Video Home System (VHS), produced by JVC and Panasonic, allowed viewers to watch movies on their television sets and eventually to record shows. (*Photo: Smithsonian*)

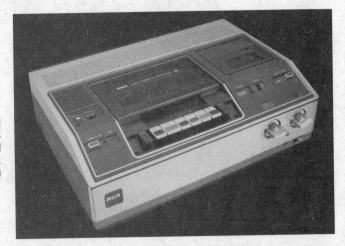

The AIDS crisis devastated gay communities and stimulated a mobilization of Americans who demanded that the government do more to fund research into this disease. Members of the Christopher Street Liberation Day Committee (CSLDC) carry a banner in New York City, June 1983. (*Photo: Barbara Alper/Getty Images*)

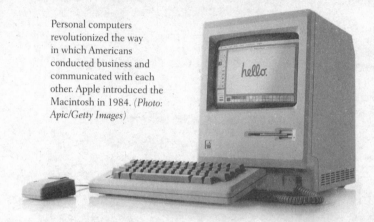

Personal computers revolutionized the way in which Americans conducted business and communicated with each other. Apple introduced the Macintosh in 1984. (*Photo: Apic/Getty Images*)

As the culture wars arose, activists and politicians in both parties tried to push back against a rising tide of pop culture content that they deemed to be obscene or profane. Dee Snider, lead singer for heavy metal band Twisted Sister, testifies before Congress in 1985 to resist these regulatory efforts. (*Photo: C-SPAN*)

Many parts of the country, including inner-city American communities such as the one in this picture of a storefront in Detroit, Michigan, did not witness the uneven benefits of the economic revival that took place under President Reagan. (*Photo: Barbara Alper/Getty Images*)

Defying expectations, President Reagan (left), who had made much of his name fighting against "détente" with communism, reached a historic arms agreement with the Soviet Union. The negotiations between Soviet leader Mikhail Gorbachev and Reagan, which started in November 1985 (pictured), culminated with the Intermediate Range Nuclear Treaty in 1987. (*Photo: Ronald Reagan Presidential Library/National Archives*)

simple enough for an individual to use in the home. Jobs caught the attention of Robert Noyce, who had created the first silicon microchip and then founded Fairchild Semiconductor, the first major business in what would become known as Silicon Valley.[31] Noyce and another scientist at Fairchild founded the Intel Corporation in 1968 and, with it, launched the semiconductor industry, which made the region into a hub of economic growth. "The Mayor of Silicon Valley," as Noyce was known, soon left his daily role as president at Intel and started to spend more time nurturing new talent in the region, including Jobs. "Steve would regularly appear at our house on his motorcycle," Noyce's wife, Ann Bowers, recalled; "he and Bob were disappearing into the basement, talking about projects."[32]

Jobs began working out of a garage in Los Altos, along with his high school friend Stephen Wozniak, another college dropout who had worked as an engineer for Hewlett Packard. Together, Jobs and Wozniak developed a prototype in the summer of 1975. To their delight, it worked. "It was the first time in history," Wozniak remembered, that "anyone had typed a character on a keyboard and seen it show up on their computer screen right in front of them." One year later, the pair had created the first personal computer, a small device with a keyboard that could connect to a television monitor. After the technology companies they had worked for expressed no interest in the product, Jobs and Wozniak decided to create the computers themselves through a new company of their own called Apple. They soon received their first order—for fifty of their crude "Apple I" computers—from a local store and frantically began building them in their garage. As sales increased, they poured the profits into developing the more sophisticated "Apple II," a much smaller version that came with a standardized keyboard and power supply. The pair incorporated the company in 1977, releasing the Apple II to first year sales of $2.7 million. The company's ads proclaimed the dawn of a bold new era, ushered in by "the home computer that's ready to work, play, and grow with you."[33]

In the early 1980s, the company introduced a number of innovations that revolutionized the field of personal computing. To distinguish its products from IBM's more successful desktop models, Apple moved beyond its simple keyboard and command lines interface to introduce the mouse as a means of navigating an on-screen graphic desktop. In

January 1984, Apple unveiled its cutting-edge Macintosh computer with a $1.5 million Super Bowl ad that revealed the company's ambitions. "I want something that will stop people in their tracks," Jobs had insisted. "I want a thunderclap." He got his wish. John Scully, a major advertising executive whom Apple had recruited from Pepsi (famous for the "Pepsi Generation" campaign that brought the soft drink to younger Americans), had a massive budget. Directed by Ridley Scott, the Hollywood legend behind the sci-fi film *Blade Runner*, the Super Bowl ad depicted a bleak Orwellian future: dressed in drab, workers tromped through bleak industrial hallways to assemble before the ominous image of a Big Brother–type figure droning on a screen. In sharp contrast, a defiant blonde woman in brightly colored clothing ran into the huge hall, escaping faceless security forces and hurling a giant hammer at the screen, shattering it and sending a shockwave through the crowd. "You'll see why 1984 won't be like '1984,'" the narrator intoned. An instant sensation, the Super Bowl ad helped transform the image of the computer from being an engine of corporate and government dominance to an instrument of personal liberation.[34] After 43 million Americans watched the ad, stunned by what they'd just seen, the legendary CBS football announcers John Madden and Pat Summerall asked each other: "Wow, what was that?"[35]

The original Macintosh offered a model for the new era of personal computing in terms of the ease and simplicity of use. Priced at $2,495, it took less than an hour to learn how to operate, compared to the twenty to one hundred hours needed to navigate other computers. "The mouse is the Macintosh's biggest selling point," one analyst noted, "because it takes almost no prior knowledge of computers to run the machine. As a result, Apple hopes the computer will appeal to a new market: executives, students and home users who want to use a computer without having to understand its inner workings."[36] Jobs argued that the difference between IBM and Apple was "like the difference between the telegraph and the telephone. Back in the days of the telegraph, there were people who talked about putting a telegraph on every desk. But it would never have happened, because people weren't willing to spend the time necessary to learn to use them."[37] Throughout the decade, Apple continued to innovate, first improving the low memory of the first model and then introducing the Macintosh II, which had color graphics and even more expansion potential, in 1987. Despite such advantages, Apple still lagged behind IBM in sales for the remainder of the 1980s. Corporations, still the biggest buyer of computers, were more willing to buy from an established company like IBM than an upstart without much history.

Other technological developments complemented the personal computer. Though few Americans knew about it, the federal government had already begun working on developing an interlocked network of computers, the internet, which would vastly increase the speed of communication. For ordinary Americans, the next best thing was dial-in services to information companies. CompuServe, founded by Jeffrey Wilkins and John Goltz, two graduate students in electrical engineering at the University of Arizona, emerged as an early innovator. The company's primary mission had been to provide computing resources to Golden United Life Insurance, but it also offered a time-sharing system for individual users. Based in Ohio, the CompuServe Network Services launched in 1979 to offer access nationwide. By the end of the decade it was the first company to offer services such as sending electronic messages called "email," home shopping, news and travel information, and "bulletin boards" devoted to discussing various issues. From the start, eleven newspapers, including the *Washington Post* and the *Los Angeles Times*, offered electronic versions of their print editions.[38]

More than simply replicating print media, CompuServe pioneered new forms of what would come to be known as "social media." Its most popular feature, for instance, was the "CB Simulator," which allowed people to communicate in real time, simulating the "citizens' band (CB) radio" that had been popularized by truckers in the 1970s. Connectivity to the outside world became a major selling point for CompuServe. "Someday," its first print advertisement read, "in the comfort of your home, you'll be able to shop and bank electronically, read instantly updated newswires, analyze the performance of a stock that interests you, send electronic mail across the country, then play Bridge with three strangers in LA, Chicago, and Dallas." Under the photograph of a couple dressed in futuristic white outfits sitting with a computer in the living room, the caption read: "Welcome to someday." The system offered subscribers access to a vast new world of information, but initially the costs were still prohibitive. Consumers who had already splurged on a personal computer now needed to invest in additional equipment, as well as pay for monthly access fees. "It only took a couple of days to realize that the biggest single obstacle I faced in trying to tap the enormous potential of my new home computer wasn't my ignorance of computer languages or my lack of imagination," one critic wrote. "Nope. More mundane than that. It was my personal checking account."[39] Despite the costs, CompuServe made its mark immediately. By 1981, the company had roughly 10,000 subscribers.[40]

The new computer networks immediately gave rise to the problem of "hacking." The term went mainstream on September 5, 1983, when the cover of *Newsweek* magazine featured a photograph of Neal Patrick, a 17-year-old boy who was part of a group that had broken into several major computer systems, including Sloan-Kettering Cancer Center and Los Alamos National Laboratory. The cover story, "Computer Capers," explained that these talented prodigies had done this just because they could. "It's terribly unethical for computer centers and networks to have the low level of security that they do," one expert warned. "It's like leaving the keys in the ignition of an unlocked car."[41] The hackers broke into businesses and institutions, sometimes for the thrill but other times for data theft and financial fraud. In one incident, the "Inner Circle," a collective of fifteen teen hackers living in eight cities, including Detroit and New York, had accessed the GTE Telemail network in Vienna, Virginia, which handled electronic communications for corporations like Raytheon as well as NASA.[42]

The phenomenon of hacking soon intersected with pop culture. In the hit film *WarGames* (1983), Matthew Broderick played a young hacker who broke into the Pentagon's computer system and nearly initiated World War III. The film concluded dramatically with the computer running every possible scenario for a global thermonuclear war before concluding that "the only winning move is not to play." The film scared Reagan so much that he asked advisors whether the film's scenario could really happen. General John Vessey Jr., chairman of the Joint Chiefs of Staff, reported that "the problem is much worse than you think." The fears generated by the movie triggered NSDD-145, the first major directive to deal with cybersecurity.[43] But the film also inspired a greater number of Americans to get involved in hacking. "The scene exploded," one observer explained. "It seemed that every kid in America had demanded and gotten a modem for Christmas. Most of these dabbler wannabes put their modems in the attic after a few weeks, and most of the remainder minded their Ps and Qs and stayed well out of hot water. But some stubborn and talented diehards had this hacker kid in *WarGames* figured for a happening dude." In real life, however, hacking often proved to have a personal price. One of the Inner Circle whiz kids, a 16-year-old with a 163 IQ named Bill Landreth (known as "the Cracker"), had hacked into approximately 100 corporate computer systems since 1979, first using a Tandy Corporation TRS-80 and then the Apple II his parents purchased as a gift. In 1984, he was convicted in federal court for computer fraud. Placed on three years' probation, he wrote a memoir of the mysterious hacking culture called *Out of the Inner Circle* (1985), which introduced many Americans to this subterranean world. Then, he mysteriously went missing himself in 1986.[44]

The chaotic open world of computing was soon replicated across the realm of telecommunications. Most significantly, the Federal Communications Commission, with President Reagan's support, brought an end to the "fairness doctrine" in 1987. The policy, in effect since 1949, had been based on the notion that the three major networks were "public trustees" licensed by the government and therefore needed to serve the entire public by airing competing perspectives on controversial issues. Since there had been a scarcity of available broadcasting space, the Supreme Court ruled in 1969 that the federal government could indeed make requirements of the networks and of radio stations in exchange for their access. That said, the doctrine had been far from perfect. FCC enforcement was notoriously weak. Many radio stations, particularly conservative religious broadcasters, had flouted the rule without punishment. Nonetheless, the doctrine served as a strong and constant disincentive for most major broadcasters to allow for openly political shows. Though it was intended to encourage a fair debate, in practice the fairness doctrine led networks to avoid employing anchors or reporters with obvious biases and instead to play most issues down the middle.[45]

By the mid-1980s, the availability of many more channels through cable weakened the notion that the networks were solely responsible for disseminating information and, as a result, weakened support for the fairness doctrine as well. Many conservatives, both inside and outside the Reagan administration, argued that the government did not have the right to regulate broadcasts. At the same time, they complained that the networks, despite their claims of moderation, were actively pushing a liberal agenda. In 1987, in *Meredith Corp. v. FCC*, a federal court ruled that the FCC had no obligation to adhere to the fairness doctrine and could end it at any time. Accordingly, the FCC, now packed with Reagan appointees, dropped it. "Our action should be cause for celebration," insisted FCC chairman Dennis Patrick. "By it, we introduce the First Amendment to the twentieth century." The Democratic Congress tried to overcome the FCC decision with legislation that mandated a version of the fairness doctrine, but Reagan vetoed the bill. Suddenly, there were new possibilities on television and radio, as hosts could now openly make political arguments from one side of the spectrum with no requirement for balance.[46]

In all, the 1980s witnessed a revolutionary transformation in the realm of communications. As old institutions from the telephone to the television became fragmented, individual consumers entered a new era in terms of how they could interact with one another and the world around them. Changes in government policy opened the door for programs that promoted specific political perspectives, while cable television and the new internet provided new homes for such programs, and much more. While many consumers marveled at the dizzying array of choices in communications and culture that now stood before them, some conservatives worried that these new opportunities threatened what they regarded as traditional values and sought to push back.

Backlash

The new fault lines cracked open by this new era of telecommunications and technology triggered a political backlash. In the summer of 1985, a pair of well-connected Washington spouses—Tipper Gore, the wife of Democratic senator Al Gore Jr. of Tennessee, and Susan Baker, the wife of Republican treasury secretary Jim Baker—launched a new group called the Parents' Music Resource Center (PMRC). Despite their different political affiliations, the two shared a common identity as concerned mothers who had been horrified by their children's exposure to sexually explicit rock songs by the performers Prince and

Madonna, two prominent stars on MTV. A sympathetic newspaper columnist explained that Gore and Baker were "no blue-nose record smashers. They are mothers who are distressed that their children are being exposed to filth, violence, sado-masochism and explicit sex whenever they switch on their favorite radio station or watched televised videos." Insisting that they were not calling for such music to be banned, the PMRC leaders instead framed themselves as consumers seeking a greater degree of command over the chaos of cultural choices that were now becoming available to them and their children, whether they wanted them or not. "It's simply gone too far, and it has to be stopped," Gore said; "at least we have a right to know what's on an album so we can exercise some control."[47]

Sensing a growing backlash, executives in the music industry responded to the PMRC complaints with incredible speed. They quickly took steps agreeing to self-regulation before the government imposed rules of its own (taking a lesson from the movie industry, which had undertaken a similar strategy with its ratings system when faced with complaints earlier in the twentieth century). For instance, at the PMRC's request, the president of the National Association of Broadcasters asked forty-five record companies to start providing written copies of lyrics so radio and television stations could know precisely what they were broadcasting. Meanwhile, Stan Gortikov, president of the Recording Industry Association of America, personally traveled from New York to Washington to meet with PMRC leaders and hear out their demands. Although he balked at some of the more excessive proposals—which ranged from requiring record stores to hide albums with explicit covers to having production companies pressure broadcasters from airing their own artists' songs and videos—he quickly agreed to the PMRC proposal to place warning labels on albums with "explicit lyric content." Within days, all of the largest record companies backed the plan, seeing it as a form of self-regulation akin to the ratings system used in Hollywood.[48]

Even with the recording industry's decision, the PMRC pressed ahead in a campaign to mandate such warning labels by law. Sensing that there could be a political payoff to taking on the industry, the Senate Commerce, Science, and Transportation Committee scheduled formal hearings to consider the proposal. Many of the committee's members, including Al Gore, were receptive to the idea of making the warnings a federal requirement, while others pressed for even greater action. "It is outrageous filth and we must do something about it," insisted Senator Ernest Hollings of South Carolina, the ranking Democrat. "If I could find some way constitutionally to get rid of it, I would." Members of the music industry, however, insisted that such intervention was wholly unconstitutional. Danny Goldberg, chairman of a smaller record company and president of the newly formed activist group Musical Majority, argued that warning labels were "absolutely a move toward censorship." Many musicians agreed, warning of a slippery slope ahead. "Right now, it's sex and violence," noted singer John Cougar Mellencamp; "before long, it'll be 'That's just too political.'"[49]

In September 1985, the two sides in this increasingly heated debate came face-to-face in the Senate hearings. Hundreds of spectators gathered for the show, with hundreds more waiting outside hoping to secure a seat. To make their concerns clear, PMRC leaders showed the assembled crowd some popular videos from MTV, including Van Halen's "Hot for Teacher" (which showed schoolboys ogling a bikini-clad teacher) and the heavy-metal group Twisted Sister's "We're Not Gonna Take It" (which critics insisted promoted violence). The PMRC claims, however, did not go unchallenged. Three prominent musicians—country artist John Denver, avant-garde performer Frank Zappa, and Dee Snider, the lead singer of Twisted Sister—were on hand to push back. Although their wildly different styles made them what the *Los Angeles Times* called "the weirdest pop music trio since Alvin and the Chipmunks," the three performers presented a determined and united front against the proposals. Denver noted that even his wholesome songs had often been misunderstood. Zappa, dressed conservatively in a dark suit with his own teenage children in tow, claimed that the lyrics in question represented only a small minority of music and the proposal to crack down on the whole industry was therefore "the equivalent of treating dandruff by decapitation." But Snider stole the show. Though he arrived wearing sunglasses and a cut-off denim vest, with long, wiry bleached hair, he insisted that the PMRC critics had badly misunderstood him and his music. Presenting himself as a devout Christian and the father of a three-year-old boy, he claimed his personal example was one that critics should praise. "I do not drink, I do not smoke, and I do not do drugs," he insisted. His songs reflected his conservative values, he said, forcefully rebutting the PMRC charges point by point. "Ms. Gore claimed that one of my songs, 'Under the Blade,' had lyrics encouraging sadomasochism, bondage and rape," Snider noted. "The lyrics she quoted have absolutely nothing to do with these topics. On the contrary, the words in question are about surgery and the fear that it instills in people. . . . I can say categorically . . . that the only sadomasochism, bondage and rape in this song is in the mind of Ms. Gore."[50] Though the Senate ultimately decided not to act, its hearings served both to publicize and polarize the issue across the nation.[51] The television show *American Bandstand* prevented the singer Sheena Easton from performing "Sugar Walls" because the PMRC had complained about the lyrics, while Marvin Gaye's record company forced him to retitle a song from "Sanctified Pussy" to "Sanctified Lady" to avoid a likely controversy.[52]

Meanwhile, as the Senate investigated obscenity in music, the Reagan White House turned its attention to pornography in magazines and films. In May 1984, after some prompting from the Religious Right, President Reagan announced the creation of a new presidential commission on pornography. There had already been such a presidential commission during the Nixon administration, but Reagan said in his announcement that he disagreed with its essential findings that sexually explicit films and magazines had no negative impact on society. "It is time to take a new look at this conclusion," the president insisted, "and it's time to stop pretending that extreme pornography is a victimless crime." After a year's worth of preparation, Attorney General Ed Meese formally launched the commission in May 1985. "No longer must one go out of the way to find pornographic materials," Meese noted. "With the advent of cable television and video recorders, pornography now is available at home to almost anyone—regardless of age—at the mere touch of a button or at the mere dialing of a telephone."[53]

The Meese Commission, as it was commonly known, was made up largely of law enforcement figures and conservative activists who had already engaged in campaigns against pornography. The commission's chairman, Henry E. Hudson, was a county prosecutor from suburban Virginia who reporters noted had shown "uncommon zeal" in shutting down adult bookstores and making arrests. "Hudson's record on pornography is clear," said Barry Lynn of the American Civil Liberties Union (ACLU). "He hates it, he wants to get rid of it, and he thinks it's a public safety menace akin to driving 100 miles an hour in a residential neighborhood." Setting aside the considerable number of social science studies on the impact of pornography, most of which concluded that it was not a significant social problem, the members of the Meese Commission resolved to do their own research. Over the next year, they personally inspected 2,325 magazines, 725 books, and 2,370 films. As it carried out its work, the commission made it clear that it was concerned not just with the production of pornographic material, but its dissemination as well. Bookstores and major convenience store chains received official letters from the commission's executive director noting that the panel had "received testimony alleging that your company is involved in the sale or distribution of pornography" and "determined that it would be appropriate to allow your company an opportunity to respond" before it drafted its report identifying such distributors. Intimidated by the government's letter, several large chains of convenience stores and drugstores, including 7-Eleven and Revco, responded by removing magazines like *Playboy* and *Penthouse* from their racks. In response, the two magazines sued the attorney general. According to Christine Hefner, president of Playboy, "this harassment of legitimate business recalls a kind of 'McCarthy blacklist,' with pornography serving as the 1980s version of the 'red menace.'"[54]

In July 1986, the Meese Commission issued its final report. At its heart, the two-volume, 1,960-page document concluded that pornography caused irreparable harm to society. Specifically, the commission concluded that porn "debased" women and directly led to acts of violence against women and children alike. Accordingly, the Meese Report called for stricter enforcement of existing obscenity laws and a broadened legal definition of obscenity to make even more kinds of sexually explicit material illegal. Following a federal court ruling against the panel, however, the commission did not publish its "blacklist" of vendors as publishers had feared. Still, individual states pressed ahead where the federal government could not, passing tougher new pornography and obscenity laws of their own and launching new waves of arrests. In October 1985, for instance, a new obscenity law in North Carolina had allowed police to seize materials and make arrests without a court order, prompting new crackdowns across the state.[55]

Meanwhile, the campaign against obscene music continued to spread. A growing concern was the genre of rap music, with its aggressive lyrics and confrontational style. In the late 1980s, much of the controversy centered on 2 Live Crew, a controversial rap group from Miami whose main claim to fame had been its sexually explicit lyrics. After listening to the band's 1989 album *As Nasty as They Wanna Be*, PMRC officials duly reported that it contained over 200 uses of the word "fuck," over 150 uses of the word "bitch," more than 100 references to male and female genitalia, and over 80 different descriptions of oral sex. While the PMRC merely wanted warning labels placed on the album, more aggressive activists pushed for its complete ban. According to the American Family Association, such music was "mind pollution and body pollution" that could only cause harm. "This stuff is so toxic and so dangerous to anybody," one attorney argued, "that it shouldn't be allowed to be sold to anybody or by anybody." Because children might hear the songs, he continued, the group's lead singer Luther Campbell was nothing less than "a psychological child molester."[56]

As with the state-level campaigns against pornography, state and local efforts against obscene music succeeded where the national campaign stalled. Such campaigns occurred across the country, from California to Pennsylvania, but they were especially prominent in southern states, serving as a reminder that however nationalizing the decade's communications might have felt, there were strong pockets of regional resistance. In a small town in Alabama, for instance, record store owner Tommy Hammond was arrested in 1988 for selling a 2 Live Crew cassette tape to an undercover officer, and then convicted and fined $500. (The conviction was reversed on appeal.) Though seemingly minor, the penalty made Hammond, as Tom Wicker noted in the *New York Times*, "the first American ever found guilty of selling recorded obscenity." Others would soon join him. Hammond's brother, for instance, was fined $3,000 and given a year's suspended prison sentence for selling an album by the rapper Too Short in another Alabama town.[57]

The controversy came to a head in Florida in 1990, with the Miami-based 2 Live Crew once again in the spotlight. Inspired by a series of private "sting" operations orchestrated by the American Family Association, local police conducted their own undercover work. In March 1990, a 19-year-old record store clerk in Sarasota was arrested for selling a 2 Live Crew album to an 11-year-old girl and charged with selling "harmful material" to a minor, a felony that carried a potential penalty of five years in prison and a fine of $5,000. That same month, a Broward County judge ruled the album "obscene" and banned its sale entirely in the county; in June, a federal judge in Ft. Lauderdale agreed, opening the door to further prosecution of record store owners and clerks who sold the album not merely to children but even to adults. "This is a case between two ancient enemies, Anything Goes and Enough Already," announced US District Court judge Jose Gonzalez, before making it clear that he came down firmly on the side of the latter. Emboldened by the court decisions, a local sheriff promised to arrest the members of 2 Live Crew if they performed songs from the album live. A few days later, his deputies did just that. Republican governor Bob Martinez, then embroiled in a tough reelection fight, took credit for the arrests, insisting he had acted to protect the interests of most of his constituents. "There's always a small percentage that that [album] will appeal to," Martinez announced. "It doesn't to me, and I think it doesn't to the majority of the people in this state or the majority of people in this nation."[58]

In truth, however, the controversy and the charges of censorship only boosted sales of the album. The fundamental problem for the culture warriors was that large numbers of Americans liked the material that they wanted to eliminate. While some found it politically attractive to try to contain these products, the consuming public generally had little interest in their efforts. Even with a number of major retail chains pulling the album off their shelves in response to conservative activists' complaints and court orders, As Nasty As They Wanna Be still went platinum, selling 1,200,000 copies in its first year of release and staying in the Top 40 of both Billboard Magazine's pop and black music album sales charts the entire time. Riding the new wave of notoriety, Campbell set to work on a new album—"this one dirtier than the last"—and quickly secured a multimillion-dollar deal with a major label. In July 1990, Atlantic Records "proudly" released the follow-up album, pointedly named Banned in the U.S.A., with an initial run of a million copies. On the inner sleeve of the album, Campbell offered a sarcastic "extra special thanks" to Bob Martinez, Tipper Gore, and "all the right-wing people" who had helped make him a celebrity. Even though a number of major record chains refused to carry the album, it quickly sold hundreds of thousands of copies and was certified as a gold record within weeks.[59]

Meanwhile, the effort to prosecute the group for performing its songs went nowhere. Typically, obscenity charges had only been leveled against individuals engaged in indecent exposure—for acts rather than words. Believing the case represented a significant escalation in a growing climate of censorship, large numbers of academics, journalists, and civil libertarians rushed to defend 2 Live Crew. Though many made their personal distaste for the group clear, they argued that the effort to crack down on sales of the album represented a slippery slope toward greater constriction of artistic expression. "It is unfortunate that, as one astute civil libertarian once said, First Amendment cases often put you on the same side with people you would never invite to your home for dinner," noted *Chicago Tribune* columnist Clarence Page. "But those who want to curb the Bill of Rights are clever enough to single out the most objectionable and artless material they can find, hoping to pave the way to later assaults on the more commonplace and meritorious." At the trial, the defense relied on expert testimony from figures such as *Newsday*'s music critic John Leland and Henry Louis Gates Jr., a professor of literature at Duke University. The jury, swayed by their arguments, quickly returned a not-guilty verdict. "There was very little argument," the foreman told reporters. "As the cross-section of the community that we are, it was just not obscene. People in everyday society use those words."[60]

Conservatives learned that American culture was rapidly becoming more liberal and more difficult to control as technology balkanized the public square. Even as the changes stimulated a backlash within both parties, the fragmentation of technology made it hard for anyone to control anything. The cultural marketplace seemed to be demanding more sex and more drugs, as well as more politics, and there was little room to push back. The fragmentation created a world with fewer points of commonality in terms of what people heard or saw, even as computing and cable technology emerged as the medium through which most people consumed their cultural goods. The fault lines that emerged in the decade would prove impossible to reverse and would soon have a transformative effect on the foundations of American society.

CHAPTER 8

Dividing America

THE FAULT LINES OF AMERICAN POLITICS HARDENED IN the late 1980s, as conservatives and liberals alike adjusted to new issues that were taking hold. Across three seemingly disparate fronts—the Cold War, which overwhelmed foreign affairs; the Supreme Court, which determined the boundaries of life at home; and the AIDS crisis, which ravaged and destroyed individual lives—the late 1980s witnessed sharp new lines of division.

First, in the realm of foreign policy, the final years of the Cold War embodied a range of tensions, at home and abroad. The Iran-Contra scandal intensified the role partisan politics played in the prosecution of American foreign policy, raising it to levels that hadn't been seen since the earliest days of the Cold War. But as those divisions worsened at home, other dividing lines abroad suddenly came down—literally so, with the toppling of the Berlin Wall in late 1989. Rather than moving beyond the internal political division that had shaped partisan politics over fighting Communism, tensions in many ways worsened as Americans no longer shared a common fear of the Soviet Union.

As the fault lines over international relations were remade, new ones were exposed at home. Long-simmering domestic disagreements over politics, race, and sexuality now came to a head at the Supreme Court. Key vacancies on the court shifted its balance of power considerably in the mid-1980s, sparking some of the ugliest confirmation hearings in the history of the institution, especially the one for Robert Bork. In the end, an uneasy truce was drawn, but conservatives and liberals alike left the episode ready to do battle again.

Third came the AIDS epidemic, America's most serious public

health crisis in more than a half-century's time. The rapid spread of the deadly disease fostered new fault lines in both senses of the term— intensifying gay rights direct action and homophobic reaction, but also sparking a debate about the victims' own culpability for the crisis.

Unfolding at the same time, these revolutionary developments effectively changed the relationships that Americans had with the world at large, with the politics and laws of their nation, and with their own bodies and the bodies of others.

The Crack-Up of the Cold War

Shortly before the 1986 midterm elections, the media uncovered a shocking story: the Reagan administration had been trading arms to Iran in exchange for its assistance in securing the release of American hostages still held in Beirut. In 1984, Reagan had withdrawn US forces from the civil war in Lebanon following the devastating bombing of the barracks of US and French forces that left 200 Marines and 21 additional service members dead. But hostages still remained, under the control of Hezbollah, a terrorist organization with ties to the Iranian government.

Rumors of secret arms deals to the Iranian regime had been bubbling up for the better part of a year, but a day before the November 1986 midterms, a Lebanese magazine put the pieces together, noting America's role in the illegal scheme. The news wasn't immediately picked up by American media outlets, but Democrats nevertheless did well in the elections, picking up more seats in the House and taking back the Senate for the first time in Reagan's presidency. Then within days, news of American involvement in arming the Iranian regime came to dominate domestic headlines. "U.S. Sent Iran Arms for Hostage Releases," read a front-page headline in the *Los Angeles Times*, over a story that detailed how "the Tehran government received planeloads of military equipment" in a deal made "with the personal approval of President Reagan."[1] The president's involvement was especially shocking because Reagan had repeatedly singled out Iran as a "terrorist state" that represented a dangerous part of "a new international version of Murder Incorporated." His promise to be tougher than Carter in resolving the Iranian hostage crisis in 1980 had been one of his principal campaign pledges. Insisting he would never negotiate with its leaders under any circumstances, Reagan directly asserted that "America will never make concessions to terrorists." Despite such strong words, it soon became clear that Reagan had given his full support to the secret negotiations with Iran.[2]

As the press dug into the details, the scandal only widened. Despite an explicit congressional ban against funding the anti-Communist Nicaraguan rebels known as "Contras," it was soon revealed that the administration had found a way to do precisely that. Marking up the price of arms sold to Iran, the CIA then diverted the excess profits to the Contras. As the public learned the details of the twin scandals now linked together as "Iran-Contra," the administration found itself under fire. When the arms-for-hostages connection came to light in November 1986, Reagan categorically denied the charges in an Oval Office address. "The charge has been made that the United States has shipped weapons to Iran as ransom payment for the release of American hostages in Lebanon, that the United States undercut its allies and secretly violated American policy against trafficking with terrorists," Reagan said sternly. "Those charges are utterly false." The public, however, did not believe the president. Polls showed that only 14 percent of Americans accepted Reagan's claims of innocence. The president tried to cut off the scandal, insisting that his National Security Advisor John Poindexter and White House staffer Lt. Col. Oliver North had undertaken the operation without his knowledge and accepting their resignations at the end of November. This was, he argued, a case of reckless advisors making mistakes, not impeachable high crimes and misdemeanors. But few Americans believed him. According to Gallup, the president's approval rating plummeted from 63 percent to 47 percent that month, the single largest drop in their history of presidential polling.[3]

With his back to the wall, the president authorized an investigation led by Texas Republican senator John Tower, the staunch conservative who had long stood as an administration ally. In early 1987, the Tower Commission issued a report that focused on the administrative mismanagement that allowed the operation to take place. The commission did not say that Reagan had done anything illegal or unethical, emphasizing instead how poorly the president had led his own White House. It was, in essence, a slap on the wrist: chiding the president without implicating him in any kind of crime. Congress, skeptical of the

Republican Tower's impartiality, pursued its own investigation through joint congressional hearings, while Independent Prosecutor Lawrence Walsh conducted a multimillion-dollar investigation of his own. Notably, Walsh was appointed under the independent counsel law that Congress passed in 1978 to check executive branch corruption in the wake of Watergate. Contradicting the Tower Commission, Walsh concluded that the illegal acts had been directed from the top levels of the White House and that North and others had only stepped forward as "scapegoats whose sacrifice would protect the Reagan Administration in its final two years." Despite the endless comparisons between "Contragate" and Watergate, Congress was unable at the time to find any "smoking gun" evidence that the president had known about the Nicaraguan portion of the operation or directly authorized it. (Iran-Contra documents were famously destroyed in the so-called "shredding party" conducted by Oliver North with the help of his then-secretary Fawn Hall.)[4]

The politics of the scandal changed dramatically as the inquiry deepened, especially when North testified before Congress on live television. Initially, the "big three" networks missed the importance of the moment. The networks revived the approach they had used for the televised Watergate hearings, rotating coverage among them a day at a time. NBC News "drew the long straw," network president Lawrence Grossman told reporters, and would therefore be the first to preempt its profitable daytime programming of game shows and soap operas to air the hearings. In contrast, CNN aired the hearings live and in full, tapping into public interest but also increasing it with its own breathless coverage. Television critics took note. "The notion that there is nothing to watch on TV during the summer is belied by the contentious morality play gathering steam in the Senate Caucus Room this week," wrote Steve Daley of the *Chicago Tribune*. "The folks at 1600 Pennsylvania Avenue in Washington made a point of telling us they had better things to do with their time than watch television, but millions of the rest of us were not in agreement with that assessment." Almost five times as many television viewers tuned in to watch North as watched the hit soap opera *General Hospital*. "The event is high drama," admitted the vice president and executive producer of special programming at ABC News. "The event is enthralling. This is a piece of historic theater that's being played out here. The key word is historic, but it is also theater."[5]

The public was fascinated with the drama of the hearings, giving cable news and the live coverage of the networks a huge ratings boom. North made the most of his time in the spotlight. Though he had not worn his Marine uniform in his role at the White House, he put it on again for the hearings, presenting an impressive military image for the cameras. Granted limited immunity from prosecution, after having initially invoked his Fifth Amendment rights, North knew he had some leeway with the committee and used it to cut a melodramatic tone. Alternately abrasive and humble in his answers, "North mixed Clint Eastwood with Jimmy Stewart, Dirty Harry with Mr. North Goes to Washington," a media critic noted. But it was all an act, "the pose of a man threatening to leap from a street-level window." Defending everything that he and his colleagues had done, North insisted the administration had merely acted for the good of the nation. Turning the tables on his critics, he blamed congressional Democrats for blocking the money the administration needed to fight Communism. "Olliemania" briefly swept the country as some seemed moved by North's testimony, seeing the White House staffer now as a populist hero. "People like the idea of the little guy beating up on the big guys," said a disc jockey at WLW radio in Cincinnati. "He's proving that you really can beat city hall." Businesses quickly cranked out Oliver North dolls, action figures, bumper stickers, T-shirts, and videotapes. In Tonawanda, New York, a local deli promoted an Oliver North sandwich—a hero. "It consists of red-blooded American beef," the owner explained. "And a little bologna."[6]

"Olliemania" did not last long, but long enough to dampen the energy behind the congressional investigation and quiet the calls for impeachment. The Democratic Congress ultimately decided that the country—only a dozen years removed from Watergate—could not afford to go through the process again. Speaker of the House Jim Wright opted to forgo impeachment, believing that Reagan would be on the defensive for the rest of his term as he struggled to survive. And indeed, though Reagan escaped an impeachment inquiry, Iran-Contra still cost him and his presidency dearly. The televised hearings, viewed by millions of Americans, had led many to conclude that Reagan had created an environment conducive to nefarious activity. For most Americans, there were only two possible conclusions, neither of them good: the president had either sanctioned the illegal actions of his closest advisors, or else he had lost control of his administration and had no idea what it was doing. For the remainder of his term, Reagan spent much of his political capital fighting off the scandal, and the public never saw him in the same light again. His approval ratings plateaued at the 50 percent mark, where they largely stayed for the next year.

For some on the right, however, the scandal offered different lessons. Republicans on the congressional committee, led by Wyoming representative Dick Cheney, released a stinging minority report that condemned the investigation as a partisan witch hunt. Echoing Oliver North, the minority argued that administration officials had rationally pursued these policies in response to excessive congressional restraints on the executive branch's pursuit of foreign policy. "Congressional actions to limit the president in this area," they argued, "should be reviewed with a considerable degree of skepticism. If they interfere with the core presidential foreign policy functions, they should be struck down." Ignoring the constitutional role set for Congress in crafting foreign policy, they argued that all decision-making power lay with the president. Republicans and Democrats were beginning to see the same set of facts through very different partisan lenses. While they had once been united on foreign affairs, increasingly there was little room for common ground.

Toward the end of his presidency, Reagan was able to revitalize his standing on foreign policy, but only through a surprising reversal of course. Abandoning his early stance of confrontation, Reagan suddenly turned in earnest to negotiation. Between 1985 and 1987, he negotiated a major arms agreement with the new Soviet premier Mikhail Gorbachev. Younger and more cosmopolitan than his predecessors, Gorbachev represented a new generation of Soviet leadership. He thought the nation was nearing bankruptcy due to the endless military spending necessitated by the long Cold War. The entire Communist system, Gorbachev believed, had to be changed. Accordingly, he pushed for transformative new policies. Domestically, Gorbachev pursued the liberalization of the economy (*perestroika*) on the belief that the weight of state management and military spending was crushing the Soviets. He also undertook a new spirit of political openness and transparency (*glasnost*).

As he looked abroad, Gorbachev saw the potential for an unlikely new partner in the old Cold Warrior Reagan. "Everything points to the fact that Reagan is trying persistently to capture the initiative in international affairs," stated a memo prepared for Gorbachev, "to create an image of America as a country that is purposefully striving to improve relations with the Soviet Union and to improve the global political climate."[7] To be sure, there were significant political risks for Reagan. Many members of the administration, including in the Pentagon, warned that Gorbachev's new pronouncements were part of a plot by Kremlin hard-liners that threatened the security of the United States. Defense Secretary Weinberger, for one, dismissed Gorbachev's new style and insisted the nation he led remained the same. "I don't think just because he wears Gucci shoes and smiles occasionally," he argued, "that the Soviet Union has changed its basic doctrines."[8] Despite his past criticism of détente and negotiations, Reagan decided to try a new direction and meet with Gorbachev. As a result, the end of the Cold War unfolded in elegant negotiating rooms instead of on battlefields.

At the first meeting in November 1985, Reagan focused on stagecraft as much as statecraft. He understood that the public perception of their meeting might matter more than the realities of what went on inside, and accordingly sought to craft images that would work to his advantage. When CBS and CNN set up live broadcasts of the two leaders' arrivals in Geneva, Reagan tried to set the tone when he stepped out in the cool weather without a coat. He offered a sharp contrast to Gorbachev, who despite being two decades younger, appeared in a hat and heavy overcoat. "Where is your coat?" Gorbachev asked. "It's inside," Reagan responded as he grabbed Gorbachev by the arm and started to walk into the Chateau Fleur d'Eau.[9] As the summit went on, other images of Reagan and Gorbachev—especially one of the two sitting in front of a fireplace—conveyed the impression that relations between the Cold War enemies had thawed considerably. Despite the public relations successes, the talks ultimately broke down over the Strategic Defense Initiative. The Soviets insisted that the plans had to be abandoned, but Reagan stubbornly refused.[10]

Although the first summit stalled, the two met again in Reykjavik, Iceland, in October 1986. This time, Gorbachev tried to move things forward by accepting a dramatic proposal Reagan had made earlier in his presidency called the "zero-zero option." It would end further expansions of their nuclear arsenals but also spark a 50 percent reduction in strategic weapons, all leading to the elimination of all nuclear weapons within ten years. "All nuclear weapons?" Reagan asked in disbelief. "Well, Mikhail, that's exactly what I've been talking about all along."[11] Once again, however, the two men reached an impasse over SDI.

As Reagan negotiated privately with Gorbachev, he still worked to maintain a public image of strength. In June 1987, as the Iran-Contra hearings in Congress were starting to take their toll on his standing, Reagan delivered a confident speech at the Berlin Wall. His advisors had urged him not to make the address, but Reagan believed he needed to look tough, not just to maintain support of his allies at home and abroad, but also to make sure the Soviets continued to negotiate. To create that image, White House advance men convinced their skeptical West German hosts to stage the address in front of the Brandenburg Gate, located on the other side of the wall in East Berlin. The West Germans worried such a move would be "provocative," but Reagan's aides insisted, claiming the gate had "the highest recognition factor." At the same time, they convinced West German officials to double the size of the crowd at the address, even though each person would have to be cleared by security forces. The Secret Service placed two panes of bulletproof glass behind Reagan, worried that snipers from the other side of the wall might attempt to assassinate him.[12] In the end, though, the stagecraft worked and Reagan secured an iconic moment. Most memorably, at the end of the speech, Reagan uttered a line that would thrill his conservative supporters at home: "Mr. Gorbachev—Tear Down This Wall!"[13]

The final breakthrough occurred in December 1987, when Gorbachev traveled to the United States to meet with Reagan once more. In an act that nearly derailed the diplomatic overture, conservatives pressured the White House to rescind an invitation to the Soviet premier to speak before a joint session of Congress. But Gorbachev, refusing to let anything deter this final moment, moved forward with determination to bring the deal to a successful resolution. The media covered every step of his trip, with Americans swarming to see the Soviet leader as if he were a Hollywood celebrity. "In a relatively brief period," a reporter marveled, "he has managed to rebut the enduring Soviet stereotype of the brutal, mindless, oafish skinhead. The man is good, really good—an instinctive, charming and smooth salesman with just the right package for Western eyes." Boutiques in the United States sold hammer-and-sickle t-shirts. Some vendors even converted leftover Oliver North dolls, unsold after the brief euphoria from the Iran-Contra hearings fizzled, into new Gorbachev figures. "Everything Soviet is suddenly very romantic," said one tour operator. "Everybody's into it." A gay newspaper, *The Washington Blade*, even held a Gorbachev look-alike contest.[14]

Gorbachev seized the moment and, in a crucial step, agreed to let arms reductions and SDI be dealt with separately. The impasse removed, Reagan and Gorbachev agreed to a historic arms agreement called the Intermediate-Range Nuclear Forces Treaty (INF) that required each country to eliminate its weapons that could travel between 300 and 3,400 miles. Significantly, the treaty was the first agreement to reduce nuclear stockpiles while eliminating an entire category of weapons.[15] As Reagan signed an agreement that contradicted the fierce anti-Communist image so many Americans had of him, public opinion remained steady. The Cold Warrior suddenly emerged as the champion of peace.

Many conservatives refused to accept the deal. Paul Weyrich, for instance, complained that "Reagan is a weakened president, weakened in sprit as well as clout, and not in a position to make judgments about Gorbachev at this time."[16] In response, Reagan castigated the Right. "I think that some of the people who are objecting the most and just refusing even to accede to the idea of ever getting any understanding, whether they realize it or not, those people basically down in their deepest thoughts have accepted that war is inevitable and that there must come to be a war between the superpowers," the president said. "Well, I think as long as you've got a chance to strive for peace, you strive for peace."[17] Although many conservatives opposed ratification of the INF, those in Congress rallied around the president, with the Senate soon ratifying the treaty by a margin of 93 to 5. Within a few years, nearly 2,700 nuclear missiles were dismantled under its terms.

The Cold War did not end on Reagan's watch. When he left the Oval Office, the Soviet Union was still intact and there remained an intense distrust of its leadership within US national security circles. But gradually, further changes started to generate support for reform within Russia and all the other Communist states. In December 1988,

Gorbachev announced at the United Nations that the Soviet Union would no longer follow the Brezhnev Doctrine of intervention in the Communist bloc and would instead allow each satellite state to determine its own path, giving them the "freedom of choice," as he said. (As some Soviet officials joked, the "Brezhnev Doctrine" had been replaced with the "Sinatra Doctrine": from that point on, Communist countries would be allowed to do it their way.) As a sign of Gorbachev's sincerity, the Soviets withdrew 50,000 troops from Eastern Europe. For residents in those nations, the announcement created excitement and hope for the possibility of liberation from the Soviet regime. It energized anti-Communist activists to push for democratic change, and lowered the defenses of the status quo.

The changing zeitgeist within the Soviet bloc was on display on July 19, 1988, when Bruce Springsteen performed to hundreds of thousands in a large plaza in East Berlin. The leaders of the German Democratic Republic, one of the most brutal and repressive Soviet clients, had been inviting Western rock artists to perform in an effort to bolster their international image. The New Jersey–born rock singer, who devoted most of his lyrics to the plight of working-class Americans struggling in the postmanufacturing economy, had been eager to sing across the Cold War divide. In the middle of the concert, broadcast to over a million people on delay on television and radio, Springsteen noted, "I'm not here for or against any government. I've come to play rock 'n' roll for you, in the hope that one day all the barriers will be torn down." The crowd roared in approval. Springsteen had been frustrated that Ronald Reagan had co-opted his antiwar song, "Born in the USA," as a jingoistic anthem for his 1984 presidential reelection campaign. Now, he could join Reagan's efforts, in a liberal way, by appealing to a global desire for human rights and performing Bob Dylan's "Chimes of Freedom." East Berliners, who had been trapped under Communism for decades, heard an American icon sing: "Tolling for the rebel, tolling for the rake. . . . An' we gazed upon the chimes of freedom flashing." For some in the audience, the concert was a revelation. "It made people . . . more eager for more and more change," noted one historian. "Springsteen aroused a greater interest in the West. It showed people how locked up they really were."[18]

The breakthrough came on November 9, 1989, when residents from

East and West Berlin rejected the wall that had separated them and literally tore it down. "This entire era in the history of the socialist system is over," wrote an assistant to Gorbachev. This was just the beginning. Violent and nonviolent revolutions spread throughout the Soviet bloc, bringing down the Communist governments in these countries. Although President George H. W. Bush hesitated from making any bold proclamations that might trigger a backlash against the United States, Soviet Communism diminished as a major force. When the Russians stopped an attempted hard-line coup in 1991, which included the arrest of Gorbachev, Boris Yeltsin, the new Russian nation's first president, led the forces that brought down the rebels. Referring to the old regulars of the Communist Party, former American ambassador to the Soviet Union Jack Matlock quipped that the coup had been the "last hurrah of the apparatchiks."[19] The Cold War was over.

The Divided Court

As the Cold War wound down abroad, the Supreme Court emerged as an important new battlefield at home. The court had often ruled on controversial, divisive issues in the past, but during the Reagan era, it increasingly served not just as a site of polarization, but a source of it. Reagan and his aides understood that if their conservative counterrevolution were to have any lasting impact, it would need to manifest not just in the Republican White House and its allies in Congress, but in the federal judiciary. In an era when Democrats still held considerable power in Congress, a reliably conservative court would prove to be essential.

The conservative shift in the Supreme Court began in May 1986, when Chief Justice Warren Burger informed the White House that he would be resigning at the end of that year's term. Burger had served as chief justice since 1969, when President Nixon selected him in an effort to undo the "permissive rulings" in the realm of law and order that had been made under his predecessor, Earl Warren. While Burger proved to be a fairly reliable conservative vote on the high court, he had failed to organize his fellow conservatives into a force that would undo the liberal decisions of the 1960s, as Nixon had once hoped. "Under Burger's leadership the court has left the great bulk of the Warren Court legacy in civil rights, federal power over the states and other areas virtually intact," the *Washington Post* reflected. "Headed but never really led by Burger, the court continued to expand on many of those rulings, ordering school busing for desegregation and establishing a constitutional right to abortion."[20] Just as Reagan had failed to dismantle many New Deal and Great Society programs, the Burger court had left much of Warren's work in place.

To fill the vacancy and the vacuum of leadership, Reagan announced his plan to elevate Associate Justice William Rehnquist to chief justice and then nominate Judge Antonin Scalia of the US Court of Appeals in Washington, DC, as a new associate. In fourteen years on the court, Rehnquist had a perfect record on the legal issues that mattered most to conservatives. He had opposed a constitutional right to abortion, voted against busing and affirmative action, aggressively sought to constrict the rights of criminal defendants, supported governmental limits on free speech, and interpreted the First Amendment as permitting prayer in public schools. Reagan's aides hoped that, as the new chief justice, Rehnquist could lead a broad constitutional counterrevolution.

Antonin Scalia, the administration understood, would be crucial to that campaign. He shared the same ideological outlook as Rehnquist, and the same boldness. A "conservative activist" on the Court of Appeals, he had been outspoken in his desire to reshape and limit the role of the federal courts, and he promised to bring to the court a good deal of mental firepower and political energy.[21] "The effect of Justice Rehnquist's elevation and Judge Scalia's nomination will be to solidify the court's right wing," the *Wall Street Journal* noted, with special attention given to the potential "demise of the abortion right" in light of the new moves. "While the new appointments won't force an immediate shift of course on affirmative action, school desegregation, separation of church and state and the rights of criminal suspects, they are expected to intensify the court's internal debates over these difficult issues."[22]

In Congress, the confirmation hearings were slightly contentious. Civil rights organizations came forward with troubling allegations about Justice Rehnquist. They reproduced a memorandum he had written when he was a clerk for the court, urging Justice Robert Jackson to uphold segregation in the landmark *Brown v. Board of Education* case of 1954. Meanwhile, new reports surfaced that Rehnquist had engaged in minority voter intimidation as a Republican poll-watcher in Arizona in the 1960s. Despite such charges, Republican senator Strom Thurmond of South Carolina steered the nomination through the GOP-led Senate. Senate Democrats were generally compliant, allowing the nomination to move through with speed. Rehnquist was ultimately confirmed by a vote of 65 to 33, the largest number of no votes ever lodged against a successful nominee for chief justice. With all the energy and attention focused on the top spot, Scalia was easily confirmed, by a vote of 98-0. Together, the two men took their new seats in September 1986.[23]

The conservative energy that Rehnquist and Scalia brought in their new roles on the Supreme Court soon had a chance to be amplified considerably. Less than a year after their confirmations, Justice Lewis Powell, another Nixon appointee, announced that he too would step down. For a decade and a half, Powell had balanced the conservative and liberal wings of the court, often serving as the decisive vote in cases that were decided by a thin 5–4 majority, as they increasingly were. Whoever filled Powell's seat, a professor at Yale Law School predicted, would become "the pivot point in the next generation of American constitutional law."[24]

The Reagan administration believed it had found the perfect candidate to take the spot and tilt the court to the right: Judge Robert Bork, the intellectual dean of the conservative legal community who would give the Right an ideological champion on the court. Reaganites also believed that it would be difficult for Senate Democrats to challenge his nomination. In terms of experience and qualifications, Bork had an impeccable resume: a tenured professor at Yale Law School, a successful corporate lawyer, the solicitor general of the United States, and, since 1981, a judge on the DC Circuit Court, the nation's second-most prestigious court. More important for the conservative movement, Bork was philosophically in tune with the Reagan Revolution. For decades, he had stood at the forefront of a group of academics attacking the Warren court as an out-of-control "imperial judiciary" that had badly overstepped its bounds and usurped the authority of the legislative branch. Bork and others had worked to build a cohort of legal scholars and professional institutions that could ultimately reshape the courts. If he became the new "pivot point" on the court, a host of liberal rulings might well be reversed. Conservative activists were thrilled at the prospect. "We are standing at the edge of history," Jerry Falwell dramatically announced. Bork's nomination, he said, "may be our last chance to influence this most important body." Members of Falwell's Moral Majority sent nearly 22,000 postcards to the Senate Judiciary Committee urging his confirmation, as other organizations of the Religious Right weighed in as well. The Bork nomination, Christian Voice argued, was their "last chance . . . to ensure future decades will bring morality, godliness, and justice back into focus."[25]

Liberals were no less energized. They sensed that Bork offered a perfect foil for mobilizing their supporters against Reagan's revolution in the courts. Bork, many remembered, had been the lone figure in the Nixon Justice Department willing to do the president's bidding. When Attorney General Elliot Richardson and Deputy Attorney General William Ruckelshaus resigned on principle, Solicitor General Bork had followed Nixon's orders and fired the Watergate special prosecutor in the infamous "Saturday Night Massacre." For Democrats, that decision disqualified Bork from serving on the bench. They immediately set out to stop him, using hyperbolic language to portray him as a clumsy ideologue. Within hours of Reagan's announcement, Senator Ted Kennedy sounded the war cry on behalf of the entire civil rights and civil liberties establishment. "Robert Bork's America," he warned ominously, "is a land in which women would be forced into back-alley abortions, blacks would sit at segregated lunch counters, rogue police could break down citizens' doors in midnight raids, school children could not be taught about evolution, writers and artists could be censored at the whim of the government, and the doors of the Federal courts would be shut on the fingers of millions of citizens for whom the judiciary is—and is often the only—protector of the individual rights that are at the heart of our democracy." The dramatic rhetoric worked perfectly. Just as the Religious Right lined up behind the Reagan administration, so too did liberal organizations line up behind Democrats, who had retaken control of the Senate in the 1986 midterms. Organizations including the NAACP, ACLU, NOW, and Planned Parenthood banded together to block Bork, devoting nearly $15 million to the cause. Norman Lear's organization People for the American Way alone spent a million on television, radio, and print advertisements to defeat a nomination the liberal group claimed "would turn back the clock of progress."[26]

With both sides of the political spectrum so heavily mobilized, the Senate hearings on Bork's nomination took on larger-than-life proportions, more like a presidential election. Reporters covered the hearings that way, increasingly framing the judicial nomination as yet another partisan conflict. As *Time* put it, "All at once, the political passions of three decades seemed to converge on a single empty chair."[27] Viewed in cold political terms, the campaign against Bork was masterful, and the one waged in his defense inept. Reagan was usually adept at going over the opposition and appealing directly to the American people, but this time, liberals beat him at his own game. Casting Bork as a reactionary, they swayed public opinion and cost him crucial votes in the Senate. Reagan's liberal adversaries triumphed by using the sort of symbolism and simplicities at which Reagan had long excelled. "They took Bork's own words and decisions and pared away subtleties, complications, and shadings," Ethan Bronner noted. "What remained was neither lie nor truth. It was half-truth. Like the half-truths of the Reagan years, it played well." Meanwhile, the White House decision to portray the combative Bork as a middle-of-the-road moderate fell flat. It was an impossible sell, made all the more so by Bork's combative tone at the hearings and the fact that Reagan disappeared during the heart of the battle to go on vacation. In October 1987, just a few days after the Stock Market crashed on "Black Monday," the Senate rejected Bork by a vote of 58–42. Conservatives were furious, believing Bork had been treated unfairly. They came out of the fight determined to do the same to liberals in the years to come.[28]

The immediate aftermath of the botched nomination was little better. As the court opened its October term with only eight members, the Reagan White House scrambled to find a new nominee. Initially, the administration tried to stay the course, nominating Judge Douglas Ginsburg, a former Harvard Law professor and an intellectual ally of Bork's who seemed ready to carry out their common crusade against the liberalism of the Warren court. But when social conservatives learned that Ginsburg had smoked marijuana and that his wife, an obstetrician, had performed abortions, they demanded he withdraw his name. And indeed, just ten days after his nomination had been announced, Ginsburg did just that.[29] Desperate for a victory, the White House changed its approach and put forth Anthony Kennedy, a more mainstream conservative. Seen as someone who would essentially replicate the swing role that Lewis Powell had played on the court, he sailed through the Senate and was confirmed unanimously on February 3, 1988.[30]

Acting Up against AIDS

The conflict over the Supreme Court extended beyond its seats to the steps outside. On October 13, 1987, just two weeks before the Bork vote in the Senate, more than four thousand protesters gathered outside the court, in what was the largest mass arrest there since a 1971 protest against the Vietnam War. Hundreds of thousands of gays and lesbians had come to Washington, DC, that weekend to lobby Congress for equality and to stage a massive march through the city. Thousands stayed on to protest the Supreme Court, which had the year before upheld the constitutionality of sodomy laws that effectively criminalized gay sex. Police arrested more than six hundred protesters who tried to enter the building. Meanwhile, a smaller group of demonstrators, including a number of AIDS victims, sat down on the steps outside. "We have AIDS," they chanted, "and we have rights."[31]

AIDS (Acquired Immunodeficiency Syndrome) represented the single greatest health crisis for the country in nearly a century. Despite its scope and significance, it had been, for much of the nation, largely invisible in its early years. Initially, the disease spread primarily through communities who had been marginalized by the mainstream, most notably gay men and heroin users. For those outside these groups, the disease seemed safely contained. In one of the first news reports on AIDS, for instance, NBC News anchorman Tom Brokaw reported: "The lifestyle of some male homosexuals has triggered an epidemic of a rare form of cancer."[32] Within that community, though, the disease was frighteningly common. New York playwright Larry Kramer later remembered, "You couldn't walk down the street without running into somebody who said: Have you heard about so and so? He just died. Sometimes you could learn about three or four people just walking the dog. I started making a list of how many people I knew, and it was hundreds. People don't comprehend that. People really were dying like flies."[33] By the mid-1980s, roughly 15,000 deaths had been attributed to AIDS.[34]

Initially, the response to AIDS was anemic. Most of the early struggle to curb the spread of the disease took place at the local level, but with considerable controversy. When municipal governments in New York or San Francisco moved to shut down bathhouses, where unprotected sex was common, some gay activists protested the measures as an effort to crack down on their community. The federal government, meanwhile, did nothing. President Reagan refused to mention the disease as his administration initially ignored it entirely. On October 15, 1982, reporter Lester Kinsolving asked White House Press Secretary Larry Speakes to comment on AIDS. "What's AIDS?" he replied. When the reporter explained that it was known as the "gay plague" many in the room started laughing. "I don't have it, do you?" Speakes joked. Walling off the White House, the press secretary insisted: "There has been no personal experience here." Accordingly, there was no need to discuss it further.[35]

Despite such denials, the president soon had his own personal experiences. In October 1985, actor Rock Hudson died from the disease. An old friend of Reagan's from Hollywood, the charismatic leading man had spent his career in the closet, hiding his homosexuality from fans and friends alike. His death shook the president. Reagan soon sought to learn more about AIDS through consultations with leading physicians, but still refused to speak out. US press coverage of the disease also increased multifold once the public knew that the beloved actor had contracted it. ABC News devoted seven minutes and twenty seconds to the news of Hudson's death, a considerable amount of airtime compared to the coverage the disease had previously received.[36] Meanwhile, the nation as a whole gained a new understanding of AIDS victims through the story of Ryan White, a fourteen-year-old Indiana hemophiliac who had contracted the disease through a blood transfusion. He successfully fought in court to attend public school after he was barred due to the hysteria of parents and kids who feared that they would contract the disease simply by being in the same building. The boy managed to survive until 1990, when he was eighteen years of age, and his public struggle with the disease placed AIDS victims in a sympathetic light for the first time. The new face of the crisis, White appeared on the cover of popular magazines like *People*. Meanwhile, a television special that dramatized his plight was watched by an estimated 15 million Americans.[37]

As the public's mood changed, so did the administration's. In February 1986, the president asked Surgeon General C. Everett Koop to coordinate a belated response to the crisis. The evangelical Koop had been a staunch social conservative who participated in the antiabortion movement of the 1970s. Gay rights activists had little confidence that he would take the disease seriously, but Koop quickly came to grasp the severity of the crisis and the need to act. Uncoupling the disease from the communities it had ravaged, Koop reminded policy makers: "We are fighting a disease, not people." In his final report published that October 1986, Koop predicted almost 200,000 Americans would die of AIDS by 1991 if nothing were done. "Acquired Immune Deficiency Syndrome is an epidemic that has already killed thousands of people, mostly young, productive Americans," the surgeon general's report declared. "In addition to illness, disability, and death, AIDS has brought fear to the hearts of most Americans—fear of disease and fear of the unknown." The solution, Koop insisted, was that the government needed to convince Americans to change their sexual behavior. The report called for three approaches, in descending order of effectiveness: "one, abstinence; two, monogamy; three, condoms."[38]

The administration launched an extensive public relations campaign in schools and on television to promote safe sex. The ads were surprisingly blunt. One, for instance, showed a couple preparing to have sex, before being interrupted by a stark TV warning about the disease and ultimately deciding to engage in safe sex. Conservative activists were horrified. The ad not only gave the government's effective sanction to extramarital sex, but also encouraged the use of contraceptive measures like condoms. More important, it absolved gay men of responsibility for the disease. Pat Buchanan, then a communications official for Reagan, called AIDS "nature's revenge on gay men" while Jerry Falwell dismissed the disease as "the wrath of God upon homosexuals."[39] Even longtime allies of the administration broke with Reagan over the campaign. Seizing on educational literature, Phyllis Schlafly accused the president of encouraging third-grade students to engage in "safe sodomy."[40]

But activists in the gay community were even more energized. In 1986, Larry Kramer addressed the Lesbian and Gay Community Services Center in New York. "If my speech tonight doesn't scare the shit out of you, we're in trouble," he began. "If what you're hearing doesn't rouse you to anger, fury, rage, and action, gay men will have no future here on earth." Within five years, he told the audience, two-thirds of them would be dead because of AIDS and a pharmaceutical-medical-industrial complex that ignored the crisis.[41] To prompt action, both within the gay community and the nation at large, activists began plastering posters emblazoned with a pink triangle, the symbol Nazi Germany had once used to identify and ostracize homosexuals. They contained a stark slogan: "SILENCE = DEATH." The small print underneath the triangle posed a challenge: "Why is Reagan silent about AIDS? What is really going on at the Centers for Disease Control, the Federal Drug Administration, and the Vatican? Gays and Lesbians are not expendable . . . Use your power . . . Vote . . . Boycott . . . Defend yourselves."[42]

These local efforts led to the AIDS Coalition to Unleash Power (ACT UP). Led by Kramer, the coalition used controversial and confrontational tactics to mobilize public attention and political pressure for some kind of federal response. While ACT UP's primary goal was political change, it also helped serve as a source of community for those suffering from the disease. It felt like you were "doing something about it," one founder recalled, "rather than being a victim." Over the next few years, ACT UP's numbers would swell, with some demonstrations involving hundreds of thousands. But the movement began small. On March 24, 1987, ACT UP held its very first demonstration at Wall Street to protest pharmaceutical companies' lack of engagement on AIDS medications and to demand that the Food and Drug Administration (FDA) accelerate approval of the limited number of drugs that had been created. "President Reagan," the crowd of 250 shouted, "no one is in charge!"[43]

A week later, Reagan finally spoke out. In a stark reversal from his earlier silence, the president declared that AIDS was now "Public Health Enemy Number One."[44] Over the remainder of his term, the government showed a new commitment to fighting the disease. Congress began earmarking funding for AIDS research in 1986, for instance, with steady increases over the remainder of the decade.[45] In 1988, meanwhile, Surgeon General Koop sent out 107 million copies of a pamphlet called *Understanding AIDS*, which dispelled many myths about the spread of the disease and clearly explained its causes.[46] As the government did more, activists ramped up their efforts to maintain the momentum. In

October 1988, ACT UP activists took control of FDA Headquarters in Rockville, Maryland. Wearing T-shirts with the slogan "WE DIE— THEY DO NOTHING," activists demanded that the agency speed up its trials of new drugs that could prolong the lives of people who had contracted the disease.[47] The government responded by doing more to include gay rights organizations in the decision-making process in clinical trials and in the drug approval process. Notably, the FDA accepted the idea of a "Parallel Track," long promoted by ACT UP, that sped up the path to approval for antiviral drugs dealing with AIDS.[48] Refusing to remain silent, the activists had bent the country, and even a conservative White House, to their cause.

Between the fight over AIDS, the ongoing struggle over the Supreme Court, and the closing of the Cold War, the Reagan era ended on a mixed note. Working with congressional Republicans, the president had been able to push public debate to the right and had made some important decisions that severely limited the ability of government to grow. His national security policy initially reenergized a defense establishment that had languished and, in an unexpected turn, his presidency ended with a major arms agreement with the Soviets. But conservatives did not get everything on their agenda. Politically, the country remained divided, and on social issues the Right often found itself losing out.

Equally important, liberalism did not go away. Indeed, Reagan's presidency served to illustrate the durability of specific programs like Social Security and general support for the welfare state. While Americans welcomed tax cuts, they also clearly expected the federal government to maintain its presence in their lives, on issues ranging from classic concerns like the economy to newer crises such as AIDS. In the same vein, even though Americans had rallied to the Republicans' message of patriotism and supported increased spending on national defense, they nevertheless resisted more aggressive calls to militarism.

In the end, both sides—Right and Left—emerged from the Reagan years with a renewed sense of purpose. Conservatives now demanded more than ever before, refusing to accept another leader who would not press their agenda fully. Liberals, meanwhile, had been buoyed by their success in limiting the Reagan Revolution and remained determined to continue the fight.

CHAPTER 9

New World Orders

IN THE BEGINNING, THE REAGAN ERA HAD BEEN MARKED by confident certainties—a politics painted with "bold colors," as the self-assured president liked to say, rather than "pale pastels"—but the years following his administration seemed much less so. The Reagan Revolution, as his supporters called it, did not provide America with the kind of long-term stability that the nation had experienced after World War II and during the Cold War. It had been much more fragile from the start, and that fundamental fragility quickly became evident as the nation wrestled with the challenges of the new decade.

For starters, the race to replace Reagan in the White House emerged as one of the ugliest presidential campaigns in American political history. In sharp contrast to the sunny optimism of the two Reagan campaigns, the race run by his vice president, George H. W. Bush, was dominated by dark themes that took negative campaigning to new lows. The campaign not only deepened the already severe fault lines between the two parties, but also alienated much of the electorate, who increasingly felt the political system no longer spoke to them.

Meanwhile, international affairs were thrown into a similar state of confusion soon after with the sudden collapse of the Soviet Union. For all the tensions that it had inspired at home, the long Cold War had managed to bring Americans together in a state of common defense against a common enemy. With its end, Americans not only searched for a new sense of meaning in the world at large but also succumbed to greater internal bickering at home. As America moved into the 1990s, political systems and assumptions that had seemed so central just a decade before once again came crashing down.

The 1988 Campaign

Vice President George H. W. Bush entered the 1988 campaign with an impeccable record as an establishment Republican. A veteran of World War II and the son of a former senator, he won a House seat in the 1960s and then held prominent roles in the 1970s as ambassador to the United Nations, head of the Republican National Committee, and director of the Central Intelligence Agency, before serving two terms as Reagan's loyal vice president. He was well respected in both parties and known as someone who valued civility in politics. Bush could be tough when necessary, but his approach had generally avoided the kind of sharp-elbowed politics that so many of Reagan's inner circle seemed to love.

Despite his distinguished record and conservative agenda, Bush found it difficult to win over the Republican faithful. In the Iowa caucuses, he finished an embarrassing third, behind Kansas senator Bob Dole and, more surprising, televangelist and political newcomer Pat Robertson. The preacher's stunning victory in the first contest of the campaign indicated that the Religious Right had transformed the party even more than experts thought. "Conservatives with whom I have spoken are filled with foreboding about the result," reported Tom Bethell of the *Los Angeles Times*. "It's not that they dislike former television evangelist Pat Robertson, or that they will not vote for him. But they can foresee the no-holds-barred, Bork-style onslaught that his candidacy will no doubt soon arouse."[1]

Fears that the culture wars would consume the Republican primaries were short-lived, however. The GOP establishment had shown resilience throughout the previous decade, pushing back against social conservatives when necessary, and they did so again. With superior funding and a stronger organization, Vice President Bush edged out his rivals in the New Hampshire primary a week later and had the nomination effectively in hand by the end of March. Along the way, Bush proved that he could be much tougher than most pundits had assumed and play dirty when needed. His rival Bob Dole became so frustrated about the Bush campaign's many misrepresentations that, in a joint interview with NBC's Tom Brokaw, Dole snapped at the vice president: "Stop lying about my record!"[2]

At the Republican National Convention that summer, Bush sought to find a balance between his personal centrism and the party's conservatism, which had steadily increased under Reagan's leadership. Though he was often mocked as an inarticulate speaker—Texas's Democratic governor Ann Richards liked to joke that Bush had been "born with a silver foot in his mouth"—the vice president delivered an impressive acceptance speech in which he promised to smooth the rougher edges off the Reagan Revolution and transform America into a "kinder and gentler nation." Despite such comments, Bush worked to assure social conservatives that he would not cede any ground in the culture wars. Most significantly, he selected a favorite of the Religious Right, Senator Dan Quayle of Indiana, to be his running mate. "He gives us what we're looking for," conservative activist Paul Weyrich noted. "We'll definitely have a place at the table."[3] During his acceptance speech, drafted by former Reagan speechwriter Peggy Noonan, Bush made it clear that he understood the key economic principles of the so-called Reagan Revolution. He brought the delegates to their feet when he assured everyone in the convention hall: "Read my lips, no new taxes!" If anyone thought that Bush was suffering from what *Newsweek* had once called the "Wimp Factor," the speech sent a signal that he could take a stand.

The Democrats, in sharp contrast, sought to downplay the polarizing issues of the culture wars at all costs. Notably, their presidential nominee, Massachusetts governor Michael Dukakis, had positioned himself as part of a generation of new Democrats who were not tied to the orthodoxies of the 1960s and could appeal to independents and moderates. In his three terms as governor, Dukakis had earned a reputation as an intelligent and efficient administrator, a "technocrat" who could solve problems coolly and calmly. Behind the scenes, Dukakis was stirred by partisan emotions, confiding to friends that Republican actions during the Iran-Contra scandal had inspired his entry into the race. But publicly, he gave no sign of such passions. Indeed, if the nation was becoming more polarized, Dukakis made it clear he wanted nothing to do with it. "This election is not about ideology," he insisted in his acceptance speech; "it is about competence." As veteran political reporter Bill Schneider noted, "Democrats are following a calculated strategy: 'Sell management. Sell competence. But for God's sake, don't try to sell liberalism.'" The appeal worked, with voters giving Dukakis an impressive

17-point lead over Bush after the Democratic National Convention. "No major party nominee with that kind of a July Gallup poll margin has ever been defeated in November," former Nixon strategist Kevin Phillips noted, "least of all by a rival saddled with Mr. Bush's record-breaking negative perceptions."[4]

To rescue his campaign, Bush fully embraced the culture wars. Though he had defeated the social conservative candidacy of rival Pat Robertson, he learned from the experience that he could not afford to isolate himself from such activists. Not wanting to leave anything to chance, he hired some of the most aggressive consultants in the business. His chief strategist Lee Atwater had made his name in the 1980s as a practitioner of a no-holds-barred style of politics. (His boss in the 1984 Reagan-Bush campaign, Ed Rollins, characterized Atwater as a "ruthless" attacker who "just had to drive in one more stake" even after his political target was already dead.) Searching for wedge issues that would revive the Republican campaign, Atwater held a series of focus groups at a shopping mall in Paramus, New Jersey. Swing voters who were considering Dukakis were told that: (1) as governor, he had vetoed a bill requiring teachers to lead students in the Pledge of Allegiance; (2) he had called himself a "card-carrying member of the ACLU"; (3) he opposed the death penalty; and (4) through a furlough program for Massachusetts prisoners, a convict named Willie Horton, sentenced to life without parole, had raped and stabbed a Maryland woman. After hearing these things, half of these voters said they had changed their minds about Dukakis and wouldn't vote for him. Atwater had found the issues that would dominate the 1988 presidential election. There would be a "Bork-style onslaught" in the campaign after all, but from the right, rather than the left, painting the centrist Dukakis as a far-left radical who didn't believe in traditional American values.[5] Even Reagan joined in the game. When reporters asked the president whether candidates like Dukakis should be required to reveal their medical records to the public, Reagan stoked rumors about Dukakis's mental health, noting: "Look, I'm not going to pick on an invalid."[6]

The strategy Atwater crafted for the Bush campaign pushed the practices of negative campaigning to new depths. The overall plan for Dukakis, Atwater later noted, was a brutal assault meant to "strip the bark off the little bastard." The comment didn't sound like one from a typical political consultant, but Atwater was anything but that. Famously, he had long been a fan of professional wrestling, which he insisted was the only "honest sport" there was, because everyone involved—the producers, the performers, the announcers, and the audience—all knew it was entirely scripted and thoroughly fake. The world of politics, in contrast, may have seemed wholesome on the surface but, behind the scenes, was full of cheaters. "He was basically saying that politics is phony, the government is phony, that a lot of personal life is phony," reporter Howard Fineman recalled. "And 'phony' was a big word with him." While Atwater respected wrestling for its honest dishonesties, he also learned a great deal about stagecraft and storytelling from the sport. As his biographer later noted, wrestling shows were "where he learned the importance of bombast, and how to immobilize a larger opponent." In the 1988 campaign, he took those lessons to heart, presenting his candidate to voters as the crusading hero and his opponent as the untrustworthy heel.[7]

The most infamous ads of the cycle focused on Willie Horton and the furlough program in Massachusetts, an issue Senator Al Gore Jr. had first raised in the Democratic primaries. Even though Dukakis had nothing to do with the case itself and the program had been launched by his Republican predecessor, the campaign strategist sought to link the candidate to the convict's crimes. "By the time we're finished," Atwater bragged to his associates, "they're going to wonder whether Willie Horton is Dukakis' running mate." One ad depicted criminals moving through a revolving door at a Massachusetts prison, while another lingered on a close-up photo of Horton, an African American man, in unsubtle racist appeals. The media picked up on the Republican themes, most famously during a presidential debate when CNN's Bernard Shaw asked Dukakis if he would still not favor the death penalty if his own wife were "raped and murdered." In the debate, as on the campaign trail, Dukakis seemed unwilling or unable to respond to the attacks. "No, I don't, Bernard, and I think you know that I've opposed the death penalty during all of my life. I don't see any evidence that it's a deterrent and I think there are better and more effective ways to deal with violent crime." The once-competent technocrat now seemed like an unfeeling robot, and his commanding lead in the polls vanished.[8]

As the campaign turned increasingly negative, reporters and voters recoiled with disgust. The presidential contest, a *Washington Post* writer noted, had become "one of those morning dreams where it's not quite a nightmare, but things just keep repeating and repeating ... Willie Horton ... silver foot in his mouth ... a thousand points of light." Equally uninspired, only 50.1 percent of eligible voters cast a ballot, the lowest level of voter participation since 1924. "We had abysmal, vacuous elections," noted the head of the nonpartisan Committee for the Study of the American Electorate, "and the people responded accordingly." For the Bush campaign, however, lower turnout was a boon. As independents dropped out of the race, partisans moved to the forefront, giving the more unified Republicans an advantage. And so, George H. W. Bush won the presidency with 53 percent of the popular vote to his opponent's 46 percent, with a more commanding 426–111 edge in the Electoral College.[9]

Operation Desert Storm

The culture war concerns that had dominated the 1988 presidential race largely faded from view in the first years of the Bush presidency, as foreign policy moved to the forefront. The new president's own preferences for international affairs dovetailed with dramatic developments overseas to force the national agenda in a different direction. Between the fall of the Berlin Wall in November 1989 and the collapse of the Soviet Union in December 1991, the Bush administration was busy adjusting the United States to its new role as the world's lone superpower and helping create new relationships across the globe. The president was extraordinarily cautious as these events unfolded, refraining from using the kind of bombastic or boastful rhetoric that might trigger a backlash from old Soviet hard-liners. In November 1989, when Germans dismantled the Cold War icon of the Berlin Wall and began the process of reunification, Bush used his diplomatic skills and promises of collective security arrangements as a way to diminish opposition to such changes inside Russia.

But as the long Cold War finally came to a close, a hot war emerged in the Middle East. On the morning of August 2, 1990, approximately 120,000 Iraqi troops invaded Kuwait, annexing the territory and establishing a provisional government. Despite the boldness of the move, the Iraqi government believed that the invasion would not prompt international outrage; a week earlier the American ambassador had told them the United States had "no opinion on Arab-Arab disputes such as your border disagreement with Kuwait." But global outrage was swift. The United Nations Security Council convened an emergency meeting, calling for an "immediate and unconditional" withdrawal. America intervened quickly, stationing 100,000 ground troops in Saudi Arabia within a week of the invasion. President Bush, not wanting to politicize the conflict, waited until after the midterm elections to seek a United Nations resolution authorizing the use of military force in the region. Once he had it in hand, the president sent in another 200,000 troops and sought Senate authorization for military action, which was granted in January 1991 by a narrow vote of 52–47.[10] The congressional vote, Bush asserted, was the "last best chance for peace."

When war came, it proved to be a bit anticlimactic. "Operation Desert Storm" lasted only six weeks, from January 17 to February 28, 1991, with a surprisingly low casualty count for the United States and its allies. Secretary of State James Baker helped assemble an impressive multinational coalition that belied Saddam Hussein's arguments that the attacks against him were simply an effort by the United States to assert its imperial power. Notably, the coalition included Russia and Middle Eastern states that traditionally would not have partnered with America against their neighbors. It offered an example of what Bush called a "New World Order" might look like: collective security arrangements that collaborated to achieve diplomatic breakthroughs and were able to use military force when necessary against sources of instability. The overwhelming force of the coalition quickly routed the Iraqis.

Only 148 Americans died in the conflict, while the larger coalition forces lost slightly more. Iraqi losses were considerably higher, with estimates of 20,000 to 100,000 soldiers and 1,000 to 3,000 civilians killed. The *Washington Post* marveled at the "absolute victory" for America: "Not since the Spanish-American War—perhaps never in this nation's nine previous wars—has the United States waged such a relentlessly successful military campaign as the 42-day juggernaut that was the Persian Gulf War." Both the short duration and light cost of the war (for the allies, at least) stemmed from the fact that US leaders limited their plans to driving Iraq out of Kuwait. Though battered and chastened, Iraqi dictator Saddam Hussein was allowed to stay in power.[11] Bush insisted on sticking to the original mission by limiting the objectives of the coalition and refusing to use force to achieve changes beyond the scope of the original mandate.

In the aftermath of the brief conflict, Bush boasted that the nation had finally overcome the crippling legacies of the Vietnam War that had long made elected officials reluctant to use force. "By God, we've kicked the Vietnam syndrome once and for all!" the president proclaimed. Moreover, in the midst of the fighting, Bush set forth a new vision for the world that would emerge in the aftermath of the Gulf War and the Cold War before it. In his State of the Union Address on January 29, 1991, the president spoke in grand tones. "What is at stake is more than one small country; it is a big idea: a new world order, where diverse nations are drawn together in common cause to achieve the universal aspirations of mankind—peace and security, freedom, and the rule of law," he announced. "Such is a world worthy of our struggle and worthy of our children's future."[12]

Part of the New World Order came in how Americans understood their world. Indeed, in retrospect, the most notable aspect of the 1991 Gulf War was the outsized role that cable television played in it. Although CNN had been around for a decade, it only emerged as a major force in the news world during the conflict. Notably, CNN was the only network with correspondents stationed in Baghdad when the military assault began; as a result, it alone had the capacity to bring viewers live, real-time reports about what was happening on the ground there. For the duration of the conflict, the military operations offered dramatic content for the twenty-four-hour news cycle, which the network presented in the same gripping fashion as a Hollywood film. Americans watched the war unfold on television from the comfort of their homes. In some ways, of course, this was nothing new. The Vietnam War had widely been known as "the living room war," as Americans watched nightly reports from the battlefield on the evening news. But the reports from that war had been slowly and steadily processed— raw footage was captured on film in the field, then flown back to network studios to be edited and processed into coherent stories, and then finally shown in short form in tight segments on one of the "big three" broadcasts days or weeks later. In sharp contrast, the war that CNN broadcast into America's living rooms came as an almost constant live feed, unfolding in real time, with neither reporters nor viewers sure of the outcome as the images played out before them.[13]

As much as the war was a victory for the allied coalition, it was also one for CNN. On the evening that the bombing began, its ratings increased twelvefold, soaring higher than any basic cable network had received in the history of the technology. The traditional networks suddenly lagged in their ability to cover the events. For weeks, viewers watched nearly continuous images of high-tech "precision bombs" falling on Iraqi targets in what some called the "video game war." Even President Bush became an avid watcher of the cable network, which he said was the quickest source of news about developments in the war zone. "I learn more from CNN than I do from the CIA," he quipped. The Iraqis watched CNN as well, as it provided information about outside events that they otherwise could not have found. ("How many Iraqis does it take to fire a Scud missile?" began a common joke. "Three. One to arm, another to fire, and a third to watch CNN and see where it lands.")[14]

With Americans enthralled with coverage of a war that went so well, and seemingly with so little cost to them, President Bush's popularity soared. In early January, a CBS/*New York Times* poll had his approval rating at 58 percent; a few days later, as the air war began, it leapt to 86 percent. His reelection in 1992 started to seem inevitable and several prominent Democrats decided that they would not run against him. "The number of people who don't like George Bush," admitted Congressman Newt Gingrich, hardly a friend, "is almost down to the number of people running for the Democratic nomination." When the president delivered a speech to a joint session of Congress on March 6, 1991, to celebrate the victory, legislators wore yellow ribbons and waved American flags to demonstrate their support. Republicans, seeking to remind the public that most Democrats had voted against using force, stuck pins on their lapels that said: "I voted with the President." It was yet another sign that partisanship did not stop at the water's edge.[15]

But polling experts warned that the wartime surge in the president's popularity, like past "rally events," would not last. "There's fragility evident in Mr. Bush's present standing," a *New York Times* editorial cautioned in early March 1991. "Despite all the popular support for his policies in the Gulf, little seems to translate into support for his other policies. In recent weeks, approval for his handling of the economy has consistently been 40 points lower than his Gulf rating."[16] The aftermath of the operation likewise created problems for the administration. The decision to leave Saddam Hussein in power, which Bush felt was the best strategy to avoid a long and protracted ground presence, didn't sit well with many Republicans who felt that US troops had not been allowed to finish the job. When Hussein violated UN-authorized "no-fly zones" to attack his enemies in Iraq in 1992, some Americans started to question whether the victory was as grand as they had thought.

Indeed, Bush's bounce in the polls proved short-lived as the economic recession of 1990 and 1991 dragged on. An estimated 4.5 million Americans lost their jobs during those years, pushing the unemployment rate to 7.8 percent in June 1992, the highest level since 1982. Major corporations across the nation initiated massive rounds of layoffs. AT&T fired 100,000 employees and General Motors another 74,000; meanwhile, both Pan Am and Eastern Airlines went under, throwing another 48,000 out of work. As American companies collapsed, Japanese ones seemed to be making startling inroads in the United States. In 1991, for instance, the Matsushita Electrical Industrial Company paid $6.6 billion to buy out MCA, the American company that owned MCA Records and Universal Studios. Executives went to great lengths to assure investors that nothing would change. "We impressed upon our clients the fact that our businesses would continue to be run in the fashion they had been run," one noted. "The idea that the Japanese [would] interfere in making movies and writing books is borderline silly."[17] Still, the sudden influx of foreign ownership quickly became a major political issue, spurring fears that the American economy was literally being sold off to some of the nation's biggest competitors. The trend sharply undercut the triumphalism of the Gulf War victory. As former Democratic senator Paul Tsongas of Massachusetts put it: "The Cold War is over, and Japan won."[18]

Though he was widely blamed for the recession, in truth President Bush did a great deal to help end it. Importantly, he parted with the economic ideas that had defined the Reagan era and, in some ways, had helped bring on the recession in the first place. First, in a significant break with the principles of supply-side economics—a school of thought that he had previously mocked as "voodoo economics"—Bush raised domestic spending to help fuel the economy through a Keynesian stimulus. Second, he authorized a federal bailout of the savings and loan industry, another casualty of the Reagan era. In the early 1980s, Reagan tripled the amount of federal insurance available to S&Ls, as his allies in Congress passed new laws that allowed those same lending institutions to engage in a range of high-risk investments. In the late 1980s, many S&Ls suddenly collapsed, ruining large numbers of depositors and forcing the federal government to launch a massive, controversial bailout. It was, at the time, the single costliest financial scandal in American history. Third, Bush broke his campaign pledge that he would never raise taxes and did so to address both the long-term federal debt and the immediate federal deficit. The economic policies of the Reagan years, when government revenues had been greatly reduced while spending increased, had exploded the federal debt from 32 percent of GDP in 1980 to 50 percent in 1989 to 53 percent by 1990. The federal deficit, meanwhile, had grown, in fits and starts, from 2.8 percent of GNP in 1980 to 4.1 percent in 1990. To address these problems, Bush acceded to a tax hike.[19]

When Bush moved forward with the deficit reduction package in spite of his "read my lips" promise, prominent conservatives rebelled against the president and vowed that they would not support him in the campaign. House Minority Whip Newt Gingrich openly led a revolt against a sitting president of his own party. One day before the House was set to vote on the measure, Gingrich dramatically walked out of a White House meeting. According to Bush, the plan had been for all the Republican and Democratic leaders to walk into the Rose Garden and outline a bipartisan deal to the press. This way, neither side could be to blame. But when they started walking out, the president noticed that Gingrich had simply disappeared. White House officials, who thought Gingrich had signed off on the deal, saw this as an "act of political sabotage," remembered Budget Director Richard Darman. "You're killing us," Bush later told Gingrich, "you are just killing us."[20] Even though Bush made a televised appeal to the nation warning of "economic chaos" that would ensue if the deal failed, the House rejected it. Following the vote, House Democrats took the opportunity to negotiate a better deal with the White House that included an even larger tax increase; it soon passed the House and Senate. Bush's rift with the Right would never heal and, according to polls, it cost him support in his bid for reelection.

Besides the economy, Bush made strides with other domestic programs. Working with a Democratic Congress, the president enacted a number of important initiatives. One area in which he made surprising inroads was environmental protection, an issue that had become increasingly prominent over the course of the 1980s. An unintended consequence of the Reagan administration's war on the EPA had been a surge of interest in private organizations dedicated to protecting the environment. The Sierra Club's membership increased by roughly 50 percent over the first half of the decade, from 246,000 in 1980 to 378,000 in 1985, while its budget likewise mushroomed from $9.5 million to $22 million. The National Audubon Society experienced similar growth, moving from 400,000 members and $10 million in funds in 1980 to 500,000 members and $24 million in 1985. By the end of the Reagan era, environmental protection had become such a popular cause that Bush tried to claim it as his own issue in the 1988 election. On the campaign trail, Bush stopped in Michigan to deliver a speech about the need for the government to address climate change. "Our land, water and soil support a remarkable range of human activity, but they can only take so much and we must remember to treat them not as a given but as a gift," he cautioned. "These issues know no ideology, no political boundaries. It's not a liberal or conservative thing we're talking about."[21]

As president, Bush looked to make good on his promise to protect the environment, taking aim at a new crisis in air pollution. As American power plants ramped up their activity in the 1980s, they sent massive clouds of sulfur dioxide into the atmosphere. The result was "acid rain," a startling phenomenon that began to take a destructive toll on eastern North America. Despite the alarm, Congress proved incapable of overcoming its partisan gridlock to find a solution. "By the end of the Reagan administration, Congress had put forward and slapped down 70 different acid rain bills," the *Smithsonian* magazine noted, "and frustration ran so deep that Canada's prime minister bleakly joked about declaring war on the United States." A breakthrough came in the Bush years, however, with the embrace of the novel idea of emissions trading. Developed in conversations between Bush's White House counsel C. Boyden Gray and leaders of the Environmental Defense Fund

(EDF), the policy would soon become known by its component parts: "cap and trade." Basically, the government would set an overall cap on emissions; individual companies would be allotted their fair share of the cap, which they could use themselves or trade off to other companies. A free-market means from the Right was thus used to reach an end long championed by the Left. While many in the administration chafed at the idea of limiting industrial production in any way, emissions trading became a key element of the 1990 Clean Air Act. When its provisions went into effect, the impact was dramatic: acid rain emissions plummeted by 3 million tons in the first year, well ahead of schedule.[22]

As the Republican president made inroads on environmental protection, he also secured landmark legislation in another field more commonly linked to Democrats: civil rights. The Americans with Disabilities Act, the most significant civil rights measure since the 1960s, had the full support of the president from the start. The new law implemented a wide array of federal protections and mandates for the physically disabled, an estimated 43 million Americans in all. "Every man, woman and child with a disability can now pass through a once-closed door to a bright new era of equality, independence, and freedom," Bush happily announced at the July 1990 signing ceremony. The measure was "historic," he claimed, as it represented nothing less than the "world's first declaration of equality for people with disabilities." In a metaphor that called to mind the collapse of Communism and the dismantling of the Berlin Wall, Bush called the new law a "sledgehammer" that would break down the barriers between the disabled and "the freedom they could glimpse but not grasp." The crowd that had gathered roared with approval. ("There was an empty wheelchair in the back row," a reporter noted, "and somebody said that the occupant must have gotten up and walked on the waves of emotion.") Moments like these—for the environment as well as civil rights—suggested that there might be hope for government action on bipartisan lines, but such instances were becoming increasingly rare.[23]

Doubting Thomas

Though the economic recession loomed as the largest domestic issue for the Bush administration, the culture wars continued to roil in

relation to the Supreme Court. The appointment of Justice Kennedy
had brought the Bork confirmation crisis to a close, but not the ongoing struggle over the courts. During 1989 and 1990, the court issued
a series of divided rulings on contentious subjects such as domestic
violence, parental rights, flag "desecration," and affirmative action, to
name just a handful. Most significantly, the court appeared ready to
reverse itself on the hot-button issue of abortion rights. In July 1989, the
justices delivered their ruling in *Webster v. Reproductive Health Services*.
The case centered on a 1986 Missouri law that had declared "human
life begins at conception." The state law banned use of public facili-
ties for virtually all abortions, significantly cut back the use of public
funds, and required physicians to perform tests on women seeking an
abortion to determine if the fetus was viable. A slim 5–4 majority not
only upheld every restriction in the Missouri law but also seemed ready
to overturn *Roe v. Wade* itself. In a rare move, Justice Harry Blackmun,
the Nixon appointee who had authored *Roe,* read his angry dissent from
the bench. "I fear for the future," he read. "For today, the women of this
nation still retain the liberty to control their destinies. But the signs are
evident and very ominous, and a chill wind blows."[24]

Concerns for the future of the court, and the country, only increased
when two liberal stalwarts from the Warren court era announced their
plans to step down. First, William Brennan, an Eisenhower appointee
who had emerged as a champion of civil liberties on the bench, retired
in 1990 and was replaced by David Souter. Drawing on a quarter-
century's record as a prosecutor, state attorney general, and justice in
New Hampshire, Souter presented himself as a moderate in his confirmation hearings and was easily confirmed in a 90–9 Senate vote.
Then, in 1991, civil rights icon Thurgood Marshall announced that
he, too, would step down. As a replacement, the Bush administration
nominated Clarence Thomas, a forty-three-year-old African American
judge on the US Court of Appeals for the District of Columbia Circuit. Unlike Souter, Thomas was an outspoken conservative, one who
had made a name for himself as a consistent critic of all civil rights
legislation and affirmative action when he served as head of the Equal
Employment Opportunity Commission during the Reagan administration. And unlike Souter, Thomas had little judicial experience, having
served on the DC Circuit Court for little over a year.[25]

Both sides of the culture wars saw Thomas's nomination as a replay of Bork's. Florynce Kennedy, a liberal African American activist, urged the National Organization for Women to revive strategies used in the earlier hearings to prevent Thomas's appointment. "We're going to Bork him," she told a NOW conference. "We're going to kill him politically!" Conservatives, however, drew different lessons from the Bork hearings. Indeed, as one observer noted, the Republican White House's strategy for advancing Thomas's nomination was essentially "reverse Bork." While Reagan's administration had emphasized Bork's experience in an effort to downplay his personal ideology, the Bush team resolved to sell Thomas on the basis of his background in hopes of overcoming any concerns about his competence. Thomas's inspirational story of overcoming racism and poverty as a poor African American from rural Georgia would prove to be the key to his nomination. "Just keep getting his personal story out," a Justice Department official told his handlers.[26]

Those who expected the Thomas hearings to match the intensity of Bork's were not disappointed. The Senate Judiciary Committee found it difficult to gain any understanding of the nominee's legal thinking. Conservative nominees had learned from the Bork hearings to keep quiet about anything substantial that might be used to oppose their nomination. When Thomas was pressed about his stances on issues likely to come before the court, he disowned or trivialized most of his former statements, especially on matters of civil rights. Unlike Bork, who had forthrightly defended his past statements and offered a clear picture of his future, Thomas refused to offer an opinion on much of anything. When he was asked about *Roe v. Wade*, which had been decided while he was in law school, Thomas said he could not "remember personally engaging" in any discussion of it as a law student; nor, he added, had he *ever* "debated the contents of it" in the eighteen years since. Such implausible statements only helped harden opposition to him.[27]

One day before the scheduled Senate vote on Thomas, the already tense confirmation hearings turned chaotic. A leaked FBI interview with University of Oklahoma law professor Anita Hill surfaced, including her allegations that Thomas had made inappropriate sexual advances when they worked together at the EEOC. The Senate Judiciary Committee had actually known about what Chairman Joe Biden called "nefarious charges," but had decided not to look further into them. The reserved thirty-five-year-old Hill, reluctant to make herself a center of controversy, had declined to make a formal affidavit. Still, the FBI interview relayed Hill's accusation that Thomas had frequently entered into inappropriate conversations with her about pornography and sex. When a story by NPR's Nina Totenberg followed, the Senate Judiciary Committee reopened its hearings to look into the charges, convincing Hill to testify. Thomas responded with a blanket denial, denouncing the accusation as "a high tech lynching for uppity blacks." The counterattack, which Thomas said he leveled from his "standpoint as a black American," effectively saved his nomination. The lynching metaphor didn't quite fit—his main accuser and many of his loudest critics, like civil rights advocate Florynce Kennedy, were black too—but it completely froze the committee's white liberals, who seemed unable to counterattack when charged with racism.

For women, in particular, the Hill-Thomas hearings represented the public emergence of an issue all too many had lived with in private. Sexual harassment, a term that had only arisen in 1975 during a claim filed against Cornell University, had become a central issue for women's rights organizations by the time of Hill's revelations.[28] Polls showed that significant portions of the female workforce had encountered sexual harassment on the job. The hit comedy *9 to 5* (starring Jane Fonda, Lily Tomlin, and Dolly Parton) had brought the problem to film audiences—ironically coming from an industry that was notorious for the very behavior the film decried. The movie came out in 1980, the same year that the EEOC released new guidelines stating that sexual harassment was unlawful under Title VII of the Civil Rights Act of 1964. The courts began to tackle the problem during the 1980s, while parts of the private sector issued stronger rules about acceptable behavior on the job. But Hill's testimony offered a dramatic reminder that progress had been halting and incomplete.

The response of the Senate Judiciary Committee underscored this disconnect. White male senators, from both parties, spent most of their time questioning the character of the African American woman before them, rather than taking her accusations seriously. Utah Republican Orrin Hatch alleged that Hill was working with "slick lawyers" who wanted to destroy Thomas's candidacy. Wyoming Republican Alan

Simpson doubted her claims. "If what you say this man said to you occurred, why in God's name when he left his position of power or status or authority over you, and you left it in 1983," he asked in disbelief, "why in God's name would you ever speak to a man like that for the rest of your life?" Democrats joined in. Biden, for instance, asked Thomas if he thought Hill had made the entire story up. For many, this line of questioning from an all-male committee confirmed the dire need for more female legislators in Washington. Organizations like NOW mobilized, reporting swelling membership rolls and contributions as a result of the outrage. The Bush administration and movement conservatives conducted a fierce campaign to discredit Hill, raising questions about her character and claims.[29] Finally, in October 1991, the Senate confirmed Thomas by a vote of 52–48, the narrowest margin for a successful confirmation of a Supreme Court nominee in the twentieth century.[30]

The confluence of race, courts, and the culture wars in the Thomas hearings found a disturbing echo six months later on the other side of the country. In early 1992, four members of the LAPD were tried on charges of using excessive force to restrain Rodney King, an African American man in their custody. While charges of police brutality had been a perennial complaint, this particular incident stood out because it had been captured on videotape. George Holliday, a thirty-one-year-old Argentinian immigrant, witnessed the attack from the balcony of his apartment. He filmed the confrontation on his Sony Handycam and then submitted the tape to a local television station, reportedly for $500. The station aired about eighty-one seconds of the film the following night; then, cable news channels picked it up and broadcast it repeatedly, with grainy images of four policemen beating a prone and passive King with their nightsticks playing on a seemingly endless loop.

As the nation watched and rewatched the videotaped images of the Rodney King beating, most Americans assumed the four policemen depicted on it would easily be found guilty. Indeed, in many ways, the single bit of videotape eclipsed the trial, showing the limitations of an old system of justice in a new world of telecommunications. "The jury system was conceived so that citizens could act as surrogates for the public, to sit in judgment of crime," noted a columnist in the Los Angeles Times. "But with cameras increasingly trained wherever news is expected—from police cars, by citizen photographers and by free-lance camera crews who prowl the streets looking for footage to sell to TV stations—in a growing number of cases the public is beginning to believe that it can see and judge the crime for itself." And indeed, those who watched the trial at home actually saw something quite different than the jury in the courtroom did. Television stations, always looking for gripping visuals, replayed the most dramatic bits of the videotape throughout the trial rather than presenting the more ordinary evidence or routine bits of testimony. As a result, the tape loomed much larger for those watching the trial at home than for those in the courtroom, where the full recording was considered, and as one piece of evidence among many. When the jury returned with not-guilty verdicts for all four policemen, the sudden disconnect was shocking. For many African Americans and Latinos in South Central Los Angeles, that shock turned to anger, and anger turned to violence.[31]

The night of the verdict, South Central erupted in a five-day uprising marked by arson and looting: the Los Angeles riots of 1992. In echoes of the Gulf War, Americans watched the chaos unfold in real time on cable and the network news. Cameras situated on helicopters broadcast disturbing images of entire blocks of buildings on fire and charcoal smoke filling the skies over the already smoggy city. Conservative critics charged that the live coverage of the initial stages of the riot only encouraged more to take part. "Helicopter one-upmanship on Wednesday night led to a two-hour invitation, delivered via an airborne mini-cam, to riot," asserted Hugh Hewitt. "The pictures from South Central conveyed a single, powerful image—the police are not responding and probably can't respond. Those inclined to loot or set fires got the message: 'Nothing will stop you tonight, so go ahead, make your day.'" In one particularly tense moment, viewers watched as a white truck driver, Reginald Denny, was dragged from his vehicle before being savagely beaten. As he lay bloodied in the street, helicopters circled overhead sending images live across the country. The images, naturally, were endlessly replayed on cable and network news, much as the original videotape of Rodney King's beating had been. "The Holliday video of the black King being beaten by white police officers immediately became a symbol of racism in America," noted television critic Howard

Rosenberg. "And by continually rerunning footage of Denny being bru-
talized, television has affixed to the Los Angeles riots a symbol every bit
as powerful. This image—of blacks victimizing a white—is infinitely
more potent and lasting than words describing Denny's rescue by four
good Samaritans, also black."[32]

The rioting did not stop until the California National Guard and US
Marines intervened. In the end, fifty-one people were killed and several
thousand more injured; property damage was estimated at over $700
million. When the smoke cleared, the nation surveyed the damages,
which offered a stark reminder that the economic policies of the 1980s
had not brought universal rewards to the nation and that racial and
ethnic divisions remained deep in American society. Throughout the
1980s, roughly a fifth of the African Americans living in South Central Los Angeles had been unemployed, with many homes led by single
mothers who depended on government support to survive. Gang violence was rampant, but efforts to solve it merely made things worse.
Incidents of police brutality had sharply increased over the decade.
When Los Angeles hosted the Olympics in 1984, Mayor Tom Bradley
had authorized Police Commissioner Daryl Gates to crack down on
criminality in order to improve the city's image. Thousands of men were
imprisoned, sometimes on the thinnest evidence. But Gates didn't stop
when the Olympics did. He had responded to the cocaine and crack
epidemic of the late 1980s, and the related gang violence, through
"Operation Hammer," which continued the forceful police response to
crime. The purpose of the program was to "make life miserable" for
the gangs of the city, with constant police sweeps that resulted in over
20,000 arrests.

As Republicans and Democrats traded barbs about which party
was responsible for the riots, the former Nixon analyst and Reagan
critic Kevin Phillips cast blame on both. In the 1960s, he noted, "liberals were widely seen as having failed to deal with major questions
of law enforcement, taxation, fiscal management, and the role of government as well as race." When they were "repudiated," Republicans
took over, but with little results. "Twelve years of Reagan and Bush
has not cured the problems," Phillips noted. "It hasn't given us morning in America. It's produced more columns of smoke rising from our
inner cities."[33]

The Election of 1992

At the 1992 Republican National Convention, firebrand Pat Buchanan, a pugnacious conservative who entered politics in the Nixon White House, electrified delegates with an address that has been known, ever since, as "the culture wars speech." Buchanan had waged a strong challenge to President Bush in the Republican primaries that year, and his address to the convention was an attempt to bring the disaffected cultural conservatives who had followed him back into the fold of the GOP. He was one of the many Republicans who believed that Reagan and Bush had abandoned the social conservatives who had driven the conservative revolution. Angrily giving voice to a host of conservative grievances about American cultural and social life, Buchanan at once looked back over the struggle for social conservatism in the 1980s and forward to a new round of warfare in the 1990s. "My friends," Buchanan announced in the critical passage of the address, "this election is about much more than who gets what. It is about who we are. It is about what we believe. It is about what we stand for as Americans. There is a religious war going on in our country. It is a cultural war, as critical to the kind of nation we will one day be as was the Cold War itself."[34]

The enemies in this domestic war were the Democrats. In his address, Buchanan directed his red-meat remarks to not just Arkansas governor Bill Clinton, the Democratic nominee for president, but also his wife Hillary, a woman the Republican decried as a champion of a "radical feminism" that would destroy America. Buchanan warned that the candidate and his wife would bring radical values of the 1960s to the White House, and then to the rest of the nation. "The agenda that Clinton & Clinton would impose on America—abortion on demand, a litmus test for the Supreme Court, homosexual rights, discrimination against religious schools, women in combat units—that's change, all right. But it is not the kind of change America needs. It is not the kind of change America wants." Buchanan declared that there was "a war for the soul of America" under way, and in that war, "Clinton & Clinton are on the other side, and George Bush is on our side."[35] Some GOP officials suggested Democrats weren't even on America's side. "These other people are not America," Republican National Chairman Richard N.

Bond told NBC's Maria Shriver.[36] Partisans inside the Houston Astrodome cheered Buchanan's combative comments, while many outside
recoiled in horror. Liberal columnist Molly Ivins joked that the speech
"probably sounded better in the original German."[37]

By the time the 1992 presidential campaign began in earnest, President Bush's approval rating had fallen sharply from its Gulf War highs.
Between the sluggish economy, the L.A. riots, and the resurgent culture
war criticisms leveled by Buchanan in the primaries, the president had
taken a thorough beating. Moreover, the rift among Republicans over
Bush's decision to raise taxes had never healed. In early June, the ABC
News-*Washington Post* poll showed his approval rating at 35 percent, a
new low for his presidency. But ultimately, his aides believed, Bush's
positive numbers didn't matter; as in 1988, the negative numbers of his
opponent did. And as luck had it, his opponent, Governor Bill Clinton of Arkansas, seemed to be the ideal target for a negative campaign.
He had avoided serving in the war in Vietnam, smoked marijuana,
and all but admitted to having an extramarital affair. For GOP strategists, he seemed like a target too good to be true.[38] In many respects,
Bill Clinton embodied the worst aspects of the cultural changes that
Republicans had been warning about for over a decade. Persistent
rumors about Clinton's sexual affairs likewise offered Republicans more
than enough ammunition to bring down this Democrat, connecting his
personal problems with a larger narrative about his party.

But Clinton was determined to avoid the culture wars charges that
had effectively destroyed Dukakis four years before. He tried to steal
the issue away from Republicans by moving to the middle on repeated
occasions, often shifting to the right. For instance, while Dukakis had
been tarred as "soft on crime," Clinton made a show of his support
for the death penalty. He even interrupted his campaign so he could
fly back to Arkansas and oversee the execution of Ricky Ray Rector,
a man who was so mentally impaired he told prison guards to save
the dessert from his last meal so he could eat it later. Meanwhile, in
his own contribution to the culture wars, Clinton condemned a fairly
obscure rapper named Sister Souljah who had said, in reaction to the
L.A. riots, "If black people kill black people every day, why not have
a week and kill white people?" Pointedly, Clinton used an appearance
before Jesse Jackson's Rainbow Coalition to denounce Sister Souljah,

who was a member of the organization, and thereby signaled that he was not beholden to "special interests" as Republicans often alleged.[39] Many liberals complained about these kinds of tactics, seeing them as cheap efforts by a slick, centrist Democrat to win over moderate voters. But they proved effective at dampening the conservative efforts to paint Clinton as a very left-of-center Democrat.

As Clinton defended himself on these social issues, he counterattacked strongly on economic themes. This was an area where he felt more comfortable tapping directly into traditional Democratic values and embracing his party's philosophy. Pointing to lingering unemployment, a steadily growing divide between the rich and the rest of America, and the unprecedented growth of the federal debt and deficit over the previous twelve years, Clinton forced the 1992 campaign back from the culture wars issues that Bush favored and instead made it a referendum on the economic consequences of the Reagan Revolution. The twelve years of Reagan and Bush had amounted, in Clinton's words, to "the worst economic record since the Great Depression." He and other Democrats argued that the president had been so focused on military issues and international affairs that he had neglected middle-class Americans who were suffering from the economic downturn at home. The president's wealthy and elitist pedigree, Clinton argued, made it more difficult for him to understand the kinds of struggles that average Americans were facing in their jobs and homes. A sign in the Democratic campaign's "War Room" captured the Clinton team's singular focus on this issue: "THE ECONOMY, STUPID."[40]

Bill Clinton's effort to emphasize economic issues was helped considerably by the campaign of a third-party candidate that year: Ross Perot. The Texas billionaire bypassed traditional party structures and self-financed an eccentric campaign. The changes that had taken place in the news media allowed a candidate to make his case directly to the voters, as long as he or she had the money to support the effort. Relying on cable television to spread his message, Perot announced his candidacy on CNN's talk show *Larry King Live,* and then saturated the airwaves with TV ads blasting Republicans' economic policies. "The total national debt was only $1 trillion in 1980 when President Reagan took office. It is now $4 trillion," he noted. "Maybe it was 'voodoo economics.' Whatever it was, we now are in deep voodoo." That summer, as Bush tried to build up his economic credentials by supporting the North American Free Trade Agreement (NAFTA) between Canada, the United States, and Mexico, Perot worked tirelessly to discredit the idea. Perot appealed to populist strains in the electorate that increasingly believed corporate America—supported by the government—was moving its factories to low-wage parts of the world without any sense of remorse. If NAFTA were passed, he warned, the only thing it would create in America was a "giant sucking sound" as even more American jobs were swept across the border to cheaper Mexican markets.[41]

Though they went about it in kinder, gentler ways than the Bush campaign of 1988, the Clinton and Perot campaigns of 1992 combined to forge a common attack on President Bush. Just as important, Perot's emphasis on deficit reduction took votes away from Bush, while also giving Clinton more room to depict himself as a champion of fiscal conservatism despite the president's support for tax hikes. Negative campaigning had effectively come home to roost. In the end, the emphasis on the economy worked and Clinton won. He took 43 percent of the popular vote, to Bush's 38 percent and Perot's 19 percent. In the Electoral College, Clinton's margin was even wider, as he won 370 electoral votes to Bush's 168.[42]

In some ways, Bill Clinton's victory seemed to turn the page from the politics of the previous twelve years. He had managed to sidestep the fault lines of the culture wars and, at the same time, win a referendum on the economic merits of the Reagan Revolution. But as it turned out, both those debates were far from over.

CHAPTER 10

The Roaring 1990s

BILL CLINTON HAD PROMISED TO SWEEP AWAY THE Reagan Revolution, but once in office he quickly discovered—much as his predecessors had—that the opposition party had entrenched itself firmly in the halls of power. Unlike the postwar decades, when near-constant Democratic control of Congress meant that Democratic presidents routinely enjoyed the benefits of single-party government, the final decades of the twentieth century were ones in which divided government had become the norm. For much of Reagan's two terms, the Republican Party at least had control of the Senate, but once that chamber switched hands in 1986, the remainder of his term—and all of George H. W. Bush's—saw Democrats control both houses of Congress once more. Clinton's first two years in office would see a rare moment of return to single-party rule, but it ultimately did him little good. In 1994, both chambers would flip back to Republicans, placing him in the same position as his predecessors.

Meanwhile, as politics became ever more polarized, new fault lines opened in several sectors of American society. The American economy recovered from the recession at the decade's start and soared to new heights, but the benefits of the boom were not broadly shared. Indeed, stark levels of economic inequality and a growing sense of middle-class insecurity only continued to worsen over the course of the 1990s. Many of the jobs that Americans now held lacked union protections and thus provided neither substantial benefits nor long-term security. Low wage, temporary jobs were growing rapidly from 1 million to 3 million workers a day between 1990 and 2000.[1] Americans were working longer hours in the 1990s but earning lower real wages than they had in the 1970s.

For many struggling to survive in the middle class, holding two or three jobs was becoming more common. "The number of people working part-time but wanting full-time work," two economists concluded in their survey of the nation mid-decade, "or who are too discouraged to look for work, has grown. Millions more are holding at least two jobs to make ends meet, making do with lower wages in some self-employed venture, or stuck in a temporary job."[2]

Social conservatism, meanwhile, increased its hold on American politics. Among other milestones, the increasingly conservative Republican Congress secured legislation defending "traditional marriage" from homosexuality and impeached the president over his lies about an extramarital affair. But outside the political arena, trends in society continued to move the other way. Sexually graphic language and pornography became ever more common in popular culture, opening up a new divide between the complaints of the culture warriors and the broad base of American consumers and voters who saw no reason to complain.

The Incredible Shrinking President

When President Bill Clinton took office in January 1993, most Americans expected his administration to focus on economic reform above all else. His campaign, after all, had strongly emphasized economic populism. "For the last 12 years, government has served the rich and special interests," Clinton noted in his campaign book *Putting People First*. "Millions of middle-class Americans have paid more to government and gotten less in return." He promised to change the system to benefit ordinary Americans who "work hard and play by the rules." The populist message resonated with voters, as Clinton took in 43 percent of the popular vote and Ross Perot, who likewise campaigned on the "broken" economy of the Reagan-Bush era, pulled in another 19 percent. With 62 percent of the nation siding with vocal critics of Reaganomics, and a Democratic Congress waiting to work with him, the new president seemed to have a clear mandate for economic reform.[3]

Clinton welcomed the task, and seemed well suited to it. In his twelve years as governor of Arkansas, he had developed a reputation as a policy wonk, someone who knew intricate details on a wide range of domestic issues. He loved to talk about the specifics of policies, often at great length, and believed that government could be effectively changed to work more efficiently for ordinary Americans. Moving away from the traditionally liberal policies of his party, Clinton had worked throughout the 1980s to craft a more centrist agenda that would lead Democrats back to the White House. He had been a prominent figure in the Democratic Leadership Council (DLC), a group that elite Democrats founded in 1985 to push their party toward the center in the age of Reagan. Cagey as a politician—critics called him "Slick Willie"—Clinton understood how to play hardball and co-opt the message of his opponents. At the same time, he was a skilled retail politician with an ability to connect with ordinary voters. Perhaps most important, he began his term with large Democratic majorities in Congress. In the House, Democrats outnumbered Republicans 258 to 176; in the Senate, they led 57 to 43.[4]

Despite the seemingly favorable climate for economic reform, Clinton soon discovered that Washington would prove tougher to change than he had once hoped. The new president and his advisors, many of whom were old friends from Arkansas, seemed out of their depth on the national stage. Meanwhile, opponents stood on both sides. A cohort of conservative Republicans, whose ranks and influence in Congress had been steadily growing since the 1970s, were determined to prevent any serious rollback of the Reagan agenda. At the same time, some liberal Democrats, inside and outside of Congress, looked uneasily to the new president, seeing his DLC past as a sign that he would abandon the party's traditional principles. During the transition period, Clinton's nominees to key cabinet positions came under fire, and spokesmen hedged on major campaign promises. Even before the president-elect had been sworn in, many in the press were already starting to write him off. "End of a Bumpy Road," announced a *New York Times* headline days before the inauguration. "Clinton Aides Wondering, 'Where's Our Honeymoon?'"[5]

Seeming slow and indecisive, the new administration stumbled into a series of unforced errors. The first significant one came on the issue of gays in the military. Early in the presidential campaign, Clinton told a gay rights group that, if he were elected, he would work to overturn the ban against gays and lesbians in the armed forces. After that comment, it was largely a nonissue, resurfacing only after the election when a reporter checked in to see if Clinton intended to follow through with his promise. The president-elect said he would, but noted that he would do so slowly and after full consultation with the national security apparatus. Despite Clinton's timid approach to the issue, General Colin Powell, a Bush appointee still serving out the remainder of his term as chairman of the Joint Chiefs of Staff, publicly rebuked the new president. Meanwhile, conservative members of his own party turned on him. Senator Sam Nunn of Georgia, the powerful chairman of the Armed Services Committee, threatened to hold up all legislation in the Senate if Clinton made any effort to lift the ban.[6]

As a result of these threats, Clinton—who had hoped to get off to a quick start on economic issues—instead found himself almost immediately mired down in matters of the culture wars. Just nine days into his presidency, he announced a compromise commonly known as "don't ask, don't tell." In essence, it reaffirmed the decades-old policy that the armed forces would bar gays and lesbians from serving, with the minor cover that military officials would not actively investigate the sexual lives of servicemen and women to expose them. While the compromise settled the immediate controversy, it badly hurt the new president's standing with multiple constituencies. Gays and lesbians felt deeply betrayed, seeing this as confirmation that critics who warned them about Clinton's slickness were right; members of the military, meanwhile, worried for reasons of their own that the new commander-in-chief was not to be trusted. Most important, middle-class voters who were looking for action on economic issues seemed baffled that the president had become preoccupied with the particular needs of a "special interest."[7]

Partisanship would not subside, consuming almost everything in Washington. For all the chatter about the appeals of centrism to pundits and the public alike, the structures of Washington had increasingly entrenched partisanship in a variety of ways. For most participants in the political process, from interest groups to individual members of Congress, there were considerable incentives that pushed them deeper into partisan warfare. Media outlets were steadily more partisan, primary voters and party activists strongly drawn to the extremes, funding outlets attracted to the most strident voices, and congressional districts gerrymandered to present more ideologically inflexible electorates at the local level. Any president seeking a centrist path would have problems in this environment, but with Clinton there was the added handicap that many conservatives saw him as the embodiment of everything they hated about the revolutions of the 1960s: he was married to a working woman; he admitted to experimenting with drugs; and he seemed to them morally suspect.

From the start, Clinton's administration became embroiled in a series of small but still damaging scandals. During the campaign, the candidate had promised to select a cabinet that "looked like America." In particular, he was determined to appoint the nation's first female attorney general, but ran into repeated problems. His first nominee, Zoe Baird, an accomplished corporate lawyer, had to withdraw her name from consideration when it was revealed that she had employed an undocumented immigrant as a nanny and failed to pay Social Security taxes for her. Clinton's second nominee, Kimba Wood, was a federal judge who had been appointed by President Reagan. But it was soon revealed that she, too, had employed an undocumented immigrant as a nanny, although she had paid proper taxes. Wood withdrew her name as well. Though it was a fairly insignificant scandal, the media played up the drama of "Nannygate." The attention to it again hurt the administration's image with ordinary voters, who increasingly came to see Clinton's talk of valuing people who "played by the rules" as empty rhetoric. Talk radio programs and cable TV shows amplified the sense of betrayal. One caller to NPR host Diane Rehm spoke for many: "I thought Clinton was supposed to be different."[8]

The Clinton administration didn't find its attorney general until March 1993, with the confirmation of Janet Reno, a Florida prosecutor with a tough reputation (and, notably, no children and thus no nanny problems). Reno's term, however, got off to a rocky start of its own. A few weeks before her confirmation, David Koresh—the leader of a religious cult known as the Branch Davidians—led his followers in a gunfight with agents of the Bureau of Alcohol, Tobacco, and Firearms, a battle that ended with the deaths of four federal agents and two members of the cult. Koresh and his followers then barricaded themselves inside their compound outside Waco, Texas, as the FBI, now under Reno's command, surrounded them in an effective siege. On April 19, 1993, the FBI battered down the compound's walls and shot tear gas inside to force the Branch Davidians out. But Koresh ordered his followers to set the building on fire, resulting in the deaths of more than seventy members of the cult, including Koresh. The raid turned into a public relations nightmare for the new administration; for members of the far Right, Waco confirmed their worst fears about the intrusive power of the federal government.[9]

Taken together, the controversies around Clinton's Department of Justice—from overblown scandals like "Nannygate" to the more serious crisis in Waco—set the stage for a presidency that would be plagued by a variety of scandals. Shaped by the now-dominant cable news and the crowded landscape of its twenty-four-hour coverage, the media searched for gripping stories that would win the attention of viewers and readers. Newspapers and weekly news magazines, desperate to stay alive in an era of dwindling advertising revenue and subscriptions, believed that investigative journalism about corruption and wrongdoing at the highest levels would attract readers. Many reporters were also genuinely committed to the lessons of Vietnam and Watergate, especially the idea that the press had to hold those in power accountable. Scandals fit the bill perfectly on all fronts. Though they came in all shapes and sizes, the media seemed intent on sensationalizing the administration's missteps, often attaching the "-gate" suffix in an effort to make mountains out of molehills. In the spring of 1993, for instance, when Clinton tried to fire the staff of the White House travel office—employees with no civil service protection who could therefore be replaced at will—the press presented the story as "Travelgate." A few years later, when the White House director of personnel asked for and received files containing FBI background checks of applicants, the revelation was reported as another major scandal: "Filegate."[10]

Even when the administration focused on economics, it still floundered. House Democrats, in particular, believed Clinton made serious missteps in moving away from the party's traditions. One of his first major moves was to oversee the ratification of the North American Free Trade Act (NAFTA), the agreement with Mexico and Canada that President Bush had signed as a lame duck in December 1992. Many top Democrats, including House Majority Leader Dick Gephardt, vehemently opposed the trade agreement as a threat to American workers and the unionized workforce. But Clinton, who embraced many of the tenets of free-market economics, insisted on sticking with the agreement. He cobbled together a bipartisan coalition to pass the legislation that would implement the terms of the treaty in August 1993. With his own party's congressional leaders standing against NAFTA, Clinton had to rely on his erstwhile enemies. Indeed, more Republicans voted to ratify the bill than Democrats: the House passed NAFTA by a vote of 234–200, with 132 Republicans and 102 Democrats in favor; the Senate approved it by a vote of 61–38, with 34 Republicans and 27 Democrats in favor.[11] Though NAFTA represented a rare bipartisan victory for the president, it ultimately cost him the support of several important allies in Congress and other constituencies, while it gained him no new ones.

As the administration stumbled repeatedly during its first year, alienating Democratic supporters in Congress and the general public alike, it increasingly came to be seen as incompetent. The president's poll numbers, notably, plummeted at an incredible rate. In February 1993, Clinton's approval rating in the *New York Times*–CBS poll had been an impressive 64 percent. Three months later, at the end of May, it had fallen all the way down to 37 percent. This drastic collapse in public support led to another round of stories in the media pronouncing a premature end to his presidency. "The pundits have stuck a fork in this administration and decided it's very nearly done," the *Washington Post* reported in late May. Most famously, in June 1993, *Time* magazine ran a cover story calling Clinton "The Incredible Shrinking President." His administration was less than six months old, but many in the media were already pronouncing it dead on arrival.[12]

In the second half of 1993, President Clinton hoped to restore his image as a moderate by pushing for some economic and political reforms. First, he worked in the summer of 1993 to address the federal debt built up in the Reagan and Bush era. This had been an issue that third-party candidate Ross Perot made central in the 1992 campaign, and Clinton, burnishing his DLC credentials, wanted to demonstrate that Democrats could be the party of fiscal responsibility. Specifically, he fought to pass a budget package that would reduce the federal debt by $500 billion over the next five years. To make this happen, however, Clinton had to abandon his campaign promise to work for a middle-class tax cut and instead implement a tax hike on corporations and individuals at the higher end. Like his predecessor, he reluctantly braced himself for the political fallout of raising taxes. Specifically, his plan called for a slight 1 percent hike in the highest corporate tax rate and an increase in the marginal tax on incomes over $250,000 to 39.6 percent. These tax hikes were then coupled with modest spending cuts. For Republicans, the plan was a nonstarter. From the beginning of Reagan's term, the party had made opposition to any tax increase a core issue. Despite the steadily growing federal debt, they believed that raising taxes would be a massive mistake because it would, in their minds, stifle investment and provide revenue for even bigger government programs. The only way to curb deficits, they insisted, was to "starve the beast" of government. House Republicans were unanimous in their opposition to the budget plan, and convinced a number of conservative Democrats to join them. As a result, the margin of victory in the House was as narrow as it could have been—218 to 216. Likewise, in the Senate, Vice President Al Gore Jr. had to serve as the tiebreaker when the chamber deadlocked at 50–50.[13]

In the long run, the 1993 budget would prove to be one of Clinton's most important accomplishments. Over the next six years, federal expenditures steadily decreased as a percentage of the gross domestic product—falling from approximately 20.4 percent in 1993 to about 17.6 percent in 2000, the lowest percentage since the late 1960s. Over the same period, thanks to tax increases, government revenues steadily rose, from $1.15 trillion in 1993 to $1.72 trillion in 1998. In that year, the federal budget showed a surplus of $70 billion—the first federal budget surplus America had seen since 1969. Even higher surpluses followed for the remainder of Clinton's time in office, averaging $156 billion a year between 1999 and 2001.[14] For the first time since 1930, the federal government ran a surplus for four straight years. Economists calculated that if the string of surpluses continued, the United States would be able to pay off the entirety of its federal debt by the year 2010.[15] The long-term impacts of Clinton's budget package were not immediately clear at its passage, of course, and in the short term the plan was seen as a political loser. The program's tax increases on corporations and individuals in the top brackets allowed Republicans to portray Clinton as an out-of-touch liberal intent on growing government at the expense of the private sector. "It is a tax-and-spend bill, pure and simple," said Republican congressman Jim Bunning of Kentucky.

"It won't reduce the deficit, but it will injure the country and decimate the economy. It's a job killing bill from the word go."[16]

The image of Clinton as a "tax-and-spend liberal" was reinforced when he unveiled his health care plan a month later, in September 1993. The crisis in American health care had become abundantly clear. Private expenditures had more than tripled over the course of the Reagan and Bush years. At the same time, more than 35 million Americans had no insurance at all while another 20 million had only partial coverage. Health care reform had long been on the liberal agenda, but it had eluded accomplished presidents such as Harry Truman and Lyndon Johnson. Despite the long odds, Clinton was determined to make it work. "If I don't get health care done," he said at the time, "I'll wish I didn't run for president."[17]

Despite the daunting odds, however, Clinton approached health care reform in an unusual way. Rather than relying on official aides, congressional hearings, or government departments, he enlisted First Lady Hillary Rodham Clinton and Ira Magaziner, an old friend with a background in management consulting, to develop a plan. Their Health Care Task Force bypassed the stakeholders in official Washington and instead conducted meetings on its own with an array of academics and medical experts. In September 1993, they unveiled their proposal, a bulky 1,342 page plan that ignored liberal calls for a single-payer plan like the one used in Canada and instead advocated an employer-based plan of managed competition. Under the plan, employers would be required to pay for 80 percent of their employees' health benefits. Regional insurance-purchasing alliances would then promote "managed competition" among private insurers, thereby using market forces to lower premiums. The government would step in and provide coverage for the unemployed, thus effectively ensuring universal coverage.[18]

The plan immediately ran into serious opposition. Smaller insurance companies worried they would be squeezed out of the market by larger competitors, while small businesses were upset that they would have to bear the brunt of much of their workers' health care costs. They banded together and spent millions of dollars on TV ads to defeat the proposal. The most effective starred a middle-aged, middle-class white couple playing characters known as "Harry and Louise." One ad showed them at their kitchen table, sorting through a stack of forms as the narrator warned that "the government may force us to pick from a few health care plans designed by government bureaucrats." "They choose," Harry said; "we lose," Louise answered.[19]

As the ad campaign helped turn public opinion against the Clinton health care plan, Republicans seized the moment. Conservatives claimed that the plan, despite its reliance on private insurance companies and free-market competition, was actually "socialized medicine." This same battle cry had been used against Harry Truman when he proposed national health care in 1946 and 1949, and used again against Medicare until Congress passed the program in 1965. House Minority Whip Newt Gingrich claimed that the Clintons were "going against the entire tide of Western history. Centralized command bureaucracies are dying. This is the end of that era, not the beginning of it." The political assault was so effective that the health care proposal was never even brought up for a vote in the Democratic Congress. Instead, it was quietly allowed to die in August 1994.[20]

In the end, Clinton emerged from these fights—over gays in the military, the progressive tax increase, and health care reform—as little more than a caricature of outdated liberalism. During his run for the presidency, he'd managed to escape the fate of Michael Dukakis. But now that he was president, Clinton had essentially been painted into the same corner.

Republican Revolution

As congressional Democrats floundered and Clinton's stock fell in 1994, the timing was right for a challenge by the GOP, under Newt Gingrich's leadership. Gingrich's rise to power had begun a decade earlier. Determined to create a bold new vision for the conservative wing of the Republican Party, the young representative from Georgia had formed the "Conservative Opportunity Society" (COS). In the new group, Gingrich gathered together a new generation of congressmen who would fight to advance an aggressive style of conservative politics. COS members had three goals: (1) tear down the Democrats; (2) advance a bold new agenda for the Republicans; and then (3) take control of the Republican Party itself. As they liked to say, only two little things stood in their way: the Democrats and the Republicans.[21]

While policies were important, the COS revolutionaries initially focused their attention more on publicity. The group's origin coincided with the installation of live television coverage in the House of Representatives. In 1979, the Cable-Satellite Public Affairs Network, or "C-SPAN," began televising sessions from the House floor. Gingrich and his allies resolved to use the new media for their own ends. Each morning, they met to decide on a topic for the day and then made brief one-minute televised speeches attacking the Democrats on that theme. Each night, when the House chamber was virtually empty, they would return to take advantage of extended time set aside for "special orders." In the spring of 1984, Gingrich and others from COS took over the floor during one of these empty evening sessions to attack the Democrats for refusing to support the Nicaraguan Contras. Charging their opponents with appeasement, Gingrich said the Democrats had a "pessimistic, defeatist, and skeptical view toward the American role in the world." He then proceeded to denounce several specific Democratic congressmen of being "blind to Communism." Gingrich singled them out by name and dared them to respond. None of them could, of course, because the rest of the chamber was empty. But on television, where the C-SPAN cameras were fixed firmly on the speaker's spot, viewers simply saw Gingrich daring his targets to defend themselves, followed by an ominous silence. When Democrats realized what had happened, they were outraged. Speaker Tip O'Neill ordered the C-SPAN cameras to start panning around the chamber when Gingrich and his allies made their speeches from then on, to show that there was no one in the room listening to them. Gingrich, however, didn't care. He said at least one person was out there watching, and that was enough.[22]

In 1989, Gingrich made his newfound power clear when he ended the career of Democratic congressman Jim Wright, who had succeeded Tip O'Neill as Speaker two years before. With only a little evidence at first, Gingrich worked tirelessly to build an ethics case to destroy Wright. He sent a member of his staff to Texas to dig up whatever dirt he could find in the congressman's personal life, compiling a thick file of clippings from newspaper stories that raised questions about Wright's business dealings and then distributing it to anyone who would listen. And, to be sure, the media listened. Gingrich repeatedly called reporters and editorial writers across the country to press the story. "The number-one fact about the news media is that they love fights," he later noted. "When you give them confrontations, you get attention." And attention, he knew, would prompt action: "We worked on the assumption that if enough newspapers said there should be an investigation . . . [then] members would say it. It would happen."[23]

Prompted by Gingrich's crusade and complaints from the good government organization Common Cause, the House Ethics Committee soon opened a formal investigation of Wright. In April 1989, it issued a multicount indictment on charges that revolved around a suspect book deal, in which Wright received an unusually high percentage of royalties, and some gifts they believed he had improperly accepted from a lobbyist in his Fort Worth district. A month later, Wright announced his resignation from Congress. In an emotional farewell address, he called on his colleagues to put to an end the "mindless cannibalism" that was starting to consume the institution. Democrats were furious. "There's an evil wind blowing in the halls of Congress today that's reminiscent of the Spanish Inquisition," Representative Jack Brooks of Texas said. "We've replaced comity and compassion with hatred and malice." But Republicans were impressed. Gingrich had proven that he was more than an ideologue. He had shown that he could play politics, portraying the Democratic majority as a corrupt establishment in ways that echoed Watergate. The day after Wright's resignation, Gingrich received a standing ovation from his GOP colleagues on the House floor.[24]

Much as Gingrich used the new media of C-SPAN to attack House Democrats, other conservatives made use of "talk radio" to attack liberalism writ large. The format had grown rapidly in the postwar era: In 1960, there were only two all-talk radio stations in America; by 1995, there were 1,130. The growth of talk radio was fueled, in large part, by the demise of the fairness doctrine, which ended the old requirement for balanced presentation of political issues and instead allowed sharper, more partisan hosts to dominate the airwaves. Conservatives were especially drawn to the format, accounting for some 70 percent of all listeners by 1995. By then, the undisputed king of talk radio was Rush Limbaugh. Routinely proclaiming himself "America's most-listened-to talk show host," Limbaugh reached an audience of 20 million Americans on 659 radio stations, as well as through a syndicated television program on 225 stations and several best-selling books too. With constant attacks on "commie-libs," "feminazis," and "environmentalist wackos," Limbaugh quickly cultivated a loyal audience of self-styled "Dittoheads" who proudly took their political cues from him. "What Rush realizes, and what a lot of listeners don't," an Atlanta station manager enthused, "is that talk-radio programming is entertainment, it is not journalism."[25]

Despite his persona as an entertainer, Limbaugh's sway with conservative listeners quickly made him a powerful force on the political right. During the 1992 presidential campaign, President George H. W. Bush courted him in hopes of winning over his right-wing listeners. In June, the president had Limbaugh to the White House for an overnight stay in the Lincoln Bedroom. In a telling detail—one that Limbaugh repeatedly stressed when retelling the story of his visit—Bush insisted on carrying Limbaugh's bag into the White House. The host's previously lukewarm coverage of the administration turned more enthusiastic. In September, Republicans convinced Limbaugh to break his "no-guests" rule for the show with interviews with President Bush and Vice President Quayle. Though the GOP lost the White House, Limbaugh saw a silver lining in Clinton's election. "I think it's a boon for me," he said, noting that a Democratic administration would give him even greater targets. "I think Rush Limbaugh represents the views of millions of Americans," noted Bush's media advisor Roger Ailes, "and it would be stupid of the Clinton administration to ignore that." Even Ronald Reagan anointed Limbaugh as his effective heir, telling him in a letter that he was now "the Number One voice for conservatism in our Country."[26]

Indeed, Rush Limbaugh quickly emerged as a chief critic of the Clinton White House. With daily coverage of the administration titled "America's Hostage Crisis"—in which he claimed the whole country had been taken hostage—he denounced Democratic policies as "the Raw Deal." Limbaugh's constant criticism of Clinton had a personal, often vicious, edge to it. Once, he joked about the "White House dog" on his syndicated television show and held up a picture of the president's 13-year-old daughter, Chelsea. But such brutal attacks on the Clintons only increased Limbaugh's appeal. In September 1993, *National Review* ran a cover story on him, titled "Leader of the Opposition." The conservative magazine speculated that Limbaugh might emerge as a Republican presidential candidate, but he remained content to work on behalf of others. Gingrich became a staunch ally, feeding Limbaugh information by fax that the radio host then spread to listeners on the air. The 1994 midterms, Limbaugh asserted, would be nothing less than "Operation Restore Democracy."[27]

To the delight of Limbaugh and his listeners, the Republicans found their way back to control of the House that year. Newt Gingrich brought together all the tools and arguments that he had been making since the early 1980s in a powerful attack on congressional Democrats and Clinton. In public, Gingrich rallied Republican candidates around what he called the Contract with America. The slick ten-point program called for, among other things, a balanced budget amendment, a line-item veto for the president, welfare rollbacks, more money for defense, term limits, stringent measures for crime control, and a 50 percent reduction in the capital gains tax. In an important touch, the more contentious social issues from the culture wars, like school prayer and abortion, were left out of the contract to avoid controversy. In private, however, Gingrich advised Republican candidates to focus not on these positive policies but on negative attacks against their opponents. Circulating a Frank Luntz memo titled "Language: A Key Mechanism of Control," he advised Republicans to use a focus-group-tested list of negative words to describe their Democratic opponents. They should call them "sick" and "destructive," say that they "lie" and "threaten" America, claim they were engaged in "greed" and "hypocrisy," and even directly call them "traitors." The sharp attacks were tailor-made for the Limbaugh era and resonated well with voters.[28]

In the end, the Republicans won a huge victory that year. They picked up eight seats in the Senate and fifty-four in the House, giving the party control of both houses of Congress with solid majorities. As the incoming Speaker of the House, Gingrich noted frankly that the conservative counterrevolution had depended on blurring lines between partisan politics and the new media. "Without C-SPAN, without talk radio shows, without all the alternative media, I don't think we would have won," he reflected. "The classic elite media would have distorted our message." A month after the election, Gingrich welcomed Limbaugh to a gathering of the incoming class of Republican freshmen hosted by the Heritage Foundation. The talk radio host, he noted, would be considered an "honorary member" of the House Republicans. "Rush is responsible for what happened here as much as any-one," enthused Vin Weber, a former congressman who then worked at a conservative think tank. A poll conducted by Frank Luntz, he noted, showed that people who listened to talk radio for more than ten hours a week had voted Republican by a margin of 3 to 1. "Those are the people who elected the new Congress."[29]

Flush with victory, Speaker Gingrich told reporters that Clinton would be "very, very dumb" to oppose the conservative agenda. Incoming Senate Majority Leader Bob Dole of Kansas would soon "control every [executive] appointment," he noted, while the GOP House would control appropriations. Still combative, Gingrich sarcastically informed reporters that he would no longer call President Clinton an enemy of "normal" Americans; instead he would denounce him as an enemy of "middle-class Americans." "I was once told to my shock that the use of the word normal is politically incorrect—a sign of how far the culture has eroded."[30]

Triangulation

For his part, President Clinton seemed deeply shaken by the 1994 elections. Even though he was not on the ballot, the midterms had seemed to all sides a referendum on his administration, one with decidedly negative results. "Exit polls showed that one third of all voters acted as they did because they disapproved of the President," the *New York Times* noted. "The polls were not specific, but something about Mr. Clinton . . . has clearly nettled many voters to the point of distraction." Searching for a way to remain "relevant" in American politics, the president turned to political consultant Dick Morris, who urged Clinton to follow a policy he called "triangulation." He told Clinton to establish a position for himself that would be distinct from both the liberals of his own party and the conservative Republicans in Congress. Throughout 1995 and 1996, Clinton did precisely this. In essence, he made strong efforts to steal the Republicans' thunder in two key places—on the conservative social issues of the culture wars, and on the continued push for the Reagan Revolution's crusade against the Great Society.[31]

To address the conservative complaints on social issues, Clinton initiated some moderate measures of his own but, just as significantly, acquiesced to conservatives' own efforts. Little more than a month after the midterms, he proposed a "middle-class bill of rights" which included some small if symbolic stances on moderate social issues. In a nod to conservatives' concerns over the lack of structure and discipline in the public schools, the president endorsed mandatory public school uniforms; in a nod to worries about violence and vulgarity in the media, he pushed for the passage of the Communications Decency Act.[32] He supported the use of V-Chips that allowed parents to monitor the content of their television to prevent kids from watching dangerous shows. Once installed on a family's television, the chip, which only cost $5, would block shows rated as violent or sexual. The technology, similar to that used for closed captioning, relied on broadcasters' transmitting rating codes explaining the content of each program.[33] Clinton embraced the innovation to support families who wanted protection from "too much indiscriminate violence, too much indiscriminate sex, and too much . . . callous degradation of women and sometimes of other people in various parts of our media today."[34]

Though Clinton advanced such measures on his own, the bulk of his support for conservative social issues came in his acquiescence to acts of Congress. The most significant change of the decade came on the contested issue of same-sex marriage. In 1996, social conservatives pushed through a landmark piece of legislation. In keeping with their view that same-sex marriage was an assault on marriage itself, they christened the law the Defense of Marriage Act (DOMA). Congressman Bob Barr of Georgia, the chief sponsor of DOMA, declared on the floor of Congress that same-sex marriage threatened straight marriage and, therefore, all of society. As he put it, "the flames of hedonism, the flames of narcissism, the flames of self-centered morality are licking at the very foundations of our society, the family unit." At heart, DOMA did two things. First, it allowed states the right not to recognize same-sex marriages from other states. Second, it established a legal definition of marriage as purely heterosexual, as a "union between one man and one woman." In a sign of how politically toxic the issue of same-sex marriage was at the time, DOMA passed quickly and by overwhelming numbers. It won in the House by a margin of 342 to 67, and in the

Senate by a margin of 85 to 14. President Clinton signed it into law in a midnight ceremony meant to minimize media attention.[35]

At the same time, Clinton made significant moves to reinvent himself as a Reagan-like opponent of Great Society programs. Like Reagan, Clinton did this both in rhetoric and reality. Most famously, in his State of the Union Address in January 1996, Clinton insisted—twice, for good measure—that "the era of big government is over." In terms of actual policy, meanwhile, he pressed two initiatives. First, he took on affirmative action. In a July 1995 speech, Clinton announced that he wanted to "reaffirm the principle of affirmative action and fix the practices. We should have a simple slogan: Mend it, but don't end it." Practically speaking, he issued an executive order to all federal departments, requiring them to make sure no quotas were in place, and that no "reverse discrimination" was occurring on their watch. Moreover, Clinton took on welfare itself. In the 1992 campaign, he'd promised to "end welfare as we know it." He dragged his feet, but Republicans revived the issue and forced his hand. The end result was another piece of legislation with a telling name, the Personal Responsibility and Work Opportunity Reconciliation Act of 1996, which essentially finished the attack that Reagan had made on Aid to Families with Dependent Children (AFDC) programs. The new law forced families off the welfare rolls by cutting off their benefits after two years, limiting their lifetime benefits to five years, and allowing people without children to receive food stamps for just three months in any three-year period.[36]

In an important detail, the 1996 welfare reform stripped benefits away from legal immigrants, a dramatic curtailment of rights. The provision reflected the ways in which hard-line opposition to immigration had been taking hold in the Republican Party over the previous decade. In 1994, Barbara Coe founded the California Coalition for Immigration Reform in her coastal community of Huntington Beach. A cantankerous nativist who called undocumented aliens "savages," Coe credited her political awakening to a revelation she had had in 1991, when she walked into a social services center in Orange County. She saw "this monstrous room full of people, babies, and little children all over the place, and I realized nobody was speaking English. I was overwhelmed with this feeling: 'Where am I? What's happened here?'" Under Coe's direction, her coalition worked to drum up resentment to "illegal immigrants" and resistance to their growing presence in California. At times, the work was low-level, as when she and allies dropped "only citizens can vote" flyers at polling places, largely to spite Latino citizens. More significantly, Coe led the drive for Proposition 187, a state ballot proposal in 1994 to prohibit undocumented immigrants from obtaining any basic social services.[37]

Governor Pete Wilson, running for reelection that year, made Proposition 187 the centerpiece of his campaign. As a California Republican, Wilson had been tagged as a potential presidential contender, one who could follow the path from the West Coast to Washington set by Richard Nixon and Ronald Reagan. But Wilson's fortunes had taken a tumble with the economic downturn early in the decade, a development that forced him to cut government services drastically and raise taxes as well. The immigration issue provided him a chance to change the subject. Noting that there was "a real sense of rage" over immigration in California, the governor did his best to exploit the panic. His campaign produced slick TV ads with an ominous warning: "They keep coming." Nationally, other Republicans recoiled from Wilson's crude campaign, with former Bush administration officials Jack Kemp and William Bennett explicitly denouncing it. Wilson brushed off their criticism. "Those are two guys who have been in Washington too long," he said. "They ought to come out to California and look at the real world." That fall, Wilson rode the issue to reelection, taking 55 percent of the vote to his opponent's 40 percent.[38]

While Republicans set the pace for national politics on immigration, welfare reform, and same-sex marriage, President Clinton seized the initiative on a seemingly unlikely topic: terrorism. On April 19, 1995, a truck bomb destroyed the Alfred Murrah Federal Building in Oklahoma City, killing 168 people and injuring 600 more. Although reporters first speculated that the deadly attack had been the result of Islamic terrorists, law enforcement agents quickly showed that it was the work of Timothy McVeigh and Terry Nichols, two men associated with white nationalist groups. The bombing drove home the fact that the mid-1990s had witnessed a sharp spike in white hate groups and radical antigovernment militias. Though not representative of the mainstream movement of conservatives, these self-styled "patriot" organizations tapped into the growing anger of whites on the right over taxation, immigration, and federal regulation of western lands. Committed to gun rights, these militias loaded up on high-powered weapons and trained in military fashion for an eventual showdown with the federal government.[39]

The Oklahoma City bombing forced the country to consider the impact of terrorists, both foreign and domestic. The president criticized extremists on the right who had filled the airwaves with hateful rhetoric for breeding a dangerous environment. "It is one thing to believe that the Federal Government has too much power and to work within the law to reduce it," he said in a May 1995 commencement address at Michigan State. "It is quite another to break the law of the land and threaten to shoot officers of the law if all they do is their duty to uphold it." Taking aim at the militia movement, the president dismissed their invocations of patriotism. "There is nothing patriotic about hating your country, or pretending that you can love your country but hate your government," he said.[40]

Beyond such rhetoric about the far Right, the bombings also sparked significant action. Clinton pushed for a broad antiterrorism bill that would vastly increase the power of the federal government, authorizing "roving" wiretaps that would follow a suspect and no longer require individual warrants for each new phone used. The legislation, known as the Antiterrorism and Effective Death Penalty Act of 1996, also prohibited certain kinds of firearms and gave the military the power to help combat the spread of some chemicals. House Republicans opposed the bill for granting too much power to government, and as a result, the legislation stalled until Gingrich brokered an agreement. The final legislation, signed into law in April 1996, one year after the Oklahoma City attacks, made terrorism a federal crime, empowered the government to crack down on fund-raising by groups associated with terrorists, and increased money for various agencies. It also allowed individuals who entered the country illegally to be deported without judicial review. The struggle over terrorism ultimately worked to Clinton's political benefit. As one reporter noted: "Clinton has neutralized Republican efforts to paint him as a woolly liberal with his emphatic vow to crack down on terrorism with expanded F.B.I. surveillance powers, which have raised the hackles of civil liberties groups."[41]

In the end, Clinton's efforts to "triangulate" the Republicans were successful. He shrewdly positioned himself in opposition to the

Republicans in Congress, who were increasingly being seen as extremists. In the 1996 presidential campaign, he faced off against Republican senator Bob Dole, an older member of Congress who had served as Ford's running mate back in the 1976 election. Dole now seemed out of step with his own party, as well as the general electorate. He struggled to survive the image of his party as one that was unable and uninterested in governance, an image that became especially pronounced after the GOP allowed the federal government to shut down not once, but twice. The Republican platform didn't help either. It was, as Garry Wills observed, "an executioner's platform for gays, abortionists and flag burners" drafted by the Pat Buchanan wing of the party. In the end, Clinton took in 46 percent of the vote, to Bob Dole's 41 percent and Ross Perot's 9 percent, becoming the first Democrat to win two terms since Franklin D. Roosevelt. With the president reelected and the ranks of House Republicans reduced, it was Newt Gingrich's turn to promise that he would work to find "common ground" with the president.[42]

Bill Clinton's triangulation had proved successful in the short term, saving his embattled presidency and securing his own reelection. It even created some political opportunities to move forward with domestic issues that had eluded him in the first term, such as the creation in 1997 of the Children's Health Insurance Program, which offered states matching funds to provide health insurance to children. The program wasn't national health insurance, but it did constitute a historic expansion of coverage. Clinton's move to the center on several issues—most notably NAFTA, welfare reform, and the crime bill—had helped the Democrats find their way back to the White House after three failed campaigns, but at the price of abandoning much of the progressive policy agenda that had long served as a core rationale for the party and a chief reason for much of its support. Increasingly, as the Democrats moved to the center, leftists and even liberals began to feel their connections to the party's coalition loosening. Meanwhile, conservatives looked for new ways to distinguish the Republican Party from the new neoliberal orthodoxy by pushing even further to the right.

CHAPTER 11

Scandalized

DESPITE PROMISES TO FIND "COMMON GROUND," REPUB-
licans responded to Bill Clinton's reelection by redoubling their efforts
to bring his administration to an end. Doggedly pursuing every possible
allegation of wrongdoing, they were aided once more by an increasingly
partisan media.

With the advent of Fox News, conservatives found a channel for their
political views on cable television, completing a long quest to overcome
the perceived biases of the "mainstream media" through new channels
of their own. What had begun in the direct-mail innovations of the
1970s and 1980s, and then accelerated with the rise of conservative talk
radio in the early 1990s, now reached its peak with a twenty-four-hour
news network that would promote conservative interests to audiences
across America and increasingly pressure the Republican Party to follow its lead. Meanwhile, new websites like the Drudge Report radically
reshaped the national conversation, serving not just as another voice for
conservative ideas but also, through its growing influence on journalists
at more traditional outlets, a way to push the conservative agenda across
the entire media.

Still, the conservatism in such news media coexisted uneasily with
an increasingly liberalized popular culture around it. As the radio star-
dom of risqué "shock jock" Howard Stern showed, the social conservatism advanced on channels like Fox News was in many ways out of step
with the relaxed attitudes to sexuality, obscenity, and lowbrow humor
on the rise in popular culture. The result was a nation that seemed
increasingly at odds with itself.

The Path to Impeachment

Roughly a month before the 1996 presidential election, the Fox News Channel made its debut. The brainchild of Australian-born billionaire Rupert Murdoch, Fox News represented the culmination of conservatives' decades-old dream to take control of a news network. "So long as there were just a handful of major networks, both cost and institutional inertia forestalled an ideological takeover," historian Nicole Hemmer noted. "It simply required too much money to buy out shareholders at NBC or CBS, who at any rate were not interested in selling." But the advent of cable news had broken the effective monopoly of the networks, with CNN pointing the way to a new path forward for media-minded conservatives. Murdoch had originally tried to buy Turner's network; when he refused to sell, Murdoch resolved to exact revenge by creating a rival of his own.[1]

Starting from scratch, the Fox News Channel followed the lead of the Fox Broadcasting Company, a fourth television network that had emerged in the mid-1980s to challenge ABC, NBC, and CBS. The new network had distinguished itself from the "big three" with edgier programs like the animated hit *The Simpsons* and the often-vulgar sitcom *Married . . . With Children*. Likewise, Fox News sought to stand as a stark alternative to the existing cable news networks, but it faced a daunting challenge. Initially, the new cable channel was only available to 17 million households nationwide (and completely blocked out of major markets like New York City, thanks to a conflict with Time Warner Cable). In contrast, CNN was available to 66 million households, and the four-month-old MSNBC, a joint venture of NBC and Microsoft, was accessible to 25 million.[2]

While Murdoch provided the money for Fox News, his handpicked chairman Roger Ailes set the tone. A longtime Republican media consultant, Ailes made his fame during the Nixon years when he succeeded in remaking the dour politician and pitching him to a new generation. The media consultant frankly assessed the chasm between his client and the climate of the decade. "You put him on television, you've got a problem right away," Ailes told the *Washington Post* in 1969. "He's a funny-looking guy. He looks like somebody hung him in a closet overnight, and he jumps out in the morning with his suit all bunched up and starts running around saying, 'I want to be President.' I mean this is how he strikes some people." To fix the problem, Ailes worked hard to repackage Nixon, using new makeup and camera angles to polish his image and new slogans and catchphrases to sell his candidacy. At the same time he built up his client, Ailes worked to tear down the competition, famously reducing the 1972 Democratic nominee George McGovern to an imagined liberal platform of "abortion, amnesty and acid." Famous from his successful image makeover of Nixon, Ailes went on to become a reliable tool of Republican candidates, working on races like George H. W. Bush's negative campaign in 1988.[3]

Despite his partisan background, Ailes insisted that Fox News would be, as its motto stated, "fair and balanced." Indeed, he promised, it would serve as a corrective to the pervasive "liberal bias" that he said dominated CNN and the networks by providing the only unbiased option. All reporting would be objective, Ailes insisted, and any opinion or analysis would be clearly labeled as such.[4] Initially, though, Fox News was little more than a pale imitation of CNN. Its early staples seemed to be echoes of standard shows seen elsewhere: *The O'Reilly Report*, with host Bill O'Reilly, former anchor of the syndicated tabloid show *Inside Edition*, now discussing a range of issues; *The Crier Report*, with Catherine Crier, in a talk format that meant to echo *Larry King Live*; and *Hannity and Colmes*, an imitation of CNN's *Crossfire* debate program that featured, in the words of one reviewer, "Sean Hannity as the conservative and Alan Colmes as his liberal sidekick." The rest of the network likewise seemed to echo existing news formats, but with one minor innovation: on-screen graphics. "The Ken-and-Barbie anchor teams do a credible job of cruising through the headlines, but there's no more depth than you'd see on your typical Action News," media critic Howard Kurtz noted. "Brief snippets and factoids keep popping up onto the screen ('Dole is a member of the Shriners and the Elks') while they are talking, which can be EXTREMELY ANNOYING when you're trying to listen."[5]

Fox News soon began to distinguish itself from the competition with its conservative slant, which became pronounced during its close attention to the scandals unfolding in the Clinton administration. When the US Senate held hearings on presidential fund-raisers in July 1997, for instance, Fox News was the only channel to broadcast them live.[6] Though Clinton's scandals proved to be a ratings draw, the highest-profile ones—a sexual harassment lawsuit from a former Arkansas state employee, Paula Jones, and the Whitewater land deal investigation—both turned out to be dead ends. A US District Court dismissed the Jones lawsuit as a nuisance case, while Independent Counsel Kenneth Starr concluded, after spending four years and nearly $40 million investigating the Clintons' real estate dealings, that he could find no evidence of their wrongdoing in Whitewater. But, importantly, both of those lines of inquiry gave Clinton's enemies the authority and ability to look into every aspect of the president's life, keeping the lines of investigation active for years. Now searching for evidence of any criminal activity, Starr eventually zeroed in on an affair the president had had with a young White House intern named Monica Lewinsky.

The president's affair had been improbably exposed by the Drudge Report, a threadbare gossip website launched in 1997. Matt Drudge, a 30-year-old whose previous job had been managing a CBS gift shop in the Studio City neighborhood of Los Angeles, began the Drudge Report out of his apartment. Originally, he sent off email newsletters that were simply a collection of links to other websites' stories of Hollywood rumors. A conservative and self-described "Clinton crazy," he soon began promoting political gossip as well. "I go where the stink is," he noted. In January 1998, he learned that *Newsweek* had held back on a story about the president's affair with a young intern, due to fears about fact checking. Drudge didn't feel bound by the traditional rules of journalism, however, and gladly broke the story on his site. The news quickly spread across the internet, and then fully entered the mainstream media's discussion when Bill Kristol, editor of the conservative *Weekly Standard*, mentioned it on ABC's Sunday news show *This Week*.[7]

Now focused on the growing rumors about the affair, Independent Counsel Starr soon uncovered that the president had lied about it, while under oath, in a grand jury deposition that was ostensibly about the Paula Jones case. Videotape of the president's testimony proved to be a sensation for network and cable news outlets alike, as more than 22.5 million people tuned in to watch when it was broadcast in September 1998. For Fox News, the experience was a revelation, as the channel experienced its best-ever ratings.[8] Indeed, the Lewinsky scandal proved vitally important for all the cable news networks, providing a short-term ratings boom and, more significantly, helping to shape newer stations like MSNBC and Fox News that were still in their formative stages. As they launched new programs and hired new talent, they did so with the president's scandal in mind. In the words of John Gibson, an early MSNBC host who would soon join Fox News, "it has helped shape the definition of a big story in the absence of cold war." The scandal proved a popular topic across the cable news networks, with frequent live coverage of breaking news. When House Republicans used the perjury charge to pass articles of impeachment against the president in late December 1998, Fox News once again set a new record for viewers.[9]

While polarization on the right helped fuel the campaign for Bill Clinton's impeachment, similar forces on the left caused that drive to stall. Liberals, who had readily believed the charges Anita Hill leveled against Republican Clarence Thomas earlier in the decade, now dismissed similar accusations against a president of their own party. Because many of the charges, about Lewinsky and other women, too, had originated in right-wing media outlets, many liberals interpreted them as another round of baseless smears in a polarized environment. Even prominent feminists, who had rallied around Hill's accusations to highlight the pernicious problems of sexual harassment, sided with the accused this time around. The president's "enemies are attempting to bring him down through allegations about some dalliance with an intern," Betty Friedan noted. "Whether it's a fantasy, a set-up or true, I simply don't care." "If anything," argued Susan Faludi, author of *Backlash: The Undeclared War on American Women* (1991), "it sounds like she put the moves on *him*." And so, just as reflexively as conservatives and Republicans rallied around the campaign to remove the president from office, so too did liberals and Democrats commit themselves to his defense. Ironically, the very polarization that prompted the endless scandals of the 1990s would, in many ways, prevent them from finding resolution.[10]

The Real World

Despite the Republican zeal for impeachment, the party proved to be badly out of step with the public. Cable networks won increased ratings, but in the grand scheme of things, a scandal that revolved around the private sexual relationships of a president didn't resonate with many Americans. If the country had shifted to the right on many domestic political issues, the liberalized cultural trends of the 1960s seemed to have won out by the 1990s.

One of the most popular radio talk shows of the decade was the syndicated program of Howard Stern. Originally the host of a late-night program on WNBC in New York, Stern featured frank talk about sex, drugs, and everything else that the Moral Majority railed against. "The idea of the show is to convey real honesty on the air," Stern explained in a 1991 interview, "to get away from the phony type of broadcasting where they bite their tongue and are afraid to say anything."[11] By 1992, Stern's program had spread across the country, becoming the number-one morning radio show in three major cities—New York, Los Angeles, and Philadelphia.[12] As Stern's empire grew, the Federal Communications Commission tried to rein him in, levying fines of over $100,000 in some instances.[13] But the owner of the company that syndicated Stern's show, Infinity's Mel Karmazin, was happy to pay the fines since Stern generated so much in profits. With 15 million daily listeners in sixteen major cities, the shock jock brought in an estimated $20 million per year to the company. By 1995, his program was the number-one morning show in most top markets and a hit with men eighteen to thirty-four.[14]

The success of the outrageous radio host reflected broader trends sweeping across American culture, as sex and violence became ever more prominent in video games, movies, and television. A study from the University of California at Los Angeles reported that "sinister combat violence" could be found in most Saturday morning cartoons, while 42 percent of the movies broadcast on network television were inappropriately violent.[15] According to another survey, two-thirds of prime-time programs featured sexual material, while daytime shows like *The Jerry Springer Show*, launched in 1991, offered discussions of once-taboo topics like bestiality and incest.[16] The erotic thriller *Basic Instinct* became a blockbuster success at the box office in 1992, ultimately earning $350 million and inspiring a stream of other sexually explicit films like *Consenting Adults, Disclosure, Showgirls,* and *Striptease.*[17] Meanwhile, MTV quickly found that the most lurid music videos in its rotation were in the highest demand.

The network also started to introduce original programming, starting with *The Real World*, a new style of "reality programming" that debuted in 1992. Copying the 1970s PBS documentary series *An American Family*, which had chronicled the dysfunction and eventual divorce of a seemingly wholesome white suburban family, MTV's show placed a diverse set of young Americans in an apartment for a few months, all wired for video and sound. Despite its generally lighthearted style, the show occasionally tackled serious subjects. The third season, for instance, featured Pedro Zamora, a 22-year-old Cuban immigrant who had come to the country as part of the 1980 Mariel boatlift, and who was now suffering from AIDS. Zamora had long been an activist and hoped his role on the show might publicize the AIDS crisis and humanize its often-ostracized victims. As he had hoped, the show raised awareness for many younger Americans, who took lessons about safe sex into their own lives. "It's his story and everybody else's that make you think. I know I wouldn't do it without a condom," said one 15-year-old.[18] When Zamora died in November 1994, President Clinton noted that the show had changed the face of HIV and AIDS in America forever."[19]

While the real-life struggles of Pedro Zamora did much to dramatize and humanize the plight of HIV/AIDS victims, fictional television programs increasingly showcased gay and lesbian characters in a more sympathetic light and in more central roles as well. In 1997, comedian Ellen DeGeneres, star of the popular ABC sitcom *Ellen* (1994–1998), came out publicly as a lesbian—first in real life, and then again as the character on her show. The decision generated a great deal of publicity and positive press for the show, with a cover story in *Time* magazine titled "Yep, I'm Gay." But it also sparked a significant backlash from the Religious Right. Jerry Falwell mocked the star as "Ellen Degenerate," while the Family Research Council urged conservative Christians to boycott the show's advertisers. ABC began running "adult content" warnings before the program and then canceled the show altogether at the end of the season. That same year, NBC launched *Will & Grace* (1998–2006), another show with a gay lead character—though, in this case, one played by a straight actor, and with his sexuality downplayed considerably. "Network executives reportedly got queasy and now Will seems not so much gay as neutered," one critic noted of its debut. "He's not only a eunuch, he's a lawyer, and a corporate lawyer at that; how much more sexless can anyone get?" Though initially cautious, the show demonstrated that gay and lesbian themes could find a footing even on network television, in the midst of a concerted conservative backlash.[20]

Meanwhile, on cable channels, even franker discussions of sex and sexuality were becoming commonplace. The HBO show *Sex and the City* (1998–2004), for instance, centered on the relationship struggles of four single women in their mid-30s and 40s. Framed through the perspectives of its lead character Carrie Bradshaw, a New York City newspaper sex columnist, the program advanced a cynical view of modern romance. "Welcome to the age of uninnocence," she noted in one voiceover. "No one has breakfast at Tiffany's and no one has affairs to remember. Instead we have breakfast at 7 a.m. and affairs we try to forget as soon as possible." The program's perspective quickly made it the top-rated comedy on cable television and a national phenomenon. "Sex and the City" tours started up in New York. Across the country, groups of women gathered for viewing parties, taken in by the show's frank discussions of sex and its focus on the woman's perspective. "I love that on the show they talk about men the way that men talk about women," noted a fan in Atlanta. "It turns the tables, and I try to think of how I can do that in my own life."[21]

Frank discussions of sex and sexuality shaped even apparently staid subjects like the computer boom. As had happened with the advent of videocassette recorders, new advances in computing were regularly wedded to the porn industry. One of the best-selling computer discs in 1986, for instance, was *Virtual Valerie*, a game that revolved around simulated sex. Even early advances on the internet were fueled by pornography, which introduced cutting-edge mechanisms like streaming video and popularized new browsers for the World Wide Web such as Mosaic and Netscape Navigator. The growth of the internet facilitated the spread of personal computers from three hundred in 1981 to a million by 1993 and then about 37 million by 1996 and 83 million by 1998.[22] Sex, once again, was often an important part of this process. Internet porn sites were receiving about 50 million hits per month by 1999, generating over $1 billion in revenue per year.[23] There were efforts to regulate the industry, particularly in response to news of child pornography rings. But regulating this new technology became extraordinarily difficult because in the internet age, access came from anywhere in the world.

Set against this increasingly permissive climate, Republican attacks on Clinton for his sexual infidelity simply failed to resonate. Polls showed that 63 percent of Americans disapproved of the campaign to impeach the president, a dissatisfaction that made itself felt in the 1998 midterm elections. Defying the norm in which the opposition party would typically gain seats in the midterms, the GOP actually lost ground in the House. The results were so shocking that they sparked an internal rebellion resulting in Newt Gingrich's resignation as Speaker. (Gingrich's standing had already been weakened by the revelation that he too was having an extramarital affair.) Despite the warning sign from voters, House Republicans remained committed to the impeachment cause. But voters recoiled again. In the week after the full House voted to impeach the president on December 19, 1998, Clinton's favorability leapt ten points in the Gallup Poll, to his all-time high of 73 percent approval. Meanwhile, the Republican Party's approval rating sank to 31 percent. Reading the public's mood better than their colleagues in the House, Republicans in the Senate soft-pedaled the impeachment trial, leading to Clinton's acquittal in February 1999.[24]

Boom and Bust

In many ways, the impeachment campaign failed because it simply couldn't compete with a bigger story: the booming economy of the late 1990s. Even though Americans had been titillated by the sordid details of the Lewinsky affair and transfixed by the political fallout, their general happiness with the status quo led them to resist Republican calls for the president's removal. In January 1999, when the Senate deliberated the matter, Gallup found that 70 percent of all Americans reported being satisfied "with the way things are going in the United States"—a dramatic improvement on the 14 percent that had said so in June 1992. That satisfaction with the status quo largely reflected their satisfaction with the economy. In January 1999, 69 percent of Americans rated the economy as either "excellent" or "good"; in June 1992, only 12 percent had.[25]

The unbridled optimism of the moment was captured in a game show that became a phenomenon: *Who Wants to Be A Millionaire?* An import from England, the show essentially replicated the format of a 1950s hit, *The $64,000 Question*, though this time the expectations were much higher and the potential payoff, of course, much grander. A top ratings draw in 1999 and 2000, the show soon became the cornerstone of ABC's programming. Indeed, the network was so excited about the ratings bonanza that it put the show on several nights a week, breaking the tradition of reserving one slot for hit shows such as this. At its peak, up to 30 million people tuned in each night.

The show's popularity spoke to a nation reveling in an economic recovery. The Dow Jones Industrial Average more than tripled between 1993 and 2000, booming from roughly 3,600 to 11,000. As impressive as those gains were, they were nothing compared to what was taking place on the NASDAQ, an exchange that focused more directly on the tech companies that drove the decade's growth. In January 1993, the NASDAQ stood at about 670; in January 2000, it stood at about 4,100—an amazing sixfold increase. Everyone seemed, on the surface at least, to be doing well. The percentages of Americans who were poor or unemployed had reached new lows by the end of the 1990s. By April 2000, the unemployment rate in America had been reduced to just 3.8 percent, the lowest rate in more than thirty years. In his State of the Union address that year, Clinton reflected the euphoria that most Americans had about the economy. "Never before," the president proclaimed, "has our nation enjoyed, at once, so much prosperity and social progress with so little internal crisis and so few external threats."[26]

Silicon Valley, the San Francisco Bay area home to the high-tech boom, quickly became the symbol of the late-1990s economy. As private capital poured funds into the surging computer industry, young professionals made huge amounts of money at rapid speed, becoming multimillionaires and, moreover, symbols of a resurgent America. Steve Kirsch exemplified the trend. As the CEO of Frame Technology, he made $30 million before selling his firm, at just 38 years of age, for $500 million more. He soon started another company called Infoseek, one of seven businesses he would found in rapid succession. Another young "serial entrepreneur," Kurt Brown, described the process as "like a roller coaster. The first time through you get sick and say, 'What am I doing?' Then you get off, a little woozy, and you need some time to let your lunch settle. But then you just want to get back on the roller coaster again—a bigger one."[27] Similar stories came out of Silicon Valley. In 1994, a 22-year-old named Marc Andreessen joined forces with Jim Clark, who had more experience in the tech sector, to found a company called Netscape, whose products would allow computer users to search for information on the internet. In 1998, after having appeared on the cover of *Time* magazine, Andreessen and Clark sold their company to America Online for $4 billion in stock.

They and others constituted, according to one journalist in the *New York Times*, a "loose tribe of young moguls, minimoguls and moguls in waiting, a brat pack whose members play together and endlessly debate business strategies among themselves."[28] Though women had constituted a significant part of the computer programming industry, Silicon Valley felt very much like a boys' club in the 1990s, in every sense of the term. Many drove extraordinarily expensive cars, flew private jets, and owned huge homes with every luxury imaginable. The desire for more kept growing as the money kept flowing into their coffers. "To feel truly rich in Silicon Valley," one of them said, "you have to be worth in the three-digit millions."[29] Not to be outdone, Massachusetts launched its own high-tech corridor along Route 128, while New York mimicked the California boomtown with its own version, "Silicon Alley."[30]

Across the country, between Silicon Valley and Silicon Alley, American cities were being remade. The most famous renovation of all was Times Square in New York. A stark symbol of decay in the 1970s, it underwent dramatic transformations in the 1990s. Under Mayor Rudy Giuliani, elected in 1993, the city completed the long process of remaking the area that had once been a center for dingy porno theaters and "peep shows" into a new site for family-friendly entertainment and upscale commerce. At one level, the NYPD implemented a harsh crackdown on the vast criminal world that had thrived on these streets for decades. Sex shops were closed; drug dealers were arrested. Meanwhile, the city government used zoning laws and tax incentives, as well as the sale of property, to bring in new businesses. The development of the area accelerated as a number of major companies, such as Disney and MTV, purchased huge swaths of real estate, and the police ensured that the millions of tourists coming there would feel as safe as they were in Disney World. The neighboring Bryant Park on 42nd Street emerged as a venue for wealthier city residents whose numbers were growing as more neighborhoods were converted to high-priced condos and co-ops. Indeed, half of the increase in income between 1992 and 1997 in New York came from people working in the financial service sector, even though they represented less than 5 percent of the work-force. The number of city residents who were categorized as being in the middle class, meanwhile, steadily declined from 35 percent in 1989 to 29 percent ten years later.[31]

As New York made clear, the economic recovery of the 1990s was anything but evenly distributed. Upper income brackets boomed as those on the lower end of the income ladder struggled to stay in place. In the offices that housed many of the thriving companies, the bor-derlands of the new economy were clear, especially in Silicon Valley. Rosalba Ceballos went to work each day in the manufacturing giant KLA-Tencor to clean offices and sweep floors, only to return home to a tiny, cramped garage outside Palo Alto where she lived with her three kids. Maria Godinez, who worked as the janitor at Sun Microsystems, lived in a house packed with four different families, totaling twenty-two adults and kids. "Unfortunately," said the head of the AFL-CIO division in the Silicon Valley, "the New Economy is looking a lot like an hourglass with a lot of high-paid, high-tech jobs at the high end and an enormous proliferation of low-wage service jobs at the bottom."[32]

Indeed, for all the attention given to the wars of Washington in the 1990s, the most pronounced division in the nation was neither cultural nor political, but economic. The pattern established in the 1980s—in which the rich became richer, the middle class shrunk, and the poor sank further behind—accelerated in the boom years of the 1990s and continued well beyond. Over these decades, the gap between the wealthiest and poorest Americans steadily grew. According to one study, the top 1 percent of the nation received more than 80 percent of the total increase in America's income between 1980 and 2005, nearly doubling their overall share of the nation's wealth. The Economic Policy Institute, meanwhile, found that CEO wages relative to those of their workers skyrocketed: in 1965, the average CEO made twenty-four times as much as an average worker; in 1978, thirty-five times as much; in 1989, seventy-one times as much. The numbers continued to soar, and by the end of the 1990s, the average CEO was making three hundred times as much as the average worker.[33]

With economic inequality came economic insecurity. As union jobs vanished, the new economy increasingly revolved around low wage jobs that did not provide much stability. The number of households whose income fell by 25 percent or more within one year, according to the political scientist Jacob Hacker, had steadily risen since the 1980s. The loss of income came from either declining wages or higher medical expenses. In the 1970s, about 3–4 percent of the population was expected to suffer through a fall in their income of 50 percent or more; that segment would reach almost 10 percent by 2004. More and more Americans declared bankruptcy, with filings increasing by 95 percent between 1990 and 1998, breaking historic records several times. With each downturn, the "new normal" that Americans could expect became worse.[34]

Even the economic improvement of the mid-1990s did not reverse the long-term trends toward underemployment in several parts of the country. By 1996, there were over 36.5 million Americans under the poverty line. Notably, these individuals were largely concentrated in central cities. National recoveries did not matter much for the residents there, as the jobs simply never came to their neighborhoods. Unemployment rates for minority youth living in cities were five times the average of those for white youth in other parts of the country. The pressures were amplified by an influx of immigrants, who increased urban populations. While overall crime rates diminished across the 1990s, urban levels remained extremely high.[35] During the decade, cities saw dramatic rises in the number of single-parent families and extremely high rates of infant mortality among African Americans. One study found that half of the poor children under six were in families whose income didn't even reach half of the poverty line. Among the African American workforce, 9.9 percent were unemployed in 1998 compared to 4.7 percent of the national workforce.[36]

As jobs disappeared, prisons grew. Stricter drug laws imposed in major states like New York (such as the Rockefeller Drug Laws of 1973) had steadily made it easier for the courts to convict those charged with possession or distribution of illegal substances. This long-term trend inside various states took on a national scope in the 1990s, most notably with the Violent Crime Control and Law Enforcement Authorization Act of 1994. Among other things, the $30 billion measure instituted harsher new rules for sentencing convicted felons and fueled new spending for prisons across the nation. Minimum sentences for many drug-related federal crimes were now formally mandated; state sentences were likewise extended, thanks to a provision that linked federal funds for prison development to state promises to make serious offenders serve at least 85 percent of their sentences. Most notably, the crime bill included a "three strikes, you're out" provision, which mandated life imprisonment for criminals convicted of a violent felony if they had at least two prior convictions.[37]

As public laws fueled mass incarceration, the privatization of the penal system created more institutional space and economic incentives for it too. Reporter Eric Schlosser aptly characterized the phenomenon as a "prison-industrial complex." "The raw material of the prison-industrial complex," he wrote, "is its inmates: the poor, the homeless, and the mentally ill; drug dealers, drug addicts, alcoholics, and a wide assortment of violent sociopaths." Prisoners were profitable, however, and fueled a massive growth in the American penal system. California, Schlosser noted, had constructed eight maximum facility prisons between 1984 and 1994 to hold its booming prison population; by 1998, that one state incarcerated more people than the six nations of France, Great Britain, Germany, Japan, Singapore, and the Netherlands combined. By 1994, the private prison industry in America had grown so large and lucrative, it had its own trade magazine: *Correctional Building News*. Although Republicans had been the first to push for the privatization of prisons, the Clinton administration strongly supported this trend and worked with the Justice Department to place undocumented immigrants in these institutions. In 1997, for instance, the Wackenhut Corporation, a Florida-based company founded by a former FBI agent, was hired by the Federal Bureau of Prisons to manage a major prison.[38]

The impact of mass incarceration fell predominantly on racial minorities. "There are today over two million Americans incarcerated in federal and state prisons and local jails throughout the United States," scholar Manning Marable noted in 2000. "More than one-half, or one million, are black men and women." The high rates of black imprisonment, he and others observed, stemmed from systemic biases that impacted black suspects at higher rates than whites, ranging from more aggressive policing in inner cities than in suburbs and "mandatory minimum" laws that set tougher sentences for crystalline "crack" cocaine (popular with poorer African Americans) than for powder cocaine (popular with affluent whites), to widely different rates of referral to juvenile courts for the races. As a result, a new generation of African Americans found itself disproportionately swept up in the carceral state. Roughly a quarter of black men in their 20s, Manning observed, were "either in jail or prison, on parole, probation, or awaiting trial." As prisons shifted their overall emphasis from rehabilitation to punishment, moreover, the realities of incarceration became a permanent marker for large segments of society who were now cast off by society as unwanted and irredeemable.[39]

Meanwhile, even those who had benefited from the 1990s boom economy began to have worries, as cracks in its façade appeared. Early excitement about computers turned to anxiety when fears of a "Y2K" bug led to predictions that on New Year's Day, 2000, entire systems would shut down as a result of coding errors. The havoc never occurred, but a financial meltdown did. Many of the companies that had led the tech boom had profited from low interest rates and free-flowing private capital rather than the value of their product, but the Federal Reserve soon clamped down on interest rates several times and the economy slowed. On March 20, 2000, the tech-sensitive NASDAQ fell dramatically. "Fast-Forward Stocks Meet Rewind Button," read a headline in the *Wall Street Journal*. The quick reversal suggested that the overhyped "momentum stocks" that had fueled the dot-com boom might easily go bust in a panic. "They drove them to ridiculous levels on the way up," a hedge fund manager said, "and they'll drive them to ridiculous levels on the way down."[40]

Indeed, it soon became clear that many companies at the center of the "dot-com" boom were not remotely worth their alleged value. One of the best examples of overvalued stock was Pets.com, a start-up that promised to sell pet supplies online. Founded by Greg McLemore in August 1998, the firm went public a year and a half later, even though it still lacked a basic business plan or any solid market research. Julie Wainwright, with a background in marketing, took over the company and poured enormous resources into public relations. The company relied almost entirely on an aggressive ad campaign. Its mascot, a sock-puppet dog with a microphone, appeared on *Good Morning America,* the Macy's Day parade, and even in a $3 million ad that aired during the Super Bowl. With its products placed on massive discounts to lure in new customers, the company made little profit of its own and was instead primarily supported by continued investments from private capital firms. In all, Pets.com spent almost $12 million on advertising in its first year, while earning just $619,000 in revenue.[41]

With shaky start-ups like this at the heart of the "dot-com" boom, the market soon collapsed and countless companies began to fold. The Dow Jones Internet Index fell by 72 percent from its all time high point of March 2000, with online companies suffering steep drops in stock prices. The burst of the bubble continued into 2001, driving stocks down, bankrupting companies, and leaving many investors with massive losses. Soon, the high-tech marketplace looked like an abandoned mall. While 17 tech companies had purchased $44 million worth of advertisements in the 2000 Super Bowl, only three did so a year later, and at much lower rates.[42] The future of the industry remained unclear, with many younger Americans, previously intoxicated by the ease of new wealth, sobered in their expectations. "What a difference a year makes," lamented the editors of the *New York Times.* "The NASDAQ sank. Stock tips have been replaced with talks of recession. Many pioneering dot-coms are out of business or barely surviving."[43] Pets.com stock had gone up to $14 initially, but toward the end it was selling for $1, finally closing at 22 cents.[44] When Pets.com shut down its operations on November 8, 2000, the former owners sold the rights to their once famous mascot to a car loan firm called Bar None for $125,000.[45] The slogan the new owners gave the once-popular puppet was "Everybody deserves a second chance."

Indecision 2000

Despite the turmoil, the stock market recovered and, more importantly, unemployment rates remained low for the remainder of Clinton's term. Throughout the year, the Gallup Poll asked Americans: "In general, are you satisfied or dissatisfied with the way things are going in the United States?" In January 2000, 69 percent of Americans said they were satisfied with how things were going. The number dipped a little as the

campaign season wore on and the typical complaints of an election surfaced, but it remained a solid majority throughout the year. Clinton's
approval ratings remained strong as well, never sinking below 55 percent
for the year. In spite of the impeachment process—or, as some mused,
because of it—voters remained supportive of the president, largely due
to the conditions of peace and prosperity that had marked the decade.[46]

Not surprisingly, the candidates running to replace Clinton that year
sought to convince the American people that they could best maintain
this status quo. The Democratic nominee, Vice President Al Gore Jr.,
promised "continued peace and prosperity," while the Republican nominee, Texas governor George W. Bush, advanced a similarly moderate
agenda he called "compassionate conservatism." Pointedly, both candidates sought to distance themselves from the partisan clashes of the
previous decade. Gore kept Clinton at arm's length, worried the president's personal scandals would tarnish his own image. Bush, meanwhile, criticized House Republicans for heartlessly "balancing the
budget on the backs of the poor" and, in a sharp break with the culture
wars, complained that all too often "my party has painted an image of
America slouching toward Gomorrah," a direct reference to (and dis-
missal of) the complaints from Robert Bork.[47]

With Gore and Bush both trying to claim the political center, the
2000 election pivoted less on matters of policy than it did on personality. An amiable, easy-going Texan, Bush struck many, in the words
of the *Wall Street Journal* columnist Paul Gigot, as a "likable light-
weight." After decades in the federal government, Gore had a stronger command of the issues, but the political reporters who significantly
shaped the narrative of the campaign disliked him intensely. His public
performances were routinely derided as "stiff" and "wooden," and his
campaign coverage soon centered around a narrative that he was an
inveterate liar. Gore brought some of this onto himself, with a tendency
to brag about his accomplishments. In 1999, for instance, he noted in
an interview: "During my service in the United States Congress, I took
the initiative in creating the Internet." This statement was, on its own
terms, true. As Vinton Cerf, the man commonly credited as the "Father
of the Internet," said in 1999, "The Internet would not be where it is
in the United States without the strong support given to it and related
research areas by the vice president in his current role and in his earlier

role as senator. . . . He was the first elected official to grasp the potential of computer communications to have a broader impact than just
improving the conduct of science and scholarship. . . . His initiatives
led directly to the commercialization of the Internet. So he really does
deserve credit." The press, however, ignored that history and treated
the claim as a whopper. Moreover, they simplified what Gore had said
into something that would seem even more ridiculous, claiming he said
simply "I invented the internet."[48] Later in the campaign, *Time* reporter
Margaret Carlson explained in an interview with talk radio host Don
Imus how and why the media settled into its narrative. Both candidates made misstatements during the campaign, she said, but the press
tended to seize on Gore's alone. "You can actually disprove some of what
Bush is saying if you really get in the weeds and get out your calculator
or you look at his record in Texas," she noted. "But it's *really* easy, and it's
fun, to disprove Al Gore. As sport, and as our enterprise, Gore coming
up with another whopper is greatly entertaining to us."[49]

   With the emphasis on personality over policy, the 2000 election
became one of the closest in American history. In the end, Gore beat
Bush by a margin of roughly 540,000 in the popular vote. But as election night wore on, it became clear that neither Bush nor Gore had the
number of electoral votes needed to declare a victory. With every state
except Florida decided, Gore had secured 267 electoral votes to Bush's
246. Both were beneath the number needed to win—270—and therefore the 25 electoral votes of Florida would determine the winner. Relying on exit polling and competing with each other to call the race first,
the networks initially awarded the state to Gore, then backed off, then
called it for Bush, and then backed off again.[50] Jon Stewart, the comedian and television host, expressed the frustration that he and others felt
with the coverage. "The great part was just the giant fuck-up network-
wise," Stewart recalled, " 'Gore's the winner. Gore's not the winner. Bush
is the winner. Bush is not the winner, nobody's the winner.' The media
declared two people president, and then declared no one president."[51]

   As the color-coded maps of election night remained frozen in place on
these networks—first for hours, then days and even weeks as the fight
over Florida stretched on—Americans quickly adopted a new shorthand for their deepening political divisions: "red states" for Republican
areas and "blue states" for Democratic ones. The assignment of the two

colors was, in truth, arbitrary. The networks had started using color-coded maps in 1976, when NBC's John Chancellor informed viewers that he would be coloring states for Republican Gerald Ford blue and states for Democrat Jimmy Carter red. Over the ensuing decades, the color schemes used in network news coverage of presidential elections changed from year to year, and network to network. (In 1984, Democratic vice presidential nominee Geraldine Ferraro noted how the "big three" networks displayed the results in different hues. "One network map of the United States was entirely blue for the Republicans," she recalled. "On another network, the color motif was a blanket of red.") In contrast, *Time* magazine used blue for the Republicans and red for the Democrats from 1988 through 2000. The networks switched the order in their 2000 coverage, however, and as Americans stared endlessly at the electoral maps, and talked about them, the color scheme became cemented in their minds. With it came a new sense of the nation as one divided into separate camps: one set of red states and another set of blue states, rather than a United States.[52]

In the 2000 race, the battle for Florida—the last state to be colored in, the one that would decide the whole election—carried on for weeks. The confusion over who had won the state stemmed from confusion over the votes at the county level. There were, closer inspection revealed, a number of serious inconsistencies and irregularities in the voting procedures of several of Florida's counties. The most famous was the dispute over the so-called "butterfly ballot" clumsily designed by Democratic officials in Palm Beach County, an awkward form that led over 3,000 Jewish retirees—one of the state's most reliably Democratic demographics—to cast ballots for the archconservative, third-party candidate Pat Buchanan instead of Al Gore.

More serious than the butterfly ballot was the statewide purge of voter rolls. Between May 1999 and November 2000, Florida secretary of state Katharine Harris ordered the names of nearly 48,000 ex-felons—barred from voting by state law—to be removed from the rolls. In theory, this was perfectly legal; in practice, however, it proved quite controversial. In addition to her official state duties, the Republican Harris also served as one of the state cochairs of the Bush campaign. As reports soon revealed, roughly 2,800 people who had names similar to those of convicted felons had been wrongly removed from the voter rolls, while nearly 8,000 additional individuals who had only misdemeanors on their records—and who thus should have kept their voting rights—were purged as well. (In one of many examples that came to light only later, among those who lost their right to vote was a 64-year-old man whose only conviction had been for falling asleep on a bus-stop bench back in 1959.)[53]

When the initial vote totals revealed that George W. Bush had a razor-thin margin of roughly 500 votes statewide, the Gore campaign pushed for selective recounts in a handful of Democratic-leaning counties. As these recounts eroded the Bush lead, the Republican campaign asked the Supreme Court to intervene. On December 12, 2000, the court handed down its pivotal decision in *Bush v. Gore.* In a bitterly divided 5–4 ruling, the conservative majority ordered an immediate halt to the recounts, awarding Florida's electoral votes—and therefore, the entire presidential election—to Bush. In the end, a presidential campaign that had begun as a race to the center concluded with an ending that only polarized the country further.[54]

CHAPTER 12

Compassion and Terror

THE SENSE OF PEACE THAT LOOMED OVER THE 2000 PRES-
idential election, with each candidate focused on small-scale domestic
issues and largely embracing limits on the use of military force overseas,
seemed incredibly dated just one year later.

While President George W. Bush sought to replicate some earlier
acts of the Reagan Revolution, he initially focused his administration on an agenda of what he called "compassionate conservatism."
He was determined to forge a different path for the Republican
Party, one that eschewed the bitter fights over social issues that had
marked the culture wars of the previous decade, but he found his
agenda stalled and then soon overshadowed by a sudden shift in foreign affairs.

The horrific, large-scale terrorist attack on September 11, 2001,
revealed the nation's vulnerabilities and swept aside the easy confidence
America had held when it seemed to be the last superpower standing in
the wake of the Cold War. The events of that one day—so significant
it became universally known by the shorthand "9/11"—immediately
transformed the national security agenda, ushering in a new paradigm that soon dominated not just America's diplomatic and military
postures abroad, but its social and political life at home. At heart, the
attacks represented a challenge not just to the psyche of the nation but
also to its national security institutions. Initially, it seemed likely that
the country would once again find unity in the face of outside threats,
but it quickly became clear that the fault lines that had emerged over
previous decades stubbornly remained.

Compassionate Conservatism

In its broadest strokes, the "compassionate conservatism" that Bush championed sought to soften the harder edges of the movement conservatism initiated by the Reagan Revolution of the 1980s and amplified by the Gingrich Republicans of the 1990s. Much as his father, President George H. W. Bush, had spoken of creating a "kinder, gentler America" during his term in office, President George W. Bush said he wanted to enable "armies of compassion"—standing in the private sector but financed by public money—to care for America's needy. "I call my philosophy and approach compassionate conservatism," he explained. "It is compassionate to actively help our fellow citizens in need. It is conservative to insist on responsibility and results. And with this hopeful approach, we will make a real difference in people's lives."[1]

Despite the signals that his presidency would depart from past practices of Republicans, some of Bush's earliest efforts were quite familiar. Though he was the son of former Republican president George H. W. Bush, George W. Bush looked instead to Ronald Reagan as a role model, so much so that an early account of his presidency was titled *Reagan's Disciple*. Returning to President Reagan's resistance to environmental regulation, for instance, the Bush administration made early moves to push back against the growing campaign to curb carbon emissions. At the end of his term, President Clinton had used executive orders to bypass a resistant Republican Congress, but his successor quickly worked to undo the measures. Most notably, in March 2001, Bush withdrew US support for the Kyoto Protocol, a landmark international agreement adopted in 1997 to curb the release of greenhouse gases into the atmosphere. An outspoken advocate of action, Vice President Al Gore had signed the measure on behalf of the Clinton administration, but the Senate never approved it. In sharp contrast, the Bush White House announced it had "no interest" in implementing the Kyoto Protocol. Rejecting the scientific consensus on the relationship between greenhouse gases and climate change, the administration and its allies insisted there was no need to act. At the same time, the Bush White House worked to reduce the oversight and enforcement role of the EPA, relegating inspection duties to the states. "The president's cuts take the environmental cop off the beat," warned Representative Robert Menendez, "and it creates a devastating blow to EPA's ability to enforce clear air, clean water and hazardous waste laws."[2]

Much as Bush stuck to the Reagan script with its drive to roll back the regulatory state, he likewise tried to copy his predecessor's playbook with a massive supply-side tax cut. Notably, the Bush tax cut—signed into law on June 7, 2001—was the first major reduction in twenty years and, at an estimated cost of $1.35 trillion, the largest single tax cut in American history. While Reagan had claimed that supply-side tax cuts were specifically suited to spur the sluggish conditions of the early 1980s, Bush argued that the budget surpluses from the Clinton-era boom meant that the government could, and indeed should, cut taxes again. "The surplus is not the government's money," Bush had said in his 2000 acceptance speech. "The surplus is the people's money." Now in office, he promised to "give the people their money back." Republicans saw the tax cut and the larger Bush budget as a means of restoring their glory years. "It would, they believe, revive and retrofit the Reagan Revolution," a reporter noted in March 2001, "by putting new spending constraints on the federal government with the tax cut; by ceding more responsibilities to state and local governments and religious institutions; and by transforming two great monuments of the New Deal and Great Society, with partial privatizing of Social Security and Medicare." Democrats, of course, had different memories of the reckoning wrought by Reaganomics and worried that the country would suffer again. "I just know that at some point that reality is going to come crashing down on all of us," Senate Minority Leader Tom Daschle noted, "and we're going to have to deal with it."[3]

Not everything, however, was about re-creating the Reagan Revolution. Early in Bush's term as president, the White House had pointed to three areas in which his administration was seeking to implement its new philosophy. "The President's vision of compassionate conservatism," an April 2002 press release noted, "effectively tackles some of society's toughest assignments—educating our children, fighting poverty at home, and aiding poor countries around the world." In these three realms, the Bush administration tried to transform its vision of compassionate conservatism into concrete policy. Specifically, the policies were known as the faith-based initiative, the No Child Left Behind Act, and the global initiative on HIV/AIDS.[4]

More than any other policy, George W. Bush's "compassionate conservatism" was embodied in what he called the "faith-based initiative." At heart, this promised to empower private religious and community organizations and enlist their charitable arms in the provision of social services, especially to the poor. This had been a major issue for Bush during his presidential campaign, one he used to distance himself from the Republican Party's traditional stances on economic and fiscal conservatism. "I know that economic growth is not the solution to every problem," he announced at one campaign event. "The invisible hand of the free market works many miracles. But it cannot touch the human heart." As a result, Bush proposed a new program of government spending to support religious bodies engaged in social welfare. "Without more support and resources, both public and private," he insisted, "we are asking them to make bricks without straw." Laying out the details of his vision, the Republican candidate proposed a combination of tax credits for charitable donations and direct government financing that would put an estimated $8 billion annually into the cause.[5]

Upon taking office, President Bush continued to emphasize the faith-based initiative as the centerpiece of his domestic agenda. Notably, the longest section of his inaugural address had been devoted to describing the program. "America, at its best, is compassionate," the new president observed. "Church and charity, synagogue and mosque lend our communities their humanity, and they will have an honored place in our plans and in our laws." Despite his high rhetoric, the faith-based initiative still remained unformed. Indeed, it soon became clear that for all the emphasis the new president had given to the issue in his speeches, nothing at all had been done to turn those words into deeds. Many members of the administration saw the promise as a political ploy, rather than serious policy. Late in the transition period, a young aide named Don Willett had stepped forward to craft plans for the program after he realized no one else had taken charge. To his surprise, he found requests for funding and staff rebuffed at every turn. In an abrupt change, just three days after the inaugural, political advisor Karl Rove told Willett that the full faith-based initiative would be unveiled to reporters in six days. The thirty-four-year-old asked how that could be accomplished when the initiative still lacked a director, a staff, an office, or even a general plan of action. "I don't know," Rove responded wearily. "Just get me a fucking faith-based thing. Got it?"[6]

The following Monday, January 29, 2001, Bush issued his first two executive orders as president. The first created a new executive branch agency, the White House Office of Faith-Based and Community Initiatives (WHOFBCI), charged with setting priorities, coordinating public education campaigns, and monitoring faith-based initiatives across the federal government. The second executive order, meanwhile, created faith-based programs for five cabinet-level departments, which would conduct internal audits to help private-sector community organizations and religious charities provide social services.[7] Despite the president's enthusiasm for the executive branch programs, the faith-based initiatives never fully formed there. Frustrated with the White House's lack of leadership, House Republicans embraced more socially conservative proposals championed by the Religious Right. These proposals were marked by little or no government oversight for grant recipients; complete freedom for them to discriminate in hiring, especially in the realm of gender and sexuality; and a license to use public funds for private religious work. As WHOFBCI Director John DiIulio later observed, the House bill "bore few marks of compassionate conservatism and was, as anybody could tell, an absolute political nonstarter." Its already slim chances of passing the Senate became even slimmer in May 2001, when Senator Jim Jeffords of Vermont switched parties, changing from a Republican to a Democrat, and taking control of the Senate with him.[8]

Without legislation to shore it up, the core of the president's original plan—the provision to secure a massive boost in private charitable giving through tax incentives—was lost as well. By mid-2001, the faith-based initiative had been effectively ended. The legislative struggle, according to one study, had transformed Bush's original "bipartisan rallying cry for the armies of compassion" into little more than "a throwback to partisan blitzkriegs of the Newt Gingrich era." The WHOFBCI soon became an empty shell. DiIulio had only originally planned on staying for six months, but his planned departure at the end of the summer was seen by many as a sign that the office had failed. His replacement, Jim Towey, essentially turned the office into a political arm of the Republicans' midterm campaign in 2002 and the president's reelection effort in 2004.[9]

Bush's plans for a new era of "compassionate conservatism" were crippled by the failure of the faith-based initiative. Other programs, however, still sought to fill the void, with some success. Chief among these was an education initiative, the No Child Left Behind Act of 2001. The law solidified the federal commitment to funding public education, representing a stark reversal to decades of conservative calls for the dismantling of the Department of Education. Reaffirming the federal role in education and even expanding it, No Child Left Behind imposed rigorous national standards in subjects like math and English. The standards served a double political purpose in that they constituted a direct attack on the authority of the teachers' unions, which had traditionally retained strong control over hiring decisions. Conservatives had long criticized public schools for allowing "social promotion"—advancing unqualified students when they should have been held back, a practice Bush had decried on the campaign trail as "the soft bigotry of low expectations." Under the new law, every public school in the nation would now be required to meet or surpass government-mandated achievement levels in core subjects or lose federal funds. Students in these failing schools would then be able to transfer to better-performing ones. Entire schools could be closed if the problems were not solved.[10]

No Child Left Behind initially had broad bipartisan support, a sign of the importance that education had for the suburban voters both parties coveted. Future Republican Speaker John Boehner was one of two sponsors in the House, while Senator Ted Kennedy, a noted liberal, was one of two in the Senate. Though the standards at the heart of the legislation were strongly opposed by teachers' unions, a key Democratic constituency, many members of the party joined Kennedy in backing the bill. In a sign of bipartisan support, the measure passed the House by a wide margin of 384 to 45, and then passed in the Senate 91 to 8. President Bush then signed it into law in January 2002. Though No Child Left Behind seemed to be a bipartisan success, partisan divisions over the program quickly took hold. Democrats were furious when, one month after signing the bill into law, Bush drastically cut its funding. Democrats and many teachers warned that NCLB was an unfunded mandate imposed on local schools by the federal government without providing school districts with any serious funding. The policy did little to advance the standing of "compassion-ate conservatism" at large.[11]

Although Bush's compassionate conservatism demonstrated that he was willing to challenge the traditional stances of the Republican Party on key issues such as funding of social services and the federal com-mitment to public education, these proposals were poorly formed at the outset and then were quickly obliterated by events in the fall.

9/11

The front page of the *New York Times,* printed in the early hours of the morning of Tuesday, September 11, 2001, featured a typical range of stories. One explained how New York State public schools were requiring dress codes, in an effort to curb the fishnet stockings and see-through clothing that were becoming more common in classrooms. Another recounted the last day of the Democratic primaries for the can-didates seeking to replace New York's Mayor Rudy Giuliani. In national news, a panel of scientific experts urged President Bush to rethink his restrictions on federally financed stem cell lines, while leaders in both parties, another piece explained, wanted Bush to make more aggres-sive moves to boost a now-struggling economy. Media critic Bill Carter, meanwhile, reported that the networks were competing to gain a big-ger share of the booming audience for morning television. Amid these front-page stories, there was one article about terrorism: an account of a teacher in Westchester County, who was being charged in a 1971 air-line hijacking, after his role in it had been discovered thirty years later in an internet search.[12]

The events that would later define September 11, 2001, seemingly came out of nowhere. Early that day, nineteen members of the Islamic terrorist organization al-Qaeda boarded four commercial airplanes in American cit-ies. Armed with box cutters they had snuck through airport security, the attackers killed the pilots and took control of the planes. They then pro-ceeded to fly three of them into major buildings: two into the twin towers of the World Trade Center in New York and a third into the Pentagon outside Washington, DC. A fourth plane, United Flight 93, was meant to target the White House, but passengers on board, hearing reports of the other hijackings over their personal cell phones, were able to seize control from the terrorists and crash the plane in a rural field in Pennsylvania. Despite those heroics, the elaborate plan still killed roughly 3,000.

Americans had witnessed acts of terrorism before, but rarely on their own shores and never on a scale like this. When the first plane hit the tower, many assumed it was a tragic accident, a pilot who had somehow been taken off course. When the second plane hit, however, and the buildings then started to crumble before the television cameras, it was suddenly clear that this had been something far more noxious—an intentional attack against the United States. As the streets of lower Manhattan filled with smoke and debris, news channels broadcast scenes of confusion to the nation. Normally cheerful morning shows switched abruptly from soft celebrity stories and weather reports to breaking news. NBC's *Today Show* segued from a conversation on a book about "America's first billionaire," Howard Hughes, to live shots of the initial crash; ABC's *Good Morning America* switched to cover the carnage by cutting away from an interview with a member of the British royal family. After the sudden shift, the networks and cable news channels alike remained focused nonstop on the ongoing developments in New York and Washington, with images of the twin towers—first smoking, then collapsing—replaying over and over again. According to a later study, Americans watched an average of 8.1 hours of coverage that day, transfixed in horror.

For those in New York, the attacks upended everything. The first responders, who had helped evacuate the buildings as they fell, found themselves unsure of what to do next. "Like dazed and bloodied soldiers," one reporter recounted, "thousands of firefighters and police officers wandered helplessly throughout the afternoon and evening on the West Side Highway, blocked by the danger of further catastrophe from attempting to enter the scene." Meanwhile, residents searched for missing friends and family members, blanketing subway stations and telephone poles with homemade posters and fliers, looking in vain for the lost.[13] "The sense of security and self-confidence that Americans take as their birthright suffered a grievous blow, from which recovery will be slow," a reporter noted in the next day's edition of the *New York Times*. "The aftershocks will be nearly as bad, as hundreds and possibly thousands of people discover that friends or relatives died awful, fiery deaths."[14]

While the nation reeled from the assault, its political leaders mounted a joint response, hastily scrambling to put a nation that had largely been at peace for a decade back on a wartime footing. The night after the attacks, President George W. Bush offered a brief but earnest declaration of the nation's resolve and noted "a quiet, unyielding anger" that had been brought up across the country. Leaders of both parties offered their support, joining together to sing "God Bless America." Indeed, national unity in the face of the crisis became their predominant concern. "We have just seen the war of the 21st century," Bush declared in a conference call with reporters two days after the attack. "There is universal approval of the statements I have made, and I am confident there will be universal approval of the actions this government takes." Democrats echoed the president, both in his condemnation of the attacks and his commitment to national unity. Senate Majority Leader Tom Daschle denounced the "despicable acts" that were "an assault on our people and on our freedom." "I know that the most important thing now," said Hillary Clinton, who had been elected in 2000 to serve as US senator for New York, "is for us to be united, united behind our president and our government, sending a very clear message that this is something that transcends any political consideration or partisanship."[15]

Americans' impulse to unite came easily, but the question of just what "unified action" might entail was much more difficult to determine. For one thing, the threat itself remained unclear. Many suspected al-Qaeda would soon wage additional attacks across the nation, perhaps against vulnerable "soft targets," such as shopping malls or movie theaters. Others speculated that hostile nations might try to take advantage of the chaos by launching a more conventional attack of their own. At the same time, the nature of the American response was equally murky. "As Washington struggled to regain a sense of equilibrium, with warplanes and heavily armed helicopters crossing overhead," R. W. Apple Jr., noted in the *New York Times*, "past and present national security officials earnestly debated the possibility of a Congressional declaration of war—but against precisely whom, and in what exact circumstances?" Ultimately, President Bush did decide to treat the attacks as an act of full-blown war rather than an isolated criminal act, an important departure from how Clinton had handled the 1993 bombing of the World Trade Center. Putting the nation on a formal war footing, his aides noted, would give the president more expansive executive power with fewer legislative restraints.[16]

Although many were skeptical about Bush's capacity as a leader, he and his experienced national security team quickly impressed many who doubted him. The president displayed a level of gravitas that was very different from the character comedian Will Ferrell had played on *Saturday Night Live,* a bumbler who stumbled over his own words and was never in real command of the issues. Faced with this crisis, Bush showed that there was another side to his public presence. On September 14, 2001, he made a surprise appearance at "Ground Zero," the site of the World Trade Center attack, standing on a pile of rubble before rescue workers who were still desperately trying to find people buried in the debris. With the television cameras relaying his every move, Bush, in impromptu fashion, placed his arm around one of the firemen. As he spoke to the rescuers, one in the back yelled out, "I can't hear you!" Seizing the moment, Bush grabbed the bullhorn and said: "I can hear you. I can hear you. The rest of the world hears you. And the people who knocked these buildings down will hear all of us soon." The moment conveyed an image of strength and defiance, fostering the belief that Bush could be a leader capable of handling this challenge.[17]

Other politicians found their footing in the crisis. New York's Mayor Rudy Giuliani, for instance, emerged with a new heroic image. His administration had been plagued by problems with policing and racism, as well as some scandals in the mayor's personal life, but his leadership in the aftermath of the attacks swept those concerns away, at least in the short term. "Giuliani has been a cranky and not terribly effective mayor, too distracted by marital and health problems to work on the city's surging murder rate," the journalist Jonathan Alter wrote in *Newsweek.* "But in this cataclysm which he rightly called 'the most difficult week in the history of New York,' the city and the country have found that most elusive of all democratic treasures—real leadership."[18]

Bipartisanship prevailed, with Democrats supporting the administration's initial plans against al-Qaeda strongholds in Afghanistan. Congress readily complied with the president's decision to claim wartime footing, passing on September 14, 2001, the Authorization for the Use of Military Force (AUMF) with only one vote against in the House and none in the Senate. The resolution authorized the president to use "all necessary and appropriate force against those nations, organizations, or persons he determines planned, authorized, committed, or aided the terrorist attacks that occurred on September 11, 2001 or harbored such organizations or persons." With such broad parameters, the response to 9/11 quickly became a full war in every sense of the term. The "war on terror" would be conducted in an aggressive and ruthless fashion, with an aim toward dismantling the entire operation of al-Qaeda leader Osama bin Laden as well as any countries that were believed to be supporting terrorist networks.[19]

That said, President Bush wanted to make clear that the war on terror was not a war against Islam. He was especially concerned about Muslim immigrants, most of whom had arrived from South Asia (Bangladesh, India, and Pakistan), Iran, and Arabic-speaking countries, reaching significant numbers in the 1990s. In contrast to Europe, where Muslim immigrants had been geographically concentrated, new arrivals in America had scattered themselves all over the country in forming communities. Approximately 90 percent of one section of Dearborn, Michigan, the Southend district, for instance, was composed of Muslim immigrants.[20] "Arabic signs hawking insurance, dental work, auto repair, bargain blue jeans and fresh fruit stretch for miles down Warren Avenue," wrote one reporter, "as 188 Arab-owned businesses have opened in the last decade."[21] In the wake of 9/11, ugly incidents of racial and religious hate crimes sprang up across the nation: a Sikh gas station owner in Mesa, Arizona, was killed by a man who went on to shoot a Lebanese clerk at another gas station, while a 46-year-old Pakistani immigrant was murdered in a grocery store.[22]

In response, the president decided to speak at the Islamic Center in Washington on September 17, 2001. When the center opened on Embassy Row in 1957, President Dwight D. Eisenhower had visited to make it clear that he considered Muslims a vital part of America's religious heritage; now another Republican returned to confirm that point. In his remarks, Bush argued that it was vital for Americans to understand that the terrorists did not represent Muslims: "These acts of violence against innocents violate the fundamental tenets of the Islamic faith." The president even quoted from the Koran: "In the long run, evil in the extreme will be the end of those who do evil." Then, in his own words, he continued to argue that American Muslims were "friends" who bore no connection to the attacks. "The face of terror is not the true faith of Islam. That's not what Islam is all about," Bush insisted. "Islam is peace. These terrorists don't represent peace. They represent evil and war." Reflecting on the president's comments, Sayyid Syeed, the secretary general of the Islamic Society of North America, noted that "Americans have shown great maturity."[23]

Meanwhile, the rest of society worked to return to business as usual, as much as possible. The National Football League, which had replaced baseball as America's favorite sport, only postponed games for one weekend before resuming the next. On September 23, New England Patriots guard Joe Andruzzi—the brother of three New York firemen—ran out of the tunnel at Foxboro Stadium waving American flags. As the crowd chanted "USA! USA!" the player ran to midfield to meet some first responders from New York. Then, at the end of the week, the comedy show *Saturday Night Live* took to the air again. The broadcast began solemnly, with the singer Paul Simon offering a stark performance of "The Boxer" as an array of New York firemen and policemen stood by. Then the cameras cut to a shot of producer Lorne Michaels speaking with Mayor Giuliani. On behalf of a nervous nation, Michaels asked for his permission: "Can we be funny?" Giuliani gave a deadpan response: "Why start now?"[24]

The War on Terror

As the nation sought to return to normal, the Bush administration launched a new chapter in American foreign policy. Its first target was Afghanistan. The Taliban regime had harbored Osama bin Laden and al-Qaeda for many years, offering a base of operations, raising funds, and nurturing the networks that carried out the 9/11 attacks and other incidents as well. In late September, President Bush announced that America was "in hot pursuit" of al-Qaeda and would follow them wherever they ran, including Afghanistan. Experts warned that the United States would become bogged down there, much as the Soviet Union had been during the 1980s, but the president insisted he understood the difficulties. It would be "very hard" to fight a "guerrilla war with conventional forces," he said. "We understand that."[25]

On October 7, 2001, the United States launched Operation Enduring Freedom, a coordinated series of massive airstrikes and special operations on the ground. An array of new technologies proved to be vital in the attack. Predator drones, computerized aircraft that operated without an on-board pilot, were capable of firing antitank missiles and capturing precise radar images of opposition forces. A new precision-guided weapon called the Joint Direct Attack Munitions, directed to its target by a Global Positioning System (GPS), had the capacity to correct and change its course of flight after being separated from the tip of a standard bomb. These technologies represented a large proportion of the fighting because Bush hoped to avoid, as long as possible, any significant presence of American troops on the ground. Initially the operation looked efficient and effective. "Use of Pinpoint Airpower Comes of Age in New War," proclaimed the *New York Times*. By December 22, 2001, the Taliban had been routed. NATO and the United States then worked with the Northern Alliance, a local anti-Taliban group, to establish a new interim government.[26]

The war against terrorism was also conducted on the home front, with a striking escalation of domestic counterterrorism programs. Americans' anxieties, already at high levels in the aftermath of the 9/11 attacks, ramped up to new levels when an anthrax scare hit Washington. Just a week after 9/11, Senate Majority Leader Tom Daschle and Tom Brokaw, anchor of the NBC Nightly News, received packages containing high-grade anthrax. "I actually saw it [the letter] and I think I even picked it up at one point, and so I may have been exposed," explained a defiant Brokaw. "I'm not sure, but I'm confident that Cipro is going to get me through this," he said, holding up a bottle of antibiotics that were suddenly much in demand.[27] As other anthrax attacks spread, five died and seventeen others became ill. Though many worried that Islamic terrorists were behind the attacks, evidence later led the government to conclude it was the work of a mentally ill microbiologist inside the United States. Regardless of their origins, the anthrax attacks only heightened the growing sense of vulnerability at home, especially as false alarms of similar incidents spread across the panicked country. In a suburb of Portland, Oregon, the police shut down the main highway after someone found a strange powder, only to discover a local running club had sprinkled wheat flour to create a path on the road. In another suburb outside Washington, DC, police burst into a church after a secretary reported that her mouth felt tingly after opening an envelope.[28] The panic over the anthrax incidents, real and imagined, only accelerated the drive to expand the reach of the federal government's response.

Despite the panic, the sudden increase in counterterrorism programs prompted resistance. Many conservative Republicans, steeped in the limited government philosophies of the Reagan era, initially opposed any expansion of federal power, even in the face of terrorism. Liberal Democrats, meanwhile, worried that the "war on terror" might repeat the excesses of prior periods of wartime in which the government violated constitutional rights in the pursuit of security. Such concerns from both ends of the political spectrum created some odd alliances against the bill. Representative Bob Barr, a conservative Georgian who had led the drive to impeach Bill Clinton, worried about increasing the reach of grand juries, while Representative Maxine Waters, an outspoken liberal from Los Angeles, agreed that "we have to draw the line" at civil liberties. "I find myself agreeing with Mr. Barr," she noted, "and that is very unusual." Outside Congress, moreover, there was institutional resistance to the new proposals for counterterrorism changes. Existing government agencies, for instance, resented the creation of new organizations that might impinge on what they defensively saw as their "turf."[29]

In spite of the concerns, the 9/11 attacks had exposed a variety of vulnerabilities, ranging from airport security that offered little protection against threats, to tourist sites in major cities that suddenly seemed incredibly exposed. Before 9/11, airline passengers were allowed to travel with small knives, scissors, and box cutters; at other sites, physical screening was virtually nonexistent. In the early weeks after the attacks, the same bipartisan support that had marked the launch of Operation Enduring Freedom abroad was repeated in the effort to create new security measures at home. Swept up in the moment, few congressmen objected when the Department of Justice requested legislation that would vastly increase the ability of the federal government to conduct surveillance on its citizens. Officially named the Uniting and Strengthening America by Providing Appropriate Tools Required to Intercept and Obstruct Terrorism Act, the law was more commonly known by the acronym that sprawling title was meant to create: the "USA PATRIOT Act." The law expanded the ability of the government to conduct roving wiretaps which traced multiple phones without multiple subpoenas, to monitor e-mail and business records, to have more authority over undocumented immigrants, to make it harder to appeal detention and also to expand the working definition of a terrorist. The USA PATRIOT Act passed the House by a decisive vote of 357 to 66 on October 24, 2001, and the Senate 98 to 1 the following day.[30]

Not all parts of the war on terror received bipartisan support. Indeed, polarization only seemed to deepen as the government's efforts expanded. Airport security proved to be a particularly tricky topic. Initially, House Republicans under Majority Leader Tom DeLay hoped to keep airport security in private hands, as it had been on 9/11. But in early November, a passenger at Chicago's O'Hare Airport made it past the private-sector screeners of United Airlines with several knives, a stun gun, and a can of pepper spray in his carry-on luggage, an incident that effectively ended the case for continuing private security.[31] The Bush White House, meanwhile, proposed that the federal government do more to guard airports but insisted that its employees, unlike all other federal workers, be exempt from civil service protections so the government could hire and fire at will. Democrats opposed this plan, arguing that the president was exploiting the need for airport security to continue a longer conservative campaign against public sector unions. In the end, Bush acceded to the demands of Senate Democrats and signed a bill that required the government to use federal workers with the standard protections.[32]

At other times, President Bush circumvented the legislative branch altogether, invoking his wartime powers as commander-in-chief to pursue terrorism without needing to subject himself to the political process. In November 2001, the president signed a directive allowing for the use of special military tribunals to prosecute alleged terrorists, rather than the traditional judicial process. Under these new arrangements, the secretary of defense was given the responsibility for selecting the judges as well as the rules of interrogation. One month later, the administration established a massive detention center at the Guantanamo Bay Naval Base in Cuba. Guantanamo, which Secretary of Defense Donald Rumsfeld called the "least worst place we could have selected," was pointedly not a

US territory. Therefore, the administration argued that US laws were not applicable there and the Geneva Conventions did not apply.

Vice President Dick Cheney led the campaign to strengthen the power of the executive branch in the war on terror.[33] A conservative Republican from Wyoming who had served in the Nixon and Ford administrations, Cheney had been extremely frustrated when Congress reasserted its authority in the 1970s. Though a former congressman himself, Cheney believed the legislative branch was inefficient and ineffective. In his view, the president had to circumvent Congress, especially on matters of national security. (This had been one of the major themes of the minority report Cheney crafted for the Iran-Contra Committee.) At his direction, a team of legal advisors that included White House Counsel Alberto Gonzales, the Office of Legal Counsel's John Yoo, and David Addington and Lewis Libby in the Office of the Vice President provided legal memoranda to justify a massive expansion of executive authority. A shrewd political strategist who had spent decades in Washington, Cheney spread support for this new philosophy by placing allies in lower-level executive branch decisions, where they could then report recommendations aligned with his own to their superiors, and thereby create the illusion of independent confirmation of his own ideas.[34]

Meanwhile, to grant US interrogators as much leeway as they could, the Justice Department released an opinion that created an extremely narrow definition of torture, thereby establishing a legal foundation for previously suspect acts now described euphemistically as "enhanced interrogation techniques."[35] In a departure from past norms, CIA interrogators could now use once-banned techniques such as "waterboarding," in which a subject's face was drenched with water while they were held down, simulating the sensation of drowning. The administration argued that waterboarding allowed it to obtain information from Khalid Sheikh Mohammed, who had plotted much of the 9/11 attack. Despite such claims, investigative reporting found that waterboarding rarely yielded substantial results, and key data had instead been obtained through other, more traditional investigatory methods. Later investigations by the Senate Intelligence Committee confirmed these findings, concluding that "the use of the CIA's enhanced interrogation techniques was not an effective means of obtaining accurate information or gaining detainee cooperation."[36]

Despite the lack of results, the aggressive stance toward terrorists still resonated in popular culture. Conservatives who had dismissed federal agents as reckless "jack-booted thugs" during the Clinton era a decade earlier, now came to welcome an image of gung-ho heroes who operated outside the law. One of the most popular television shows of the period, which first aired in November 2001, was the war-on-terror drama 24. The thriller revolved around a fictional counterterrorist unit headed by the elite agent Jack Bauer (played by Kiefer Sutherland), whose heroic exploits unfolded in real time, with a digital clock ticking away seconds on screen. Over the course of the show, Bauer saved the nation from repeated Islamic terrorist plots, using whatever means were necessary. "I have killed two people since midnight," he threatened an innocent bystander in one scene. "So maybe . . . maybe you should be a little more afraid of me than you are right now."

In a sign of the sweeping influence of popular culture, 24 didn't merely reflect the policies of the war on terror; it actively shaped them. "The military loves our show," boasted cocreator Joel Surnow. Officials at Guantanamo Bay later admitted that they took "lots of ideas" from the show's interrogation scenes, and legal authorities soon began invoking the show as a rationalization for extreme measures such as waterboarding prisoners, terrorizing them with dogs, and even subjecting them to sexual humiliation.[37] John Yoo, the constitutional lawyer who authored the so-called "torture memos," invoked the drama in his book *War by Other Means*: "What if, as the Fox television program '24' recently portrayed, a high-level terrorist leader is caught who knows the location of a nuclear weapon?" Even the Supreme Court was swayed by the show's framing of national security issues. "Jack Bauer saved Los Angeles. . . . He saved hundreds of thousands of lives," Justice Antonin Scalia reflected in a speech on the constitutionality of such measures. "Are you going to convict Jack Bauer?"[38] Fiction was now shaping fact.

While 24 popularized a fictionalized war on terror on the Fox broadcast network, its sister station Fox News emerged as an important promoter for the real war on terror. The conservative cable news network had found its footing during the Clinton impeachment process, but it flourished in the aftermath of 9/11. In sharp contrast to its rival CNN, which consciously framed its coverage for a diverse international audience, Fox News increasingly played to viewers at home with populist, nationalistic themes. Patriotic messages and American flags became fixtures on its broadcasts, as the entire network threw itself behind the administration's case for the war on terror. Fully committed to the cause, Fox News saw its ratings spike. In January 2002, it finally surpassed CNN as the most-watched cable news network. "What Fox is doing," a conservative media analyst applauded, was demonstrating "that one can be unabashedly patriotic and be a good news journalist at the same time."[39]

For some, the lesson ran the other way, with criticism of the war on terror depicted as somehow inherently dangerous or unpatriotic. Less than a week after 9/11, the comedian Bill Maher, host of ABC's late-night talk show *Politically Incorrect*, caused a media firestorm when he argued that, however despicable they might be, it was wrong to call terrorists "cowardly" as many were then doing. "*We* have been the cowards lobbing cruise missiles from 2,000 miles away," Maher insisted. "That's cowardly. Staying in the airplane while it hits the building, say what you want about it, it's not cowardly." Backlash to Maher's comments was immediate. ABC initially stood by the host, but more than a dozen affiliates pulled the program and major advertisers like FedEx and Sears dropped their support too. Asked about Maher's remarks, White House Press Secretary Ari Fleischer only inflamed the controversy. "It's a terrible thing to say," he said. "There are reminders to all Americans that they need to watch what they say, watch what they do, and this is not a time for remarks like that; there never is." Maher tried to backtrack, but the damage had been done. The following spring, ABC announced that his show would be canceled.[40]

Back in Iraq

Confident after the success it had had toppling the Taliban in Afghanistan, the administration suggested that further interventions overseas were coming. In January 2002, the president used his State of the Union Address to warn about an "axis of evil" that included North Korea, Iran, and Iraq, three "rogue states" that he said were harboring terrorists and seeking to obtain weapons of mass destruction. Despite the invocation of these three nations, the real focus for the White House remained squarely on Iraq. Many leaders in the administration, especially holdovers from the first Bush administration, such as Cheney, remained determined to take out Saddam Hussein.[41] Even while the 9/11 attacks were still unfolding, Defense Secretary Donald Rumsfeld saw an opportunity to use the event to take on Iraq, a nation whom many in the administration had been eager to strike from the start. Notes from his aides revealed his desire for a sweeping response: "Best info fast. Judge whether good enough to hit S. H. [Saddam Hussein] at same time not only U.B.L. [Usama Bin Laden]. Go massive. Sweep it all up. Things related and not." Such voices in the administration convinced the president to act in the same vein. In March 2002, according to one report, Bush popped into a meeting on Iraq that his National Security Advisor Condoleezza Rice was having with several senators. Learning the topic of discussion, the president declared bluntly: "Fuck Saddam. We're taking him out."[42]

Publicly, the president and his supporters continued to make their case about the threat posed by Hussein. The administration worked hard to disseminate information about these weapons programs, even if much of it was based on suspect intelligence. In the 2002 midterm election, national security stood front and center. "Really good policy," White House political advisor Mark McKinnon explained, "is really good politics. It's the right thing to do for the right reasons. It also throws a huge blanket over the entire domestic agenda. The domestic agenda right now is security. It's covering up everything else." The Republican National Committee nationalized the campaign by emphasizing how successful the GOP had been in taking on the Taliban, erasing the overwhelming support provided by Democrats. In some races, this emphasis turned ugly. In Georgia, for instance, Republicans attacked Senator Max Cleland, a Vietnam veteran who had lost his right arm and both legs, as being "soft" on national security because he opposed the administration's initial proposal to create a Department of Homeland Security with nongovernment workers. One campaign spot featured a photograph of Senator Cleland alongside Osama bin Laden and Saddam Hussein. For some Republicans, the ad was a step too far. "It's worse than disgraceful," said Senator John McCain of Arizona, a fellow Vietnam veteran. "It's reprehensible."[43]

In the middle of the 2002 campaign, the administration requested from Congress a resolution authorizing the use of force in Iraq. To rationalize the need for a preemptive military operation, the White House argued that Hussein possessed a devastating arsenal of "weapons of mass destruction" that might be used against the United States and key allies like Israel. The vice president's office pushed back against media skepticism about the administration's claims that Iraq actually possessed substantial amounts of weapons of mass destruction. Still, a number of prominent Republicans, including those from the first Bush presidency, warned that the costs of trying to remove Hussein would be too high. Some Democrats questioned the need for a second war against a nation that had had nothing to do with 9/11. But many others, including senators who were potential 2004 presidential candidates, such as Hillary Clinton and John Kerry, feared the political costs of saying no and thus supported the president's plan with qualifications. In October, Congress passed a resolution authorizing the use of force in Iraq.

Following the midterm elections, which saw Max Cleland go down to defeat and gave Republicans control of both chambers, the lame-duck Congress established the Department of Homeland Security (DHS). The new cabinet-level department would now centralize and coordinate government operations in the war on terror but also work to encourage readiness in the civilian population. The department unveiled a color-coded system of Homeland Security Advisory alerts, which were meant to inform Americans about the daily threat level but only seemed to confuse them more, as the designations seemed arbitrary and unclear. Comedians soon mocked the system—"champagne-fuscia means we're being attacked by Martha Stewart," Conan O'Brien joked—and the general public soon learned to ignore it. Other DHS actions prompted a similar mix of alarm and derision. In a callback to the nuclear bomb shelters that had proliferated in the early Cold War era, DHS officials now urged Americans to prepare their homes for chemical and gas attacks. In February 2003, DHS Secretary Tom Ridge and the US fire administrator urged citizens to stockpile three days of water and food, plus radios and batteries, in order to weather an attack. Homeowners should also buy enough plastic sheeting and duct tape, officials instructed, to be able to seal off all the doors and windows of the home as well. Hardware stores soon reported skyrocketing sales of the supplies, especially duct tape. "Everything that was on that newscast," a manager of a Virginia Home Depot noted, "we are selling a lot of it." And indeed, the "war on terror" opened a new range of business ventures, ranging from companies that pitched consumers an array of survival goods, including "nuke pills" and "apocalypse houses," to major venture capital funds that saw financial fortunes to be made in the chaos.[44]

As the administration moved forward aggressively toward intervention in Iraq, it showed the world another side with a new commitment to the international fight against global HIV/AIDS. In the early years of his presidency, it seemed likely Bush would lead a retreat from the Clinton administration's fight against AIDS at home and abroad, as he only made cautious steps in supporting the international fight against the disease. In May 2001, Bush announced the United States would contribute $200 million to the Global Fund to Fight AIDS, Malaria and Tuberculosis; in June 2002, he promised to increase funding to that UN-backed program to $500 million. Such funds were "desperately needed," experts noted, but not nearly enough. "That is a drop in the ocean," noted Dr. Peter Lamptey, director of the AIDS Institute at Family Health International. "The U.S. could do a lot more, and the amount they are spending is disappointing, very disappointing."[45]

In his January 2003 State of the Union Address, Bush surprised such critics by announcing that his administration would significantly ramp up its commitments by dedicating $15 billion over the next five years to the global fight against AIDS. Many reacted with skepticism, but Bush quickly went to work, lobbying aggressively for the legislation and marshaling biblical language to win over religious conservatives. "When we see a plague leaving graves and orphans across a continent, we must act," he urged. "When we see the wounded traveler on the road to Jericho, we will not—America will not—pass to the other side of the road."[46] He found strong support from a number of congressional Republicans, including Senate Majority Leader Bill Frist, a doctor who had taken the lead in the Senate when his party regained control of both chambers of Congress. Only four months after the initial proposal, the full $15 billion in funding had been secured. The initiative—officially known as the President's Emergency Plan for AIDS Relief (PEPFAR)— was directly responsible for a massive increase in the number of people on the African continent who would receive the anti-retroviral drugs that keep HIV from developing into AIDS. Roughly 50,000 Africans had access to these life-saving drugs before PEPFAR. By the end of Bush's term in office, that number had risen to 1.2 million, continuing to rise thereafter. Millions of lives were saved as a result. In the eyes of most observers, it stood as the clearest sign that "compassionate conservatism" was more than an empty slogan.[47]

At the same time, the Bush administration continued its steady march to war. With troops in Afghanistan still trying to maintain order and solidify the new government and Osama Bin Laden still at large, the Bush White House faced an uphill climb in selling a new military operation. For many in the administration, making the case for the war in Iraq revealed a new set of powers and also a new realm of possibilities. In the summer of 2002, reporter Ron Suskind had a startling conversation with a senior Bush advisor, who noted dismissively that journalists were stuck "in what we call the reality-based community," which he defined as those who "believe that solutions emerge from your judicious study of discernible reality." "That's not the way the world really works anymore," this White House advisor insisted. "We're an empire now, and when we act, we create our own reality. And while you're studying that reality—judiciously, as you will—we'll act again, creating other new realities, which you can study too, and that's how things will sort out. We're history's actors," the Bush official concluded confidently, "and you, all of you, will be left to study what we do." In such ways, the political leaders of the Bush White House steadily waved away the insights of experts. Instead, they began with their own conclusions and, only later, found the evidence to prop up those claims. The path to Iraq showed the successes of such an approach, but also its limits.[48]

In the months leading up to the war, the administration accelerated the campaign to convince Americans that Iraq posed a threat to them. In February 2003, Secretary of State Colin Powell, one of the most trusted officials in American politics, testified on television before the United Nations Security Council to present data "proving" that Iraq had a serious, operational weapons program. Though most of the evidence was based on flimsy intelligence, the images and transcripts were enough to bolster support for the war in the United States, especially coming from Powell. "People may disagree with him, but they never question his integrity or dead honesty," Reagan's secretary of state George Shultz noted at the time. "If he says something, they know he believes it—and means it." With Powell putting his credibility behind the administration's claims, the United States managed to put together an international coalition of supporters, despite the objection of long-standing allies such as France.[49]

As war seemed increasingly inevitable, a significant opposition took shape. The protests against the war in Iraq proved larger than any anti-war movement since the nuclear freeze campaigns of the 1980s and the protests against the Vietnam War in the 1960s. But this time, the protests took on new forms. Notably, the internet offered activists a tool to reach huge numbers of Americans with information and messages about protests. A group in Vermont called TrueMajority.org, for instance, raised $1 million and grew its ranks to 350,000 members from the time Congress passed the resolution authorizing the use of force to the time of the actual invasion. Meanwhile, MoveOn.org, an organization formed in 1998 by technology entrepreneurs Joan Blades and Wes Boyd to oppose the impeachment of Bill Clinton, evolved into the principal platform to fight the war. The organization used email, social network sites, and online balloting, as well as more traditional television and print ads, to put pressure on politicians to oppose President Bush's operation. On February 15, 2003, there were protests in hundreds of cities around the globe, with an estimated 12–14 million people taking part in the largest international protest ever. In New York, approximately 400,000 took the streets on a freezing day, shouting "Not in our name!"[50]

Despite the size and scope of such protests, the media paid little attention. Antiwar sentiment was significantly marginalized, especially on the cable news networks. On MSNBC, for instance, the outspoken liberal Phil Donahue's nightly program had emerged in late 2002 and early 2003 as one of the few places where antiwar opinions were expressed with any regularity or sympathy. Three weeks before the invasion of Iraq, MSNBC executives canceled the show. Publicly, the network cited low ratings, but privately it had a different rationale. "Donahue represents a difficult public face for NBC in a time of war," one executive explained in an internal memo. "At the same time, our competitors are waving the flag at every opportunity." Dissent was simply "not good for business," Donahue later recalled. Instead of the liberal's antiwar platform, MSNBC announced it would fill the timeslot with an expanded two-hour edition of a much more popular program, *Countdown: Iraq*.[51]

The backlash to antiwar critics spread far beyond the world of journalism. On March 10, 2003, the Dixie Chicks, a popular country music trio, condemned the rush to war during a concert in London and criticized the president. "Just so you know," lead singer Natalie Maines told the crowd, "we're on the good side with y'all. We do not want this war, this violence, and we're ashamed the president of the United States is from Texas." The singer's comment originally passed with little notice, but within a few days that had all changed. "Reports of the remark spread to the United States through Web sites," the *New York Times* marveled, "notably the Drudge Report and a conservative site called Freerepublic.com, and in no time, the Dixie Chicks . . . found themselves the subject of radio boycotts and public CD burnings." Maines apologized, but the backlash and boycotts remained strong, leading to a 20 percent drop in the band's airplay.[52]

After months of anticipation, the war in Iraq began on March 20, 2003. Following the lessons from the first Gulf War, the Bush White House did everything it could to use cable and network news media to dramatize and publicize the effort. The military brass kept the media on message with daily briefings from its Coalition Media Center in nearby Qatar. General Tommy Franks provided slick, media-friendly briefings on a quarter-million-dollar stage constructed by a set designer who had previously worked for Disney, MGM, and the illusionist David Blaine. The first round of airstrikes, promoted by the Pentagon as the "Shock and Awe" campaign, provided live televised images of "surgical strikes" on targets in Iraq. The full might of the military was now on display, with the human casualties completely obscured. It was, columnist Frank Rich complained, "a victory of TV's show business instincts over news. It was the irresistible clichéd climax to the first 72 hours of TV war coverage with its triumphal story line bereft of gore." Amazed by the fawning coverage given by the media in the initial days of the war, a former Pentagon spokesman could only marvel: "If you hired actors, you could not have gotten better coverage."[53]

Most significantly, when the ground attack began, troops entered Iraq with reporters "embedded" in their units, ensuring that American audiences would literally experience combat from the perspective of

American troops alone. "It's been an extraordinary experience for all of us," CBS News president Andrew Heyward raved. "This really has been, not just a quantitative change, but a qualitative change in war journalism." The new practice of "embeds" changed not just how the war was seen at home, but how it was fought in the field. Embedded NBC reporter Chip Reid recalled a debate he saw between two US marines over what to do with some Iraqi civilians they encountered, with one calling for all the Iraqis to be shot and the other counseling caution, as the NBC cameras recorded it all. "I thought at the time they were partly performing for us," Reid remembered. "I don't know how different the conversation would have been if we hadn't been there, but I suspect it would have been different." A later analysis from BBC News made it clear that, for all their claims of providing unvarnished access to the front lines, broadcasts from "embeds" had in fact been highly sanitized. There was, the report concluded, a conscious desire not to present viewers at home with images that were too graphic or potentially upsetting. The administration also prohibited reporters from covering the returning bodies of soldiers, with the stated intention of protecting the privacy of the families but the strategic hope of blunting the kind of backlash that developed earlier over images of body bags coming back from Vietnam.[54]

Initially, the war went quite smoothly, generating nothing but good news for audiences at home. As in Afghanistan, the American-led coalition made quick inroads against Iraqi forces and soon brought down the Hussein regime. The joint military and media campaigns reached their peak on May 1, 2003. In a carefully scripted photo-op, President Bush, a former Texas Air National Guard pilot, dramatically landed a plane on the USS *Abraham Lincoln*. The aircraft carrier had been positioned off the California coast, half a world away from the combat zone, especially for the event. The images of Bush, striding confidently across the aircraft carrier in a flight suit, proved irresistible for many in the media. *New York Times* columnist Maureen Dowd compared him to Tom Cruise's Navy fighter pilot from the action film *Top Gun*. "Maverick was back, cooler and hotter than ever," she raved, "throttling to the max with joystick politics." On MSNBC, Chris Matthews was likewise thrilled about the president's performance. "Americans love having a guy as president, a guy who has a little swagger, who's physical," he said.

After changing back into a business suit, the president then delivered a more serious speech from the carrier deck, in which he declared the end of combat operations in Iraq. Behind him on the upper reaches of the aircraft carrier stretched a huge banner: "Mission Accomplished."[55]

Once again, the loudest cheerleaders for the war were at Fox News. Shedding any pretense of objectivity, the network unabashedly took the administration's perspective, appropriating the Pentagon's name for the war, "Operation Iraqi Freedom," and using it as the title for its own coverage. As one newspaper noted with alarm, "the United States quickly becomes 'our' in reporters' parlance." The network led its viewers to see support for the war as the only patriotic choice, encouraging them to send in pictures of their families supporting the troops. "There are so many pictures of protesters out there," noted Steve Doocy, cohost of the morning show *Fox & Friends*. "We want to show pictures of pro-Americans." Notably, leading figures on the network insisted there was nothing wrong with their pro-administration approach. "So am I slanted and biased? You damn well bet I am," anchor Neil Cavuto said in response to such criticism. "You say I wear my biases on my sleeve? Better that than pretend you have none, but show them clearly in your work."[56]

Despite such positive spin from supporters in the media, it quickly became clear that there were real problems in Iraq. Notwithstanding the president's speech on the *Abraham Lincoln*, combat operations continued and in many cases became more complicated. Soon after coalition forces took control of the country, for instance, severe looting took place at the antiquities museums of Baghdad. Secretary Rumsfeld shrugged off the problem with a flippant answer: "Stuff happens." Much more serious was the fact that after a thorough search of the entire country, no evidence of weapons of mass destruction was found anywhere. The rationale for the entire war had proved to be false. Commentators started to conclude that the evidence used by US officials had been faulty and misleading, and that there had been a rush to war. At the same time, it soon became clear that preinvasion predictions that Iraq's oil wealth would effectively pay for the conflict had been wildly overoptimistic. When the administration went to Congress in October to seek $87 billion in supplemental funding, even Republican members began to balk. John Pitney, a political scientist, captured the growing problem for the administration well: "The president's poll numbers are down, the casualty rate [in Iraq] is up, and Republicans are nervous."[57]

Meanwhile, other problems mounted for the Bush White House. First, a congressional commission conducted hearings to determine whether the 9/11 attacks could have been prevented. The commission reviewed the Presidential Daily Briefings provided by the intelligence community and concluded that there had been strong suggestions about the possibility of an attack. On May 1, 2001, for instance, the CIA had informed the White House that a terrorist operation was being planned; on June 22, it had explained an al-Qaeda strike was "imminent." Most damning, on August 6, 2001, Bush had received a briefing paper authored by counterterrorism official Richard Clarke entitled "Bin Laden Determined to Strike in U.S." When some administration officials pushed back, the CIA gave the president a detailed analysis insisting the intelligence was very sound. Providing a sobering account of the mistakes made before 9/11, Clarke published a book describing how such warnings had been ignored.[58]

Another scandal that rocked the administration centered on the Abu Ghraib detention center outside Baghdad. Photographs released on CBS's *60 Minutes 2* on April 28, 2003, showed US soldiers humiliating and brutalizing prisoners in the facility. One picture showed a male prisoner hooded with his hands tied with wire; another depicted guards forcing a different male prisoner to mimic sexual activity with another. One of the most disturbing photographs showed Private Lynndie England displaying a "thumbs up" sign to the camera as she gleefully pointed to a naked Iraqi man who was being forced to masturbate while his head was covered by a bag. Investigative reporting by Seymour Hersh in *The New Yorker* indicated that these events had not been an aberration by renegade soldiers but rather an outgrowth of a systematic program of torture. He reported one case where an Iraqi prisoner was "stressed . . . out" so badly by CIA officials that "the man passed away. They put his body in a body bag and packed him in ice for approximately twenty-four hours in the shower. . . . The next day the medics came and put his body on a stretcher, placed a fake IV in his arm and took him away." Hidden from public record, according to Hersh, the victim never even had an official number.[59] Such exposés implicated the harsh interrogation policies that the Pentagon had been using since 9/11. "It's a blinding glimpse of the obvious to say we're in a hole," admitted Deputy Secretary of State Richard Armitage. "For many of our European friends, what they saw on those horrible pictures is tantamount to torture. . . . In the Arab world there is general dismay and disgust, but in some places we were not real popular to start with."[60] In a review of press opinion in Germany, *Der Spiegel* concluded: "In editorials, most newspapers on Friday call for Guantanamo to be closed—once and forever." Despite public outrage, Bush refused to let Secretary of Defense Rumsfeld resign.[61]

As controversy mounted and the war wore on, Bush found his public support flagging. His approval rating, which had skyrocketed from the mid-50s to nearly 90 in the wake of the 9/11 attacks, had slowly come back down to the 50s in the months that followed. It jumped back into the 70s during the early months of the Iraq war, but once again, as the initial thrill wore off and Americans confronted the true costs of the conflict, the president's popularity sagged. By December 2003, the CBS News-*New York Times* poll had his approval rating at 52 percent; it briefly shot up again to 58 percent when Saddam Hussein was finally captured by American troops, but the fluctuations only showed how precarious his position would be as he headed into his reelection campaign.[62]

In the end, the series of events that began with 9/11 radically transformed the nation. In terms of its national security approach, the United States thoroughly overhauled its military and diplomatic footing, vastly expanded the reach of the federal government with new programs, ramped up its counterterrorism infrastructure and, most notably, engaged in two major wars. But beyond the obvious changes of the post-9/11 world, the threat of terrorism saturated the landscape, impacting popular culture and deepening the lines of partisan division as well. While much of the strategy initiated by the Bush administration and its bipartisan supporters in Congress would remain contested, by the time Bush left office the policies initially put into place to combat al-Qaeda had become firmly entrenched. The Cold War had been replaced by the war on terror. And much as the struggle against Communism had shaped the domestic life of the mid-twentieth century, the fight against terrorism would shape the contours of life in the twenty-first.

CHAPTER 13

The Politics of Mass Destruction

As HE TURNED TO HIS REELECTION CAMPAIGN IN 2004, George W. Bush retreated from "compassionate conservatism" and rediscovered the divisive issues of the culture wars to rally his base. Increasingly playing to the political struggles over abortion and LGBTQ rights, the president rallied the Religious Right and, in so doing, deepened the nation's divisions over gender and sexuality. A new wave of liberal critics rose to challenge the president, working across a range of media, but ultimately his plan worked.

However, scorched-earth politics came at a cost. Bush won reelection by the narrowest margin for an incumbent president in over a century's time, and found himself increasingly vulnerable in his second term. As the Iraq War soured abroad, at home the administration found itself under fire for its mishandling of Hurricane Katrina and other crises. Democrats soon turned the tables on the president, politicizing national security issues in the 2006 midterms in much the same way that Republicans had in 2002. Divided more and more by domestic politics and foreign affairs, the nation became driven to starker levels of polarization and partisanship.

Return to the Culture Wars

As the 2004 election drew near, Bush's advisors convinced him he needed to rally religious conservatives. Accordingly, the president picked up many of the old issues of social conservatives and pressed them to new heights. The struggle over abortion, for instance, quickly moved to the forefront of his agenda. Bush had, of course, already shown his support for the right-to-life movement with some symbolic steps. Its political allies were given prominent positions in the administration, including John Ashcroft as attorney general and Tommy Thompson as secretary of health and human services. More significantly, on the anniversary of *Roe v. Wade*, Bush resurrected a ban on federal funding for any organizations that provided abortion services abroad, a restoration of a Reagan executive order known by pro-choice critics as the "global gag rule."[1]

In addition to these executive actions, Bush worked to secure two landmark pieces of pro-life legislation at home. In November 2003, the president signed into law the measure known by antiabortion activists as the "partial-birth abortion ban." Although the specific procedure was incredibly rare, the ban was seen by all sides as a major step in the long campaign of religious conservatives to roll back abortion rights. The following year, in April 2004, the president signed another major piece of antiabortion legislation: the Unborn Victims of Violence Act (UVVA), which held that, if a pregnant woman were murdered, the fetus would be legally considered a second victim. Once more, the practical applications of the law were quite limited, but the larger ramifications were nevertheless quite considerable. "What the UVVA does is give legal recognition to life in the womb," noted a spokesperson for Focus on the Family.[2]

As Bush moved to advance the Religious Right's agenda on abortion in 2003 and 2004, he likewise moved to meet their demands to block gains in LGBTQ rights. The president had long wanted to avoid the controversial issue and had successfully done so for years. As he well knew, public attitudes on LGBTQ rights had grown considerably more liberal over the last decades. The portion of Americans who considered homosexuality an "acceptable lifestyle" had risen from 34 percent in 1982 to 50 percent in 1999, while attitudes to civil rights protections showed even broader support. The percentage of Americans who believed gays and lesbians should have the right to equal job opportunities, for instance, rose from 56 percent in 1977 to 88 percent in 2003. Such polls showed that religious conservatives, who saw such protections as unwarranted "special rights" for gays and lesbians, were on the losing side of cultural changes. When the Supreme Court handed down the *Lawrence v. Texas* decision striking down bans on sodomy in June 2003, it sparked a renewed backlash on the right. "We think this is the start of the court putting San Francisco values on the rest of the country," noted an analyst with the Culture and Family Institute. In particular, they feared federal courts would extend the logic of *Lawrence* and legalize same-sex marriage as well. "That's where we are headed," worried Richard Lessner of the Family Research Council. "We're convinced this case was brought to provide the foundation for same-sex marriages." When Massachusetts became the first state to legalize same-sex marriage, prompted by a court decision in 2004, the Religious Right's worst fears seemed to be coming true.[3]

To prevent other states from following suit, religious conservatives focused on a new campaign for a constitutional amendment that would formally define marriage as a partnership between one man and one woman. In the eyes of the Religious Right, the drive for this amendment took on heroic proportions. James Dobson of Focus on the Family said the fight would be nothing less than "our D-Day, or Gettysburg, or Stalingrad." The Traditional Values Coalition mailed out literature at a rate of 1.5 million pieces monthly, while other organizations like the Family Research Council and Focus on the Family fully devoted themselves to the cause. That fall, the Arlington Group—a new umbrella organization formed specifically for the fight against same-sex marriage—announced plans to distribute literature to 70,000 congregations and reach millions more through radio and television. The strong engagement of religious conservatives in the Republican base forced Bush to abandon his hands-off approach to LGBTQ rights. In February 2004, the president formally called for passage of the Federal Marriage Amendment (FMA). "Activist judges and local officials have made an aggressive attempt to redefine marriage," Bush insisted. "If we are to prevent the meaning of marriage from being changed forever, our nation must enact a constitutional amendment to protect marriage in America." The FMA campaign stalled in the Senate after a few weeks, but religious conservatives kept the base focused on the campaign through ballot referenda on same-sex marriage in eleven states. "Make no mistake, my friends," said Gary Bauer, "the sanctity of marriage will be the defining issue of 2004."[4]

As the Right mobilized for another round of the culture wars, so did the Left. Seeing the success conservatives had had in the 1990s using innovative media forms like talk radio, the internet, and cable to challenge a Democratic administration, liberals tried to form the same sort of media resistance now that there was a Republican in the White House. In March 2004, Air America Radio debuted, offering a new network of liberal talk-radio programming that was meant to copy and counterbalance the success of right-wing radio hosts like Rush Limbaugh and Sean Hannity. Early hosts included left-leaning comedians like Al Franken, Marc Maron, and Janeane Garofalo, liberal journalists like Sam Seder and Rachel Maddow, and Chuck D of the hip-hop group Public Enemy. Despite the early promise and enthusiasm, Air America had trouble finding stations and securing a regular audience. While it began operations on only five stations, Limbaugh and Hannity were on hundreds each. Moreover, reviewers noted that the liberal hosts were temperamentally different from the conservatives they hoped to mimic. "Satire and sarcasm come more easily than rage to Mr. Franken," one noted. "And rage—unbound by reason or reticence—is what fuels most successful political talk shows." On-air problems were nothing compared to the behind-the-scenes chaos. Over its first two months of operation, the *New York Times* reported, the "fledgling talk-radio network has replaced five top executives, been taken off the air in two of its top three markets and lost several crucial producers." The network struggled with funding from the start and, in October 2006, had to file for bankruptcy.[5]

Liberal programming found greater success on television, a medium better suited to sarcasm and satire. Most notably, *The Daily Show with Jon Stewart* on the cable channel Comedy Central quickly emerged as a favorite site for bewildered liberals seeking to make sense of the age of George W. Bush. The show, which launched in 1996 but really took off in 1999 when Stewart started hosting, won both critical and public acclaim. The winner of several Emmy and Peabody Awards, the show averaged over a million viewers a night in early 2004. Democratic politicians soon took note, with Senator John Edwards of North Carolina announcing his presidential candidacy on the program. "You know, we're a fake show," Stewart responded. "So this may not count." Despite such claims, more and more Americans were in fact getting their infor-

Modern political campaigns became nastier and more divisive as polarization rigidified in the electorate. Lee Atwater, one of the masterminds of the new campaign style, orchestrated a brutal attack against 1988 Democratic nominee Michael Dukakis to bolster the standing of Vice President George H. W. Bush. This photo op, staged by Dukakis's campaign, backfired when Atwater used the image to paint the Democrat as weak on defense. (*Photo: Steve Liss/LIFE Magazine/Getty Images*)

President George H. W. Bush, who received praise for the care with which he handled the collapse of the Soviet Union, faced his first major military crisis when Iraq invaded Kuwait. Bush believed that it was time for the nation to overcome the "Vietnam Syndrome" that had prevented the use of military force since the 1960s. The president enjoyed Thanksgiving dinner with troops on November 22, 1990, shortly before they were sent into combat. (*Photo: George H. W. Bush Presidential Library*)

The bombing of Baghdad during the Gulf War on January 17, 1991, was covered around the clock by cable news and gave many citizens the impression that new technology offered a "bloodless" way to reassert American power overseas. (*Photo: Laurent Van Der Stockt/Gamma-Rapho/ Getty Images*)

Supreme Court nominations grew more divisive as the parties moved farther apart on Capitol Hill. Anita Hill, a law professor at the University of Oklahoma, testifying in 1991 that Bush's nominee Clarence Thomas sexually harassed her. (*Photo: C-SPAN*)

Racial tensions exploded during the Los Angeles riots in 1992 following the acquittal of four white Los Angeles police officers for the beating of African American motorist Rodney King. (*Photo: Gary Leonard/ Corbis/Getty Images*)

Conservative radio host Rush Limbaugh sits at his desk at Talk Radio 700 KSEV during the 1992 Republican National Convention in Houston. (*Photo: Shepard Sherbell/CORBIS SABA/Getty Images*)

In 1993, President Bill Clinton pushed through Congress the controversial North American Free Trade Agreement that had been signed by his predecessor, President George H. W. Bush. When the two men joined hands to kick off the agreement in September 1993, many Democrats were upset with the president for endorsing a free trade agreement that they believed would cost American workers many jobs. (*Photo: Bill Clinton Presidential Library*)

First Lady Hillary Clinton headed the task force for President Clinton's unsuccessful health care plan in 1993. (*Photo: Jeffrey Markowitz/Sygma/ Getty Images*)

In 1994, Republican Newt Gingrich capitalized on the backlash against President Clinton's health care proposal with the Contract with America. Republicans retook control of Congress for the first time since 1954. (*Photo: Joshua Roberts/ AFP/Getty Images*)

The bombing of a federal building in Oklahoma City in 1995 brought the dangers of white extremism to the forefront of public attention. (*Photo: FEMA Photo Library*)

Howard Stern was a mainstream phenomenon by the mid-1990s, reflecting the liberalization of popular culture that angered so many activists on the right. His depictions of women, gays and lesbians, and minorities also angered many on the left. Here Stern is interviewed by the comedian Joan Rivers. (*Photo: The LIFE Picture Collection-Time & Life Pictures*)

The news became more openly partisan in the 1990s with the establishment of media outlets that reported information from one political perspective. Conservatives proved to be particularly effective at setting up these operations. Rupert Murdoch shakes hands with Roger Ailes after naming Ailes the head of Fox News in New York City in January 1996. (*Photo: Allan Tannenbaum/Getty Images*)

The House of Representatives votes to impeach President Bill Clinton for perjury and obstruction of justice on December 19, 1998. *(Photo: C-SPAN)*

Two newspapers have very different interpretations of the 2000 election the morning after. *(Photo: Henny Ray Abrams/AFP/ Getty Images)*

Pedestrians walk across the Brooklyn Bridge away from the burning World Trade Center towers before their collapse on September 11, 2001. *(Photo: Henny Ray Abrams/AFP/ Getty Images)*

President George W. Bush talks to Vice President Dick Cheney on the telephone during a flight on Air Force One on 9/11. *(Photo: George W. Bush Presidential Library)*

The unity over the administration's response to 9/11 quickly fell apart, especially after the administration sent troops into Iraq to topple Saddam Hussein. The war turned into a military and political quagmire, as American forces were frequently targeted by improvised explosive devices. Here a car bomb has detonated in South Baghdad, 2005. *(Photo: US Army)*

Hurricane Katrina devastated New Orleans in August 2005. The effects fell hardest on the African American community. President George W. Bush's slow response hurt his political standing. *(Photo: Gary Nichols/US Navy)*

President Barack Obama, speaking to the prime minister of Iraq in February 2009, was determined to repair the damage that he believed President Bush had caused overseas with the war in Iraq. *(Photo: President Obama Presidential Library)*

Tea Party protest in St. Paul, Minnesota, on April 15, 2010. After pushing through Congress an economic stimulus, the Affordable Care Act, and the Dodd-Frank financial reforms, President Obama stimulated a fierce right wing backlash. Tea Party activists helped elect a Republican House in 2010. *(Photo: Fibonacci Blue/Flickr)*

A mural in the Pilsen neighborhood of Chicago, Illinois, in 2011. Chicago, like many American cities, was transformed by new waves of immigration in the late twentieth century. By the year 2000, over a quarter of Chicago's population was Hispanic. *(Photo: Adam Jones, PhD/ Wikimedia Commons)*

Black Lives Matter became a national movement in the wake of the killing of Michael Brown, an unarmed African American teenager, in Ferguson, Missouri, in 2014. Here, Black Lives Matter protesters demonstrate at Hofstra University before the first 2016 presidential debate. *(Photo: Brian Allen/Voice of America)*

President Obama and President-elect Trump, who represented two very different directions for the country, meet following the historic and shocking 2016 election. *(Photo: Jim Watson/AFP/Getty Images)*

 Donald J. Trump ✔
@realDonaldTrump

Follow ∨

The FAKE NEWS media (failing @nytimes, @NBCNews, @ABC, @CBS, @CNN) is not my enemy, it is the enemy of the American People!

3:48 PM - 17 Feb 2017

One of the major themes of President Donald Trump's 2016 campaign was the untrustworthiness of the mainstream media. He used social media to convey this theme. President Trump continued to attack the media as president; in this tweet from February 2017, Trump calls the media the "enemy of the American People." *(Photo: Twitter)* mation from a growing number of "soft news" shows that blended enter-tainment, comedy, and political news. Studies showed that more than a fifth of all Americans under the age of thirty learned about develop-ments in the 2004 presidential campaign from satirical sources like *The Daily Show* or the opening monologues of late-night talk-show hosts. Riffing on CNN's slogan—"the most trusted name in news"—*The Daily Show* dubbed itself "the most trusted name in fake news."[6]

Rather than simply lampooning the "real" news networks, Jon Stewart went a step further and confronted them, both on his own show and, in time, on theirs. In October 2004, he appeared on CNN's *Crossfire*, a program that—as its title implied—featured a rapid-fire debate between two combative partisans, one from the left, one from the right. *Crossfire* had been a staple of CNN's programming since its debut in 1982, with the pairs of partisan hosts changing over time. Sitting between Paul Begala, a former Clinton aide arguing "from the left," and Tucker Carl-son, a conservative journalist speaking "from the right," Stewart directly attacked the program itself. "It's hurting America," the comedian told the hosts, turning surprisingly earnest. "You have a responsibility to public discourse, and you fail miserably." When Carlson tried to laugh it off, saying, "You need to get a job at a journalism school, I think," Stewart shot back: "You need to go to one." The episode quickly went viral on the internet, where it found repeated replays. As one media critic noted, Stewart's outburst "stood out because he said what a lot of viewers feel helpless to correct: that news programs, particularly on cable, have become echo chambers for political attacks, amplifying the noise instead of parsing the misinformation." As the backlash against *Crossfire* grew, CNN announced at the start of the next year that the long-running show would be canceled.[7]

As an alternative to cable news in the Bush era, liberals increasingly turned to the internet. Vermont governor Howard Dean—previously a centrist from the Clinton wing of the party—drew in support from younger and more liberal Democrats through his unapologetic and unambiguous opposition to the war in Iraq. Dean's campaign ulti-mately fizzled, in part from a celebratory scream that echoed across cable television, but it nevertheless made a lasting contribution to the mechanisms of political campaigns. Joe Trippi, who came to politics from a background in the computer industry, served as the architect of the Dean movement. He recognized the impact that new sites like Friendster (2002), MySpace (2003), LinkedIn (2003), and Facebook (2004) had in connecting disparate populations around shared professional interests or personal tastes and worked closely with computer gurus Matthew Gross and Zephyr Teachout to pioneer the use of social networking sites to attract a range of supporters. "We were the Wright brothers," Trippi recalled. "We had great ideas, and we were doing it in a very primitive way with what was possible." They used early social media sites like Meetup.com to bring supporters together for grassroots campaign events at local coffee houses and neighborhood bars. "A lot of the people on the net had given up on traditional politics precisely because it was about television and the ballot box, and they had no way to shout back," Dean noted. "What we've given people is a way to shout back, and we listen—though they don't even have to shout anymore." In addition to mobilizing supporters, the campaign used the internet to raise campaign funds. In the third quarter of 2003 alone, Dean raised nearly $15 million online—setting a single-quarter record for a Democratic presidential candidate and showing the true power of online politics.[8]

Beyond the Dean campaign, a thriving community of liberal bloggers had developed politically active communities online. Several formed in the aftermath of the 2000 election, such as Josh Marshall's *Talking Points Memo* (TPM), which debuted during the Florida recount. By the time of the 2004 election, the liberal "blogosphere" was fully formed. A number of prominent new voices—Markos Moulitsas of *The Daily Kos*, Duncan Black of *Eschaton*, and Jesse Taylor and Ezra Klein of *Pandagon*—took their laptops directly to the presidential conventions that year to report live in makeshift war rooms that seemed like low-budget guerilla versions of the cable news networks' operations. In many ways, these liberal blogs represented the real answer to right-wing radio. "Left-wing politics are thriving on blogs the way Rush Limbaugh has dominated talk radio," the *New York Times Magazine* noted in a September 2004 piece titled "Fear and Laptops on the Campaign Trail," "and in the last six months, the angrier, nastier partisan blogs have been growing the fastest."[9]

As liberals and leftists ramped up their activism across these new forms of media, the Democratic Party rallied around Massachusetts senator John Kerry as its presidential nominee. A decorated Vietnam veteran, Kerry had risen to national fame after returning home and leading other veterans in protest against a war they had come to see as a mistake. Kerry and the Democrats hoped his military record would inoculate him from the kind of attacks that the Republicans had made in the 2002 midterms and, more pointedly, offer a contrast to President Bush, who had secured safe domestic assignments during Vietnam. But Republicans mounted a fierce pushback, portraying Kerry as a flip-flopping liberal elitist with no clear stance on terrorism. Nominally independent organizations such as the Swift Boat Veterans for Truth even challenged Kerry's record of military service, publicly claiming that the wartime incidents in a navy swift boat for which he had been awarded the Silver Star, the Bronze Star, and three Purple Hearts were fabrications. (The term "swiftboating," meaning a smear campaign against a candidate, soon became part of the political lexicon.) Ultimately, the allegations blunted Kerry's ability to use his military record and made the race incredibly close.

In the general election, both sides mobilized their bases with increasingly charged rhetoric. While the Left had ramped up its activism, it proved no match for the Right. Notably, in the key targeted demographics of the Religious Right, President Bush improved his 2000 performance by small but significant margins. His standing with white evangelical voters increased from 72 to 78 percent and Catholic voters from 47 to 52 percent. These national shifts were even more pronounced in swing states like Ohio, where a state referendum on same-sex marriage brought large numbers of socially conservative voters to the polls to vote against same-sex marriage and, at the same time, for the Republican ticket. "I see people marching like a holy army to the voting booth," Pastor Rod Parsley told his 12,000-member evangelical church in Columbus. "I see the Holy Spirit anointing you as you vote for life, as you vote for marriage, as you vote for the pulpit!" The call to "defend" marriage from the LGBTQ rights movement clearly resonated, as Ohio Catholics rallied to the Republican ticket. Thousands of Bush campaign field workers dispersed to Catholic churches across the state, making sure they were registered to vote and motivated to do so. Their impressive ground game succeeded in getting conservative congregations to the polls. On election day, Bush broadened his share of the Ohio Catholic vote from 50 to 55 percent. Notably, that gain of 172,000 votes was more than his 130,000-vote margin of victory in a pivotal state.[10]

While the Religious Right proved to be a vital part of the Republican coalition, many observers exaggerated the election returns as a mandate for their agenda. In particular, some pundits pointed to National Election Pool (NEP) exit polling that suggested some 22 percent of voters claimed "moral values" were more important to them than any other issue. GOP strategists seized on the poll as a sign of success, arguing that 80 percent of these "values voters" chose the Republican ticket. Yet the data were not so straightforward, and the Republican argument that the election demonstrated a new "moral values" mandate was overblown. As Andrew Kohut of the Pew Research Center noted, the "moral values" answer ranked high in the exit polling because it was an attractive and ambiguous catchall. Combining separate categories like "terrorism" and "the Iraq war" as a single "national security" category, for instance, would have represented 34 percent of respondents; likewise, a broad "economic" category would have taken 33 percent. Despite such analysis, prominent social conservatives still spun the results their own way. "President Bush now has a mandate to affect policy that will promote a more decent society, through both politics and the law," argued William Bennett. "Now is the time to begin our long, national cultural renewal."[11]

To the frustration of the Religious Right, however, Bush moved away from their agenda after the election and instead signaled that his priority would be to focus on the privatization of Social Security. "I earned capital in this campaign, political capital," the president noted after his reelection, "and now I intend to spend it." Bush devoted the early months of 2005 to shoring up support for privatizing the New Deal program, devoting much of his State of the Union address to the proposal and then holding a series of public events to persuade voters. The more they heard about the idea, however, the less they liked it. Gallup reported that disapproval of the president's handling of Social Security actually increased as he pitched the plan, from 48 to 64 percent over the first half of the year. As the proposal stalled in Congress, it seemed clear that the president had indeed spent most of the political capital he acquired in the campaign. The Religious Right, furious that Bush had devoted his energies to Social Security instead of a federal marriage amendment, refused to be ignored again. "Business as usual isn't going to cut it, where the GOP rides to victory by espousing traditional family values and then turns around and rewards the liberals in its ranks," asserted Robert Knight of Concerned Women for America. "If the GOP wants to expand and govern effectively, it can't play both sides of the fence anymore. It needs a coherent message, which came through loud and clear in the election."[12]

Religious conservatives soon found a cause in the case of Terri Schiavo. The Florida woman had collapsed in 1990 and entered what physicians called a "persistent vegetative state." After several years with no signs of improvement, her husband Michael Schiavo petitioned to have his wife finally taken off the artificial system of life support. But her parents, devout Catholics, argued that such actions were violations of their family's faith and fought him in court. They enlisted the support of pro-life activists and sympathetic politicians like Florida governor Jeb Bush, the president's brother. Their protests in Terri Schiavo's name transformed an isolated family dispute into a national political controversy. In March 2005, Florida courts authorized Michael Schiavo to remove the feeding tubes that had been keeping his wife alive for the previous fifteen years. Republicans swiftly intervened. Congress passed a special law that required her case to be reviewed once more by the federal courts, which Bush then signed in a dramatic, late-night ceremony.[13]

While the Schiavo case energized the Religious Right, the government's intervention served to alienate even larger numbers. An ABC News poll showed that Americans supported Michael Schiavo's position, 63 percent to 28 percent. They also opposed congressional involvement in the family's dispute, 70 percent to 27 percent. Notably, even 54 percent of self-described conservatives and 61 percent of Republicans supported the husband's decision to end life support. Many in the party saw the entire incident as evidence of the Religious Right's exaggerated influence. "This Republican Party of Lincoln has become a party of theocracy," argued Representative Chris Shays, a moderate Republican from Connecticut. "There are a number of people who feel that the government is getting involved in their personal lives in a way that scares them."[14]

Hurricane Katrina

In many ways, Bush's embrace of the Religious Right in the middle years of his administration undercut his efforts at establishing a new vision of "compassionate conservatism" in America. For liberals impressed by the inroads Bush had made on issues like the AIDS initiative and the faith-based initiative, Bush suddenly seemed like a traditional culture warrior who could not be trusted. But there were costs inside Bush's own party, too. Libertarians had hoped that Bush would reduce the role of government in Americans' lives, but his embrace of social conservatism meant that the federal government was taking an active role in what struck them as entirely private decisions—whether to have a child, whom to marry, how to die on their own terms. While the Bush administration alienated those voters by seeming in these instances to be *too* eager to intervene in the lives of ordinary Americans, it soon wound up alienating even more voters by appearing to be too reluctant to intervene in other cases. This was especially true in the aftermath of Hurricane Katrina's devastation of New Orleans.

In late August 2005, Katrina struck the Gulf Coast. A massive category-5 storm, it ravaged a wide stretch of the coastline, causing destruction from Texas to central Florida. But New Orleans was particularly hit hard, as it lay in the path of the hurricane when it was at its fiercest. The levees that protected the city from the surrounding seas ultimately failed, and soon large sections were underwater. In the end, Hurricane Katrina proved to be the most expensive natural disaster in American history, with property damage estimated at $108 billion. It was one of the deadliest hurricanes in American history as well, with 1,833 deaths attributed to the storm and the subsequent floods.[15]

In a larger sense, another victim of Hurricane Katrina was the image of "compassionate conservatism" itself. Early in his administration, Bush had tried to convince Americans that their basic needs could be handled by local governments and private charities, with the federal government merely offering funding and direction. But the hurricane—and, more important, the federal government's inept and inert response in the weeks that followed—convinced many Americans that there *was* an important role to be played by the government in protecting its citizens during a disaster and caring for their needs directly in its aftermath.[16]

The hurricane had been a natural disaster, but not a complete surprise. Federal agencies like the National Weather Service and the National Hurricane Center provided early warnings that the storm would be a massive catastrophe. As a video later released made clear, officials at these agencies alerted the White House before the storm that the costs would be immense. Specifically, they warned that the levees in New Orleans could fail, leading to catastrophic destruction there. Despite these warnings, leaders at the local, state, and federal levels proved to be badly unprepared. The Democratic mayor of New Orleans and the Democratic governor of Louisiana both were ineffective leaders during the crisis, which was only made worse when much of the New Orleans Police Department abandoned the city. As the region was overwhelmed by the massive destruction of homes, a large number of deaths, and widespread flooding, power outages, and food shortages, local leaders simply froze, unsure of what they could do.[17]

Hurricane victims huddled inside the New Orleans Superdome, which had been designated as a relief center. But it was understaffed and lacked basic supplies like food and water. Without power or backup generators, it had no air conditioning or running water. Those who had hoped to find relief in the Superdome soon came to feel it was a prison. Despite the horrible conditions there, National Guardsmen refused to let them leave for days, afraid that they would be swept away in the floodwaters outside. A state of panic set in, with rumors of rapes and even a suicide sweeping through the Superdome, with no sign of relief in sight. The siege mentality was made all the clearer as policemen from the New Orleans suburb of Gretna established a roadblock on the bridge between the city and their suburb. Residents and tourists in New Orleans who tried to flee the chaos of the city were turned back at gunpoint. According to multiple witnesses, the Gretna police threatened to shoot anyone who approached them.[18]

As the situation worsened in New Orleans, the cable news networks broadcast scenes of devastation and destruction across the nation. Four days after the storm, Americans were stunned to see dead bodies still lying in the street or floating in the floodwaters. The Superdome, once a symbol of American achievement, now seemed like a Third World nightmare. And yet the federal government was nowhere to be seen. Even field reporters for Fox News, the conservative network that routinely backed the Bush administration, were outraged at what they saw. Prominent figures there, such as anchor Shepard Smith and journalist Geraldo Rivera, reported live from scenes of destruction that clearly left them in a state of shock.[19]

As the nation watched reports like these, they were stunned to see that the Bush administration was essentially doing nothing. As the hurricane hit, the president stayed isolated at his ranch in Crawford, Texas. After two days there, he finally flew east, but to Washington rather than the storm-ravaged Gulf Coast. On his trip back to the White House, Bush had Air Force One fly low over the region so he could look at the damage along the way. The White House released photos of the president doing this, in an effort to show that he was concerned, but the imagery only made it seem that the president was even more detached and distant.[20]

Bush remained unengaged for days, believing that the officials he had placed in charge of the Federal Emergency Management Agency (FEMA) had the situation in hand. But those officials lacked the training, the skills, and even the will to lead the massive rescue and cleanup operation that was mandated by the storm. During the Clinton years, FEMA had gained a strong reputation as an efficient and effective responder to a variety of disasters, including several massive hurricanes and the 1995 domestic terrorist attack in Oklahoma City. After 9/11, however, Bush made the formerly independent agency part of the new Department of Homeland Security. That massive new department, however, was concerned first and foremost with preventing man-made disasters from acts of terrorism, making FEMA's focus on natural disasters seem secondary. The agency's funding was reduced, with a number of key functions farmed out to private contractors; as a result, a number of longtime employees soon left.

The greatest signs of FEMA's reduced importance in the Bush administration were the men the president chose to lead it. Originally, he placed his campaign manager Joe Allbaugh in charge, despite his lack of experience in emergency management. In 2003, Allbaugh was replaced by Michael Brown, another friend from Republican politics with even less experience. Indeed, before FEMA, Brown's last job had been as a lawyer for the International Arabian Horse Association.

Not surprisingly, he proved wholly unqualified at the new position. Brown dithered during the early days of Katrina and, in a live interview, claimed to have been unaware of the suffering in the Superdome, despite the nonstop coverage on cable news. The furor over Brown's incompetence was matched by new outrage over Bush when the president enthusiastically praised him in a public appearance: "Brownie, you're doing a heckuva job!"[21]

Bush's standing in the polls showed how much damage the storm had done to his presidency. In the aftermath of 9/11, when Gallup asked if Bush had strong qualities as a leader, Americans said yes by an overwhelming margin of 83–11. Four years later, in the wake of Katrina, the numbers had dropped to 48–49. Bush's approval ratings, which had been at about 45 percent approval right before the storm, steadily sank in the aftermath. They rose briefly in late 2005, before dropping again into the low 30s by the spring of 2006.[22]

Blowback

As Bush's standing plummeted, liberal voices found a broader audience. *The Daily Show* continued to score top ratings, with one of its star correspondents, Stephen Colbert, spinning off his own successful Comedy Central show in October 2005. Much as *The Daily Show* was designed as a spoof of the straight-news programs of cable news networks, *The Colbert Report* lampooned their prime-time opinion shows. Performing as a conservative blowhard modeled on Bill O'Reilly of Fox News, Colbert sarcastically skewered cable media pundits. In his debut episode, the host offered a new term to describe the figures he mocked: "truthiness." "Truthiness is sort of what you want to be true, as opposed to what the facts support," he noted in an interview. "Truthiness is a truth larger than the facts that would comprise it—if you cared about facts, which you don't, if you care about truthiness." George W. Bush, to Colbert's character, was the exemplar of "truthiness." Mocking the administration's arguments for invading Iraq, for instance, the host noted: "Doesn't taking Saddam out *feel* like the right thing?" The term quickly caught on, and "truthiness" was chosen as the 2006 "Word of the Year" by the *Merriam-Webster Dictionary*.[23]

Suddenly a media sensation, Colbert was asked to provide the entertainment in April 2006 for the White House Correspondents Dinner. Much like his show, his dinner routine mocked the president and the press in equal measure. "I know there's some polls out there saying this man has a 32-percent approval rating," Colbert said in character, with Bush at his side. "But guys like us, we don't pay attention to the polls. We know that polls are just a collection of statistics that reflect what people are thinking 'in reality.' And reality has a well-known liberal bias." At the same time, Colbert mocked the media's handling of the Bush White House. "Let's review the rules. Here's how it works: The president makes decisions. He's the decider. The press secretary announces those decisions, and you people of the press type those decisions down. Make, announce, type. Just put 'em through a spell check and go home," he said. With so much free time, Colbert continued, reporters could do other things: "Write that novel you got kicking around in your head. You know, the one about the intrepid Washington reporter with the courage to stand up to the administration? You know, fiction!" Neither the president nor the press in the ballroom seemed to appreciate the withering sarcasm leveled by Colbert, but the speech quickly became a viral sensation online.[24]

As comic pundits like Stephen Colbert and Jon Stewart proved that criticism of the president could be popular and profitable, "real news" followed suit. Notably, MSNBC, the station that had previously assumed antiwar dissent was a ratings killer, belatedly emerged as a critic of the administration, especially on its handling of the war on terror and the war in Iraq. Keith Olbermann, a former sports anchor at ESPN, emerged as MSNBC's new star, hosting a nightly program called *Countdown with Keith Olbermann*. On August 30, 2006, the host introduced viewers to his first "special comment," tearing into administration figures with vitriol previously unseen from the Left on cable television. "The man who sees absolutes where all other men see nuances and shades of meaning is either a prophet or a quack," the host said, staring sternly into the camera. "Donald H. Rumsfeld is not a prophet." The new feature soon became a staple of Olbermann's show, prompting strong ratings as a result. The MSNBC host had become, in the double-edged praise of a *New York Magazine* title, the "Limbaugh for Lefties."[25]

As criticism mounted in the press and its public approval collapsed, the Bush administration also faced serious setbacks in the war on terror. Controversies over the counterterrorism programs arose with revelations of violations of human rights and international treaties. Guantanamo Bay, or "Gitmo," became a symbol for many Democrats of how the administration had violated the law in pursuit of terrorists. Even the Supreme Court struck a blow to the administration here. In its June 2006 decision in *Hamdan v. Rumsfeld*, the court ruled 5–3 that the special military commissions at Guantanamo violated both the Geneva Conventions and the Uniform Code of Military Justice. (Chief Justice Roberts, appointed by Bush the previous year, recused himself because he had been involved in an earlier stage of the case.) Contradicting the legal claims constructed by Vice President Dick Cheney and his allies in the executive branch, the court's majority held that detainees had both the right to legal counsel and the right to challenge their arrest within the parameters of the US law. "The ruling destroys one of the key pillars of the Guantanamo system," noted Gerald Staberock, director of the International Commission of Jurists in Geneva. "Guantanamo was built on the idea that prisoners there have limited rights. There is no longer that legal black hole."[26]

The war in Iraq also continued to disintegrate. With Saddam Hussein's repressive regime out of power, internal ethnic conflict increasingly tore the region apart. Unlike the swift and seemingly decisive victories of the "shock and awe" bombing campaigns and the initial invasion, American troops found themselves fighting an ever more complex and frustrating war. Increasingly, they came under attack through the use of improvised explosive devices (IEDs). Set up as booby traps or detonated through radio-controlled detonators, IEDs were often buried in unpaved roads, hidden inside dead animals, or placed alongside railroad tracks. These homemade bombs originally cost about $1,200 to make, but by 2009 they could be assembled for under $300, as insurgents learned how to use American military material that had been left behind in the initial invasion. "There's more ammunition in Iraq than any place I've ever seen in my life, and it's not securable," complained General John P. Abizaid, head of the US Central Command.[27]

As the administration's political problems escalated, Democrats seized the initiative. Polls in late 2006 showed that two-thirds of the public said the war in Iraq was not going well and directly disapproved of the president's handling of the issue. In a stunning reversal of the 2002 midterms, it was the Democrats who now politicized national security concerns and the Republicans who found themselves playing defense. With TV ads spotlighting their resistance to the war and highlighting the administration's failures, the opposition party turned the tables. "For the first time in modern memory, Democrats are actually on the offensive when it comes to national security," marveled a political consultant. "It is really stunning." To be sure, other issues helped the opposition party recover its footing, from the mishandling of Hurricane Katrina to a series of ethical scandals involving the House GOP leadership. But anger and frustration over the war on terrorism and the war in Iraq remained central.[28] Campaigning against the Iraq war, Democrats took control of both houses of Congress that fall. They won thirty-one seats in the House and five in the Senate, flipping both chambers back to Democratic control and returning America to its new norm of divided government. "It was a thumping," a chastened Bush admitted at a White House news conference soon after the election. "I'm confident that we can work together," he announced. "I'm confident that we can overcome the temptation to divide the country between red and blue."[29]

Seeking to forge a compromise between the parties, President Bush looked to an issue on which he had solid credentials: immigration. As governor of Texas during the 1990s, Bush had resisted calls for restrictions on immigration and immigrants' rights as championed by hardliners in his party. In pointed contrast to Governor Pete Wilson of California, the sympathetic Bush told reporters that immigrants were good people who "come to Texas to provide for their families. . . . They come for love." As president, Bush had worked to win over Latino voters to the Republican Party and now saw immigration reform as the key to his plans. The administration rallied around a bipartisan proposal in the Senate that struck a compromise between those who wanted increased border patrols to cut down on new waves of illegal immigration and those who sought a path to citizenship for the twelve million undocumented immigrants already in the nation. While the measure won significant support from politicians in both parties, a revolt by conservatives—who complained that the bill represented "amnesty" for those who had entered the country illegally—effectively killed the measure that summer. Talk radio had been a "big factor" in derailing the plan, noted Senator Jeff Sessions of Alabama, an outspoken opponent. Supporters had hoped to pass it quickly, he said, "before Rush Limbaugh could tell the American people what was in it." But conservative media had shored up the resistance on the right and killed the bill.[30]

Unable to win over hard-liners in his own party, Bush looked to foreign affairs, where he had a freer hand. In a sign of his new conciliatory stance toward Democrats, but also a recognition that the administration's approach in Iraq needed new leaders, Bush now accepted the resignation of his long embattled defense secretary, Donald Rumsfeld. Publicly, the president announced he wanted to "stay the course" in Iraq, but the White House soon shifted its strategies. Rather than pulling back from the conflict, as many of his critics expected, however, the president doubled down. In early 2007, Bush announced a major change known simply as "the surge." Under the leadership of the new defense secretary, Robert Gates, and General David Petraeus, the military launched a significant escalation with 21,500 additional troops. The strategy involved much more than an increase in the size of the military presence, as troops redirected their energy away from fighting insurgents to trying to win over the loyalty of local Iraqis. Though Bush's popularity still fell and support for the wars declined, the new strategy succeeded. The situation on the ground started to stabilize with the number of deaths decreasing. As early as April 2007, military officials claimed that areas such as the Anbar province, recently thought to be lost to insurgents, were now under US control as local Sunni recruits started to turn decisively against al-Qaeda leaders.[31]

Meanwhile, the domestic war on terror continued to expand as well. In 2007, the administration secretly launched the PRISM program. Through this covert operation, the National Security Agency (NSA) began to collect internet communications in a sweeping virtual dragnet meant to capture interactions among potential terrorist threats. The program involved nine of the largest internet companies in Silicon Valley: Microsoft, Yahoo, Google, Facebook, PalTalk, AOL, Skype, YouTube and Apple. Ironically, just as Americans were starting to feel more liberated by their ability to communicate easily through cell phones and social media sites, the federal government was working with key companies among them and strengthening its ability to pry into Americans' daily lives. Employing the provisions of the Foreign Intelligence Surveillance Act, the NSA gradually expanded the scope of its program, working closely with telecommunications and internet firms to obtain a huge bank of collected data. Secret until 2013, the NSA program represented a massive expansion of federal surveillance and spying.[32]

In many ways, the private program of domestic spying revealed a growing level of public mistrust between Americans. In sharp contrast to the bipartisan spirit that had briefly flourished in the wake of the 9/11 attacks and the nation's early interventions in Afghanistan and even Iraq, the Bush presidency came to a close marked by levels of partisan polarization that were even deeper than the ones it had inherited. Potential areas of agreement—like immigration reform—had resulted in failure, encouraging both sides to retreat from the middle and shore up their bases. The fault lines of politics had once again been amplified by new fault lines in media, as the Left finally caught up to the Right in establishing a sustained and successful partisan media presence. With both sides more evenly matched, the domestic politics of mass destruction now carried the dangers of mutually assured destruction too.

CHAPTER 14

Polarized
Politics

WHEN ILLINOIS STATE SENATOR BARACK OBAMA DELIV-
ered the keynote address at the 2004 Democratic Convention, few knew
who he was. On the morning of the speech, the *Philadelphia Daily News*,
echoing the famous question posed about Jimmy Carter in 1976, asked:
"Who the Heck Is This Guy?" Even inside the Democratic campaign,
the choice had been a late surprise. John Kerry's campaign manager,
Mary Beth Cahill, only decided to tap the young African American politician for the keynote speech after hearing him deliver a response to
President Bush's weekly radio address a month earlier.[1]

Although few Americans knew anything about this young Harvard Law School graduate then running for a vacant Senate seat, millions found themselves enamored by the fresh perspective he offered
at the convention. In an era of political dynasties like the Bushes and
the Clintons, a new face stood out. After recounting his own personal
background, Obama challenged the claim that the nation was irreparably
divided between "red states" and "blue states." Rejecting the portrait of
division and disagreement that dominated the way that political pundits
regularly spoke of the country, Obama insisted that there was more commonality throughout the electorate than people acknowledged. "There's
not a black America and a white America and Latino America and Asian
America; there's the United States of America." He continued: "The pundits like to slice and dice our country into red states and blue states. . . .
But I've got news for them, too. We worship an awesome God in the blue
states, and we don't like federal agents poking around our libraries in the
red states. We coach little league in the blue states, and, yes, we've got
some gay friends in the red states." The message resonated particularly

with younger Americans who had grown up in an era of stark polarization and longed for something new. The speech became a sensation, launching Obama into the US Senate that year and, moreover, propelling him toward the presidency.

Obama's decision to confront the fault lines of polarization—political, racial, economic, and sexual—and the overwhelming response it generated, highlighted the ways in which Americans were still searching for common ground after decades of growing apart. There were reasons to hope, as he did then, that the people of the United States were, in fact, united around basic values and a shared sense of national purpose. But as his own presidency would make clear, the deep divisions in the country proved difficult to bridge, and indeed many of them only continued to grow.

The Meltdown

In 2008, the once-unknown Obama was himself the Democratic presidential nominee, facing off against Arizona senator John McCain. Despite Obama's optimism four years before, the nation had only become more deeply divided over the war in Iraq in the intervening years. With President Bush's approval ratings in the low 30s and sinking fast, many Democrats were excited about their candidate's odds. During the primaries, Obama had mounted a surprising and successful challenge to the presumed frontrunner, Senator Hillary Clinton of New York, who couldn't match Obama's grassroots organizational prowess and social media presence. More substantially, Obama presented a stark contrast between himself and Clinton by pointing to her vote in favor of the resolution authorizing the use of force in Iraq. Though not in Congress when the Iraq War began, Obama reminded voters that he had delivered speeches against the war from the very start. Wrapping up the nomination with relative ease, Obama became the first African American to stand as the presidential nominee on a major party ticket.

Senator McCain, who had presented a strong challenge to Bush in the 2000 primaries, proved to be a weak candidate this time around for the Republicans. Unable to escape the shadows of the Bush presidency, his campaign seemed sluggish from the start. His selection of

Alaska governor Sarah Palin as his running mate—the second woman to appear on a major party ticket—initially seemed an inspired choice, a fresh face that excited Republicans much as Obama had energized Democrats. But as she made controversial statements that appealed to the most conservative, and sometimes radical, elements in the Republican base, Palin's evident inexperience quickly became a liability. To the alarm of her handlers, she stumbled with the most basic information during high-profile media events. When Katie Couric of CBS News asked Palin to explain her claims that she had foreign policy insights due to her state's geographic proximity to Russia, the vice presidential candidate offered an odd response. "Our next-door neighbors are foreign countries," Palin said, "there in the state that I am the executive of. As [Russian president Vladimir] Putin rears his head and comes into the air space of the United States of America, where do they go? It's Alaska." Comedians had a field day. On *Saturday Night Live,* Tina Fey delivered a devastating impersonation of the governor, obliviously yelling: "I can see Russia from my house!"[2]

More substantively, the financial meltdown in the fall of 2008 ruined the Republican ticket's chances. The worst economic crisis since the Great Depression, it revolved around the collapse of a housing sector that had soared during the early 2000s. Lenders had embraced a new trend of "subprime mortgages," extending extremely risky loans to borrowers who normally would not have qualified, ballooning the national market into a dangerous bubble. When interest rates on subprime mortgages rose in 2005 and 2006, millions of new homeowners started to feel the pinch. In 2007, the number of foreclosures rose by about 79 percent from the previous years. The housing bubble burst across the country, but some areas were hit particularly hard. Nevada, for instance, emerged as "ground zero" of the foreclosure crisis. More than 77,000 Nevadans lost their homes during 2008, with experts predicting that over the next two years one out of every eleven homes in the state would face foreclosure. Even those who managed to hang on to their house, studies suggested, would see a steep drop in their property values as a result. Homeowners increasingly believed they'd been duped by the banks. Buddy Yates, a 60-year-old preacher in North Las Vegas, lost his three-bedroom home when he couldn't keep up with the $2,365 monthly mortgage payment. Foreclosure, he insisted, had been the banks' plan all along. "When they sold you the home, they knew you weren't going to be able to make the payment," he said. "They don't have compassion for the family who's in the home."[3]

Back on Wall Street, the burst of the housing bubble not only destroyed a significant segment of that particular market but also revealed that the entire financial sector was riddled with fundamental problems. In 1999, Congress had repealed the Glass-Steagall Act, a New Deal measure passed to separate commercial and investment banking and thereby avoid the catastrophic collapses that had propelled the Great Depression. With the regulations of Glass-Steagall removed, commercial banks were able to engage in much riskier investments. Many of them bought up mortgage debts, bundling them and selling them to investors as mortgage-backed securities. Moreover, the repeal of Glass-Steagall also allowed these banks to grow in size considerably through a series of major mergers. The changes here were remarkably swift. In the early 1990s, there had been about three dozen significant financial institutions in the United States; two decades later, they had all merged into just four massive banks.[4]

As such changes allowed banks to grow to an unprecedented size, other developments encouraged them to take greater risks. As chairman of the powerful Senate Banking Committee in the late 1990s and early 2000s, Texas Republican Phil Gramm did everything in his power to reduce government oversight in the financial and business worlds. In 2000, Gramm pushed through the Commodity Futures Modernization Act, which essentially prohibited the regulation of financial instruments known as "derivatives" that would prove vitally important in bringing about the housing bubble and the financial meltdown that followed. Meanwhile, when SEC chair Arthur Levitt sought to introduce new rules that would eliminate conflicts of interest in accounting firms—something that had played a major role in the 2001 collapse of the energy trading giant Enron and sparked a large number of corporate scandals—Gramm responded by threatening to slash the SEC's budget. He demanded that Levitt and the SEC stay out of Wall Street's way: "Unless the waters are crimson with the blood of investors, I don't want you engaging in any regulatory flights of fancy."[5]

Such changes in Washington encouraged Wall Street firms to take greater risks with less worry of ever getting caught. But there was still a reckoning. In March 2008, the giant global investing firm Bear Stearns went under, sparking a massive banking crisis. The government intervened to keep the firm afloat, but that only delayed the inevitable meltdown. On September 15, 2008, Lehman Brothers, the fourth largest investment bank in the United States, declared bankruptcy—the single largest bankruptcy in all of American history. This time, the government decided that it would not, or could not, save Lehman Brothers from failure. As it went under, anxiety swept through other institutions on Wall Street. Merrill Lynch, also in deep trouble, was swallowed up by Bank of America in another panicked merger. And it looked quite likely that American International Group (AIG), a giant multinational insurance corporation, would soon go bankrupt too. "My goodness," remarked Peter Peterson, who had headed Lehman in the 1970s and served as Nixon's secretary of commerce. "I've been in the business 35 years, and these are the most extraordinary events I've ever seen." Panic set in across the financial sector. The Dow Jones Industrial Average, which stood at 11,400 in mid-September 2008, plummeted 3,000 points over the next month, losing more than a quarter of its total value. As the financial hysteria spread, fueled by round-the-clock coverage on cable news, many worried that the nation might be headed into a second Great Depression.[6]

With a Republican in the White House, the financial collapse further damaged the standing of the party in power. Although the GOP's economic policies typically revolved around free-market approaches like tax cuts and deregulation, President Bush turned to federal relief. He tried to forestall the financial crisis with an emergency stopgap, the Troubled Assets Relief Program (TARP), which would use government funds to purchase assets and equity from private firms that were in trouble. As Bush noted in his speech introducing the proposal, it was a bit jarring for Americans to hear a Republican leader—who had previously called for a reduction in the role of government, especially in the financial sector—now call for a massive new bailout of Wall Street. Democrats vowed to cross party lines and support the president, but rank-and-file Republicans in the House refused to do so. TARP, in their minds, represented "big government conservatism" at its worst. With conservatives holding out, TARP initially failed in the House by a vote of 228 to 205 on September 29. The following Monday, the stock market plunged by

777 points. As the situation spiraled out of control, an analyst on the financial news channel CNBC was asked what positions he would recommend. He responded grimly: "cash and fetal."[7]

The TARP issue threw the 2008 presidential election into chaos. McCain, who had stated his support for TARP, temporarily suspended his campaign on September 24 due to the crisis. The move only angered Republicans, who believed it made him seem unsure how to handle the situation. Even the White House was shocked. "We'd devised TARP to save the financial system," Secretary of Treasury Henry Paulson recalled. "Now it had become all about politics—presidential politics. . . . I wondered what McCain could have been thinking."[8] In stark contrast, Obama's response suggested a steadier hand. "It's my belief," Obama said, "that this is exactly the time that the American people need to hear from the person who in approximately 40 days will be responsible for dealing with this mess." The Democratic candidate lobbied key constituencies in his coalition, such as the Congressional Black Caucus, to support the measure. In the end, the House did pass the TARP program on October 3, 2008, authorizing the extension of $700 billion to the financial services industry. It proved to be the most expensive intervention in markets to that point in American history.[9]

As the financial sector began to stabilize, Obama won the election handily. The Democratic candidate secured a margin of 53 percent to 46 percent in the popular vote and had an even larger landslide of 365 to 173 in the electoral college. Notably, Obama had crafted a new coalition that included African Americans, immigrants, women, suburbanites, and younger voters who saw themselves as socially liberal but fiscally conservative. In many ways, his victory offered Democrats the first glimpse of a new base to replace the old New Deal coalition that had crumbled in the 1970s. Meanwhile, Democrats not only maintained control of both houses of Congress but also increased their margins, picking up 21 seats in the House for an edge of 257 to 178, and 8 seats in the Senate for a new margin of 59 to 41. It was so significant a defeat for the GOP across the board that observers wondered if it meant the end of the Republican Party. "We were in disarray," Representative Pete Sessions of Texas remembered. "People were comparing us to cockroaches, saying we weren't even relevant." If the GOP were a brand of dog food, one retiring Republican said, it would get pulled off the shelves.[10]

In contrast, Democrats were thrilled with the election returns, especially over the milestone they had reached in electing the nation's first-ever African American president. The landmark moment led off media coverage of the election, with wild expectations for what the milestone meant. "Barack Hussein Obama was elected the 44th president of the United States on Tuesday, sweeping away the last racial barrier in American politics with ease," began the *New York Times'* front-page report. "As the returns became known," it continued, "many Americans rolled into the streets to celebrate what many described, with perhaps overstated if understandable exhilaration, as a new era in a country where just 143 years ago, Mr. Obama, as a black man, could have been owned as a slave." Those who had paved the way for the nation's first black president were overwhelmed by the moment. At a victory celebration in Chicago's Grant Park, cameras caught the Rev. Jesse Jackson wiping away tears of disbelief.[11] Gallup reported that two-thirds of those polled believed Obama's election was among the top three moments of progress for African Americans in the past hundred years; the same proportion said the election made them feel more confident there would be breakthroughs in race relations in the coming years.[12]

The Persistence of Partisanship

Having broken down the racial barrier to the presidency, Obama hoped he could do the same with other fault lines of national division. Notably, he remained optimistic that he could adhere to his campaign promises about ushering in a "postpartisan era." As he formed his cabinet, for instance, the president-elect worked to bring an unprecedented number of Republicans into his circle. He kept Bush's Secretary of Defense Robert Gates in that role, brought on Republican congressman Ray LaHood to serve as secretary of transportation, and tried to recruit a third Republican, New Hampshire senator Judd Gregg, to serve as secretary of commerce. Gregg initially accepted, but then reneged when GOP partisans complained. The incoming president, Gregg said apologetically, "has been a person who has reached out and aggressively reached out, across the aisle," but ultimately Gregg had "irresolvable conflicts" with Obama's agenda. Taking stock of these early moves, conservative observers marveled at Obama's apparently sincere drive for bipartisanship. Bush strategist Karl Rove, who had stoked partisan animosities in a "play-to-the-base" strategy in the previous two elections, called Obama's economic team "reassuring." Other Bush alumni agreed. "Obama is doing something marvelously right," noted Michael Gerson, a former speechwriter for the Bush White House. "He is disappointing the ideologues."[13]

While the new president secured a level of bipartisanship in his cabinet that hadn't been seen since the unity government of the Second World War, he quickly found Congress to be more resistant to the call for "postpartisanship." Legislators in both parties had little incentive to cross the aisle, as their gerrymandered districts created homogenous voting bases and the fractured media fostered political echo chambers. Increasingly, both of these factors led congressmen toward confrontation rather than compromise. When Obama met with the Democratic caucus in December, he told legislators that he hoped to restore civility to political debate and reach out to Republicans to work with them on legislation. Democratic leaders looked at the president in disbelief, concluding that he simply didn't grasp the depth of the two parties' hatred for each other. Republicans likewise waved such comments away as nothing but empty rhetoric. "He believes he's a game changer, but I don't believe the game has changed," argued Representative Tom Cole. "It's captivating, it's intoxicating, but it's not going to last."[14]

From his very first day in office, the president found it hard to win Republican support on virtually any piece of legislation. Even with the nation still struggling with the economic crisis, the GOP refused to budge. The most important item in the president's early agenda, for instance, was the economic stimulus bill. During the transition period, the incoming administration had done several things to make the bill more attractive to Republicans. First of all, while most economists argued for a Keynesian plan that relied solely on government spending, the proposed legislation instead dedicated roughly a third of the overall $787 billion in the plan to tax cut proposals that had been previously advanced by Republicans. Second, Obama officials spent a great deal of time meeting with both the GOP leadership and moderates in the House and Senate to seek their advice and act on their recommendations. Third, as a result of these meetings, the administration struck a number of liberal proposals from the stimulus bill, things like family planning funding, in an effort to win Republican votes. Liberals complained that such political concerns weakened the economic impact of the plan. "Whatever the explanation," wrote the economist Paul Krugman, "the Obama plan just doesn't look adequate to the economy's need. To be sure, a third of a loaf is better than none. But right now we seem to be facing two major economic gaps: the gap between the economy's potential and its likely performance, and the gap between Mr. Obama's stern economic rhetoric and his somewhat disappointing plan."[15]

House Republicans had a different perspective. After hearing from constituents who thought TARP had been a sellout by big government Republicans who had teamed up with liberal Democrats to bail out Wall Street, they were in no mood to spend anything near the levels that the president proposed. More important, the Republican leadership had decided that it would be politically beneficial to oppose the measure. House Whip Eric Cantor of Virginia, for one, thought that the GOP should do everything it could to deny Obama the honeymoon period that presidents are traditionally afforded and instead fight him immediately and at every turn. "We're not here to cut deals and get crumbs and stay in the minority for another 40 years," Cantor told his fellow Republicans in a December 2008 meeting. "We're not rolling over. We're going to fight these guys. We're down, but things are going to change."[16]

To win the battle, Cantor decided that the most important thing Republicans could do would be to keep their members united in opposition to the president's proposals. If they closed ranks, the GOP could thus deny Obama the ability to claim *any* sign of bipartisanship, no matter how small. In early January 2009, the House Republican leadership team held a retreat in Annapolis, Maryland. Representative Pete Sessions, the new GOP House campaign chair, showed the assembled members a PowerPoint presentation. The first slide asked: "If the Purpose of the Majority is to Govern, What Is Our Purpose?" The next answered: "The Purpose of the Minority is to become the Majority." House Republicans' goal for the next two years would not be promoting their own policies or making Democratic bills more acceptable to their base; it would be doing whatever it took to win back the House. The House Republicans decided to become, in the words of Minority

Leader John Boehner, "an entrepreneurial insurgency," focused solely on fighting the Democrats. In a sign of how far they were prepared to go, Congressman Sessions suggested that the Republicans could learn lessons from the disruptive tactics of the Taliban, then waging an insurgency against American troops in Afghanistan. Meanwhile, Senate Republicans took the same tactic. At their own meeting in January 2009, Minority Leader Mitch McConnell of Kentucky laid out a plan that echoed Cantor and Sessions's proposals in the House. As Senator George Voinovich of Ohio later recalled, the plan was simple— whatever Obama proposed, they would oppose: "If he was for it, we had to be against it."[17]

As negotiations over the economic stimulus began in earnest, Democrats finally realized that all of Obama's outreach had been for nothing. Congressman David Obey of Wisconsin, then chairman of the House Appropriations Committee, met with his Republican counterpart, Congressman Jerry Lewis of California, to explain what Democrats had in mind and to ask what Republicans wanted to include. "I'm sorry," Lewis responded, "but leadership tells us we can't play." Obey was stunned. "What they said right from the get-go was, 'It doesn't matter what the hell you do, we ain't gonna help you. We're going to stand on the sidelines and bitch.'" When asked by reporters, Lewis confirmed the story. "The leadership decided there was no play to be had," he told *Time*. Because Obama had made big promises on bipartisanship, the GOP realized they could effectively break those promises for him simply by refusing to cooperate. As Congressman Tom Cole, a deputy whip in the House, explained, when it came to the economic stimulus, what the Republicans wanted most of all was "the talking point [that] 'The only thing bipartisan was the opposition.'"[18] And in the end, the Republicans got their talking point. Even in the midst of a severe economic crisis, not a single Republican in the House voted for the stimulus bill, which passed 244–188.

In the Senate, Republicans had more power given the rights of the minority, especially after recent developments that effectively set a sixty-vote threshold for all major bills. And as Minority Leader Mitch McConnell later said: "The single most important thing we want to achieve is for President Obama to be a one-term president." The GOP Senate campaigned for larger tax breaks than the president had proposed when they took up the bill in early February, and were able to force Senate Democrats down from the $900 billion they were demanding. Throughout the negotiations, conservative organizations placed immense pressure on senators to avoid cooperating with the administration. The president remained optimistic that he would be able to persuade a substantial number of Republicans to vote in favor of the plan based on the logic of the legislation and the urgent need for reform. "I've done extraordinary outreach, I think, to Republicans," he explained.[19]

On February 10, the Senate passed the bill by a vote of 61 to 37. The final vote had been close. The roll call went on for hours, as Democrats could not muster the sixtieth vote to end a filibuster. Senator Ted Kennedy was away struggling with a serious illness, so Ohio Senator Sherrod Brown had to be flown back to Washington from his mother's wake so he could cast the deciding vote. Three moderate northeastern Republicans—Arlen Specter, Olympia Snowe, and Susan Collins—represented the total amount of bipartisanship that the president was able to win from the GOP. Notably, all three were immediately dismissed by the Right as "RINOs" or "Republicans In Name Only." The abuse got so bad for these three moderates that Specter switched to the Democratic Party in April 2009. Snowe, meanwhile, decided not to run for reelection in 2012, citing "an atmosphere of polarization and 'my way or the highway' ideologies" that had taken over the Senate during her last term.[20]

The final stimulus legislation, formally known as the American Recovery and Reinvestment Act, was signed into law on February 17, 2009. The legislation included more than $575 billion in new spending for health care, infrastructure, education, and energy as well as an expansion of unemployment compensation. At the same time, there was roughly $211 billion in a diverse array of tax cuts. Although some progressives argued that its spending totals were not nearly enough, and that the legislation was skewed too much in favor of the tax breaks, President Obama and his supporters insisted that this was the best that they were going to get. "None of this will be easy," he cautioned. "The road to recovery will not be straight. We will make progress, and there may be some slippage along the way." Still, he remained confident: "We have begun the essential work of keeping the American dream alive in our time."[21]

For those on the right, however, Obama's efforts represented not an effort to save the American dream, but a scheme to sabotage it. The same week the president signed the stimulus into law, CNBC reporter Rick Santelli attacked another administration proposal meant to help homeowners hurt by the housing collapse avoid foreclosure. "The government is promoting bad behavior!" he shouted from the floor of the Chicago Board of Trade on live television. Obama, he said, "should put up a website" where Americans could vote "to see if they want to subsidize losers' mortgages!" As the traders around him booed the idea, Santelli suggested that Americans needed to rise up in protest, perhaps in a "Chicago Tea Party." The video clip, replayed endlessly on cable news, quickly went viral on the internet. Within hours, it became the lead clip on the Drudge Report; after a few days, CNBC reported that the segment had been viewed nearly 1.7 million times, a record for its website.[22]

Santelli's proposal for "tea party" protests against the Obama administration quickly spread. As the income tax deadline of April 15, 2009, approached, plans for roughly 750 different demonstrations were coordinated, thanks to the financial backing of FreedomWorks, a group led by former GOP House Majority Leader Dick Armey. The conservative personalities at Fox News quickly adopted the cause as their own, advertising the rallies on the network as "FNC Tea Parties" and broadcasting live from several. "Bring your kids and experience history," Glenn Beck encouraged Fox viewers, inviting them to join him for a protest at the Alamo in San Antonio. "Our kids are being sold into slavery," he insisted, and they had a duty to stop it. Other Fox personalities followed suit. Host Neil Cavuto and conservative commentator Michelle Malkin headlined the protest in Sacramento, for instance, while Sean Hannity aired his program live from the protests in Atlanta. CNN and MSNBC covered the protests more critically, understanding them as a product of their competition. Susan Roesgen of CNN, covering a Chicago protest, shouted at demonstrators and said the gatherings were "anti-government, anti-CNN." In the end, media critic David Carr concluded, "The Tax Day Tea Party was all but conceived, executed and deconstructed in the hothouse of cable news wars." Despite its origins in cable news, though, the "tea party" protests tapped into a wellspring of populist resentment.[23]

Emboldened by the protests in the public and the press, Senate Republicans went to new lengths to stall the work of the Obama administration. The use of "holds" on presidential appointments, for instance, reached new heights, keeping the administration from staffing key positions. For instance, throughout the middle months of 2009, as the government sought to rebuild the financial sector, the Treasury Department had a stunning number of high-ranking policy positions still vacant because Obama's nominees had been stalled in the Senate. As a result, Treasury Secretary Timothy Geithner had to reckon with the largest financial crisis since the Great Depression with a skeleton staff: no deputy treasury secretary, no undersecretary for international affairs, no undersecretary for domestic finance, no assistant secretary for tax policy, no assistant secretary for financial markets, no assistant secretary for financial stability, and no assistant secretary for legislative affairs. Astonishingly, six of these roles were still unfilled at the start of 2010. Paul Volcker, who led the Federal Reserve during the Carter and Reagan administrations, was stunned. "How can we run a government in the middle of a financial crisis," he asked, "without doing the ordinary, garden-variety administrative work of filling the relevant agencies?"[24]

Meanwhile, the Senate drastically increased the use of the filibuster. For most of the chamber's history, filibusters and the cloture motions needed to end them were exceedingly rare. In the 1970s, they happened once or twice a month; over the 1980s and 1990s, they became much more frequent. Over these decades, the filibuster turned into a normal tool of partisan combat, a method of obstruction on major legislation as well as smaller issues, even a mechanism to achieve personal vendettas.[25] As with every aspect of partisanship, this rapidly accelerated after 2008 as a new generation of senators—many of whom had gotten their start in the rougher politics of the House a decade or so earlier—arrived in the Senate ready to use these methods without remorse and without restraint. In the Obama era, the number of cloture motions increased to roughly two or three a week. Much like the increased use of holds, the rise in filibusters and forced cloture votes had a significant impact on the administration's ability to make appointments, especially to the judiciary. Filibusters against judges had happened in the past, but usually only against nominees for whom there was serious opposition. In this new era, filibusters became commonplace, even against candidates for whom there was literally no opposition at all. Judge Barbara Keenan, picked to fill a vacancy on the US Court of Appeals for the Fourth Circuit, found her nomination widely praised and then advanced to the full Senate by a unanimous vote in the Senate Judiciary Committee. Nevertheless, it still took 169 days for her to go from nomination to confirmation, due to a filibuster that delayed things considerably. The motion for cloture to end the filibuster passed 99–0, and she was confirmed by the full Senate again by a vote of 99–0. "By our estimate," political analysts Norm Ornstein and Tom Mann marveled, "a process that the Senate could have handled in a few weeks, from formal nomination to committee hearing to confirmation, took almost half a year and wasted dozens of hours of floor time." Scorched earth politics had now become the norm.[26]

Health Care and Financial Reform

Meanwhile, the president decided to tackle a policy problem that Democratic presidents had been pursuing for half a century: national health care reform. Harry Truman had tried to enact a federal health insurance program twice during his administration, but his plans had been defeated when the American Medical Association mobilized in opposition and branded them "socialized medicine," a kiss of death during the Cold War. Two decades later, Lyndon Johnson worked with huge Democratic majorities in Congress to pass Medicare, an addition to the Social Security system that would provide health insurance to the elderly, as well as Medicaid, a means-tested program for the poor. The advances made a significant difference in the provision of health care, but millions of working Americans were still left without access to insurance. In 1993 and 1994, Bill Clinton had attempted to push through a Democratic Congress a system of regulated health care markets to lower costs. Though there was strong public support, Republicans in Congress mobilized against the bill and effectively killed it.

Despite the long odds and an already crowded agenda, Obama decided that he would make health care reform a policy priority. The rising cost of insurance premiums had been a major factor in escalating business and government expenses. Between 2002 and 2008 alone, average family premiums had increased by 58 percent. To bring down these costs, the administration looked to innovative state models like the one tried in Massachusetts. There, Republican governor Mitt Romney passed a measure that imposed an individual health insurance mandate on residents and created a statewide insurance exchange. A free-market alternative to state-run health care, Romney's plan won plaudits from across the political spectrum. The Obama White House assumed that embracing a similar approach to reform, with the same mix of government mandates and private insurance, could work in Washington just as it had in Boston.

The president articulated his vision to a joint session of Congress in February 2009, and by July a number of bills were circulating. Rather than sending legislators a specific plan, as Clinton had done to no success, Obama provided broad outlines but asked legislators to write the bill themselves. The White House, seeking to contain the kind of opposition that sank Clinton's legislation, placed control in Congress's hands and made it clear it was willing to make concessions from the start. Senate Democrats again tried to work with Republicans like Olympia Snowe to find potential areas for bipartisan compromise. The Patient Protection and Affordable Care Act that resulted was, in essence, made up of components from two conservative models from the past—first, the proposals that Senate Republicans had made as an alternative to Clinton's 1993 plan and, second and more significant, the program that Governor Romney had launched in 2006 in Massachusetts. In the gruff assessment of MIT's Jonathan Gruber, who had helped draft both the Romney and Obama plans, there was "zero difference" between the two. "They're the same fucking bill."[27]

Indeed, analysis of the two showed they had a great deal in common. The individual mandate, a requirement that citizens obtain health insurance or else pay a fine, was the linchpin to both pieces of legislation, with an unmistakably conservative lineage. It had first been proposed by the Heritage Foundation in 1989 and had been championed in ensuing years by Republican leaders including George H. W. Bush, Dan Quayle, Newt Gingrich, and Bob Dole.[28] In July 2009, Romney himself urged Obama to embrace the individual mandate in an op-ed piece in USA Today.[29] That same summer, Republican Senator Chuck Grassley of Iowa insisted that the individual mandate was uncontroversial and that there was a broad bipartisan consensus behind the idea—

because liberals had finally come around to accept an idea that was once only championed by conservatives. But once Obama embraced the idea too, some of these same men denounced it. Indeed, just months after he repeatedly insisted that the individual mandate was constitutional, Grassley reversed himself and claimed it was fundamentally "unconstitutional."[30]

Even though the Affordable Care Act had a seemingly conservative lineage, Republicans fought it all the way. As they had with the stimulus, congressional leaders resolved to do all they could to deny the president a single Republican vote, solely to keep him from being able to claim a bipartisan accomplishment. As Senate Minority Leader McConnell explained to the *New York Times* in a March 2010 interview, "It was absolutely critical that everybody be together because if the proponents of the bill were able to say it was bipartisan, it tended to convey to the public that this is O.K., they must have figured it out. It's either bipartisan or it isn't."[31] But this was something Senate Republicans admitted only after the law had been passed. Until then, they kept up appearances of bipartisanship, both in an attempt to maintain good public relations but also to slow the progress of the bill down considerably. As a result, the Affordable Care Act was subject to seemingly endless debate and discussion. The House held 79 different hearings over the course of a year, with testimony from 181 different witnesses; the Senate, meanwhile, had roughly another hundred hearings, roundtables, and other meetings. During that time, liberal proposals like a single-payer approach or a "public option" that would compete with private insurance companies were dismissed. Meanwhile, large numbers of Republican amendments were accepted.[32]

The key site of this last effort at bipartisanship was the Senate Finance Committee, where chairman Max Baucus of Montana, a red-state moderate Democrat, and Senator Grassley of Iowa, the ranking Republican, seemingly worked together to find common ground for the bill that would attract Republican votes. Baucus and Grassley held dozens of congressional hearings. They released joint "policy option" papers that were meant to suggest compromises. And in the end, they held thirty-one different meetings with the so-called "Gang of Six"—Baucus and Grassley, plus two moderate Democrats and two moderate Republicans—in order to find a compromise that would attract GOP votes. For his part, Baucus accepted every single proposal from the Republicans in the Gang of Six. But in return, none of them voted for the bill.[33]

The opposition was even more evident at the grass roots. When legislators went back to their districts in August 2009 they encountered fierce resistance to the legislation. The Tea Party movement, a campaign of grassroots conservatives that had formed in opposition to TARP, now took on this bill. Believing that the key to successful opposition lay in local politics, they focused on targeting members in their individual districts to negate any sense of common ground they might have had with colleagues in Washington. They mobilized supporters during the town hall meetings that legislators held in their home districts, getting into heated exchanges with the cameras rolling. In several instances, the encounters turned hostile. When Florida Democrat Kathy Castor met with constituents in Tampa, for instance, conservative protesters flooded the event. When hundreds were turned away after the room reached capacity, they banged on the door and yelled "Tyranny!" Pennsylvania Republican senator Arlen Specter, a seventy-nine-year-old legislator, had to leave a meeting after he was booed and shoving broke out in the crowd. The Tea Party anger was fueled by conservative media, which offered ongoing coverage of these protests. While organizers insisted the rallies were "nonpartisan," Fox News again ran numerous stories about the alleged threats the administration proposal posed to health care. Sarah Palin, now a frequent guest on the network, picked up on a provision enabling doctors to discuss possible end-of-life options for elderly patients. She branded them as "death panels" in August 2009. From there, the term spread across the still rising set of conservative media outlets on radio, TV, and the internet.[34]

President Obama tried to dispel the growing rumors and rancor by delivering an address to a joint session of Congress in September 2009. When the president assured legislators that, contrary to conservative complaints, undocumented immigrants would not be insured by the plan, South Carolina Republican Joe Wilson interrupted the president's speech, yelling out "You lie!" Wilson was formally rebuked by the House for his unprecedented breach of decorum, but the vote broke down along party lines. Unbowed, Wilson proceeded to highlight the fact that he'd called the president a liar in his fund-raising pitch—even though fact checkers like Politifact quickly showed that Wilson was misinformed, and the president had not lied. No matter. Within weeks, Wilson had raised over a million dollars off his outburst.[35]

As the final touches were placed on the health care bill, House Democrats added to the legislation a "public option" that meant consumers would be able to purchase insurance through the federal government if they did not like what was available in the private market. The main goal was to create pressure on private companies to lower costs so that they could meet the federal competition. The public option became a rallying cry for many liberals who believed that this aspect of the plan best carried forward the single-payer insurance idea that had fallen by the wayside. The House passed the bill by a vote of 220 to 215. In the Senate, it became bogged down in partisan battle. To overcome a filibuster, Democratic leaders conducted negotiations with members whose support would be essential. Ted Kennedy had died of brain cancer on August 25, 2009, leaving Democrats without their most vocal supporter on the Hill and one vote short of the sixty-vote threshold for ending filibusters. Accordingly, the administration turned to conservative Democrats like Ben Nelson of Nebraska. The administration won Nelson's support by agreeing to provide higher rates of Medicaid funding in Nebraska, a concession opponents mocked as the "Cornhusker Kickback." Though derided as pure pork, it did the job. The Senate voted to end the filibuster on December 23, 2009, by 60 to 39, and then passed the bill the following day, 60 to 39 again.[36]

On January 19, 2010, Massachusetts voters elected Republican Scott Brown to fill Kennedy's seat. The election changed the political calculus considerably, giving the GOP enough votes to sustain a filibuster. It also served as a symbolic blow to supporters of health care reform. In response to the upset, the president backed away from his insistence that the Senate include a public option in its final bill. Moreover, he decided to hold a televised meeting—a health care summit—where he fielded questions from House Republican legislators about the bill for more than an hour. His performance won widespread praise as he was able to deflect some of the staunchest points of criticism, while his opponents in the House likewise drew praise for the civilized discussion. "President Obama denied he was a Bolshevik," the New York Times report began, "the Republicans denied they were obstructionists, and both sides denied they were to blame for the toxic atmosphere clouding the nation's political leadership."[37]

Senate Democrats, working closely with Speaker of the House Nancy Pelosi, decided that strong-arm tactics would be needed to move the bill through the Senate. On March 11, 2010, Senate Majority Leader Harry Reid announced that the bill would be considered as part of the budget reconciliation process, which prohibited filibusters. Republicans were livid. They complained that this would undercut democratic debate and stifle the rights of the minority. "If this bill is passed," McConnell said, "in the next election every Republican candidate will be campaigning to repeal it." The House passed the final bill by a narrow margin of 219 to 212 on March 21, 2010. It did not receive a single Republican vote, the first time that any major piece of domestic reform had passed on strictly partisan lines. The Senate passed the bill on the next day; Obama signed it into law on March 23, 2010.[38]

The partisan battles that began with the 2008 financial meltdown, and accelerated with health care reform, then came full circle as Congress set to work to construct new financial regulations to prevent another meltdown in the future. President Obama promised to overhaul the financial system in a way that was comparable to what occurred during the New Deal. The proposal, first introduced by the president in June 2009, contained a number of measures that aimed at preventing another sudden collapse. Massachusetts congressman Barney Frank and Connecticut senator Christopher Dodd then sponsored a bill that would reduce the number of high-risk investments that were permissible. Among other things, Dodd-Frank set to impose stricter regulations on financial markets, including restrictions on the sale of derivatives, and the creation of a new consumer protection board that would guard middle-class investors. As the bill moved slowly through Congress, the Senate added a provision called the Volcker Rule—in honor of former Federal Reserve chairman Paul Volcker—which reimposed the New Deal–era restrictions that had prevented depository banks from engaging in proprietary trading. After considerable delays, the Senate finally passed the bill 60 to 39 in June 2010, once again largely along party lines. The House likewise passed the bill in a partisan fashion, with Republicans standing in united opposition.

Despite the partisan fighting over the financial reforms, Obama insisted they would bring stability to the struggling economy. Dodd-Frank, he assured the nation, would "protect consumers and lay the foundation for a stronger and safer financial system, one that is innovative, creative, competitive, and far less prone to panic and collapse." While the legislation left considerable space for interest groups to rework and challenge the law, stimulating an entire industry of financial service lawyers who were devoted to lobbying Washington for lenient treatment under the policy, the framework put into place some of the toughest regulations in decades. The Consumer Financial Protection Bureau, the brainchild of Harvard professor and future senator Elizabeth Warren, was a centerpiece of the bill. It aimed to protect middle-class citizens from the kinds of abuses in mortgages that had produced the collapse as well as in credit card lending. It also created two new government bodies, the Financial Stability Oversight Council and the Office of Financial Research, that were given the authority to monitor and regulate this sector of the economy. Under the legislation, the government gained the power to close down financial companies that found themselves in economic trouble as had occurred with Lehman Brothers.[39]

As conservatives attacked the Obama administration's regulations as too strict, those on the left increasingly charged that they weren't tough enough. A vivid example of the costs of deregulation came from outside the financial sector. In April 2010, an explosion on the BP oil rig *Deepwater Horizon* left eleven people dead and polluted the Gulf of Mexico in the worst oil spill in US history. In 2011, left-wing activists, worried about similar damages from lax regulation on Wall Street, mobilized to protest the economic inequality that increasingly defined the nation. Complaining that Wall Street had been bailed out after its poor behavior with few individual members of firms there facing any kind of punishment for their actions, leftists formed a new organization called Occupy Wall Street. For nearly two months, starting in September 2011, they gathered in Zuccotti Park in New York's financial district. Inspired by the youth revolution in Egypt that brought down the authoritarian government of President Hosni Mubarak that year, the protesters relied on social media to attract supporters and spread their message. Protesting the institutions and policies that allowed 1 percent of the country to control so much of the nation's resources, Occupy activists asserted: "We are the 99 percent." That slogan, which became an effective rallying cry, had been inspired by the work of French economist Thomas Piketty. The Occupy movement attracted support from a number of other prominent public intellectuals, too, such as Princeton philosopher Cornel West, who helped ensure media attention. "Every few days, a luminary would come to Zuccotti Park and give a speech that would circulate around the Internet," one of the activists recalled. "All of a sudden it was cool to be a lefty again."[40]

While the protests came under criticism for lacking sufficient organization or a clear political agenda, supporters claimed they had moved the problem of economic inequality to the center of the national conversation. Many observers agreed. "They are redefining and rebalancing our political discourse," former New York governor Eliot Spitzer noted. "To all those who are dissatisfied because the Occupy movement did not grow into the complete political theory or social agenda that some wished, I say: Give credit where credit is due." And indeed, mainstream politicians started to talk more frequently about the issue, with Democrats shifting away from the centrism of the Clinton era and more readily addressing the need to close the gap between those thriving at the top of the economy and the "99 percent" struggling beneath them. Polls showed that the public was increasingly warming to this message. According to a Pew survey released in January 2012, more than two-thirds of Americans agreed that there was a strong conflict between the rich and the poor. Economic inequality, the editors of the *New York Times* observed, had become "the greatest source of tension in American society."[41]

Increasingly, pundits, reporters, and scholars turned their attention to the topic. When Thomas Piketty's *Capital in the Twenty-First Century* (2013) was published in English in 2014, the nearly 700-page economic tome became an unexpected best seller. "With its dire warning about a possible New Gilded Age of extreme inequality, Piketty's daunting monograph hardly seems like fun summer reading," one reviewer marveled, "yet the book is currently No. 1 on Amazon.com." Chronicling the conditions that had inspired the Occupy protests, Piketty's book offered intellectual heft to their critique with statistics and charts suggesting that the protests had been right on target.[42]

The Politics of Hostage Taking

Though the Democrats found their footing on policy, Republicans increasingly had the edge on politics. Riding a new wave of Tea Party anger, the GOP did extremely well in the 2010 midterms, retaking control of the House, but not the Senate. Just as important, Republicans' massive investments in state campaigns paid off. Coming out of the 2010 election, the GOP had strong control of many state legislatures and would therefore be in position to craft redistricting plans that would secure Republican congressional incumbents for years to come. Even Obama told reporters the election had been a "shellacking."[43]

Republican leaders like new Speaker of the House John Boehner capitalized on the fervor among Tea Party Republicans, characterizing Obama as a dangerous leftist to stir conservatives into an electoral frenzy. But the growing discord and division revealed a troubling new development in American political discourse. Increasingly, the two parties were not simply drawing different conclusions from the same facts; instead, they were starting out with wildly different versions of what those facts were in the first place. "It was modern day media, and social media, that kept pushing people further right and further left," Boehner noted in a frank interview after his retirement. While the process had been long under way, it became sharply more pronounced in Obama's first term. "People started to figure out," Boehner noted, that "they could choose where to get their news. And so what do people do? They choose places they agree with, reinforcing the divide."[44] The fractured media landscape affected more than politics. Many conservatives, for instance, simply rejected the scientific consensus about climate change, believing it to be a liberal hoax.

Despite his concerns about the fraying fabric of political life, Speaker Boehner and others in the House leadership made a calculated bet that they could harness the renegades' energy. They believed they could use them to build a voting bloc that would stifle the administration, yet be able to contain them when the time came. Boehner was aware of the risks, though. His fellow Ohio Republican Jim Jordan, a key member of the Tea Party caucus, had always been a "legislative terrorist," he later admitted.[45] But Boehner believed the time had come to take chances. Senate Minority Leader McConnell was thinking the same thing. "We're determined to stop the agenda Americans have rejected," McConnell warned, "and to turn the ship around."[46]

The politics of polarization had helped the Republicans return to power, but it soon became clear that it could also tear them apart. Boehner and McConnell underestimated the difficulty that they would have controlling their own members, particularly when the rank and file practiced a style of cutthroat politics that thrived in the modern political climate. The GOP majority in the House, most notably, proved to be riven by internal fractures. Boehner had been a key player in the conservative counterrevolution led by Newt Gingrich, helping draft the "Contract with America" that propelled the GOP to victory in 1994. But sixteen years later, as his caucus moved sharply to the right, the new Speaker seemed more of a centrist by comparison. The rest of the incoming Republican House leadership—Majority Leader Eric Cantor, Majority Whip Kevin McCarthy, and Budget Committee Chairman Paul Ryan—had presented themselves as rebels who would go to even greater lengths than the Gingrich generation to reduce the size and scope of government. In 2010, the three had even published a book about themselves called *Young Guns: A New Generation of Conservative Leaders.* Though Boehner served as Speaker, the Republican caucus he ostensibly led was much more aligned with the "Young Guns" beneath him. This was especially true of the freshman class of eighty-seven new Republicans, many of whom had been elected with the backing of Tea Party organizations and conservative funders like the Koch brothers.[47]

The contrast in style and substance between Boehner's old guard and the new generation became immediately apparent after the election, as Congress turned its attention to raising the debt ceiling. Historically speaking, this was a routine procedure. Between 1960 and August 2011, Congress raised the debt ceiling seventy-eight times in all—forty-nine times with a Republican in the White House, twenty-nine times with a Democrat. Raising the debt ceiling did not authorize new spending, but rather allowed the government to pay the bills for spending measures that Congress had already approved. Over the years, it became increasingly common for members of the opposition party to use the debt ceiling vote as a chance for some political theater, to lecture the incumbent administration about its wasteful ways and present themselves as fiscally responsible instead. As a US senator, Barack Obama himself took part in this ritual, chiding the Bush administration and then voting against raising the debt ceiling, knowing the votes were there to raise it anyway. Despite the theatrics, both parties always knew the debt ceiling would be raised, because failure to do so would mean defaulting on the national debt and likely triggering a massive financial crisis.[48]

In 2011, the routine housekeeping of the debt ceiling reached a crisis point. Many of the incoming freshmen, at the Young Guns' encouragement, had spent the 2010 campaign pointing to the debt ceiling as the embodiment of Washington's problems. "This 'need' to raise the debt ceiling is caused by one thing," a Republican challenger in Alabama claimed: "Out-of-control spending in Washington." "This Congress has done nothing but spend future generations of this country into a black hole," insisted another from Wisconsin. Despite the campaign rhetoric, the incoming GOP speaker believed his party, as the majority party, had a duty to govern responsibly. "We're going to have to deal with it as adults," Boehner said two weeks after the 2010 midterms. "Whether we like it or not, the federal government has obligations, and we have obligations on our part." But the Young Guns disagreed. At a January 2011 retreat, Cantor asked his caucus to use the debt limit vote as a way to force the Obama administration to make massive spending cuts. "I'm asking you to look at a potential increase in the debt limit as a leverage moment when the White House and President Obama will have to deal with us," he told them. "Either we stick together and demonstrate that we're a team that will fight for and stand by our principles, or we will lose that leverage."[49]

Notably, prominent personalities in conservative media outlets encouraged a defiant stance. "Hells no," said Sarah Palin, the former Republican vice presidential nominee turned Fox News contributor, "I would not vote to increase that debt ceiling. Otherwise it just shows the American public we're not serious yet, we're still going to incur more debt." Host Sean Hannity mocked the "doomsday rhetoric" of congressional Democrats who argued "the American economy would crumble" with a default. "I say let them default," Eric Bolling argued on *Fox & Friends*. "What's going to happen?" Meanwhile, on the Fox Business Channel, hosts and reporters on financial programs likewise encouraged a showdown. Lou Dobbs dismissed the looming deadline for raising the debt ceiling as a "false date" and the idea the government might default as "pure fiction." "If I were in the Congress," host Andrew

Napolitano said on *Freedom Watch*, "I would encourage everybody to vote against raising the debt ceiling."[50]

As a result, the Democratic White House and Republican Congress spent much of 2011 engaged in a long series of negotiations over something that had never really been negotiated before. But the entire process, driven as it was by reflexive partisanship, seemed impossible to solve with bipartisan deals. In July 2011, the Senate seemed close to an agreement, one that would have involved significant spending cuts and some small tax increases. But it fell apart as soon as the president signed on. As an aide to the Republican leadership explained in an email to *Politico*, "The president killed any chance of its success by 1) Embracing it. 2) Hailing the fact that it increases taxes. 3) Saying it mirrors his own plan." Negotiations proved no better in the House, where compromise became such a toxic issue that, at one point, Boehner refused to return the president's phone calls. In the end, Obama agreed to a last-minute deal that gave Republicans most, but not all, of what they had demanded. Congress raised the debt ceiling and, in return, received a new deficit reduction deal that relied entirely on spending cuts with no offsetting tax increases on the other side. The agreement also established a bipartisan super-committee of senators and representatives to make recommendations for further cuts. If they could not reach agreement by a specified date, according to the law, automatic cuts would go into effect through sequestration. This threat of automatic, draconian cuts was thought to be the best incentive for overcoming partisan inaction.[51]

While Republicans hailed the conclusion to the crisis as a political success, the economic costs were evident. The stock market experienced its most volatile week and greatest losses since the 2008 financial meltdown. Soon after, Standard and Poor's downgraded the credit rating of the United States for the first time in history, noting that "the political brinksmanship of recent months highlights what we see as America's governance and policy making becoming less stable, less effective, and less predictable than what we previously believed." Federal Reserve chairman Ben Bernanke agreed, noting that the debt ceiling crisis had "disrupted financial markets and probably the economy as well." According to the Government Accounting Office, the threat of default had increased government borrowing costs by $1.3 billion that year alone. Despite the economic damage, congressional Republicans believed they had won a major victory. Senate Minority Leader Mitch McConnell, for his part, was perfectly candid about his belief that gamesmanship was now more important than governing. "I think some of our members may have thought the default issue was a hostage you might take a chance at shooting. Most of us didn't think that," he told reporters. "What we did learn is this—it's a hostage that's worth ransoming."[52]

The Election of 2012

As the next presidential campaign drew near, Massachusetts governor Mitt Romney quickly emerged as the Republican frontrunner. In many ways, Romney seemed out of step with the new trends in his party's congressional caucus and base. His father, former Michigan governor George Romney, had been a prominent moderate Republican during the Nixon era, and in many ways, his son replicated that role. Indeed, his record as a successful GOP governor in the blue state of Massachusetts offered evidence that he not only knew how to lead but also to reach across the aisle with results. In addition to his public sector record, Romney, like his father before him, could point to a career as a successful businessman in the private sector. With the economy recovering, but at an extremely slow pace, those business credentials appealed to conservatives as well as moderates.

Despite his own moderate inclinations, however, Romney increasingly found himself forced to run to the right during the primary campaign in order to placate the rising influence of the Tea Party movement in the Republican base. Placed in the position of having to defend his own role in passing health care reform in his state, Romney awkwardly tried to separate himself from one of his significant accomplishments. Sidestepping the similarities between the two plans, he argued that the difference in size between his plan and Obama's plan was the key. "Our plan was a state solution to a state problem," he insisted in May 2011. "His is a power grab by the federal government." In particular, Romney argued that imposing the individual mandate—an element he had installed in Massachusetts and then urged Obama to implement nationally—was a sign the government was imposing its will on the people. "The Obama administration fundamentally does not believe in [the] American experiment," he charged. "They fundamentally distrust free enterprise and the idea that states are where the power of government resides."[53]

As the general election began, Mitt Romney and his running mate Paul Ryan—one of the House Young Guns—continued to target the Affordable Care Act, making the promise to "Repeal and Replace" the law a major part of their pitch. But their assault on the new law as an unconstitutional power grab by the federal government was ultimately undercut by the Supreme Court. On June 28, 2012, the court upheld the Affordable Care Act by a vote of 5–4 in the case *National Federation of Independent Business v. Sebelius*. Notably, Chief Justice John Roberts, a conservative appointee of George W. Bush, cast the decisive vote with the majority. Though it upheld the law in general, the court did strike down a requirement that states had to expand their Medicaid coverage. Many Republican-led states, which had not yet enacted the expansion, now refused to do so; several also refused to set up their own state-level health care exchanges. As a result, according to the law, the federal government stepped in to set them up for them. Despite the ruling, Romney remained committed to the cause and used it as a rallying cry for conservatives. "Our mission is clear," he said. "If we want to get rid of Obamacare, we're going to have to replace President Obama."[54]

As Romney minimized his real accomplishments in the public sector to discredit the Affordable Care Act, his private sector success came under attack as well. One of his challengers in the GOP primaries, former Speaker of the House Newt Gingrich, mounted a blistering attack on Romney's business credentials at Bain Capital. While Romney had long bragged about his work at the investment firm, Gingrich asserted that Romney's actions looted companies and left workers without jobs, as Bain often took money out of industries and sent it overseas instead. An anti-Romney documentary tied to Gingrich's attacks denounced Romney as a "predatory corporate raider," highlighting the lives of workers allegedly ruined by Bain's actions. In the general election, Obama picked up on these attacks, running ads that likewise focused on workers who lost their jobs when Bain closed down their factories and steel mills. "It was like a vampire," one unemployed steelworker recalled in one spot; "they came in and sucked the life out of us." "It was like watching an old friend bleed to death," another said. This line of attack, in the primary and the general election, set up an image of Romney as an uncaring plutocrat who made his considerable wealth off the misfortune of others. That image only deepened when a Democratic campaign operative secretly recorded Romney giving a speech to donors. In it, Romney dismissed "47 percent" of Americans who he claimed "pay no income tax" and therefore are "dependent on the government." They would likely support Democrats, he said, because they thought of themselves as "victims" who were "entitled to food, to housing, to you name it." The reaction to the tape was devastating. "After months of doggedly trying to seem more likeable," Maureen Dowd noted, "Romney came across as a mean geek, a Cranbrook kid at the country club smugly swaddled in class disdain."[55]

As the Romney campaign faltered in the final months, many on the right refused to believe it. Signs that suggested the Obama administration was doing well, such as improving economic figures, were dismissed in disbelief. When the nonpartisan Bureau of Labor Statistics reported that the national unemployment rate, which had been slowly dropping over the year, ticked down another 0.3 percent in September, former General Electric CEO Jack Welch insisted the data must have been faked. "Unbelievable jobs numbers," he noted in an angry post on the social media site Twitter, known as a "tweet." "These Chicago guys will do anything . . . can't debate so change numbers." While the "B.L.S. truthers" doubted the economic numbers, others on the right refused to believe the reports from independent polling outfits. A blogger named Dean Chambers, skeptical of the polls showing Obama had a consistent lead in the closing months of the campaign, launched a new site called UnSkewedPolls.com. There, he took the work product of professional pollsters, reweighted the results to reflect the more Republican-leaning electorate of his imagination, and then published the "unskewed" results that showed Romney well in the lead. Many on the right latched on to the altered data to confirm their own feelings that the Republicans were winning.[56]

Despite the belief on the right that Romney would win and win easily, Obama was reelected by a fairly comfortable margin, winning 332 electoral college votes and 51.1 percent of the popular vote. Having bought into their own narrative about the campaign, some Republicans initially refused to believe the election returns as they came in. On Fox News, GOP strategist Karl Rove pushed back against early indications of an Obama win, sifting through exit polling to find signs of hope. "Is this just math that you do as a Republican," anchor Megyn Kelly asked him, "to make yourself feel better?" When the network called the key battleground state of Ohio for Obama, Rove pleaded with his colleagues to reverse the call, insisting the state would ultimately go to the GOP. In an improvised bit of drama, Kelly took the cameras, and viewers, back down a hallway to check in with the network's analysts, to see if they would change their mind. They didn't. Shortly after 11pm eastern, Fox and all the other networks called the race for the Democrats. The Romney campaign, which was so confident it hadn't even written a concession speech for its candidate, was stunned by the results. "I don't think there was one person who saw this coming," a senior campaign advisor noted. "He was shellshocked."[57]

In the end, Obama became the first president to win a majority of the popular vote in back-to-back elections since Reagan. But, notably, in another sign that divided government had become the new norm, voters sent roughly the same Congress back as well. Democrats kept control of the Senate, though by thin margins; the GOP held on to the House. Polarization and partisanship had proved to be sturdier than Obama had initially assumed, and in the aftermath of the election, these problems only became more pronounced. For some on the right, the lesson of the Republicans' 2012 loss was that the party needed to change not its electoral message, but its electorate. Accordingly, a spate of new laws and executive actions at the state level sought to restrict access to the ballot, making it harder for large numbers of Americans to exercise their right to vote.

Most notably, the drive to require voter identification cards at polling places, already well under way since the 2010 midterm victories, accelerated after Romney's loss. Ostensibly, voter ID laws were presented as a nonpartisan reform, meant to crack down on an alleged epidemic of voter fraud. But no such epidemic existed. (According to the most comprehensive study of the issue, out of over one billion votes cast in American elections between 2000 and 2014, there were only 31 potential cases of voter fraud that would be solved by voter ID.) In truth, as many Republican officials acknowledged, voter ID laws were pursued with partisan intent. In Pennsylvania, for instance, the state's House Majority Leader Mike Turzai bragged in the summer of 2012 that he had helped institute "voter ID, which is going to allow Governor Romney to win the state of Pennsylvania." Because racial minorities were both the most likely group to lack the mandated forms of identification and an overwhelmingly Democratic constituency, Republicans believed these voter ID measures would effectively lower Democratic turnout. At the local level, where votes were actually cast and counted, some Republican officials admitted this motive, in crude but clear terms. In North Carolina, for instance, a GOP precinct chairman told a *Daily Show* correspondent that the state's voter ID law would prevent "lazy blacks" from voting. "The law is going to kick Democrats in the butt."[58]

The campaign for voting rights restrictions received a surprise boost the following summer, when the Supreme Court struck down key sections of the Voting Rights Act of 1965. Controversial at the time of its passage, the landmark civil rights legislation quickly secured broad bipartisan support. (In 2006, for example, Congress renewed the act's provisions for another twenty-five years. In the House, the vote was 390–33; in the Senate, 98–0.) Despite that strong backing, conservative critics attacked the law as an outdated vestige of the civil rights era. In *Shelby County v. Holder* (2013), a slim 5–4 majority on the Supreme Court agreed with these critics, throwing out two key provisions of the Voting Rights Act, including the requirement that states and localities with a past record of discriminatory voting laws obtain "preclearance" from the federal government before instituting any changes. Writing for the conservative majority, Chief Justice Roberts argued that such requirements, which "made sense" at the time of the law's creation, were badly outdated because, "nearly 50 years later, things have changed dramatically." For liberals on the court, however, that logic was backward. Things had changed, they argued, because of the Voting Rights Act; if the law were undone, so too would those changes be undone. "Throwing out preclearance when it has worked and is continuing to work to stop discriminatory changes," Justice Ruth Bader Ginsberg chided in her dissent, "is like throwing away your umbrella in a rainstorm because you are not getting wet." And indeed, after the decision, the campaign for new voting rights restrictions took off with surprising speed. Between the 2012 and 2016 elections, seventeen different states—comprising 189 electoral votes among them—instituted new restrictions, including laws that made it more difficult to register to vote, cut back early and absentee forms of voting, and required strict forms of government-issued IDs.[59]

In many ways, the 2012 election and its aftermath served as an ominous warning of trends to come. As Romney's "47 percent" gaffe revealed, class resentments were growing at both ends of the economic ladder. Racial divisions, which had grown in the attacks against the first African American president, intensified with the drive for voting rights restrictions. Complaints about "fake" job numbers and "skewed" polls, meanwhile, signaled that Americans increasingly could not agree even on basic facts and figures. The fault lines of division and discord had only deepened across Obama's first term, and despite his reelection, the president would soon discover—as many of his predecessors had learned—that his political standing was far from secure.

CHAPTER 15

The Trump Effect

THE PARTISAN POLARIZATION THAT DOMINATED OBAMA'S first term only continued to spread in the years that followed.

Ominously, the divisions in DC came to be seen across the nation as a whole. The fault lines in race relations, long submerged by the fiction that America had become a "postracial nation" after the accomplishments of the civil rights era and, more recently, the election of the first black president, burst back into public view. Responding to a rash of killings of African Americans at the hands of police and private forces, the Black Lives Matter movement presented the strongest challenge to racism in decades. At the same time, white supremacist organizations increasingly made their presence felt as well, forming a new "Alt Right" culture that spoke to aggrieved whites on the fringes.

As racial divisions reached their worst point in decades, the country was rocked by a presidential campaign that severely aggravated other fault lines in the United States. The 2016 contest between the insurgent candidacy of Republican Donald Trump and the predictable politics of Democrat Hillary Clinton proved to be one of the ugliest in modern American history, a hard-edged contest that sent aftershocks through the entire nation.

Acts of Terror

One of the most contentious issues in Obama's second term stemmed from an event in the waning weeks of the 2012 election. On the anniversary of the 9/11 attacks, Islamic militants inside Libya attacked an

American diplomatic compound in Benghazi, killing US Ambassador Christopher Stevens and three other Americans. Attacks on American embassies were nothing new—during the Bush administration, for instance, thirteen had been attacked, resulting in sixty deaths—but in the heightened partisanship of the 2012 campaign, this one became particularly politicized. In the second presidential debate, Mitt Romney accused Obama of refusing to label the attack as a "terrorist act" in an effort to downplay the problem for electoral gain. But as the moderator, CNN's Candy Crowley, noted, Obama had in fact called it an "act of terror" in a Rose Garden address the day after the attack.[1]

Still, charges persisted well past the election that the Obama administration had either failed to protect the embassy or engaged in a cover-up afterward to hide its mistakes. House Republicans launched several investigations into the Benghazi incident, but ultimately found no evidence of wrongdoing. Allegations that there had been a "stand-down order" sent to troops in the region who might have helped save those at Benghazi were dismissed as baseless by the House Armed Services Committee's majority report in February 2014. Meanwhile, the House Intelligence Committee concluded in November that there was "no intelligence failure" behind the attack either. These Republican-led committees faulted the Obama White House for inadequate security plans and chided the administration for contributing to the initial confusion over the causes of the attack, but ultimately dismissed the allegations of misconduct or criminal cover-up. Despite such thorough investigations by their fellow Republicans, many in the party refused to accept their conclusions. "I think the report's full of crap," Senator Lindsey Graham of South Carolina told CNN, dismissing the findings of the House Intelligence Committee. Newt Gingrich likewise speculated that the body must have been "co-opted by the C.I.A." With party elders insisting the reports were meaningless, many rank-and-file Republicans readily agreed.[2]

Accordingly, to placate the demands of the base, Speaker Boehner authorized yet another congressional inquiry, the Select Committee on Benghazi. This time, former secretary of state and likely 2016 Democratic presidential contender Hillary Clinton found herself as its focus. South Carolina Republican Trey Gowdy, a former federal prosecutor known for his confrontational style, was picked to head the special body. Elected to the House in 2010, Gowdy had defeated Republican Bob Inglis by insisting that the incumbent—a congressman with a lifetime rating of 93 percent from the American Conservative Union—had sold out his base and strayed too far toward the center. For two years, the Gowdy Committee conducted an exhaustive $7 million inquiry that ended, like the ones before it, with no damning conclusions. Its close scrutiny of Hillary Clinton, however, did yield the discovery that, while secretary of state during Obama's first term, she had maintained a private email server through which sensitive materials had passed.[3]

Beyond Benghazi, new revelations about US surveillance techniques came to light. In May 2013, a contractor with the National Security Agency (NSA) named Edward Snowden leaked classified material revealing that the agency's domestic surveillance program was far more extensive than most had previously assumed. His revelations showed that, among other things, the government had spied on cell phone calls of foreign leaders. The new information shocked Americans across the political spectrum: libertarian Republicans saw this as an intrusion of government power, while liberal Democrats were disillusioned to see Obama had followed the same line on surveillance as his predecessor. These stories, combined with the news of the extensive use of drone attacks against targeted terrorists, revealed that Obama had not only left in place many of the counterterrorism programs that he had inherited from President Bush but had even expanded them. More revelations became public as Snowden published his findings from the documents online, gaining widespread attention from the news media.[4]

The other area of national security that proved extremely problematic for the Obama White House was a new militant organization, the Islamic State of Iraq and Syria (ISIS). The administration had felt vindicated by its decimation of the al-Qaeda terrorists who waged the 9/11 attacks, a process that culminated with a daring raid in May 2011 that resulted in the assassination of Osama bin Laden. But as soon as that threat had been addressed, a new one surfaced in ISIS. In the wake of the pullout of US troops from Iraq, Sunni Arabs there and in Syria had started to amass military power and gradually take control of territory. As their group's name indicated, their main goal was nothing less than the creation of a new Islamic state in the Middle East. ISIS captured attention by taking hostages and beheading them. Videos of the violence spread quickly via social media, YouTube, and other internet outlets, stirring up fear and anger.[5]

As with al-Qaeda, ISIS proved to be a complicated target—one that took territory across the Middle East while also launching terrorist strikes outside the region, most notably in the West. On November 12, 2015, in an interview with ABC's *Good Morning America*, Obama confidently assured host George Stephanopoulos that ISIS had been "contained" in the region. "They have not gained ground in Iraq, and in Syria they'll come in, they'll leave, but you don't see this systemic march by ISIL [an alternate term for ISIS] across the terrain." The next day, however, ISIS terrorists unleashed a massive set of coordinated attacks in Paris, where suicide bombings and shootings left 130 dead and 368 wounded. Obama's insistence that ISIS had been "contained," freed of context, made him sound badly out of touch. His characteristically dispassionate approach to handling crises didn't resonate with Republicans and even some Democrats, who felt the brutal attacks deserved a more spirited response from the commander-in-chief.[6]

On the domestic front, the president faced a different kind of insurgency, coming from the right wing of the GOP. Emboldened by their past successes, Tea Party activists now made it clear that they would mount a primary challenge against any Republican legislator who strayed from their preferred positions. Meanwhile, conservative donors poured money into the forces opposed to any compromise. When President Obama was able to get an immigration bill through the Senate with Republican support in June 2013, for instance, the House defeated the measure, despite widespread predictions that it would pass. Issues like climate change regulation likewise languished on Capitol Hill. The budget battles flared again in 2013 with renewed threats of default. House Republicans insisted on draconian spending cuts, indicating a willingness to spark economic chaos if their demands were not met. The congressional "super committee" proved unable to reach agreement on spending cuts, triggering sequestration of funds that amounted to $1.2 trillion over ten years. In October 2013, when Congress could not reach agreement on federal spending due to a dispute over funding health care, the federal government shut down for sixteen days until a deal was reached. A Pew poll showed that Republicans and Democrats were more divided along ideological lines than at any point in the past two decades.[7]

The confrontational style of politics continued to pay off at the polls, however, and the strength of the Republican Right solidified in the 2014 midterms. At the state level, Republicans now controlled nearly two-thirds of all governorships and state legislatures. Nationally, the GOP retook the Senate for the first time since 2006, and expanded its numbers in the House as well. Republicans now claimed the largest majority in the House since the eve of the Great Depression, with their ranks moving steadily to the right. But the new approach came with its own costs. In a stunning development, Majority Leader Eric Cantor— the second-most powerful Republican in the House and the leader of the all-out conservative resistance to Obama's agenda there—was unseated in a primary challenge by David Brat, an economics professor at Randolph-Macon College who had the backing of the Tea Party. Ironically, a politician who had long championed stark partisanship as the key to his party's survival was destroyed by it himself.[8]

In spite of their apparent strength, the Republican majorities in Congress again grew more visibly riven by internal fighting. Frustrated with the ineffectiveness of his institution and increasingly unable to control the Tea Party–aligned "Freedom Caucus" in the GOP ranks, Speaker Boehner announced in September 2015 that he would resign, throwing the chamber into further turmoil. His apparent successor, Majority Whip Kevin McCarthy, then came under fire as well. Seeking to burnish his credentials with the far Right, the California Republican made controversial comments about the most recent round of House Benghazi hearings. The GOP had insisted there was no partisan motive behind the investigation, but McCarthy bragged to Fox News's Sean Hannity that his role in creating the Gowdy Committee showed he could be counted on as a reliable party man. "Everybody thought Hillary Clinton was unbeatable, right?" McCarthy said. "But we put together a Benghazi special committee, a select committee. What are her numbers today? Her numbers are dropping." After the awkward admission that the inquiry was little more than a political hit, McCarthy was forced to withdraw from the Speaker's race. The search for a replacement dragged on for weeks, further exposing tensions between the more moderate members of the Republican leadership and an angry, growing base of Tea Party supporters in the "Freedom Caucus" on the far right. Only in late October 2015 did the party find someone willing to serve as Speaker: Representative Paul Ryan of Wisconsin, the last "Young Gun" standing, who had served as Romney's running mate in 2012.[9]

Black Lives Matter and the Alt Right

Outside the Beltway, the country seemed to be at war with itself, too, but often literally so. Indeed, the most polarizing issue in the 2010s dealt with growing incidents of gun violence. On December 14, 2012, a mass shooting at Sandy Hook Elementary School in Newtown, Connecticut, resulted in the brutal deaths of twenty young children, mostly first graders, as well as a half-dozen adults. Visibly shaken by the attacks, President Obama—who met personally with the grieving parents of the slain children—vowed to make gun control a "central issue" of his second term. "I will put everything I've got into this," he announced. But he soon found that Republicans refused to act. "The Second Amendment is non-negotiable," insisted Representative Tim Huelskamp of Kansas. "Let me be clear, I will fight any efforts to take our guns," Representative Dan Benishek of Michigan echoed. "Not on my watch." Frustrated with Congress's refusal to act, Obama resigned himself to signing a number of executive orders designed to limit gun violence. Even this action was condemned. "Using executive action to attempt to poke holes in the Second Amendment is a power grab," complained Senator Chuck Grassley of Iowa.[10]

Leaders of the gun lobby, most notably Wayne LaPierre of the National Rifle Association, also pushed back. In a press conference a week after the shootings, LaPierre used the incident to argue that the nation actually needed *more* guns, not fewer. "How many more copycats are waiting in the wings?" he asked. "A dozen more killers, a hundred more?" Schools needed armed guards, he insisted, and individuals had to arm themselves as well. The plea worked. Gun sales spiked in the year after Sandy Hook, with manufacturers reporting 30–50 percent increases in their profits. Congress failed to act in any meaningful way on gun control, while several states actually relaxed existing gun laws, working on the theory that "the only way to stop a bad guy with a gun is a good guy with a gun." By the end of 2015, "open carry" laws allowing individuals to carry firearms in public were legal in forty-five states. These changes in the gun climate, with fewer restrictions on gun rights and fewer regulations on the access and display of weapons, were a staggering blow to Obama's prestige. But they were, more importantly, a blow to the public's confidence in the political system. Even with polls showing that large majorities of the public favored tighter gun control measures, the gun lobby proved to be more powerful.[11]

As private gun sales soared, another debate sprang up around public uses of force by law enforcement. On February 26, 2012, Trayvon Martin, a seventeen-year-old African American, was shot and killed inside a gated community in Sanford, Florida. Martin had been staying with relatives in the neighborhood and, on the night of the incident, was walking home from a nearby convenience store. A local neighborhood watch member named George Zimmerman, who had become increasingly agitated by reports of crime in the community, mistook Martin for a burglar and phoned 911. The police dispatcher told Zimmerman to stand down, but he nevertheless followed Martin and confronted him, sparking a struggle between the two. Though Martin was unarmed, Zimmerman drew his 9mm semiautomatic pistol and shot the teenager dead. Despite the circumstances of the shooting, Zimmerman claimed he was innocent, invoking the state's recently added "Stand Your Ground" self-defense law, which authorized deadly force if an individual believed he was in danger of bodily harm. Thanks to the law, Zimmerman was acquitted on charges of second-degree murder in July 2013.[12]

In response, activists on social media launched a new awareness campaign marked by the Twitter hashtag #BlackLivesMatter. The BLM movement gained national attention, staging massive demonstrations and street protests in response to a new wave of African Americans who had died at the hands of police in suspect circumstances. The Martin incident had captured public attention, but there were countless more like it. In July 2014, for instance, Eric Garner died after members of the NYPD placed him in an illegal chokehold; cell phone video showed the forty-three-year-old, who was being detained for selling cigarettes illegally, repeatedly telling officers "I can't breathe." A month later in August, an unarmed eighteen-year-old African American teen named Michael Brown was shot and killed by police in Ferguson, Missouri;

this time, video showed the teen's body lying uncovered in the street for four hours after the shooting.[13]

Activists staged protests in Ferguson, demanding criminal prosecution of the officer who shot Brown and shouting "Black lives matter! Black lives matter!" Most of the protesters were peaceful, but a small group engaged in acts of arson and looting. The local police department, which, like many across the country, had been significantly militarized over the previous decade, responded with an overwhelming show of force, using tear gas and rubber bullets to disperse crowds. Ironically, the images of heavily armed and armored law enforcement officers squaring off against peaceful protesters only served to illustrate the very problem of police brutality that BLM sought to expose. At one point, CNN broadcast images of a police officer taunting protesters: "Bring it, all you fucking animals! Bring it!" Another Ferguson officer pointed his semiautomatic rifle at protesters, screaming "I will fucking kill you!" Even reporters, on scene to document the unrest, found themselves arrested in the massive police response. Nevertheless, they managed to spread news of the chaos through social media.[14]

Ferguson remained a major flashpoint for the Black Lives Matter movement, but countless other incidents occurred in its aftermath. Some of these stood out due to distinguishing details, such as the notorious November 2014 death of Tamir Rice, a 12-year-old black boy playing in a park, who was shot twice by Cleveland officers who mistook his toy pistol for a real gun. In the fallout from the shooting, the city settled a $6 million lawsuit with the Rice family; no charges were ever brought against the officers.[15] While such incidents stood out in the public eye, activists were more disturbed by what seemed an increasingly steady drumbeat of African Americans killed by policemen. On April 2, 2015, Eric Harris was killed in Tulsa, Oklahoma, by a sheriff's deputy who mistook his pistol for a taser; video from police body cameras recorded the deputy's shock: "I shot him! I'm sorry!"[16] Two days later, on April 4, Walter Scott was killed in North Charleston, South Carolina, by an officer who stopped Scott's car for a broken taillight; the officer said he had fired his weapon because he feared for his life, but cell phone video showed him firing eight shots at Scott's back as he fled.[17] Eight days later, on April 12, Freddie Gray suffered a spine injury while in the custody of Baltimore police officers who had apprehended him for carrying a knife; he died a week later. Arresting officers insisted Gray's injury stemmed from an accident incurred in transit, but once again cell phone videos provided by witnesses proved the story to be untrue.[18] Ten days later, on April 22, William Chapman was killed in a Wal-Mart parking lot in Portsmouth, Virginia, by an off-duty cop who wrongly suspected the eighteen-year-old boy of being a shoplifter.[19] The constant reports of incidents like these made the depth and degree of police brutality inescapable, so much so that BLM protests began to get results. In a notable departure from past norms, officers in all these April 2015 incidents were subjected to criminal investigations and, with the exception of the Gray case, convicted as well.[20]

These changes in the court of public opinion and the courts of law stemmed, in large part, from changes in technology. The proliferation of cell phone cameras and police body cameras gave unimpeachable accounts of circumstances surrounding many of the suspect deaths. In years past, as the Kerner Report revealed in 1968, these incidents had been common in African American communities, but there were rarely any records. With cell phone videos easily obtained and shared, however, reports of police brutality spread much more quickly and effectively. In previous eras, police officers had been able to rely on their professional reputation to convince courts that their version of a violent incident was the truth; ubiquitous video evidence now made that impossible. Moreover, as images and videos circulated on social media, they helped establish BLM as a mass movement. Organizers like Johnetta Elzie and DeRay McKesson had been drawn to Ferguson by social media images from the site of Michael Brown's killing. In turn, they used outlets like Vine, Twitter, and Instagram to spread word about additional incidents and BLM counterprotests, using social media to speed the growth of a movement that, a half century before, would have taken months or years of grassroots organizing. Describing demonstrations across Baltimore after Freddie Gray's death, a reporter noted that this "protest looked much like the ones that have characterized the growing movement against police violence. Bodies moved in the dark, but the faces—protesters and police officers alike—were lit up by the thin, lunar glow of cellphone screens."[21]

While new technologies such as cell phone cameras and social media outlets helped launch Black Lives Matter, they also propelled a counter-movement by white supremacists. On June 17, 2015, a twenty-two-year-old white man named Dylann Roof armed himself with a semiautomatic Glock and eighty-eight hollow-point bullets, and then killed nine worshippers at Charleston's Emanuel African Methodist Episcopal Church. Roof's radicalization to white supremacist politics had come years before. "The event that truly awakened me was the Trayvon Martin case," he wrote in an online manifesto. "It was obvious that Zimmerman was in the right," Roof decided after reading a Wikipedia article about the case. "But more importantly, this prompted me to type in the words 'black on White crime' into Google, and I have never been the same since that day." The search engine led Roof to the online world of the "Alt Right," where white supremacist websites spread stories that portrayed white Americans as the nation's real victims, subjected to the violence of black criminals and supplanted at work by immigrants. "I realized something was very wrong," Roof concluded. "How could the news be blowing up the Trayvon Martin case while hundreds of these black on white murders got ignored?" Convinced by his new online community that his fellow whites were suffering an epidemic of black violence, he set himself on the path to mass murder. "Somebody had to do something," the unrepentant Roof told FBI agents after his arrest. "Because, you know, black people are killing white people every day, on the streets. And they rape white women, a hundred white women a day."[22]

Echoes of Roof's online radicalization were heard elsewhere. In the summer of 2015, for instance, antiabortion activists released videos purporting to show officials at Planned Parenthood discussing plans to harvest and then sell both organs and fetal tissue from aborted fetuses. The videos sparked a new national controversy over abortion provisions, with accusations swirling that the organization was engaged in the sale of "baby parts." (Further investigations in multiple states cleared Planned Parenthood of wrongdoing.) As the video circulated widely on social media, the issue took on increasingly heated tones. Suddenly, on November 27, 2015, Robert Dear Jr. opened fire at a Planned Parenthood clinic in Colorado Springs, killing three people, including a police officer. During his arrest, the gunman, in apparent reference to the video, told officers: "no more baby parts."[23]

In many ways, the fault lines over these issues—abortion, race, police brutality, gun control—had long divided the American populace. But in the social media age, such divisions took on an exaggerated scope and tone. Incidents in one location were immediately nationalized, and sensationalized too. Videos of violence, purported to be committed by policemen or Planned Parenthood, spread quickly on the internet, resonating through echo chambers and finding audiences already primed for outrage. The short format of Twitter and Facebook, meanwhile, provided immediacy and intimacy for such incidents, but stripped away nuance along the way. Once again, technologies that had once promised to bring Americans together only served to drive them further apart.

Make America Great Again

The deepening sense of division in the nation would only worsen with the presidential campaign of 2016. On one side of the partisan divide, Democrats rallied around Hillary Clinton, who had lost out to Obama in the 2008 primaries but then went on to join his administration as secretary of state. Vice President Joe Biden had opted not to run, but Clinton nevertheless found herself facing a surprisingly spirited challenge by the socialist independent Senator Bernie Sanders of Vermont. Though he formally caucused with Democrats in the Senate, Sanders maintained his independence and used it now to criticize the party and the electoral system writ large. Powerful economic interests had "rigged" American politics, he charged in the primary campaign, maintaining an outsized influence through campaign contributions and corporate lobbying. The Democratic Party, which had traditionally stood as a counterweight against corporate interests, had steadily been co-opted, he charged. Singling out Clinton's habit of making high-priced speeches to Wall Street firms like Goldman Sachs, Sanders portrayed her as a tool of big business. Meanwhile, the Vermont senator made a powerful case for leftist policies, calling for the party to return to its roots by championing greater government assistance in health care, college education, and jobs. His candidacy found strong support across the nation, as progressive activists rallied around his unapologetic case for the Left. In the end, however, Clinton's long-standing ties to Democratic Party leaders, delegates, and other key constituencies helped her win out.[24]

Though the Left had been significantly energized by the primary campaign, much of that passion dissipated when Sanders failed to win the nomination. His supporters charged that the Democratic National Committee had unfairly sided with Clinton as the safer choice and had effectively "disfranchised" independent voters with closed primaries that only allowed registered Democrats to participate. "A lot of people have a feeling that the corruption and the rigged primary system are horrible," a California canvasser noted. "With the voters we were talking to, there was a strong sense that party politics isn't working." Seeing the disappointing end to their primary campaign as confirmation of Sanders's claims that the system was "rigged," many refused to take further part in party politics. "That's one of the places this supposed movement falls short," noted Markos Moulitsas, founder of the *Daily Kos* website and a longtime activist on the left, "lots of people who don't want to be sullied from all the supposed corruption in the party but refusing to do the hard work of taking over a party from the inside." Unwilling to change the Democratic Party from the inside, these disaffected voters had no real alternative outside of it. Unlike the world of media, which had been radically fragmented over the previous few decades—with the "big three" television networks competing with hundreds of alternatives on cable and talk radio and the traditional handful of major newspapers challenged on the internet from across the spectrum—the world of politics was still stubbornly rooted in the "big two" political parties. Increasingly, neither party was very popular. In May 2016, for instance, the Democratic Party had a 48 percent favorability rating, and the Republican Party an even lower 36 percent. But thanks to a combination of institutional advantages and inertia, they maintained the same stranglehold on national politics they had held since the mid-nineteenth century.[25]

In contrast to the tight Democratic duel between Clinton and Sanders, Republicans amassed the largest number of presidential primary contenders in the history of American politics. The crowded GOP field soon included seventeen major candidates, including four US senators (Ted Cruz of Texas, Lindsey Graham of South Carolina, Rand Paul of Kentucky, and Marco Rubio of Florida) as well as several then-current or former governors (such as Jeb Bush of Florida, Chris Christie of New

Jersey, Mike Huckabee of Arkansas, Bobby Jindal of Louisiana, John Kasich of Ohio, Rick Perry of Texas, and Scott Walker of Wisconsin). Although several seemed to be formidable candidates with years of experience, many soon proved to be severely flawed as campaigners and, in many respects, out of touch with the direction of politics.

Against this crowded field of traditional politicians, New York businessman Donald Trump stood out. Skilled at self-promotion, the flashy real estate mogul had made himself into a celebrity during the 1980s and 1990s. His frequent appearances on the shock-jock radio programs of Don Imus and Howard Stern, as well as his constant presence in the pages of tabloids and celebrity magazines, transformed the Trump name into a familiar brand. By the mid-2000s, however, that name had been tarnished after six bankruptcy filings (including on major projects such as the Trump Taj Mahal Casino in Atlantic City and the Plaza Hotel in New York) and several high-profile business flops (including Trump Airlines, Trump Steaks, Trump Vodka, Trump Ice, Trump Casinos, Trump Mortgage, *Trump* magazine, and Trump: The Game).[26]

As Trump struggled with these setbacks, he received an invitation from reality television producer Mark Burnett to serve as the host for a new program. Trump was initially dismissive, arguing that reality TV was simply "for the bottom-feeders of society." But he was eventually won over by Burnett's pitch for *The Apprentice*, a show that would present a polished image of Trump as the embodiment of business success. Burnett loved Trump as a character. Though he was struggling financially at this point in his career, Trump still presented himself as a brash, take-no-prisoners businessman who knew how to make decisions. After being promised that everything would be taped in Trump Tower, Trump saw the light: "My jet's going to be in every episode," he realized. "The Taj is going to be featured. Even if it doesn't get ratings, it's still going to be great for my brand." The show launched on NBC in January 2004, with the New York mogul serving as host for the next fourteen seasons. "For millions of Americans, this became their image of Trump: in the boardroom, in control, firing people who didn't measure up to his standard," noted one profile. "Trump lived in grand style, flew in a Trump-emblazoned jet or helicopter, and traveled from Trump Tower on Fifth Avenue to Mar-a-Lago in Palm Beach, Fla."[27]

With his fame and fortune refreshed, Trump moved into the world of politics. He had long been a political gadfly, donating to members of both parties and running for president in 2000 as a long-shot candidate with the Reform Party. But during the Obama era, he steadily made common cause with forces on the far right. Most significantly, Trump emerged as the highest-profile proponent of the so-called "birther" conspiracy that alleged that Obama had not been born in the United States and thus was not a "natural-born citizen" eligible for the presidency. Rumors about Obama's heritage surfaced in the 2008 campaign, but were largely dispelled when the candidate produced his birth certificate from his home state of Hawaii, which local Republican officials verified. When Trump first considered running for president in early 2011, he revived the issue as a way of discrediting the incumbent, pushing the conspiracy theory in countless interviews. "I want to see his birth certificate," Trump announced on Fox News's *On the Record*. "Why doesn't he show his birth certificate?" he asked on ABC's *The View*. "I'm starting to think he was not born here," he concluded on NBC's *Today Show*. As he pressed the issue, Trump surged ahead in early polls on the 2012 Republican field, moving from fifth place to a practical tie for first. After six weeks of open speculation about his legitimacy not just as a president but as an American, Obama released an additional long-form version of his birth certificate. Angry at having been subjected to a level of scrutiny that struck many as inherently racist, the president insisted that "we do not have time for this kind of silliness."[28]

Despite the repeated (and unprecedented) release of the president's birth certificates, Trump kept the issue alive, sensing that he had struck a chord with a Republican base that regarded Obama as an enemy. Using the social media platform of Twitter, Trump pressed the issue for the next four years. "An 'extremely credible source' has called my office and told me that Barack Obama's birth certificate is a fraud," he asserted in 2012. Increasingly, his tweets about Obama's birth certificate implied that there had been an immense criminal cover-up. "How amazing," he tweeted in 2013, "the State Health Director who verified copies of Obama's 'birth certificate' died in plane crash today. All others lived." "Attention all hackers," Trump posted in 2014. "You are hacking everything else so please hack Obama's college records (destroyed?) and check 'place of birth.'"[29] News outlets routinely noted that Trump's claims were far-fetched and reminded viewers that officials had vouched for the president's birth certificates, but neverthe-less Trump pressed on. In a 2012 interview with CNN's Wolf Blitzer, he noted there was a ready audience for such conspiracies. "A lot of people do not think it was an authentic certificate," Trump said. "And, frankly, if you would report it accurately [sic], I think you'd probably get better ratings than you're getting."[30]

When he officially entered the 2016 presidential campaign, Trump showed he had a keen sense of the political issues and public specta-cles that would get good ratings. On June 16, 2015, he made a dramatic campaign announcement at Trump Tower, the Fifth Avenue skyscraper where casts of *The Apprentice* had lived and worked for over a decade. Gliding down a gilded elevator, Trump gave a raucous, if often ram-bling, speech that captured the themes he would present on the cam-paign trail. "Our country is in serious trouble," he began. "We don't have victories anymore. We used to have victories, but we don't have them." Americans, he insisted, were losing on all fronts. Economically, Trump claimed that rival nations like China were outperforming the United States, due to unfair trade deals that disadvantaged Americans. Distanc-ing himself from the free-trade orthodoxy of his party, Trump sought to win over disaffected members of the white working class who felt NAFTA and similar deals had hurt them. At the same time, connect-ing his candidacy to an issue that had been central to a growing part of the Republican Party since the 1990s, he argued that Americans were endangered by the twin threats of Islamic terrorism and illegal immi-gration. "When Mexico sends its people, they're not sending their best," Trump mused in a particularly memorable passage. "They're sending people that have lots of problems, and they're bringing those problems with us. They're bringing drugs. They're bringing crime. They're rapists. And some, I assume, are good people." To stop the flow of illegal immi-gration, Trump promised to "build a great wall" along the entire south-ern border of the nation. "And I will have Mexico pay for that wall."[31]

Trump's announcement prefigured the coming campaign. As reporter Jeremy Diamond noted, "spectators got a flavor for the type of candidate Trump plans to become—one who shoots from the hip and doesn't care for a script—and the ideas he'll promote." Political pundits noted dismis-sively that Trump's ideas were either light on details or wrong on them, and that he had starkly reversed himself on major issues like abortion,

LGBTQ rights, tax policy, and national defense. But consistency and coherency were beside the point. "If Mr. Trump's ideology has proved flexible," Alex Burns noted in the *New York Times*, "the cornerstone of his worldview has not: He has consistently been a passionate believer in Donald Trump, and his own capacity to bully and badger his way into the best possible deal." Ultimately, Trump ran on the same persona that he had crafted on *The Apprentice*, in which he was the epitome of success, a natural leader who would solve all the nation's problems, efficiently and effectively. "The irony is that although Trump may be offering himself up as the anti-politician," Russell Berman noted at *The Atlantic*, "there is nobody who does a better job at telling people what they want to hear, regardless of how accurate or nonsensical it is."[32]

The Trump phenomenon took its clearest form in the rallies he led across the country. "The candidate's angry rhetoric—on subjects like undocumented Mexican immigrants, political correctness and 'thugs' in Baltimore—has made his run a magnet for disaffected supporters and for identity politics protesters determined to steal the spotlight and disrupt his events," *Politico* noted. "Trump's relish for confrontation, where other politicians would seek to minimize it, has only fueled the fire." While events by other Republicans and Democrats remained calm, Trump's regularly erupted in ugly, violent incidents. At an October 2015 rally in Richmond, Virginia, Trump supporters ripped signs from Latino immigration activists; one spit in a protester's face. In November, an African American protester at a Birmingham rally was punched, kicked, and choked. At a December event in Las Vegas, when a black protester was being forcibly removed by security, Trump supporters screamed "light the motherfucker on fire!" Rather than try to reduce the violence, Trump rationalized it. After the Birmingham incident, for instance, he defended the crowd's assault on the protester, saying "maybe he *should* have been roughed up, because it was absolutely disgusting what he was doing." A few weeks later, as a black protester was ejected from a Worcester, Massachusetts, event for yelling "Trump is a racist!" the candidate reveled in the moment. "Isn't a Trump rally much more exciting than these other ones?"[33]

The news media seemed to agree. Primetime viewership across the three main cable news channels—CNN, Fox News, and MSNBC— had dropped by a third between 2008 and 2014. But in 2015, the Pew Research Project showed that the three cable news networks saw "a ratings bump not seen in years." "The Trump Effect," media analyst Erik Wemple noted, had resulted in a surge in profits, thanks to full coverage of Trump's rallies and countless call-in and in-person interviews on their programs. (Fox News experienced a 21 percent increase in profits; CNN, 17 percent; MSNBC, 10 percent.) More than traditional candidates, Trump understood the dynamics of the modern media. He was obsessed with cable news and capitalized on the rhythm of the medium. By saying the most outlandish things possible, he made it impossible for the press to ignore him, and he steadily became more provocative each time to keep their attention. Many producers and reporters, worried about appearing biased against Trump, went overboard trying to give him fair coverage and making sure his surrogates received ample airtime. Journalists who were intent on appearing "objective" often felt the need to downplay his outlandish behavior by pointing to the existence of comparable extremism on the Democratic side. While the cable networks benefited from their extensive coverage, so did the candidate. According to a March 2016 study by mediaQuant, a firm that tracked press coverage of candidates and estimated the value of airtime provided, Trump benefited from nearly $3 billion in free media during the GOP primaries. Some of this coverage was critical, but most amounted to uninterrupted coverage of his hour-long rallies, broadcast from start to finish, with little effort to fact-check the claims as they came. Notably, Trump received more free media than all the other sixteen Republican candidates *combined*, and eight times as much as his closest competitor.[34]

Trump's approach to that competition represented another departure from political norms. Traditionally, presidential primaries were mild-mannered contests between like-minded members of a party. But early on, Trump showed he would reject the normal niceties in his campaign when he said the party's 2008 presidential nominee John McCain, a former POW from the Vietnam War, wasn't truly a hero. "He was a war hero because he was captured," Trump said dismissively. "I like people who weren't captured." Pundits assumed the rash comment—coming from a man who secured five separate deferments to avoid serving in Vietnam himself—would bring Trump's campaign to an unceremonious end. Those assumptions, however, were based on memories of a political process that was long gone. Trump was much more in tune with the polarized political world as it was in the current day and age. Rather than apologize, Trump stood his ground, a stance his supporters welcomed. Emboldened by the response, Trump kept attacking his rivals. At his rallies and in the debates, he abandoned the usual honorifics for insults, mocking Governor Jeb Bush as "low energy," Senator Marco Rubio as "Liddle Marco," and Senator Ted Cruz as "Lyin' Ted." In interviews, Trump insulted businesswoman Carly Fiorina's physical appearance and claimed neurosurgeon Ben Carson had a "pathological temper" akin to a "child molester." He even accused Ted Cruz's father of having ties to John F. Kennedy's assassin Lee Harvey Oswald, a claim based on a conspiracy theory run in the *National Enquirer*, a tabloid published by an ardent Trump backer. His rivals tried to take the high road at first, but as Trump continued to make headway with his attacks, a few began to respond in kind. In late February 2016, for instance, Rubio mocked Trump's "spray tan" and ridiculed his "small hands." For many in the media, such mudslinging made for good television. CBS chairman Les Moonves captured the prevailing spirit well. The primary campaign had turned into a "circus" full of "bomb throwing," he said, but ultimately "Donald's place in this election is a good thing" because he boosted their ratings and profits. "It may not be good for America," Moonves shrugged, "but it's damn good for CBS."[35]

Though some speculated that "the Trump Effect" reflected a morbid curiosity that would never be replicated at the polls, Trump soon made it clear that he could compete for votes. Running as an "outsider" against a crowded field of more conventional career politicians, the reality-TV star essentially employed his own form of "narrowcasting" to win over a small but fiercely loyal slice of the Republican base. (The remaining establishment candidates, meanwhile, found themselves fighting over the same set of voters.) As a result, Trump finished just behind Cruz in the Iowa caucuses, and then went on to win the first three primaries in New Hampshire, South Carolina, and Nevada outright. Relishing his new role as frontrunner, he played up his self-image as a winner and portrayed his nomination as inevitable. "If you listen to the pundits, we weren't expected to win too much, and now we're winning, winning, winning the country," he said after taking Nevada. "And soon the country's going to start winning, winning, winning." And, indeed, Trump kept winning, taking seven of eleven states on "Super Tuesday" and nine of thirteen states over the rest of March. By early May, Donald Trump was the GOP's presumptive presidential nominee.[36]

Even after his early victories, Trump still lacked strong support from social conservatives who were essential to the party's general election plans. To win them over, he brought roughly a thousand conservative religious leaders to Trump Tower for a summit meeting in June. There, he promised them that, as president, he would work hard to roll back abortion rights and to defend the ability of Christians to discriminate against LGBTQ people on religious grounds. Most important, Trump promised them he would appoint "the right kind of Supreme Court justice." The archconservative Justice Antonin Scalia had passed away in February; in a stunning development, Senate Republicans announced they would simply refuse to hold hearings or votes for any nominee put forth by President Obama, keeping the seat vacant so the *next* president could make the appointment. For social conservatives, this seat on the Supreme Court was ultimately more important than the presidency. The court in recent years had delivered closely divided decisions not just on policy matters like the Affordable Care Act but on the polarizing social causes of the culture wars. It allowed businesses to be exempt from regulations that for-profit owners objected to on religious grounds by a 5–4 margin in *Burwell v. Hobby Lobby* (2014), for instance, but then legalized same-sex marriage by a 5–4 margin in *Obergefell v. Hodges* (2015). That decision, in particular, concerned religious conservatives because it signaled the court might be following popular opinion on cultural issues; 60 percent of Americans supported same-sex marriage at the time of the ruling. Given the balance of the court, the Religious Right realized that Scalia's replacement could effectively set a course for social conservatism for the next generation. Ahead of the Trump Tower summit, the candidate offered a list of eleven potential nominees, picked for him by the Federalist Society. According to *World* magazine, which regularly surveyed evangelical leaders, Trump's promise to appoint pro-life justices to the Supreme Court doubled his level of support. "It makes ginormous difference," one noted. "If Donald Trump wins, he would have to look back and credit that day for mobilizing evangelicals."[37]

Even though Trump shored up his standing with the base, the next month's Republican National Convention displayed a party divided. Notably, all but one of the GOP's past presidential nominees refused to take part. Both George H. W. Bush and George W. Bush made it clear they would never support the man who had humiliated Jeb Bush. McCain said he had to focus on his own reelection, while Romney had steadfastly urged his party to see that Trump was "a phony, a fraud" and reject him. (Only Bob Dole, the 93-year-old former nominee from 1996, agreed to attend.) Large numbers of elected officials likewise chose to skip the convention, offering intentionally thin excuses. Nevada Senator Dean Heller's office mused that he might have to irrigate his ranch that week, while Senator Jeff Flake insisted he had to mow his lawn back home in arid Arizona. Senator Ben Sasse of Nebraska was even blunter, noting that he would instead take his kids "to watch some dumpster fires across the state, all of which enjoy more popularity than the current front-runners."[38]

The Republican convention in Cleveland lived down to their expectations. The streets outside Quicken Arena filled with protesters and counterprotesters; thanks to Ohio's open-carry gun legislation, several had semiautomatic weapons. Inside the arena, the mood was no brighter. Trump had campaigned heavily against "corruption" in Washington, promising to "drain the swamp" if he were elected. Hillary Clinton became the embodiment of the culture he decried. Primetime speakers promoted a dark, dystopian vision of an America besieged by problems, with Clinton linked to virtually everything wrong with America. The opening night, for instance, featured several videos and speeches about the Benghazi attacks, including an emotional address from a visibly distraught mother of one of the victims, who said, "I blame Hillary Clinton personally for the death of my son." That same night, another set of grieving mothers—billed as "Victims of Illegal Immigrants"—told how their children had been killed by undocumented Latinos. "A vote for Hillary," one asserted, "is putting all of our children's lives at risk." As allegations piled up, New Jersey governor Chris Christie told the convention that as a "former federal prosecutor" he would present the case against Hillary Clinton "to you, sitting as a jury of her peers, both in this hall and in your living rooms around our nation." Recounting the Benghazi attacks and the revelations that she had a private email server, Christie repeatedly asked, "Guilty or not guilty?" With a roar, they shouted back: "Guilty!" Later, former general Michael Flynn moved the convention's show trial from prosecution to sentencing, leading another angry chant from the stage: "Lock her up! Lock her up!"[39]

Trump's acceptance speech stuck with the dystopian spirit. "Our Convention occurs at a moment of crisis for our nation," he warned. "The attacks on our police, and the terrorism in our cities, threaten our very way of life." Crime rates had steadily declined over decades to historic lows, but the candidate nevertheless spoke at length about "chaos in our communities" which he claimed had been caused by immigrants and domestic criminals. Returning to a story he told often on the trail, Trump recounted how a twenty-one-year-old Nebraska woman had been killed by an undocumented drunk driver from Honduras, becoming, in his words, yet another "sacrifice on the altar of open borders." Having described a nation in crisis, its people endangered by enemies inside and outside its borders, Trump insisted: "I alone can fix it."[40]

"But Her Emails!"

Unlike the drama of the Republican convention, Hillary Clinton's path to her party's nomination had been surprisingly quiet. Her historic journey to become the first female nominee of a major party had electrified women and young girls across the country, but she was nevertheless eclipsed by the "Trump effect" in the media. Clinton's decades in the public eye—as First Lady, US senator, and secretary of state—had made her increasingly cautious in her dealings with the press and also made the press less interested in her as well. In stark contrast to the fiery, freewheeling Trump, Clinton took a much more conventional profile as a candidate and offered far less drama on the campaign trail. As a result, Clinton found herself sidelined by the national media, much as Trump's primary opponents had been. In May 2016, for instance, as Clinton unveiled new campaign themes in a major address in Las Vegas, all three of the cable news networks instead carried a live shot of an empty podium in North Dakota where they promised Donald Trump would soon appear.[41]

Meanwhile, when Clinton *did* receive media attention, it often only amplified the attacks that Trump and other Republicans made on her. According to a study by Harvard's Berkman Klein Center, media coverage of Clinton focused on her scandals more than it did on her policy proposals by a margin of nearly 4-to-1. (In contrast, coverage of Trump focused more on his policies than his various scandals, by a margin of nearly 2-to-1.) As the report noted, nightly news programs had devoted about three times as much coverage to Clinton's emails as they had to her policies. There were, in fact, two different email stories: first, the revelation that she had used a private email server as secretary of state and, second, the release of hacked DNC emails by WikiLeaks, an international nonprofit publicly dedicated to exposing government secrets, but privately tied to Russia, according to US intelligence agencies. Each email scandal led nowhere on its own: Clinton's private server contained classified materials, but had not been hacked; the released DNC emails, meanwhile, merely revealed routine exchanges typical for a campaign. But conflated in the public's mind as a single sweeping scandal, "Hillary's emails" became a major line of attack for Trump. In late July, a week after the "lock her up!" chants at the GOP convention, the candidate urged Russian hackers to keep digging into his rival's private server. "I will tell you this, Russia," he said. "If you're listening, I hope you're able to find the 30,000 emails that are missing."[42]

In significant ways, Trump's attacks on the campaign trail were echoed and amplified by social media. First and foremost, the candidate made extensive use of Twitter throughout the campaign, retweeting posts from his millions of followers and, occasionally, sparking controversy when several were revealed to have white supremacist sympathies. Second, the comments sections of conservative websites like Breitbart News and right-wing Reddit threads worked to spread easily digestible internet "memes" that pushed Trump's claims to a wider audience. Third, and perhaps most significantly, Facebook played a major role in the spread of such false information. Much of the problem seemed to be innocent mistakes by individual users, but later inquiries showed that there had been deliberate efforts to deceive, stemming from Russia. For instance, congressional investigations revealed that, seeking to sway US voters, a Kremlin-backed propaganda company bought $100,000 in Facebook ads, a purchase that might have reached 70 million users. Meanwhile, several Facebook groups pushing anti-immigration, anti-refugee and anti-Clinton arguments were later found to have connections to Russia as well. One of them, Heart of Texas, an account with nearly a quarter-million followers, even organized conservative rallies. Ultimately, the co-opting of Facebook by a foreign government revealed not just how social media made voters vulnerable to outside influences, but also how social media had, in many ways, supplanted the traditional media itself. As media columnist Margaret Sullivan noted, Facebook "has never acknowledged the glaringly obvious—that it is essentially a media company, where many of its 2 billion active monthly users get the majority of their news and information. . . . When its information is false, when it is purchased and manipulated to affect the outcome of an election, the effect is enormous. When the information purveyors are associated with a foreign adversary—with a clear interest in the outcome of the American election—we're into a whole new realm of power."[43] The Obama administration had known about these efforts by Russia as early as the summer of 2016, but the president refused to go public—rejecting a proposal by FBI Director James Comey to write an op-ed about what they knew—for fear of looking like he was intervening in the election. Despite an extensive investigation by US intelligence agencies, information about Russian intervention, and its possible connections to high-ranking officials in the Trump campaign, still remained outside the public purview.

Even with this array of attacks against her, Clinton entered the fall campaign confident of her chances. She had led Trump in the polls for most of the year and, after their conventions, her lead only continued to widen. At the start of August, CNN's poll showed her leading Trump by nine percentage points; a few weeks later, Reuters/IPSOS had her up twelve. As pollsters and pundits rushed to point out, in the previous sixteen presidential elections, the candidate who led in the polls after the two parties' political conventions won every single time. In a mid-August report, an American correspondent for the BBC asked the question then on many observers' minds: "Has Donald Trump Already Blown It?" The media's assumptions about the inevitable outcome of the presidential race invariably shaped their coverage of the closing months of that race itself. "The press covered Hillary Clinton like the next president of the United States," media critic James Poniewozik reflected at the end of the election. "The press covered Donald Trump like a future trivia question (and a ratings cash cow)."[44]

To keep his chances alive, Trump shook up his campaign team in mid-August. Campaign head Paul Manafort, a political operative with Russian connections who had been brought in months before to manage the convention chaos, was abruptly sidelined. In his place came a new team. Roger Ailes, recently removed from Fox News over allegations of sexual harassment, became a new campaign advisor, while Stephen Bannon, chairman of Breitbart News, was hired as the campaign's chief executive. In many ways, the moves reflected the larger displacement of the traditional Republican Party apparatus by the brash new upstarts of right-wing media. As the *New York Times* noted, "It was not lost on Republicans in Washington that two news executives whose outlets had fueled the anti-establishment rebellion that bedeviled congressional leaders and set the stage for Mr. Trump's nomination were now directly guiding the party's presidential message and strategy." Longtime conservatives saw the development as a disaster. Bill Kristol, who had pushed for the addition of right-wing favorites like Dan Quayle and Sarah Palin to past presidential tickets, saw this new union as a step too far. As he observed, "It's the merger of the Trump campaign with the kooky right."[45]

In particular, Bannon's appointment represented a sharp turn to the fringes, given his role as chairman of Breitbart News. "We're the platform for the alt right," he proudly told Sarah Posner of *Mother Jones* during the Republican convention. As conservative pundit Ben Shapiro confirmed, under Bannon's leadership the right-wing website had "become the alt-right go-to website, with [technology editor Milo] Yiannopoulos pushing white ethno-nationalism as a legitimate response to political correctness, and the comment section turning into a cesspool for white supremacist mememakers." Emphasizing the threats posed to Americans by free trade, Islamic terrorism, and Mexican immigration, Breitbart advanced a stark message of white nationalism and populism. It even contained a section titled "Black Crime," filled with the kind of stories that had radicalized Dylann Roof and other white supremacists like him. As the head of Marco Rubio's presidential campaign noted, Trump and Breitbart "both play to the lowest common denominator of people's fears. It's a match made in heaven."[46]

Despite the criticism, Trump's decision to double-down on the themes of white resentment did help shore up his campaign. By late August, Clinton's lead in the polls had been more than halved, dropping from twelve points to five in a few weeks. Her campaign made many mistakes on its own, never clearly articulating an agenda, while failing to appreciate how Trump's attacks on free trade were resonating with the white working and middle class, especially in the Midwest. Focusing instead on the vital role that appeals to white nationalism had in Trump's revival, Clinton decided to address the issue directly in a speech in Reno, Nevada, at the end of August. "Everywhere I go, people tell me how concerned they are by the divisive rhetoric coming from my opponent this election," she said, recounting ugly incidents from both Trump's past and the present campaign. "A man with a long history of racial discrimination, who traffics in dark conspiracy theories drawn from the pages of supermarket tabloids and the far, dark reaches of the internet, should never run our government or command our military." Trump's worst instincts, Clinton continued, were now moving to the forefront with the rise of Steve Bannon. "The de facto merger between Breitbart and the Trump Campaign represents a landmark achievement for the 'Alt-Right,'" she noted. "A fringe element has taken over the Republican Party." Though Clinton sought to expose white nationalists on the far right, many of them welcomed the attention, using the moment to raise funds and recruit members. "Thanks for the free PR Hillary," one wrote on Twitter. "The #AltRight will long remember the day you helped make us into the real right."[47]

As such reactions showed, the line between the traditional Republican Right and the new "Alt Right" had become increasingly blurred in the Trump campaign. At a Manhattan fund-raiser in early September, Clinton singled out the worst elements in her opponent's base. "You know, just to be grossly generalistic, you could put half of Trump's supporters into what I call the basket of deplorables, right?" she said to laughter and applause. "The racist, sexist, homophobic, xenophobic, Islamophobic— you name it. And he has lifted them up." Such people were "irredeemable," she noted, unlike "the other basket" of Trump supporters, "people who feel that the government has let them down, the economy has let them down, nobody cares about them, nobody worries about what happens to their lives and their futures, and they're just desperate for change." Despite her two categories, Trump supporters seized on the "basket of deplorables," which they saw as an echo of Mitt Romney's "47 percent" line, and made it a new rallying cry. "Hillary calling tens of millions of American men & women 'deplorable' is inexcusable and disqualifying," Sarah Huckabee Sanders noted on Twitter the next morning, where

#BasketOfDeplorables was trending. That afternoon, Trump's running mate, Governor Mike Pence of Indiana, used a speech at the Values Voter Summit to claim she had insulted all Trump voters. "Hillary, they are not a basket of anything," he chided. "They are Americans and they deserve your respect." Trump's base embraced the label. "On the shopping web-site Etsy," *USA Today* reported, "one can find Deplorable t-shirts, key chains, car decals, buttons, pendants, coffee mugs and even a deplorable pocket watch." Trump supporters added "Deplorable" to their user names on Twitter and sported it on shirts and signs at the candidate's rally. At one event in Asheville, North Carolina, a white man stood outside with a homemade banner: "DEPLORABLE LIVES MATTER."[48]

Even as his base rallied around him, Trump proved unable to take the lead. The presidential debates, which played to Clinton's strengths as an experienced policy wonk and away from Trump's advantages as an off-the-cuff stump speaker, helped Clinton maintain her advantage for most of the fall. Then, in early October, the wheels of the Trump train seemed to come off, with the release of a secret recording made just before a 2005 Trump interview with the entertainment news program *Access Hollywood*. Speaking off-camera but on-mic with host Billy Bush (a first cousin to George W. Bush), Trump graphically discussed his sexual conquests and casually confessed that he had committed sexual assault. "I'm automatically attracted to beautiful [women]—I just start kissing them," he bragged. "And when you're a star, they let you do it. You can do anything." "Whatever you want," Bush chimed in. "Grab 'em by the pussy," Trump replied. "You can do anything."[49] Significantly, the tape came out on the same day that the leaders of the intelligence agencies finally decided to make a public statement about their discoveries on Russian meddling in the election. "The US Intelligence Community is confident that the Russian Government directed the recent compromises of e-mails from US persons and institutions," they announced. "These thefts and disclosures are intended to interfere with the US election process." The remarkable statement offered serious warnings about a direct attack on American democracy. But few paid attention; all eyes and ears were on Trump's secret tape.[50]

For most pundits and political professionals, the revelations in the recording seemed serious enough to destroy Trump's candidacy. GOP leaders in Congress distanced themselves and the party from his comments, with Mitch McConnell calling them "repugnant" and Paul Ryan saying he was "sickened." Most seriously, Republican National Committee Chairman Reince Priebus even traveled to Trump Tower to plead with the candidate to drop out, to spare himself humiliation and to spare the larger party a devastating defeat. If he stayed in, Priebus pled, Trump would "go down with a worse election loss than Barry Goldwater's" infamous landslide defeat in 1964. Despite the revolt from Republican leaders, Trump's base stood by him, convincing the candidate to stay in the race. Notably, leaders of the Religious Right remained vocally committed to Trump, overlooking his sexually graphic comments and focusing instead on the larger prize of the Supreme Court. "People of faith are voting on issues like who will protect unborn life, defend religious freedom . . . and appoint conservative judges," Ralph Reed insisted. "I think a 10-year-old tape of a private conversation with a TV talk show host ranks pretty low on their hierarchy of their concerns." And indeed, polls soon revealed that the *Access Hollywood* recording had done little to impact the overall race. Clinton still led by four to six points.[51]

As the candidates headed into the closing days, the issues with Clinton's email resurfaced and radically transformed the race. A half hour after the release of the *Access Hollywood* recording, WikiLeaks responded by releasing a new batch of hacked Democratic emails, this time from the private account of Clinton's campaign chairman John Podesta. As with the hacked emails from the DNC, the new round of messages were largely mundane. (One of them, for instance, contained Podesta's recipe for risotto.) But the manner of WikiLeaks' release, trickling emails out in small batches, each and every day through the end of the election, guaranteed renewed and sustained media coverage of "Democratic emails." More significantly, on October 28, FBI director James Comey told Congress that the investigation into Clinton's private server, which he previously indicated had been completed, was being revived in light of new evidence. (Comey felt pressure to make this statement since he feared that, by not doing so, his agency would be accused of hiding information to favor Clinton.) Coverage of the election's closing days was thus dominated by speculation about Clinton's emails and the FBI investigation. The front page of the *New York Times* the next day, for instance, was filled above the fold with coverage, including an all-caps headline: "NEW EMAILS JOLT CLINTON CAMPAIGN IN

RACE'S LAST DAYS." The news struck a nerve with voters. "Within a day of the Comey letter," Nate Silver later noted, "Google searches for 'Clinton FBI' had increased 50-fold and searches for 'Clinton email' almost tenfold." Over the next week, Clinton's lead dropped dramatically, down to just two to three points in national polls.[52]

Despite the late bombshell, most observers still expected Clinton to win. On Election Day, *Time* ran predictions from a range of news outlets and pollsters. All of them agreed that the Democratic ticket would prevail, differing only on the exact odds and the precise margin of victory. But the prognosticators proved to be in for a surprise. When the early returns came in on election night, they showed Trump exceeding the experts' expectations as Clinton underperformed across the board. As the forecasts tilted to the Republican, *Politico* ran a banner headline shortly before 10pm: "Trump Gives Clinton a Scare." Soon after, Ohio was called for Trump, and CNBC.com noted the growing sense of uncertainty: "DOW FUTURES NOSEDIVE 600 POINTS ON ELECTION JITTERS." As the election night dragged on, the sense of shock and surprise only deepened. By the time he opened his live special on the Showtime cable channel at 11pm, Stephen Colbert could only marvel wearily: "What a year . . . tonight has been."[53]

By the next morning, it was clear that the 2016 race had been, in the words of Fox News anchor Bret Baier, "the most unreal, surreal election we have ever seen." Clinton won the popular vote, taking in nearly 3 million more votes nationwide than her opponent. (In keeping with the final polls that had predicted she would win the national popular vote by 2–3 percent, she did just that: winning 48.2 percent to 46.1 percent.) Despite her advantage, Clinton's votes were disproportionately concentrated, while Trump's were more evenly dispersed. As Clinton ran up the numbers in safe blue states, Trump managed to eke out longshot wins in several of the key battlegrounds, especially in the Rust Belt where Clinton had been predicted to dominate. Trump won Wisconsin, Michigan, and Pennsylvania by such razor-thin margins—less than a single percentage point in all three states—that a switch of just 77,000 votes in those states (out of 136 million votes cast nationally) would have thrown the election to Clinton.[54]

As election night came to a close, President-elect Donald Trump appeared before his stunned supporters to make a surprise victory speech. He looked back over a "very, very hard-fought campaign" and looked ahead to what his presidency might bring. "Now it is time for America to bind the wounds of division—have to get together," the president-elect asserted. "To all Republicans and Democrats and independents across this nation, I say it is time for us to come together as one united people." Those lines had, by that point in time, become something of a ritual in the remarks of winning candidates, an acknowledgment that their rise to power had been marked by partisan passions and, often, much worse. The high hopes for reconciliation in such comments speak to the best elements of American political life. But the simple fact of its constant repetition—the endless insistence, election after election, year after year, decade after decade, that this is "the time for us to come together"—speaks to the worst.[55]

Epilogue

DESPITE DONALD TRUMP'S CALL FOR AMERICANS TO "come together as one united people," the fault lines that led to his presidency only widened more over his first year in office.

In one sense, the fracturing of the United States would have continued apace no matter who was in the White House. Trump had been, in many ways, the result of trends decades in the making; he was ultimately more of a product of a polarized political environment and an increasingly hard-edged media climate than a producer of it. And indeed, many of the new president's early moves—from a cabinet cobbled together from Republican office holders, conservative businessmen, and senior military figures to the appointment of conservative justice Neil Gorsuch to the Supreme Court; from a systematic campaign to deregulate business on through the attempted repeal of Obamacare and the successful passage of a massive new tax cut—were ones that virtually any Republican administration would have initiated, and ones that Democrats and others on the left would just as likely have criticized.

And indeed, in some ways, the early days of the Trump administration seemed a mere continuation of the earlier back-and-forth between Democratic and Republican partisans. As the centerpiece of his first hundred days, the new president sought to repeal the Affordable Care Act and fulfill a longtime Republican campaign promise. But as soon as he began his legislative campaign to undo the centerpiece of Obama's legacy, opponents mobilized throughout the nation. One group of former Democratic congressional staffers, who called themselves Indivisible, self-consciously adopted the tools of the Tea Party to block the legislation. They had seen how effective conservatives had been in waging a scorched-earth resistance when Obama was president and now sought to turn the tables. Accordingly, they organized at the local level, put pressure on members in their home districts, and used social media campaigns and television-friendly protests to protect the ACA. Drawing broad support, Indivisible and its allies were ultimately successful in stalling the repeal bill. Trump was undaunted, however. Just as Indivisible looked back to the Tea Party for inspiration, Trump took another page from the conservative playbook by borrowing tactics used by Ronald Reagan, relying on administrative subterfuge to undermine the law instead. By allowing the program to be poorly implemented and then inserting a repeal of the individual mandate into separate legislation for a massive corporate tax cut, Trump succeeded in undercutting the law in significant fashion. In all, the back-and-forth over the ACA seemed quite similar to past political disputes and divisions.

Likewise, in economic policy, Trump again seemed to replicate many traditional Republican approaches. Initially, the new president signaled that he would depart from past practices and look to lift up those who had increasingly fallen behind in an era of ever-increasing economic inequality. "The forgotten men and women of our country will be forgotten no longer," Trump announced in his inaugural address. "I will fight for you with every breath in my body, and I will never let you down." Making good on a campaign promise, the new administration quickly acted to draw down American involvement in free-trade agreements, which Trump had repeatedly claimed hurt American workers. With the portion of the American labor force represented by unions half of what it had been in the early 1980s, the nation's workforce seemed receptive to anyone willing to champion their needs. Within days in office, he pulled the United States out of the Trans-Pacific Partnership (TPP) and discussed leaving NAFTA as well. More significantly, Trump embraced a new system of tariffs, arguing that the move was needed to defend American industries from unfair foreign competition. Economists noted that such actions might prompt retaliatory measures from economic competitors like China, and that an ensuing trade war would imperil US exports and thereby actually hurt American workers, but the president waved away their concerns. Such moves went against the grain of the GOP's economic orthodoxy, but the centerpiece of Trump's economic agenda—a massive tax cut, with the bulk of the relief going to corporations and individuals in the top bracket—remained firmly in the mainstream of Republican politics. After some false starts, the Republican Congress passed the tax cut in December 2017. Among other things, the new law lowered the top tax rate, slashed corporate tax rates from 35 to 21 percent, and set the estate tax to expire in six years. As many economists noted, the tax cut significantly benefited the wealthiest and would thus only widen the gap in income inequality. "As for Trump's forgotten people," one account of the tax plan concluded, "they are still left behind."[1]

But in more fundamental ways, the Trump administration, like the Trump campaign, represented a stark departure from the norms of American politics and government. The new president thrived on drawing out the tensions in American life, engaging in what Richard Nixon's aides had long ago championed as "the politics of positive polarization." From the moment of his inaugural address—with its invocation of a chaotic state of "American carnage"—the chief executive made it clear that he had no intention of dialing down the confrontational tone of the campaign or "acting presidential," as many observers assumed he would. President Trump remained a man who had made his name in the world of reality television and tabloid journalism, and he conducted his presidency accordingly. A consummate promoter, he understood that in a media climate with competing outlets, the lines between reality and fiction were constantly blurred, with an insatiable demand for content. Social media, in particular, loomed large for him. ("I doubt I would be here if it weren't for social media, to be honest with you," he told Fox Business Channel in a 2017 interview. It was a vital way to "get the word out.") Throughout his first year, the president continued to send out a barrage of messages via Twitter that continually captured the attention of social media and, through it, dictated the 24/7 cycles of cable news. With dramatic, controversial, and pointed messages, Trump routinely set the agenda for national debate and discussion, moving the conversation from one controversy to another in rapid, often exhausting succession. Through both intentional acts of provocation and unintentional missteps, his new administration and its allies in the media worked to aggravate the fault lines running through modern America, particularly in the divisive issues of gender, immigration, race, and guns.[2]

The lines of gender were the first to explode. On January 21, 2017, more than a half million Americans took part in the Women's March on Washington, a protest that dwarfed the inaugural crowds in the city the day before and, indeed, represented the single largest demonstration ever in DC. Similar marches took place in major cities and small towns across the country that same day, involving an estimated 4.2 million Americans, plus millions more worldwide. In a defiant tone, many marchers wore pink knitted hats with cat ears, styled as "pussyhats," in a callback to the president's infamous *Access Hollywood* comments. These Women's Marches signaled the emergence of a renewed movement of engaged women who resolved now to make their voices heard, not just in opposition to the administration but also in response to a wider range of incidents of sexual discrimination, harassment, and assault. The emotions and energy from the marches did not dissipate, but rather flowed into other arenas of American society. Notably, in October 2017, accusations of sexual misconduct by Hollywood producer Harvey Weinstein inspired many other women to break their silence about similar incidents they had endured, in what came to be known as the #MeToo movement, named after the viral Twitter hashtag that launched it. As credible accusations accrued, several prominent men in the realm of media and politics found themselves toppled from positions of power in rapid-fire succession over the ensuing months. On November 29, NBC announced that longtime cohost of the popular *Today* show, Matt Lauer, had been fired after accusations of sexual misconduct; the very next day, Minnesota Public Radio fired iconic humorist Garrison Keillor on similar grounds. In politics, the phenomenon transcended party lines. Pressured by his fellow Democrats, Minnesota Senator Al Franken announced his resignation from office on December 7, while Alabama Republican Roy Moore, the frontrunner for a special election to the Senate, lost in a stunning upset after nine women leveled accusations against him. Taking stock of the reckoning the #MeToo movement had wrought, *Time* named "The Silence Breakers" its 2017 Person of the Year.[3]

As the women's movement gained strength over the course of 2017, so too did new lines of resistance over the administration's immigration policies. On January 27, the president issued an executive order banning the entry of citizens from Libya, Iran, Iraq, Somalia, Sudan, Syria, and Yemen for ninety days. In response to what opponents termed a "Muslim ban," mass protests sprang up at airports across the country on January 28. Occurring only a week after the Women's Marches, these protests by tens of thousands signaled that resistance to the administration might be the new norm. The president's approach to the crisis likewise set a new pattern. After a federal court temporarily blocked the order, Trump took to Twitter to lash out at the "so-called judge" for making a ruling that was "ridiculous and will be overturned!" Defying earlier predictions that he would ease off social media once in office, Trump increasingly relied on it as a way to respond rapidly (and critics argued, rashly) to unfolding events and to rally his supporters to his side. However, his use of Twitter in the travel ban controversy showed that social media could be a double-edged sword. Several courts soon cited details from Trump's tweets to dispel the government's official rationales for a revised ban, striking it down again.[4]

Much as the "Muslim ban" proved divisive, so were the administration's actions against undocumented immigrants. A centerpiece of the Trump campaign had been the candidate's repeated pledge to build an "impenetrable, physical, tall, powerful, beautiful southern border wall" and, just as important, his promise that "I will make Mexico pay for that wall. Mark my words." Despite Trump's insistence, Mexico immediately made it clear it would *not* pay for the wall, prompting the president to search for domestic sources instead. Immigration groups, however, mobilized to make it difficult for the president to take action unilaterally. Members of Congress from regions that were not blood red on electoral maps worried about the consequences of moving away from the themes of diversity and pluralism that had marked the nation for decades. As a result, even though Trump's own party controlled both houses in Congress, he was unable to secure any funding for the border wall for much of 2017, ultimately securing only a fraction of the estimated total cost in a 2018 omnibus budget bill. Undaunted, he then proposed in a tweet that because "our Military is again rich," the nation should "Build WALL through M!" (Two advisors explained that "M" stood for "military.")[5]

As the border wall remained out of reach, the Trump White House turned its attention to undocumented immigrants already inside the nation's borders. Between January and September 2017, the US Immigration and Customs Enforcement (ICE) ramped up its activity in significant ways, arresting nearly 110,000 people suspected of illegal immigration, a 42 percent increase over the same span in the previous year. Despite the surge in arrests, the number of deportations actually decreased in comparison to the prior year. Nevertheless, the new wave of arrests made their mark, especially when suspects in highly publicized cases were picked up at their churches or at their children's schools. On top of the arrests, the Trump Justice Department announced in September 2017 that it would end the policy of Deferred Action for Childhood Arrivals (DACA), an Obama-era executive program that had allowed undocumented immigrants who had entered the United States as children to stay. The end of DACA suddenly placed some 800,000 recipients, known as "Dreamers," at risk of being deported in several months, unless Congress could work out a legislative solution. None seemed imminent.[6]

As the administration accelerated its campaigns against undocumented immigrants, white nationalists in the "alt right" became increasingly emboldened. During a weekend in August 2017, these groups gathered for a large "Unite the Right" rally in Charlottesville, Virginia. On Friday night, hundreds of young white men marched with torches through town to the campus rotunda, shouting Nazi slogans like "blood and soil!" and "Jews will not replace us!" Encountering a smaller group of black counterprotesters around a statue of Thomas Jefferson, the alt-right marchers taunted them with a cry of "white lives matter" before trading punches. The next day, the scene turned even uglier, as white nationalists gathered downtown with shields and clubs while small groups of militiamen, taking advantage of Virginia's open-carry law, arrived with long rifles. Though the police finally intervened and dispersed the crowd, violence nevertheless broke out when one alt-right protester intentionally drove a car into a procession of counterprotesters, wounding several and killing one. Rather than condemning white nationalists for the rally and their role in the violence, President Trump insisted that there were "some very fine people" in the ranks of the alt-right protesters and that "both sides" deserved blame for the deadly confrontations.[7] The rising nationalist forces inside the United States were part of an international phenomenon that took hold across the Western world, including Britain, Germany, and Italy. Much like America, these nations, and others, turned inward, with growing protests against immigration, international alliances, and transnational economic institutions.

Beyond Charlottesville, the nation as a whole continued to be consumed by violence, as the occurrences of mass shootings increased at an alarming rate. "Of the 30 deadliest shootings in the US dating back to 1949," CNN reported in November 2017, "18 have occurred in the last 10 years. Two of the five deadliest took place in just the last 35 days." On October 1, a gunman armed with more than two dozen weapons, including fourteen semiautomatic rifles, opened fire on a Las Vegas music festival, killing fifty-eight and wounding more than five hundred. Then, on November 5, another gunman armed with a semiautomatic rifle walked into a small church in Sutherland Springs, Texas, and murdered twenty-six worshippers there. The dull drumbeat of smaller mass shootings continued—six dead at an elementary school in California, five killed at a carwash in Pennsylvania—before another large-scale event sparked a new response. On Valentine's Day 2018, a former student returned to his high school in Parkland, Florida, with a semiautomatic rifle, killing seventeen students and teachers and wounding another seventeen. While prior mass shootings led to little lasting public reaction, this one soon seemed different. Within days, student survivors launched a new activist movement, the Never Again campaign, with calls for stricter background checks for gun buyers and a plan for a nationwide protest. Part of a generation raised on social media and skilled at engaging publicly, several of the students took their campaign directly to cable news programs, personalizing the gun control movement and propelling it forward with previously unseen focus and force. On March 24, 2018, the March for Our Lives movement they launched unfolded with sizable rallies across the country, involving more than two million Americans at roughly eight hundred marches nationwide. Though Congress proved unresponsive to the calls for gun reform once again, the state of Florida passed legislation that imposed gun control laws there, prompting a court challenge by the NRA.[8]

While the new administration found itself assailed by critics on all these fronts, the most serious—and most divisive—threat to the Trump White House came in the form of a deepening investigation into the presidential campaign. Confronted by both congressional and FBI investigations into whether Russia had intervened in the election, the president abruptly fired FBI director James Comey in May 2017. The White House initially claimed Comey had been fired for his poor handling of the Clinton email investigation, but soon President Trump admitted in an interview that the Russia investigation lay at the heart of it all. "When I decided to just do it," he told NBC's Lester Holt, "I said to myself, I said 'you know, this Russia thing with Trump and Russia is a made-up story, it's an excuse by the Democrats for having lost an election that they should have won.'" As a result, the Department of Justice felt obligated to respond. Attorney General Jeff Sessions had already recused himself from the matter, due to his own dissembling over contacts with Russia during the election, so Deputy Attorney General Rod Rosenstein led the way, appointing a special prosecutor, former FBI director Robert Mueller, to conduct his own investigation. Working with a team of experienced federal investigators, Mueller quickly levied indictments against Russian nationals and even secured guilty pleas from several prominent members of the Trump inner circle, including former National Security Advisor Michael Flynn and campaign manager Paul Manafort. As the investigation intensified, Trump undertook a blistering campaign to undercut its legitimacy. He accused several FBI officials, including some lifelong Republicans, of trying to bring him down because they had secretly supported Hillary Clinton. After criticizing FBI deputy director Andrew McCabe on Twitter, Trump had him fired too, just days before his planned retirement. In reaction, an angry McCabe told reporters: "This is a part of an effort to discredit me as a witness" in the investigation into the Comey firing. Meanwhile, Trump assailed investigative journalists for producing what he called "fake news" and accused the government's own intelligence agencies of spreading inaccurate information as well.[9]

As Trump dug in, large numbers of Republicans rallied around him. The congressional investigation by the House Intelligence Committee, led by Representative Devin Nunes, a staunch Trump ally who had served on the administration's transition team, seemed little interested in probing the darker corners of the Russia scandal. When, in March 2018, Nunes proposed closing the House inquiry, without even interviewing any of the individuals already indicted by Mueller, it was clear the inquiry was little more than an effort at partisan public relations. "I want [the House investigation] to end, because we have gone off the rails of being able to objectively do our job," Representative Tom Rooney (R-Florida) told the press, adding that he had "finally come to the realization that we are not going to put together any kind of a bipartisan product." Within weeks, the House Intelligence Committee showed how polarized Congress had become. Casting aside the unanimous conclusions of the intelligence community that Russia had, in fact, intervened in the election with the intent of aiding the Trump campaign, the GOP majority shut down the investigation, asserting that it had found "no evidence of collusion, coordination or conspiracy between the Trump campaign and the Russians."[10]

Trump's presidency came to highlight the hyperpartisanship of the era. Despite historically low *national* approval polls that ranged from the low 30s to low 40s across his first year and a half in office, his support among Republicans remained strong in the 80s. Even more so than Richard Nixon in 1974, Trump could count on continued Republican support—as well as conservative media—to insulate him from the outrage that helped bring his predecessor down after scandals such as the Saturday Night Massacre. The polarization of the past four decades had divided the country but, in an odd paradox, that polarization provided for a stable floor even with the most unconventional, unorthodox, and divisive president the nation had ever seen. For many Republicans, the simple fact that Trump enraged Democrats proved to be enough reason to rally around him. This partisanship, of course, was intensified by a conservative media establishment that increasingly went beyond echoing the Republican Party line to actively shaping it. Reporters soon realized that Trump's morning flurry of statements on Twitter tracked closely with the commentary of the *Fox & Friends* morning show, and likewise, the "Trump TV Presidency" seemed to take cues from *Fox News*'s evening hosts. The president dined often with Sean Hannity, and had Lou Dobbs participate in Oval Office meetings over a speakerphone. Others from conservative cable news programs were formally made part of the administration, with CNBC host Larry Kudlow made head of the National Economic Council and Heather Nauert, a former *Fox & Friends* host, appointed as an undersecretary of state. The Sinclair Broadcast Group—a conservative network of local channels whose already broad reach expanded considerably with favorable decisions by the Trump administration's FCC—then amplified the arguments coming out of the administration and its allies in cable news. Sinclair-owned stations, which soon reached nearly three-fourths of all American households, broadcast politically charged editorials by former Trump aide Boris Epshteyn and required local anchors to read Sinclair-prepared scripts that echoed Trump's complaints that the news media often spread "fake stories." Meanwhile, Trump's allies on the internet and social media were willing to go even further, peddling arguments that veered beyond conservative activism into the realm of conspiracy theories. In short order, the line between fact and fiction became so thin that it was hard to see the difference.[11]

The first year of the Trump presidency revealed the enormous wear and tear that forty years of bitter division has inflicted on the republic. Yet a divided nation did not mean a broken nation. As the leadership in Washington became ever more gridlocked, ordinary citizens—from all sides—took to the streets to take a stand for their rights and to remind the nation of its responsibilities. The Trump and Sanders campaigns had brought large numbers of previously apathetic Americans into the political process for the first time in decades, and the Trump administration inspired new waves of engagement from a variety of other marginalized groups. This was, as the students from Parkland repeatedly insisted, what democracy looked like. At the moment of this writing, the end result of the new wave of political mobilization is still unseen. Perhaps these processes, now largely a mechanism of protest, will turn into avenues toward democratic compromise and the resolution of the many questions that have pushed Americans apart since the time that Richard Nixon stepped down from office. The tumult over Watergate and Vietnam destroyed many institutions and policies that helped bring us closer together in the post–World War II era, but as this book has shown, new structures and systems took their place. The same process, of course, can happen again.

The question that the United States of America now faces as a divided country is whether we can harness the intense energy that now drives us apart and channel it once again toward creating new and stronger bridges that can bring us closer together. Whether the fault lines of the past four decades will continue to fracture, or whether these rifts will finally start to heal, is a chapter yet to come.

ACKNOWLEDGMENTS

WE WOULD LIKE TO THANK A NUMBER OF PEOPLE WHO
have provided invaluable support to this project.

The book began in 2012, when the two of us launched a course at
Princeton University focusing on American history since 1974. Over
the years, we kept refining the lectures until we realized that we had
a book on our hands. Several graduate students who served as teaching
assistants in the course, and the undergraduates who took the class,
helped us to sharpen our understanding of the period and to refine our
arguments considerably.

The process of turning those lectures into book chapters was much
more challenging than we expected, especially as the period "since
1974" kept becoming more and more complicated, but this has been an
incredibly rewarding experience. Our editor at Norton, Jon Durbin, has
been a source of enthusiasm and support from the very beginning, urging us to produce a book that would excite general readers and educate
university students. We hope that we have lived up to his hopes.

Along the way, we have benefited considerably from the insight
and expertise of our colleagues, both at Princeton and throughout
the historical profession. In particular, we owe a tremendous debt
to James Anderson, Kathryn Brownell, Nathan Connolly, Joe Crespino, Linda Gordon, Norman Markowitz, Margaret O'Mara, Kim
Phillips-Fein, and Eric Rauchway for providing thorough readings of
the manuscript at various stages of the process and giving us incredibly constructive criticism.

David Walsh, a doctoral student at Princeton, provided us invaluable service helping us to fact-check the manuscript and to obtain permission for the images and photographs. Although it was an arduous process, he was persistent and made sure that we obtained everything that we needed. Lily Gellman at Norton offered us insightful feedback while prepping the manuscript. Gary Von Euer, our copy editor, polished the final draft into something more presentable, and then Jake Blumgart provided one final round of fact checking before the book went into production.

While we are extremely grateful to all of these individuals, we dedicate the book to our families. In particular, Kevin thanks his wife, Lindsay, and their kids, Maggie and Sam. Julian thanks his wife, Meg, and their kids, Abigail, Sophia, Nathan, and Claire. As we devoted our energies to bringing alive the recent past, they kept us grounded in the present and hopeful about the future.

NOTES

Introduction

1. Thomas J. Sugrue, *Not Even Past: Barack Obama and the Burden of Race* (Princeton, NJ: Princeton University Press, 2010), 12.
2. Carla Herreria, "President Barack Obama Bids America a Heartfelt Farewell," *Huffington Post*, 11 January 2017; Marina Fang, "Obama's Farewell Address to Lay a Path Forward Under Trump," *Huffington Post*, 2 January 2017; "Obama's Farewell Address Tonight: A Look Back on His Impact," *MSNBC.com*, 10 January 2017; Paige Lavender, "The Obamas Got Emotional During the President's Farewell Address," *Huffington Post*, 10 January 2017; Alana Horowitz Satlin, "No One Is Sadder About Barack Obama Leaving Office Than These Pets," *Huffington Post*, 11 January 2017.
3. Sean Hannity, "Obama Farewell Can't Hide a Disastrous Legacy," *FoxNews.com*, 11 January 2017; "Hannity" Transcript, "Laura Ingraham Rips Obama's Farewell Address; Austan Goolsbee Defends President's Accomplishments," *FoxNews.com*, 10 January 2017; Charlie Spiering, "Obama's Farewell Campaign Speech: 'Post Racial' America Was Never 'Realistic,'" *Breitbart.com*, 10 January 2017.
4. Historian Dan Rodgers called this era the "Age of Fracture." His book, which has been extraordinarily valuable to our understanding of the intellectual currents in this era, stresses fragmentation and fracture while we trace more coherent lines of division. See Daniel T. Rodgers, *Age of Fracture* (Cambridge, MA: The Belknap Press of Harvard University Press, 2012).

Chapter 1: A Crisis of Legitimacy

1. "Most Think Nixon Did Right Thing," *Chicago Tribune*, 11 August 1974; "Ford Calls Resignation 'Courageous,'" *Los Angeles Times*, 11 August 1974; Anthony Lewis, "The Resignation Proves Impeachment Works," *New York Times*, 11 August 1974; "Tragedy and Triumph," *New York Times*, 11 August 1974; Joseph Kraft, "The Larger Meaning of Mr. Nixon's Presidency," *Washington Post*, 11 August 1974.
2. "Text of Ford's Pardon Statement," *Atlanta Constitution*, 9 September 1974.
3. Laura Kalman, *Right Star Rising: A New Politics, 1974–1980* (New York: Norton, 2010), 14; David Gergen, *Eyewitness to Power: The Essence of Leadership: Nixon to Clinton* (New York: Simon & Schuster, 2000): 118.
4. Douglas Brinkley, *Gerald R. Ford* (New York: Times Books, 2007), 69.
5. "Talk of the Town," *The New Yorker*, 23 September 1974, 27.

6. Dominic Sandbrook, *Mad as Hell: The Crisis of the 1970s and the Rise of the Populist Right* (New York: Anchor, 2011), 21.

7. Craig Unger, *American Armageddon: How the Delusions of the Neoconservatives and the Christian Right Triggered the Descent of America—And Still Imperil Our Future* (New York: Simon & Schuster, 2007), 100.

8. Gerald Ford, "Statement on the Federal Campaign Act Amendments of 1974," 15 October 1974, The American Presidency Project.

9. Julian E. Zelizer, *On Capitol Hill: The Struggle to Reform Congress and Its Consequences, 1945–2000* (New York: Cambridge University Press, 2004), 163; John A. Lawrence, *The Class of '74: Congress after Watergate and the Roots of Partisanship* (Baltimore: Johns Hopkins University Press, 2018).

10. Marilyn B. Young, *The Vietnam Wars, 1945–1990* (New York: HarperCollins, 1991).

11. John Darnton, "Reporter's Notebook on City Fiscal Crisis," *New York Times*, 10 November 1975.

12. Cited in Jeff Nussbaum, "The Night New York Saved Itself From Bankruptcy," *The New Yorker*, 16 October 2015.

13. "Ford to City: Drop Dead," *New York Daily News*, 30 October 1975; Kim Phillips-Fein, *Fear City: New York's Fiscal Crisis and the Rise of Austerity Politics* (New York: Metropolitan Books, 2017), 177–89.

14. Jonathan Mahler, *Ladies and Gentlemen, the Bronx Is Burning: 1977, Baseball, Politics and the Battle for the Soul of a City* (New York: Farrar, Straus and Giroux, 2006), 228.

15. http://pix11.com/2013/07/12/remembering-the-1977-new-york-blackout-on-anniversary/.

16. Cited in Bruce Schulman, *The Seventies: The Great Shift in American Culture, Society, and Politics* (New York: Free Press, 2001), 107.

17. Joseph S. Nye Jr., Philip D. Zelikow, and David C. King, *Why People Don't Trust Government* (Cambridge, MA: Harvard University Press, 1997), 81.

18. Adam Cohen, "After 30 Years, the Mood of 'Nashville' Feels Right Again," *New York Times*, 6 June 2005.

19. "The Half-Dead Monster," *Wall Street Journal*, 2 February 1976.

20. Lee Drutman, *The Business of America Is Lobbying: How Corporations Became Politicized and Politics Became More Corporate* (New York: Oxford University Press, 2015), 58; William C. Berman, *America's Right Turn: From Nixon to Clinton*, 2nd ed. (Baltimore: Johns Hopkins University Press, 1998), 70; Jacob S. Hacker and Paul Pierson, *Winner-Take-All Politics: How Washington Made the Rich Richer—and Turned Its Back on the Middle Class* (New York: Simon & Schuster, 2010).

21. Mark Green, "Financing Campaigns," *New York Times*, 14 December 1980.

22. Bruce McCabe, "The World of R. C. Woodstein," *Boston Globe*, 4 October 1974.

23. Diane White, "The Hard Line in Soft News," *Boston Globe*, 14 November 1974; "Covering Watergate: Success and Backlash," *Time*, 8 July 1974; Wayne Warga, "Answering a Call to the Post," *Los Angeles Times*, 15 August 1975.

24. William Safire, "The Vietgate Solution," *New York Times*, 12 September 1974; Gilbert A. Lewthwaite, "'Winegate' Trial Ends With Jail, $4 Million in Fines," *Baltimore Sun*, 19 December 1974; Jonathan Steele, "Korean Gifts Scandal Hits US Congress," *Guardian*, 30 November 1976; Michael Schudson, *Watergate in American Memory: How We Remember, Forget and Reconstruct the Past* (New York: Basic Books, 1993).

25. Charles B. Seib, "Pack Reporting Unhealthy," *Austin American Statesman*, 19 February 1977; Timothy Leland, "Controversy in Investigative Journalism," *Boston Globe*, 27 June 1977.

26. Tom Wolfe, "Birth of the 'New Journalism': An Eyewitness Report," *New York*, 14

February 1972; Colman McCarthy, "Did Bad News Kill the Messenger?" *Newsday*, 29 December 1978.

27. Jann S. Wenner, "Worry About the Quality of News Reporting," *New York Times*, 19 December 1976.

28. Jill Lepore, "Bad News," *The New Yorker*, 20 June 2014.

29. Lee Marguiles, "Networks: And Then There Were Four?" *Los Angeles Times*, 31 January 1977; Les Brown, "Is a Fourth Network About to Hatch?" *New York Times*, 8 May 1977.

30. Jerry Parker, "Medium's Message of 'Network,'" *Los Angeles Times*, 19 November 1976; *Network* (1976).

31. Tom Shales, "'Network': Hating TV Can Be Fun," *Washington Post*, 24 October 1976.

32. Parker, "Medium's Message of 'Network'"; Joan Barthel, "Paddy Chayefsky: 'TV Will Do Anything for a Rating. Anything!'" *New York Times*, 14 November 1976.

Chapter 2: A Crisis of Confidence

1. James T. Patterson, *Grand Expectations: The United States 1945–1974* (New York: Oxford University Press, 1996), 451.

2. Meg Jacobs, *Panic at the Pump: The Energy Crisis and the Transformation of American Politics in the 1970s* (New York: Hill and Wang, 2016).

3. David A. Andelman, "Gasoline Supply Drops Across U.S.," *New York Times*, 9 December 1973.

4. Robert Buckhorn, "Gasoline Lifeblood for Car-Happy Americans," *The Middlesboro Daily News*, 11 March 1974.

5. Rachel Carson, *Silent Spring*, 40th anniversary ed. (Boston: Mariner, 2002), 5.

6. Samuel P. Hays, *Beauty, Health and Permanence: Environmental Politics in the United States, 1955–1985* (New York: Cambridge University Press, 1987).

7. "Spreading Oil Fouls Beach, Harbor at Santa Barbara," *Baltimore Sun*, 6 February 1969; Jennifer Latson, "The Burning River That Sparked a Revolution," *Time*, 1 August 1969; Kevin Starr, *Coast of Dreams: California on the Edge, 1990–2003* (New York: Vintage, 2004); Bruce J. Schulman, *The Seventies: The Great Shift in American Culture, Society and Politics* (New York: Simon & Schuster, 2001), 30.

8. Dwight Tewes, "Against the 55 Limit," *Chicago Tribune*, 13 October 1975; Al Martinez, "55 M.P.H. Limit Drivers Race to Obey Law," *Los Angeles Times*, 2 January 1974.

9. Schulman, *The Seventies*, 126.

10. James T. Patterson, *Restless Giant: The United States from Watergate to Bush v. Gore* (New York: Oxford University Press, 2005), 7.

11. Tony A. Freyer, "Managerial Capitalism Contested," in *The Columbia Reader of Post–World War II History*, ed. Marc Carnes (New York: Columbia University Press, 2007), 441.

12. Yanek Mieczkowksi, *Gerald Ford and the Challenges of the 1970s* (Lexington: University Press of Kentucky, 2005), 212.

13. Torry D. Dickinson and Robert K. Schaffer, *Fast Forward: Work, Gender, and Protest in a Changing World* (Oxford, UK: Rowan and Littlefield, 2001), 56.

14. Laura Kalman, *Right Star Rising: A New Politics, 1974–1980* (New York: Norton, 2010), 57.

15. William B. Hamilton, "Hard Times Not New to New Bedford," *Boston Globe*, 2 March 1975.

16. Lee Smith, "Hard Times Come to Steeltown," *Fortune*, December 1977, 86–93.

17. Peter Biskind, *Easy Riders, Raging Bulls: How the Sex-Drugs-Rock N' Roll Generation Saved Hollywood* (New York: Simon & Schuster, 1999), 251.

18. Freyer, "Managerial Capitalism Contested," 441.

19. "U.S. Economic Gloom Is Mirrored Abroad," *Baltimore Sun,* 5 January 1975.

20. Bethany Moreton, "Make Payroll, Not War: Business Culture and Youth Culture," in *Rightward Bound: Making America Conservative in the 1970s*, ed. Bruce J. Schulman and Julian E. Zelizer (Cambridge, MA: Harvard University Press, 2008), 62.

21. William Lazonick, "Creating and Extracting Value: Corporate Investment Behavior and American Economic Performance," in *Understanding American Economic Decline*, ed. Michael A. Bernstein and David E. Adler (New York: Cambridge University Press, 1994), 102.

22. Mieczkowski, *Gerald Ford and the Challenges of the 1970s*, 138.

23. Richard Reeves, "Ladies and Gentleman, The President of the United States," *New York Magazine*, 25 November 1974.

24. Philip Jenkins, *Decade of Nightmares: The End of the Sixties and the Making of Eighties America* (New York: Oxford University Press, 2006), 47.

25. Derek Thompson, "80 Percent of Americans Don't Trust Government, Here's Why," *The Atlantic,* 19 April 2010; Gary Orren, "Fall From Grace: The Public's Loss of Faith in Government," in *Why People Don't Trust Government,* ed. Nye, Zelikow, and King, 80.

26. Sophie Gilbert, "The Year Political Advertising Turned Positive," *The Atlantic,* 9 June 2015.

27. Douglas Brinkley, *Gerald R. Ford* (New York: Henry Holt, 2007), 136.

28. Kalman, *Right Star Rising*, 57.

29. Christopher Lydon, "Carter Issues Apology on 'Ethnic Purity' Phrase," *New York Times,* 9 April 1976.

30. Thomas Patterson, *Out of Order* (New York: Knopf, 1993).

31. Julian E. Zelizer, *Jimmy Carter* (New York: Times Books, 2010), 1.

32. Bernstein, "Understanding American Economic Decline," in *Understanding American Economic Decline,* 21.

33. Greg Adamson, *We All Live on Three Mile Island: The Case Against Nuclear Power* (Sydney, Australia: Pathfinder, 1981), 49.

34. "Memorial Day Gas Shortage," 28 May 1979, WTVK; "Gas Prices in 1979," March 1979 (n.d), WEWS News; Jacobs, *Panic at the Pump,* 196–232.

35. MacNeil-Lehrer Report, https://www.youtube.com/watch?v=G7SnaMphvug).

36. Daniel Yergin, *The Prize: The Epic Quest for Oil, Money and Power,* rev. ed. (New York: Free Press, 2008), 672.

37. "N.Y. Man Charged in Gas Line Slaying," *Chicago Tribune,* 2 June 1979.

38. Kevin Mattson, *What the Heck Are You Up To Mr. President? Jimmy Carter, 'America's Malaise,' and the Speech That Should Have Changed the Country* (New York: Bloomsbury, 2010), 112–13.

39. Yergin, *The Prize,* 674.

40. Jacobs, *Panic at the Pump,* 239.

41. Editorial, "The Hustle Expands," *Wall Street Journal,* 6 August 1979.

42. William J. Eaton, "Analysts Said 20 Years of Mistakes Led to Plight," *Los Angeles Times,* 10 August 1979.

43. Warren Brown, "A Plant and Its City Fall Victim to Chrysler's Decline," *Washington Post,* 14 November 1979.

44. Charles B. Camp, "No. 3 Auto Firm's Plea for Federal Aid Shakes Industry, Washington," *Wall Street Journal,* 3 August 1979.

45. Steven Rattner, "Debate On in Capital," *New York Times,* 2 August 1979.

46. "Many Top Executives Oppose Chrysler's Plea for Federal Assistance," *Wall Street Journal,* 17 September 1979.

47. "GM Chairman Spurs Debate as He Faults Chrysler Bailout Bid," *Wall Street Journal,* 6 August 1979.

48. William H. Jones, "Chrysler Aid Plan Is Not Unique," *Washington Post,* 2 August 1979.

49. U.S. Congress, Senate Committee on Banking, Housing and Urban Affairs, *Hearings on the Chrysler Corporation Loan Guarantee Act of 1979,* 96th Congress, 1st session, 1979.

50. "Chrysler's Crisis Bailout," *Time,* 20 August 1979.

51. "Chrysler Quits Roundtable Over Bailout Position," *Washington Post,* 27 November 1979.

52. Jefferson Cowie, *Stayin' Alive: The 1970s and the Last Days of the Working Class* (New York: New Press, 2010), 18.

Chapter 3: A CRISIS OF IDENTITY

1. President Lyndon B. Johnson, Remarks at the Signing of the Immigration Bill, Liberty Island, New York, 3 October 1965.

2. William F. Chafe, *Civilities and Civil Rights: Greensboro, North Carolina, and the Black Struggle for Freedom* (New York: Oxford University Press, 1981), 109–20; Glenn T. Eskew, *But for Birmingham: The Local and National Movements in the Civil Rights Struggle* (Chapel Hill: University of North Carolina Press, 1997), 1–7; David J. Garrow, *Protest at Selma: Martin Luther King, Jr., and the Voting Rights Act of 1965* (New Haven, CT: Yale University Press, 2015), 78.

3. David Levering Lewis, *King: A Biography* (Champaign: University of Illinois Press, 2012), 85; Clay Risen, *The Bill of the Century: The Epic Battle for the Civil Rights Act* (New York: Bloomsbury, 2014); Ari Berman, *Give Us the Ballot: The Modern Struggle for Voting Rights in America* (New York: Farrar, Straus and Giroux, 2015); Julian E. Zelizer, *The Fierce Urgency of Now: Lyndon Johnson, Congress and the Battle for the Great Society* (New York: Penguin, 2015).

4. Elizabeth Hinton, *From the War on Poverty to the War on Crime: The Making of Mass Incarceration in America* (Cambridge, MA: Harvard University Press, 2016).

5. *The Kerner Report: The National Advisory Commission on Civil Disorders* (Princeton, NJ: Princeton University Press, 2016).

6. Peniel E. Joseph, *Waiting 'Til the Midnight Hour: A Narrative History of Black Power in America* (New York: Henry Holt, 2006), 130–31, 178–81, 243–44.

7. Kevin M. Kruse, "Lost Causes Not Yet Found," *The Nation* (24 April 2008); Clay Risen, *A Nation on Fire: America in the Wake of the King Assassination* (Hoboken, NJ: John Wiley & Sons, 2009).

8. Joseph, *Waiting 'Til the Midnight Hour,* 276–78; Thomas J. Sugrue, *Sweet Land of Liberty: The Forgotten Struggle for Civil Rights in the North* (New York: Random House, 2008), 495; Leah Wright Rigueur, *The Loneliness of the Black Republican: Pragmatic Politics and the Pursuit of Power* (Princeton, NJ: Princeton University

Press, 2015); "Financial Crisis Perils Activities of N.A.A.C.P.," *New York Times*, 21 December 1978.

9. Donald H. McGannon and Vernon E. Jordan, "Introduction," in *When the Marching Stopped: An Analysis of Black Issues in the '70s* (New York: National Urban League, 1973), iii–iv, cited in Sugrue, *Sweet Land of Liberty*, 494–95.

10. Bayard Rustin, "From Protest to Politics: The Future of the Civil Rights Movement," *Commentary* 39, no. 2 (February 1965): 25–31; Charles H. Loeb, "Congressional Black Caucus," *Cleveland Call and Post*, 13 February 1971.

11. Joseph, *Waiting 'Til the Midnight Hour*, 277–80; Sugrue, *Sweet Land of Liberty*, 498–99.

12. Sugrue, *Sweet Land of Liberty*, 500–501.

13. Kevin M. Kruse, *White Flight: Atlanta and the Making of Modern Conservatism* (Princeton, NJ: Princeton University Press, 2005), 105–30; Douglas Massey and Nancy Denton, *American Apartheid: Segregation and the Making of the Underclass* (Cambridge, MA: Harvard University Press, 1993).

14. Kruse, *White Flight*; Jan Blakeslee, "'White Flight' to the Suburbs: A Demographic Approach," *Focus: Institute for Research on Poverty Newsletter* 3 (Winter 1978–1979): 1.

15. William L. Van Deburg, *New Day in Babylon: The Black Power Movement and American Culture, 1965–1975* (Chicago: University of Chicago Press, 1992), 6.

16. Van Deburg, *New Day in Babylon*, 192–247; "Television History Made By 'Roots,'" *Norfolk Journal and Guide*, 5 February 1977; "Nationally, An Amazing Reaction to 'Roots,'" *Baltimore Sun*, 29 January 1977.

17. Bruce J. Schulman, *The Seventies: The Great Shift in American Culture, Society, and Politics* (New York: Free Press, 2001), 65; Klaus P. Fischer, *America in White, Black and Gray: A History of the Stormy 1960s* (New York: Continuum, 2006), 350–51; James S. Olsen, *Equality Deferred: Race, Ethnicity, and Immigration in America Since 1945* (Belmont, CA: Wadsworth, 2003), 65.

18. Armando B. Rendón, *Chicano Manifesto: The History and Aspirations of the Second Largest Minority in America* (New York: Macmillan, 1971), 354; Rodolfo Acuña, *Occupied America: The Chicano's Struggle Toward Liberation* (San Francisco: Canfield Press, 1972), 222.

19. Ignacio M. García, *United We Win: The Rise and Fall of La Raza Unida Party* (Tucson: University of Arizona Press, 1989); "Congressional Caucus Is Formed to Speak for Hispanic Population," *New York Times*, 9 December 1976; Raul Yzaguirre, "MexAmerica," *Washington Post*, 5 April 1978; "Hispanic Wins Mayor's Race in San Antonio," *Washington Post*, 5 April 1981; "Denver Elects Hispanic," *Boston Globe*, 22 June 1983.

20. Madeline Y. Hsu, *The Good Immigrants: How the Yellow Peril Became the Model Minority* (Princeton, NJ: Princeton University Press, 2015); Mark Brilliant, *The Color of America Has Changed: How Racial Diversity Shaped Civil Rights Reform in California, 1941–1978* (New York: Oxford University Press, 2010); Ellen D. Wu, *The Color of Success: Asian Americans and the Origins of the Model Minority* (Princeton, NJ; Princeton University Press, 2014), 242–47.

21. Noel Ignatiev, *How the Irish Became White* (New York: Routledge, 1995); Matthew Frye Jacobson, *Whiteness of a Different Color: European Immigrants and the Alchemy of Race* (Cambridge, MA: Harvard University Press, 1998); Matthew Frye Jacobson, *Roots Too: White Ethnic Revival in Post–Civil Rights America* (Cambridge, MA: Harvard University Press, 2006); Michael Novák, *The Rise of the Unmeltable Ethnics: Politics and Culture in the Seventies* (New York: Macmillan, 1972), 270; Thomas J. Sugrue and John D. Skrenty, "The White Ethnic Strategy" in *Rightward Bound*, 171–92.

22. John Higham, *Strangers in the Land: Patterns of American Nativism, 1860–1925* (Rutgers, NJ: Rutgers University Press, 1955), 264.

23. Mae M. Ngai, *Impossible Subjects: Illegal Aliens and the Making of Modern America* (Princeton, NJ: Princeton University Press, 2003), 21–56.

24. Reed Ueda, *Postwar Immigrant America: A Social History* (Boston: Bedford's/St. Martin's Press, 1994), 58, 64–73.

25. Ueda, *Postwar Immigrant America*, 62, 78–80; Uzma Quaraishi, "Multiple Mobilities: Race, Capital and South Asian Migrations to and through Houston, Texas" (Ph.D. diss., Rice University, 2013).

26. Paula Ioanide, *The Emotional Politics of Racism: How Feelings Trump Facts in an Era of Colorblindness* (Palo Alto: Stanford University Press, 2007), 133.

27. Douglas Massey and Karen A. Pren, "Unintended Consequences of US Immigration Policy: Explaining the Post-1965 Surge from Latin America," *Population and Development Review* 38, no. 1 (2012): 1–29.

28. Matthew D. Lassiter, *The Silent Majority: Suburban Politics in the Sunbelt South* (Princeton, NJ: Princeton University Press, 2006), 170–73; James T. Patterson, *Grand Expectations: The United States 1945–1974* (New York: Oxford University Press, 1996), 451; James T. Patterson, *Restless Giant: The United States from Watergate to Bush v. Gore* (New York: Oxford University Press, 2005), 296–97.

29. Joyce A. Baugh, *The Detroit School Busing Case: Milliken v. Bradley and the Controversy over Desegregation* (Lawrence: University Press of Kansas, 2011).

30. Baugh, *The Detroit School Busing Case*.

31. Kruse, *White Flight*, 255.

32. 418 U.S. 717 (1974); Matthew D. Lassiter, "De Jure/De Facto Segregation: The Long Shadow of a National Myth," in *The Myth of Southern Exceptionalism*, ed. Matthew D. Lassiter and Joseph Crespino (New York: Oxford University Press, 2009), 25–48.

33. "Police Clash with 1,000 in Boston," *Baltimore Sun*, 12 December 1974.

34. Jason Sokol, *All Eyes Are Upon Us: Race and Politics from Boston to Brooklyn* (New York: Basic Books, 2014), 206–7; Louis P. Masur, *The Soiling of Old Glory: The Story of a Photograph That Shocked a Nation* (New York: Bloomsbury, 2008); Lara Kalman, *Right Star Rising: A New Politics, 1974–1980* (New York: Norton, 2010), 137.

35. Martin Luther King Jr., *Where Do We Go From Here? Chaos or Community* (New York: Harper & Row, 1967).

36. J. Harvie Wilkinson, *From Brown to Bakke: The Supreme Court and School Integration: 1954–1978* (New York: Oxford University Press, 1981), 253–57; Schulman, *The Seventies*, 70.

37. 438 U.S. 265 (1978); Schulman, *The Seventies*, 70.

38. Sugrue, *Sweet Land of Liberty*, 507–8; John D. Skrentny, "Introduction," in John D. Skrentny, ed., *Color Lines: Affirmative Action, Integration and Civil Rights Options for America* (Chicago: University of Chicago Press, 2001), 11.

39. Schulman, *The Seventies*, 70–71.

40. Schulman, *The Seventies*, 71.

Chapter 4: A CRISIS OF EQUALITY

1. Elaine Tyler May, *Homeward Bound: American Families in the Cold War Era* (New York: Basic Books, 1988).

2. Beth Bailey, "She 'Can Bring Home the Bacon': Negotiating Gender in Seventies America," in Beth Bailey and David Farber, eds., *America in the Seventies* (New Brunswick, NJ: Rutgers University Press, 2004), 108–9.

3. James T. Patterson, *Restless Giant: The United States from Watergate to Bush v. Gore* (New York: Oxford University Press, 2005), 54–55; Peter N. Caroll, *It Seemed Like Nothing Happened: America in the 1970s* (New Brunswick, NJ: Rutgers University Press, 1990); "The American Woman: On the Move, but Where?" *U.S. News and World Report*, 8 December 1975, 57.

4. Louis Menand, "The Sex Amendment: How Women Got In on the Civil Rights Act," *The New Yorker*, 21 July 2014.

5. Ruth Rosen, *The World Split Open: How the Modern Women's Movement Changed America* (New York: Penguin, 2000), 72–73; *Wall Street Journal*, 22 June 1965.

6. Rosen, *World Split Open*, 80–81; Nancy MacLean, *Freedom is Not Enough: The Opening of the American Workplace* (Cambridge, MA: Harvard University Press, 2006), 129.

7. Marjorie J. Spruill, "Gender and America's Right Turn," in *Rightward Bound: Making America Conservative in the 1970s*, ed. Bruce J. Schulman and Julian E. Zelizer (Cambridge, MA: Harvard University Press, 2008), 77; Bruce J. Schulman, *The Seventies: The Great Shift in American Culture, Society and Politics* (New York: Da Capo Press, 2001), 169.

8. Spruill, "Gender and America's Right Turn," 78; Rosen, *World Split Open*, 332; Schulman, *The Seventies*, 170; Robert O. Self, *All in the Family: The Realignment of American Democracy since the 1960s* (New York: Hill and Wang, 2012), 293.

9. Self, *All in the Family*, 292–94; Rosen, *World Split Open*, 332.

10. Bailey, "She 'Can Bring Home the Bacon,'" 114–15; Vivian Cadden, "Women's Lib? I've Seen It on TV," *Redbook* (February 1972): 93.

11. Daniel K. Williams, *God's Own Party: The Making of the Christian Right* (New York: Oxford University Press, 2010), 110; Donald T. Critchtlow, *Phyllis Schlafly and Grassroots Conservatism: A Woman's Crusade* (Princeton, NJ: Princeton University Press, 2005), 221–22; Ruth Murray Brown, *For a "Christian America": A History of the Religious Right* (New York: Prometheus Books, 2002), 69–78.

12. Schulman, *The Seventies*, 169; Carroll, *It Seemed*, 271.

13. *Congressional Record* (Feb. 28, 1972), 5804.

14. Jaeah Lee and Maya Dusenbery, "Charts: The State of Women's Athletics, 40 Years After Title IX," *Mother Jones*, 22 June 2012.

15. "The American Woman: On the Move, but Where?," 57; David Frum, *How We Got Here: The '70s: The Decade That Brought You Modern Life (for Better or for Worse)* (New York: Basic Books, 2000), 250; *Harvard Crimson*, 4 October 1974; Schulman, *The Seventies*, 161; Nancy Weiss Malkiel, *"Keep The Damned Women Out": The Struggle for Coeducation* (Princeton, NJ: Princeton University Press, 2017).

16. "Mrs. King Sportswoman of the Year," *New York Times*, 21 December 1972; Parton Reese, "Tennis Decides All Women Are Equal, Too," *New York Times*, 20 July 1973.

17. George R. Goethals, Georgia Jones, and James MacGregor Burns, eds., *Enyclopedia of Leadership*, Vol. 1 (Thousand Oaks, CA: Sage, 2004), 796.

18. Schulman, *Seventies*, 159–61.

19. Charles Maher, "Women Move in on Sports Mike," *Los Angeles Times*, 20 January 1975; Doug Mead, "Twelve Women Who Pioneered the Era of Female Sports Broadcasters," *Bleacher Report*, 21 August 2000; "Being Miss America Doesn't Help Sports Reporting, Phyllis George Finds," *Baltimore Sun*, 11 August 1975.

20. *Newsweek*, 30 August 1971, 63, cited in Patricia Bradley, *Mass Media and the Shaping of American Feminism, 1963–1975* (Jackson: University of Mississippi Press,

2003), 224; Paul Farhi, "New Face of TV News First Seen in the '70s," *Washington Post*, 23 July 2006.

21. Arthur Unger, "Women on TV: The Same Old Image," *Christian Science Monitor*, 29 November 1977.

22. "42 Times *Ms.* Made History," *Ms.*, 11 August 2014.

23. Frum, *How We Got Here*, 151–52; Patterson, *Grand Expectations*, 53; Thomas Borstelmann, *The 1970s: A New Global History from Civil Rights to Economic Inequality* (Princeton, NJ: Princeton University Press, 2011), 84; "The American Woman: On the Move, but Where?" 58–59.

24. Carroll, *It Seemed*, 279; Frum, *How We Got Here*, 107.

25. Self, *All in the Family*, 156.

26. David J. Garrow, *Liberty and Sexuality: The Right to Privacy and the Making of Roe v. Wade* (Berkeley: University of California Press, 1998), 403–6.

27. 410 U.S. 113; Self, *All in the Family*, 158.

28. Self, *All in the Family*, 131; Frum, *How We Got Here*, 248.

29. David K. Johnson, *The Lavender Scare: The Cold War Persecution of Gays and Lesbians in the Federal Government* (Chicago: University of Chicago Press, 2004).

30. Self, *All in the Family*, 97–98.

31. John D'Emilio and Estelle B. Freedman, *Intimate Matters: A History of Sexuality in America*, 2nd ed. (Chicago: University of Chicago Press, 1997), 321–23; "Gays on the March," *Time*, 8 December 1975, 33.

32. D'Emilio and Freedman, *Intimate Matters*, 323–24; *New York Times*, 25 October 1977; "Gays on the March," *Time*, 8 December 1975, 32.

33. Harold Schmeck, "Psychiatrists Approve Change on Homosexuals," *New York Times*, 9 April 1974; "Shedding Blinders," *New York Times*, 16 July 1975; D'Emilio and Freedman, *Intimate Matters*, 324; Frum, *How We Got Here*, 206; *Chicago Tribune*, 5 October 1975.

34. Gregg Kilday, "Gays Lobby for a New Media Image," *Los Angeles Times*, 10 December 1973; "Male-Female," *Philadelphia Inquirer*, 7 November 1974; Les Brown, "Advertisers Worried By Pressure Groups," *Minneapolis Tribune*, 11 September 1977; Daniel Henninger, "Squeaky Clean or Just a Rinse?" *Wall Street Journal*, 12 September 1977; "ABC Sweeps Weekly Ratings," *Atlanta Constitution*, 22 September 1977.

35. D'Emilio and Freedman, *Intimate Matters*, 346–47; Carroll, *It Seemed*, 291; Jeff Prugh, "Miami Repeals Gay Rights by Overwhelming Margin," *Los Angeles Times*, 8 June 1977.

36. William Overend, "Gay Rights: Is a Backlash Forming?" *Los Angeles Times*, 29 July 1977; Self, *All in the Family*, 243–44; Carroll, *It Seemed*, 292; Adam Nagourney and Dudley Clendinin, *Out for Good: The Struggle to Build a Gay Rights Movement in America* (New York: Touchstone, 1999).

37. David Johnson, "S.F. Mourns Slain City Worker," *Los Angeles Times*, 25, 27 June 1977; Self, *All in the Family*, 245–46.

38. *The Life and Times of Harvey Milk*, Rob Epstein, director (New Yorker Films, 1984); Carroll, *It Seemed*, 293.

39. "Powell Defends Meeting," *New York Times*, 27 March 1977; Mary Thornton, "Grass Roots Lobbying for Gay Rights Bill," *Boston Globe*, 19 June 1977; Carroll, *It Seemed*, 293.

Chapter 5: TURNING RIGHT

1. *Christianity Today*, 16 August, 8 November 1968; Neil J. Young, *We Gather Together: The Religious Right and the Problem of Interfaith Politics* (New York: Oxford University Press, 2015), 106, 112 .

2. Colin Duriez, *Francis Schaeffer: An Authentic Life* (Wheaton, IL: Crossway, 2008), 186.

3. William Martin, *With God on Our Side: The Rise of the Religious Right in America* (New York: Broadway Books, 1996), 193; *Christianity Today*, 16 February 1973, 16 January 1976; Scott Flipse, "Below-the-Belt Politics: Protestant Evangelicals, Abortion, and the Foundation of the New Religious Right, 1960–75," in *The Conservative Sixties*, ed. David Farber and Jeff Roche (New York: Peter Lang, 2003), 138–39.

4. Robert O. Self, *All in the Family: The Realignment of American Democracy Since the 1960s* (New York: Hill and Wang, 2012), 373.

5. Self, *All in the Family*, 289, 373–74.

6. Edith Herman, "Houston's Over: Now All Eyes Turn to Washington," *Chicago Tribune*, 27 November 1977; "What Next for U.S. Women," *Time*, 5 December 1977, 26; Rosen, *World Split Open*, 291–94.

7. Donald Critchlow, *Phyllis Schlafly and Grassroots Conservatism: A Woman's Crusade* (Princeton, NJ: Princeton University Press, 2008), 245; Sally Quinn, "The Pedestal Has Cashed," and David Broder, "The Real Significance of Women," *Washington Post*, 23 November 1977; Judy Klemesrud, "Equal Rights Plan and Abortion Are Opposed by 15,000 At Rally," *New York Times*, 20 November 1977; "What Next for U.S. Women," *Time*, 5 December 1977, 26; Marjorie J. Spruill, *Divided We Stand: The Battle over Women's Rights and Family Values That Polarized American Politics* (New York: Bloomsbury, 2017).

8. "The Reagan Way Against Sex Discrimination," *Christian Science Monitor*, 26 December 1980; *Wall Street Journal*, 17 September 1980; Daniel K. Williams, *God's Own Party: The Making of the Christian Right* (New York: Oxford University Press, 2010), 110.

9. Christina von Hodenberg, *Television's Moment: Sitcom Audiences and the Sixties Cultural Revolution* (New York: Berghahn, 2015), 168; Elana Levine, *Wallowing in Sex: The New Sexual Revolution of 1970s American Television* (Durham, NC: Duke University Press, 2007), 197.

10. Janis Johnson, "Electronic Evangelism," *Atlanta Constitution*, 27 August 1977; Fred Fejes, *Gay Rights and Moral Panic: The Origins of America's Debate on Homosexuality* (New York: Palgrave, 2008), 103–4.

11. Michael Sean Winters, *God's Right Hand: How Jerry Falwell Made God a Republican and Baptized the American Right* (New York: HarperCollins, 2012), 98, 136; Martin, *With God on Our Side*, 198–201; Jerry Falwell, *Listen, America!* (New York: Bantam Books, 1980), 130–31; Williams, *God's Own Party*, 156.

12. Martin, *With God On Our Side*, 200–2; Joan Sweeney, "Evangelicals Seeking to Establish Political Force," *Los Angeles Times*, 19 May 1980; Leslie Bennetts, "Abortion Foes, at Conference, Plan Strategy of Political Activism," and George Vecsey, "Militant Television Preachers Try to Weld Fundamentalist Christian's Political Power," *New York Times*, 21 January 1980.

13. Linda Floyd, "For Evangelists, The Political Gospel Is God and Country," *The Philadelphia Inquirer*, 24 August 1980; Kenneth A Briggs, "Evangelicals Hear Plea," *New York Times*, 21 August 1980; Martin, *With God On Our Side*, 214–16.

14. Kevin M. Kruse, *One Nation Under God: How Corporate America Invented Christian America* (New York: Basic Books, 2015), 277; Daniel Schlozman, *When Movements Anchor Parties: Electoral Alignments in American History* (Princeton, NJ: Princeton University Press, 2015), 2.

15. Berman, *America's Right Turn*, 28.

16. Sara Diamond, *Spiritual Warfare: The Politics of the Christian Right* (Boston: South End Press, 1999), 58; Michael Schaller and George Rising, *The Republican Ascendancy: American Politics, 1968–2001* (New York: Harlan Davidson, 2002), 68.

17. Jason Stahl, *Right Moves: The Conservative Think Tank in American Political Culture*

Since 1945 (Chapel Hill: University of North Carolina Press, 2016), 70–73; John B. Judis, *The Paradox of American Democracy: Elites, Special Interests and the Betrayal of Public Trust* (New York: Random House, 2013); James A. Smith, *The Idea Brokers: Think Tanks and the Rise of the New Policy Elite* (New York: Free Press, 1993); David M. Ricci, *The Transformation of American Politics: The New Washington and the Rise of Think Tanks* (New Haven, CT: Yale University Press, 1994).

18. Jacob S. Hacker and Paul Pierson, *Winner Take All Politics: How Washington Made the Rich Richer—and Turned Its Back on the Middle Class* (New York: Simon & Schuster, 2010).

19. Kiron Skinner, Annelise Anderson, and Martin Anderson, *Reagan's Path to Victory: The Shaping of Ronald Reagan's Vision* (New York: Free Press, 2004).

20. James Mann, *The Rebellion of Ronald Reagan: A History of the End of the Cold War* (New York: Viking, 2009), 246.

21. Adam Clymer, "G.O.P. Presidential Aspirants Tour Nation to Denounce Carter's Foreign Policy," *New York Times*, 20 February 1979.

22. Robert G. Kaiser, "After the Summit: A Wave of Bipartisan Euphoria," *Washington Post*, 19 September 1978; Ray Moseley, "U.S. Embassy in Iran Under Attack," *Chicago Tribune,* 14 February 1979; "Gunmen Seize U.S. Embassy," *Los Angeles Times,* 14 February 1979; Adam Clymer, "G.O.P. Presidential Aspirants Tour Nation to Denounce Carter's Foreign Policy."

23. John Carman, "Bad News in Iran Has Meant Good News for ABC's Ratings," *Minneapolis Star*, 30 November 1979; Patterson, *Restless Giant*, 124–25.

24. William Endicott, "Reagan Toughens Stand on Crisis in Iran," *Los Angeles Times*, 28 November 1979; "Reagan Fires Salvo at Carter's Handling of Iran Hostage Crisis," *Atlanta Constitution*, 28 March 1980; Douglas Shuit, "Carter Dillydallies on Hostage Crisis, Reagan Charges," *Los Angeles Times*, 28 March 1980.

25. Pete Bowles and Jim Scovel, "Jury Convicts Four in ABSCAM Trial," *Newsday,* 30 August 1980; Paul Houston, "House Expels Myers Over Abscam Probe Conviction," *Los Angeles Times*, 3 October 1980; Thomas B. Edsall, "Abscam, Heavy Campaign Spending Cut Into Democrats' Lead in House," *Baltimore Sun*, 5 November 1980.

26. Linda Greenhouse, "Supreme Court Clears Abscam Videotapes for TV," *New York Times*, 15 October 1980; Thomas Collins, "ABSCAM Tapes Go Public," *Newsday*, 15 October 1980; Tom Shales, "The Abscam Tapes on TV," *Washington Post*, 15 October 1980.

27. Beverly Moore, "Reagan Hits 'Too Much' Government," *Atlanta Daily World*, 13 April 1979.

28. Thomas Edsall, *Chain Reaction: The Impact of Race, Rights and Taxes on American Politics* (New York: Norton, 1992), 129–31.

29. Robert O. Self, *American Babylon: Race and the Struggle for Postwar Oakland* (Princeton, NJ: Princeton University Press, 2003), 316–26; Patterson, *Restless Giant*, 133.

30. Peter N. Caroll, *It Seemed Like Nothing Happened: America in the 1970s* (New Brunswick, NJ: Rutgers University Press, 1990), 325; Patterson, *Restless Giant*, 66; Jefferson Cowie, *Stayin' Alive: The 1970s and the Last Days of the Working Class* (New York: New Press, 2010), 300.

31. Michael Barone, "What the Voters Were Saying," *Wall Street Journal*, 22 November 1978; Louis Harris, "Reading Signs on Taxes," *Newsday*, 17 November 1978.

32. Patrick Riordan, "The Born-Again," *Philadelphia Inquirer*, 17 July 1980; "Text of Reagan's Speech Accepting GOP Nomination," *Los Angeles Times*, 18 July 1980; Kruse, *One Nation Under God*, 275–77.

33. Janice Castro and Elizabeth Rudolph, "'Like a Suburban Swimming Pool,'" *Time*, 17 November 1980; Haynes Johnson, "A Reagan Revolution, Perhaps, but Not an Ideological Mandate," *Washington Post*, 9 November 1980.

34. Johnson, "A Reagan Revolution, Perhaps."
35. For a more detailed look at the limits of the "Reagan Revolution," see Meg Jacobs and Julian E. Zelizer, *Conservatives in Power: The Reagan Years, 1981–1989* (Boston: Bedford, 2010).
36. Michael Kelly, "David Gergen, Master of the Game," *New York Times*, 31 October 1993.
37. John Ehrman, "Debating the Reagan Presidency: Domestic Politics and Issues," in *Debating the Reagan Presidency*, ed. John Ehrman and Michael W. Flamm (Lanham, MD: Rowman & Littlefield, 2009), 15.
38. Kelly, "David Gergen, Master of the Game."
39. H. W. Brands, *Reagan: The Life* (New York: Anchor, 2015), 260–61.
40. Sidney Blumenthal, "Defining 'Reaganomics,'" *Boston Globe*, 2 November 1980.
41. Daniel T. Rodgers, *Age of Fracture* (Cambridge, MA: The Belknap Press, 2011), 66.
42. "Friedman Doubts Employment Goal in Nobel Lecture," *Los Angeles Times*, 14 December 1976.
43. Arthur Laffer, "Taking the Side of Supply," *Los Angeles Times*, 8 February 1981.
44. Phillips-Fein, *Invisible Hands*, 180–82; Paul Craig Roberts, "Supply-Side Economics," *Wall Street Journal*, 22 January 1981.
45. Paul Krugman, "The Tax-Cut Con," *New York Times Magazine*, 14 September 2003; William Greider, "The Education of David Stockman," *The Atlantic*, 1 December 1981.
46. Ronald Reagan, "Address Before Joint Session of Congress on the Program for Economic Recovery," 18 February 1981, the American Presidency Project.
47. Richard J. Cattani, "Debate on budget figures heats up—and Reagan slips a bit in polls," *Christian Science Monitor*, 19 March 1981.
48. Howell Raines, "Reagan Wounded in Chest by Gunman," *New York Times*, 31 March 1981.
49. Robert M. Collins, *Transforming America: Politics and Culture During the Reagan Years* (New York: Columbia University Press, 2007), 71.
50. Robert H. Michel to Colleagues, 29 May 1981, Ronald Reagan Archives, Lee Atwater Files, Box 2, File: Economic Recovery Program.
51. Thomas Edsall, "Reagan Triumphant in Tax-Cut Bill," *Washington Post*, 30 July 1981; W. Elliot Brownlee, *Federal Taxation in America: A Short History* (Washington, DC: Woodrow Wilson Center, and New York: Cambridge University Press, 1996): 115–19.

Chapter 6: FIGHTING RIGHT

1. Julian E. Zelizer, *The Fierce Urgency of Now: Lyndon Johnson, Congress and the Battle for the Great Society* (New York: Penguin Press, 2015), 131–62.
2. Lou Cannon, *President Ronald Reagan: The Role of a Lifetime* (New York: Public Affairs, 2000), 243.
3. David Rosenbaum, "First Major Cuts in Social Security Proposed in Detailed Reagan Plan," *New York Times*, 13 May 1981.
4. Joseph D. Whitaker, "Social Security Increase: The Margin of Survival," *Washington Post*, 1 July 1981; Wendell Rawls Jr., "Fears Over Reduced Social Security Afflict Elderly," *New York Times*, 25 May 1981.
5. Douglas B. Harris, "The Rise of the Public Speakership," *Political Science Quarterly*, No. 2 (Summer 1998): 193–212.
6. Chris Matthews, *Tip and the Gipper: When Politics Worked* (New York: Simon & Schuster, 2013), 130.
7. Warren Weaver Jr., "Coalition Plans Drive Against Move To Trim Social Security Benefits," *New York Times*, 14 May 1981.

8. Fred Barnes, "Reagan Puts Off Social Security Bid," *Baltimore Sun*, 29 September 1981; William Safire, "Third Rail," *New York Times*, 18 February 2007.

9. "Abortion Foes Meet with Reagan After March in Capital," *New York Times*, 23 January 1981; Janet Cooke, "Abortion Foes Stage 8th Annual 'March for Life,'" *Washington Post*, 23 January 1981.

10. Steven R. Weisman, "Reagan Nominating Woman, an Arizona Appeals Judge, to Serve on Supreme Court," *New York Times*, 7 July 1981; George Skelton, "Reagan Tries to Assuage Critics of Court Nominee," *Los Angeles Times*, 9 July 1981; William Link, *Righteous Warrior: Jesse Helms and the Rise of Modern Conservatism* (New York: St. Martin's Press, 2008), 230–32.

11. Elizabeth Dole to Edwin Meese and James Baker, 9 March 1982, Ronald Reagan Archives, Elizabeth Dole Files, Box 18, File: Conservatives—General 1982.

12. William Greider, "The Education of David Stockman," *The Atlantic*, December 1981.

13. Paul Taylor, "Rightist Group Says Reagan Has Strayed," *Washington Post*, 20 January 1983.

14. "Think About It," *New York Times*, 16 June 1983.

15. "Michigan, Youngstown Top Jobless Rolls," *Chicago Tribune*, 20 October 1982; Cannon, *The Role of a Lifetime*.

16. "Reagan's Son Collects '2 or 3' Jobless Checks," *Los Angeles Times*, 15 October 1982.

17. Stephen E. Nordlinger, "Unemployment Hits 42 Year High," *Baltimore Sun*, 9 October 1982.

18. "O'Neill Charges Reagan Planned Current Recession," *Los Angeles Times*, 6 November 1981.

19. Patrick Caddell, "Why the Democrats Might Win Big," *Washington Post*, 17 October 1982.

20. Meg Jacobs, "The 1980 Election," in *America at the Ballot Box: Elections and Political History*, ed. Gareth Davies and Julian E. Zelizer (Philadelphia: University of Pennsylvania Press, 2015), 200.

21. Howell Raines, "Poll Finds Reagan Gains on Economy," *New York Times*, 17 April 1983; Jack Lesar, "Blacks Gained in '70s, Unemployment Got Worse," *Baltimore Afro-American*, 27 August 1983.

22. Ronald Reagan, "Remarks on Signing the Social Security Amendments of 1983," 20 April 1983.

23. Dorothy Nelkin and Michael S. Brown, *Workers at Risk: Voices from the Work Place* (Chicago: University of Chicago Press, 1984), 126; Seth S. King, "Director Rates OSHA 'Far Better Than It Was,'" *New York Times*, 29 October 1982; Meg Jacobs and Julian E. Zelizer, *Conservatives in Power: The Reagan Years, 1981–1989* (Boston: Bedford, 2010), 38–41.

24. Robert Sangeorge, "Environmentalists Across-the-Board Oppose Reagan Policies," UPI, 20 June 1982.

25. Steven Weisman, "Watt Quits Post: President Accepts with 'Reluctance,'" *New York Times*, 10 October 1983; For more on Watt and Reagan's Interior Department, see James Morton Turner and Andrew C. Isenberg, *The Republican Reversal: Conservatives and the Environment from Nixon to Trump* (Cambridge, MA: Harvard University Press, 2018), 62–72.

26. "Conservationists Say EPA Shake-Up Not Enough," *Galveston Daily News*, 29 March 1983; Turner and Isenberg, *The Republican Reversal*, 101–4.

27. Juan Williams, "A Question of Fairness," *The Atlantic*, February 1987; Ernest Holsendolph, "Skills, Not Bias, Seen as Key for Jobs," *New York Times*, 3 July 1982; Leah Wright Rigueur, *The Loneliness of the Black Republican: Pragmatic Politics and the Pursuit of Power* (Princeton, NJ: Princeton University Press, 2014), 302–4.

28. Ronald Reagan, "Statement on the Observance of Peace Through Strength Week," The American Presidency Project, 22 September 1984.

29. Ronald Reagan, "Address to the National Association of Evangelicals," The American Presidency Project, 8 March 1983.

30. Beth A. Fischer, *The Reagan Reversal: Foreign Policy and the End of the Cold War* (Columbia: University of Missouri Press, 1997), 85.

31. Clyde Farnsworth, "They Call Him Cap the Knife," *New York Times*, 3 May 1985.

32. Richard Halloran, "Weinberger Tells of New Conventional Force Strategy," *New York Times*, 6 May 1981.

33. Greg Schneider and Renae Merle, "Reagan's Defense Buildup Bridged Military Eras," *Washington Post*, 9 June 2004.

34. Paul L. Montgomery, "Throngs Fill Manhattan to Protest Nuclear Weapons," *New York Times*, 13 June 1982.

35. Lawrence C. Wittner, "Reagan and Nuclear Disarmament," *Boston Review*, 2000.

36. Jacobs and Zelizer, *Conservatives in Power*, 149.

37. "Million Protest U.S. Missiles," *Chicago Tribune*, 23 October 1983.

38. Glenn Collins, "The Impact on Children of 'The Day After,'" *New York Times*, 7 November 1983.

39. John Corry, "'The Day After': TV as Rallying Force," *New York Times*, 20 November 1983.

40. "U.S. Says Soviets Shot Down Airliner," *Washington Post*, 2 September 1983.

41. Robert McFadden, "U.S. Says Soviet Downed Korean Airliner," *New York Times*, 2 September 1983.

42. Julian E. Zelizer, *The Arsenal of Democracy: The Politics of National Security from World War II to the War on Terrorism* (New York: Basic Books, 2010), 323–24.

43. Robert Gates, *From The Shadows: The Ultimate Insiders Story of Five Presidents and How they Won the Cold War* (New York: Simon & Schuster, 1997), 270–74.

44. Robert Gates, *From The Shadows*, 273.

45. Robert Dallek, *Ronald Reagan: The Politics of Symbolism*, 153.

46. Ronald Reagan, "Address to the Nation on Defense and National Security," 22 March 1983.

47. Frances FitzGerald, *Way Out There in the Blue: Reagan, Star Wars and the End of the Cold War* (New York: Touchstone, 2000), 185–86.

48. "America's Olympics," *Time*, 17 October 1983.

49. Francis X. Clines, "Reagan Delivers a Pep Talk," *New York Times*, 29 July 1984.

50. Michael Weinreb, "The American Ideal," ESPN.com, 8 July 2009.

51. Michael Beschloss, "The Ad that Helped Reagan Sell Good Times to the Nation," *New York Times*, 7 May 2016.

52. "America Is Back," 1984, LivingRoomCandidate.com.

53. Robert Lekachman, "Atari Democrats," *New York Times*, 10 October 1982; Steven M. Gillon, *The Democrats' Dilemma: Walter F. Mondale and the Liberal Legacy* (New York: Columbia University Press, 1992), 333–34; "The Exchange Between Hart, Mondale," *Boston Globe*, 12 March 1984.

54. Dick Simpson, Melissa Mouritsen, and Betty O'Shaughnessy, "Chicago: The Election of Rahm Emanuel," in *Local Politics and Mayoral Elections in the 21st Century America: The Keys to City Hall*, ed. Sean Foreman and Marcia Godwin (New York: Routledge, 2015), 88.

55. Jamelle Bouie, "Keep Hope Alive," *Slate*, 26 November 2016.

56. Jesse Jackson, "Address Before the Democratic Convention," 18 July 1984.

57. Walter Mondale, "Acceptance Speech to the Democratic Convention," 1984.

58. Joseph A. McCartin, *Collision Course: Ronald Reagan, the Air Traffic Controllers, and the Strike That Changed America* (New York: Oxford University Press, 2013).

59. Ronald Reagan, "Radio Address to the Nation on the Presidential Campaign," 13 October 1984.

60. Ronald Reagan, "Address at Point du Hoc, Normandy," 6 June 1984.

61. Ronald Reagan, "Remarks at Reelection Celebration in California," 6 November 1984.

62. Robert Pear, "President Signs Landmark Bill on Immigration," *New York Times,* 7 November 1986.

63. Garry Wills, "The Politics of Grievance," *New York Review of Books,* 19 July 1990; Christopher Lehman-Haupt, "A Vision Beyond the New Gilded Age," *New York Times,* 21 June 1990; "The Rich, the Poor, and the Growing Gap Between Them," *Economist,* 15 June 2006; Robert Jackson, "Income Gap Grew in 1980s, Study Says," *Los Angeles Times,* 28 August 1992; Sam Roberts, "Gap Between Rich and Poor in New York City Grows Wider," *New York Times,* 25 December 1994; Jacob S. Hacker, Gregory A. Huber, Philipp Rehm, Mark Schlesinger, and Rob Valletta, "Economic Security At Risk: Findings From The Economic Security Index," The Rockefeller Foundation, 2010; Kevin Phillips, *The Politics of Rich and Poor: Wealth and the American Electorate in the Reagan Aftermath* (New York: HarperCollins, 1989), 8.

64. Michael Hiltzik, "Why Boesky Insider Trading Case Rocked Wall Street," *Los Angeles Times,* 1 December 1986; Peter Behr, "Boesky's Widening Net," *Washington Post,* 18 December 1986; Daniel Hertzberg, "Drexel's Michael Milken Called a Focus of Probe of Suspect Boesky Scheme," *Wall Street Journal,* 5 February 1987; Helen Dudar, "Michael Douglas, as Villain, Hits It Big on 'Wall Street,'" *New York Times,* 6 December 1987.

Chapter 7: CHANGING CHANNELS

1. Advertisment, *Huntsville Rewound,* online archive.

2. "F.C.C. Gets in on Cable TV," *Wired,* 1 August 2011; Neil Genzlinger, "My Father the Cable Pioneer," *New York Times Magazine,* 24 August 2012; Brian Lockman and Don Sarvey, *Pioneers of Cable Television.*

3. Neil Genzlinger, "My Father the Cable Pioneer," *New York Times,* 24 August 2012.

4. Penny Pagano, "Cable TV Officials See 1987 as 'Watershed' Year," *Los Angeles Times,* 20 January 1987.

5. Larry Brody, *Turning Points in Television: Great Moments on the Small Screen* (New York: Citadel Press, 2005), 149.

6. "How Cable Works," *New York Times,* 5 July 1981; Bill Jauss, "The Future of Sports Television Connected to a Cable," *Chicago Tribune,* 13 June 1979.

7. Susan Howard, "TV Executive Focuses on Larger Goals," *Hartford Courant,* 29 April 1979; Bill Jauss, "The Future of Sports Television Connected to a Cable"; "We Pause for a Moment . . . ," *Washington Post,* 9 September 1979.

8. Brian Winston, *Media, Technology and Society: A History from Telegraph to Internet* (London: Routledge, 1998), 313.

9. Jimmie L. Reeves and Michael M. Epstein, "The Changing Face of Television: Turner Broadcasting System," in *The Columbia History of American Television,* ed. Gary Edgerton (New York: Columbia University Press, 2007), 333; Richard Zoglin, "The All-News Mastermind: Reese Schonfeld Is the Man Behind Cable News Network," *Atlanta Constitution,* 13 August 1979.

10. Hank Whittemore, *CNN the Inside Story: How a Band of Mavericks Changed the Face of Television News* (Boston: Little, Brown, 1990), 111–12.

11. Whittemore, *CNN,* 2–36, 120–21.

12. Whittemore, *CNN,* 243–44; Zoglin, "The All-News Mastermind."

13. John F. Berry, "Skepticism Greets Hype Surrounding Cable News Debut," *Washington Post,* 1 June 1980.

14. Sally Bendell Smith, "An ABC Strategy Goes Wrong," *New York Times*, 9 December 1984.

15. "Snooze News," *New York Magazine*, 28 June 1982.

16. Aaron Barlow, *The Rise of the Blogosphere* (Westport, CT: Praeger, 2007), 119.

17. Robert J. Donovan and Ray Scherer, *Unsilent Revolution: Television News and American Public Life, 1948–1991* (New York and Washington: Cambridge University Press and the Woodrow Wilson International Center for Scholars, 1992), 266–68.

18. Gabriel Weinmann, *Communicating Unreality: Modern Media and the Reconstruction of Reality* (Thousand Oaks, CA: Sage, 2000), 191.

19. Craig Marks and Rob Tannenbaum, *I Want My MTV: The Uncensored Story of the Music Video Revolution* (New York: Dutton, 2000), 1.

20. Marks and Tannenbaum, *I Want My MTV*, 25.

21. Marks and Tannenbaum, *I Want My MTV*, 22.

22. Gloria Ohland, "Music TV Will Play to Tastes of Rock 'n' Roll Generation," *Minneapolis Star*, 15 September 1981.

23. "Music Television: Report #1," *Billboard*, 10 October 1981; Andy Greene, "MTV Turns 30," *Rolling Stone*, 28 July 2011.

24. "David Bowie Accusing MTV of Racism in '83," *Los Angeles Times*, 12 January 2016; Steve Greenberg, "Where Is Graceland? 1980s Pop Culture Through Music," in *Living Through the Eighties*, ed. Gil Troy and Vincent J. Cannato (New York: Oxford University Press, 2009), 159; Philip W. Wiggins, "Turner Will Sell Cable Music Channel to MTV," *New York Times*, 29 November 1984.

25. Carleton Jones, "Cable Tries to Please All The People All The Time," *The Sun*, 16 August 1981.

26. John Paul Newport, "The Coming VCR Glut: The Prices Make You Think It's Here Already?" *Fortune*, 19 August 1985.

27. Ralph Blanchard, *The Digital Challenge for Libraries: Understanding the Culture and Technology of Total Culture* (New York: iUniverse, 2005), 92.

28. Peter Temin and Louis Galambos, *The Fall of the Bell System: A Study in Prices and Politics* (New York: Cambridge University Press, 1987); James A. White, "Baby Bell's First Months Marked by Some Confusion as People Adjust," *Wall Street Journal*, 24 May 1983.

29. "The First Cellular Phone Went on Sale 30 Years Ago for $4,000," *Mashable*, 13 March 2014.

30. Roger Rosenblatt, "The Computer: Machine of the Year," *Time*, January 1983.

31. Leslie Berlin, *The Man Behind the Microchip: Robert Noyce and the Invention of Silicon Valley* (New York: Oxford University Press, 2005), 130.

32. John Bessant and Joe Tidd, *Innovation and Entrepreneurship* (New York: Wiley, 2015), 407.

33. Walter Isaacson, *The Innovators: How a Group of Hackers, Geniuses, and Geeks Created the Digital Revolution* (New York: Simon & Schuster, 2015), 351; "The Home Computer That's Ready to Work, Play, and Grow with You," *Scientific American*, September 1977.

34. Walter Issacson, *Steve Jobs* (New York: Simon & Schuster, 2012), 162–63.

35. Eric Hintz, "Remembering Apple's '1984' Super Bowl Ad," *Smithsonian Museums Blog*, 22 January 1984.

36. David E. Sanger, "For Apple, a Risky Assault on I.B.M.," *New York Times*, 23 January 1984.

37. David Salisbury, "Apple Plans to Take Byte Out of Competition with New Macintosh," *Christian Science Monitor*, 24 January 1984.

38. Chip Brown, "F.E.A.R.com," in *Breach of Faith: A Crisis of Coverage in the Age of*

Corporate Newspapering, ed. Gene Roberts and Thomas Kunkel (Fayetteville: University of Arkansas Press, 2002), 203; Michael A. Banks, *On the Way to the Web: The Secret History of the Internet and Its Founders* (New York: Apress, 2012); "CompuServe Closes after 30 Years," Network World, 8 July 2009.

39. Don Nunes, "Computers Are Expensive to Feed," *Washington Post*, 7 June 1982.

40. Dylan Tweney, "First Online Service For Consumers Debuts," *Wired*, 24 September 2009.

41. William J. Broad, "Rising Use of Computer Networks Raises Issues of Security and Law," *New York Times*, 26 August 1983.

42. Matt Novak, "The Untold Story of the Teen Hackers Who Transformed the Early Internet," *Paleofuture*, 14 April 2016.

43. Fred Kaplan, "'War Games' and Cybersecurity's Debt to a Hollywood Hack," *New York Times*, 19 February 2016.

44. Douglas Thomas, *Hacking Culture* (Minneapolis: University of Minnesota Press, 2002), 26; Paul Korzeniowski, "All-Star Teen Hacker's Team Beat Hundreds of Systems," *Computerworld*, 8 July 1985.

45. For a more detailed history of the end of the fairness doctrine, see Julian E. Zelizer, "How Washington Helped to Create the Modern Media: Ending the Fairness Doctrine," in *Media Nation: The Political History of News in Modern America*, ed. Bruce Schulman and Julian E. Zelizer (Philadelphia: University of Pennsylvania Press, 2017), 176–89.

46. Bob Davis, "FCC Abolishes Fairness Doctrine, Arousing Debate," *Wall Street Journal*, 5 August 1987.

47. Raspberry, "Filth on the Air," *Washington Post*, 19 June 1985; Gil Troy, *Morning in America: How Ronald Reagan Invented the 1980s* (Princeton, NJ: Princeton University Press, 2005), 273.

48. William Raspberry, "Filth on the Air"; Stephen Holden, "Recordings Will Carry Advisory About Lyrics," *New York Times*, 9 August 1985; "Nineteen Big Record Firms Agree to Warning Labels," *Wall Street Journal*, 12 August 1985.

49. Jon Pareles, "Debate Spurs Hearings on Rating Rock," *New York Times*, 18 September 1985; Irvin Molotsky, "Hearing on Rock Lyrics," *New York Times*, 20 September 1985.

50. Kory Grow, "Dee Snider on PMRC Hearing: 'I Was a Public Enemy,'" *Rolling Stone*, 18 September 2015.

51. Jon Pareles, "Debate Spurs Hearings on Rating Rock"; Irvin Molotsky, "Hearing on Rock Lyrics."

52. Roger Sadler, *Electronic Media Law* (Thousand Oaks, CA: Sage, 2005), 286.

53. "Reagan Orders 'New Look' at 'Victimless Crime,'" *Baltimore Sun*, 22 May 1984; Rita Ciolli, "New U.S. Panel to Take on Porn," *Newsday*, 20 May 1985; "Meese Names Panel to Study Pornography," *Los Angeles Times*, 20 May 1985.

54. "Meese Names Panel to Study Pornography"; Howard Kurtz, "Pornography Panel's Objectivity Disputed," *Washington Post*, 15 October 1985; James Kilpatrick, "Hooray for Meese Commission on Porn," *Orlando Sentinel*, 17 July 1986; "Meese, Panel Sued by Playboy," *Chicago Tribune*, 20 May 1986; "Penthouse Sues Meese, U.S. to Block Listing of Outlets," *Wall Street Journal*, 19 May 1986.

55. Philip Shenons, "Justice Dept. Pornography Study Finds Materials Tied to Violence," *New York Times*, 14 May 1986; Robert L. Jackson, "Pornography Case Judge Rebukes Panel," *Los Angeles Times*, 4 July 1986; "North Carolina Is Cracking Down on Pornography," *New York Times*, 13 October 1985.

56. James Davison Hunter, *Culture Wars: The Struggle to Define America* (New York: Basic Books, 1991), 232.

57. Tom Wicker, "Lyrics and the Law," *New York Times*, 1 February 1990.

58. Steve Hochman and Chuck Phillips, "Florida Clerk Faces a Felony Charge for Selling Rap Record," *Los Angeles Times*, 17 March 1990; Steve Hochman, "Record Chain Clears Shelves of Rap Album," *Los Angeles Times*, 23 March 1990; Laura Parker, "Rap Singers Charged with Obscenity," *Washington Post*, 11 June 1990; "Gov. Takes Credit for Rappers' Arrests," *Los Angeles Times*, 11 June 1990.

59. Chuck Phillips, "A Rapper Under Siege Fires Back," *Los Angeles Times*, 25 March 1990; Richard Harrington, "An Obscene Amount of Attention," *Washington Post*, 13 June 1990; Richard Harrington, "2 Live Crew, Banned and Boring," *Washington Post*, 26 July 1990; Chuck Phillips, "Despite Chains' Boycott, Campbell Album Sells," *Los Angeles Times*, 2 August 1990.

60. Clarence Page, "Today 2 Live Crew, Tomorrow Maybe This Column," *Chicago Tribune*, 13 June 1990.

Chapter 8: DIVIDING AMERICA

1. Michael Wines and Doyle McManus, "U.S. Sent Iran Arms for Hostage Releases," *Los Angeles Times*, 6 November 1986.

2. Malcolm Byrne, *Iran-Contra: Reagan's Scandal and the Unchecked Abuse of Presidential Power* (Lawrence: University Press of Kansas, 2014).

3. Frank Newport, "History Shows Presidential Job Approval Ratings Can Plummet Rapidly," *Gallup News*, 11 February 1998.

4. Lawrence E. Walsh, *Firewall: The Iran-Contra Conspiracy and Cover-Up* (New York: W. W. Norton, 1997).

5. Maureen Dowd, "The Fawn Hall Story," *Washington Post*, 9 June 1987; "Networks to Rotate Hearings Coverage," *Baltimore Sun*, 15 July 1987; Steve Daley, "Television Could Make Ollie's Day," *Chicago Tribune*, 9 July 1987; Peter J. Boyer, "North Outdraws the Top Show on Daytime TV," *New York Times*, 11 July 1987.

6. Daley, "Television Could Make Ollie's Day"; Richard Herzfelder, "Cashing In on Ollie," *Washington Post*, 16 July 1987.

7. Alexander Yakovlev, Memorandum Prepared on Request from M. S. Gorbachev and handed to him on March 12, 1985, National Security Archive, George Washington University.

8. "Quotation of The Day," *New York Times*, 12 December 1987.

9. J. David Woodard, *The America that Reagan Built* (New York: Praeger, 2006), 97.

10. Howard Rosenberg, "TV Girds for the Geneva Miniseries," *Los Angeles Times*, 18 November 1985.

11. Seyom Brown, *Faces of Power: Constancy and Change in United States Foreign Policy From Truman to Obama*, 3rd ed. (New York: Columbia University Press, 2015), 463.

12. Romesh Ratnesar, "20 Years After Tear Down This Wall," *Time*, 11 June 2007.

13. Robert J. McCartney, "White House Persuasion Won High Profile Speech in Berlin," *Washington Post*, 11 June 1987.

14. Henry Allen, "The Cult of Comrade Gorbachev," *Washington Post*, 30 November 1987.

15. David Hess and Bill Arthur, "Senate Ratifies INF Treaty, 93–5," *Los Angeles Times*, 28 May 1988.

16. Julian E. Zelizer, *Arsenal of Democracy: The Politics of National Security—From World War II to the War on Terrorism* (New York: Basic Books, 2010), 351.

17. David Hoffman, "Reagan Lashes Conservative Foes of Treaty, Foresees '88 Summit," *Washington Post*, 4 December 1987.

18. Derek Scally, "Did the Boss Bring Down the Berlin Wall?" *Irish Times*, 13 July 2013; Kate Connolly, "The Night Bruce Springsteen Played East Berlin—And the Wall Cracked," *Guardian*, 5 July 2013.

19. R. W. Apple, "After the Coup," *New York Times,* 22 April 1991.

20. Al Kamen, "President Intends to Nominate Appellate Judge Scalia," *Washington Post,* 18 June 1986.

21. Kamen, "President Intends to Nominate Appellate Judge Scalia."

22. Stephen Wermiel, "Judicial Shakeup: Changes on High Court Are Likely to Increase Conservatives' Clout," *Wall Street Journal,* 18 June 1986.

23. Rita Ciolli, "Rehnquist Denies He Harassed Voters," *Newsday,* 31 July 1986; Norman Hill, "Rehnquist's Rights Record Is a Disgrace," *Philadelphia Tribune,* 22 August 1986; Glen Elsasser, "Rehnquist, Scalia Get Senate Confirmation," *Chicago Tribune,* 18 September 1986; Stuart Taylor Jr., "Rehnquist and Scalia Take Their Places on Court," *New York Times,* 27 September 1986.

24. George J. Church, "The Court's Pivot Man," *Time,* 6 July 1987.

25. Andrew Hartman, *A War for the Soul of America: A History of the Culture Wars* (Chicago: University of Chicago Press, 2015), 152–54; James Davison Hunter, *Culture Wars: The Struggle to Define America* (New York: Basic Books, 1991), 252.

26. Ethan Bronner, *Battle for Justice: How the Bork Nomination Shook America* (New York: W. W. Norton, 1989), 84; Hunter, *Culture Wars,* 252–53.

27. Richard Lacayo, "The Battle Begins," *Time,* 13 July 1987.

28. Bronner, *Battle for Justice,* 146, 297.

29. "Ginsburg's Wife Did 2 Abortions in Residency," *Los Angeles Times,* 2 November 1987; James Gerstenzang, "Ginsburg Withdraws, Citing Furor Over Use of Marijuana," *Los Angeles Times,* 8 November 1987.

30. Al Kamen, "Kennedy Confirmed, 97–0," *Washington Post,* 4 February 1988.

31. Lena Williams, "600 in Gay Demonstration Arrested at Supreme Court," *New York Times,* 14 October 1987.

32. Cathy J. Cohen, *The Boundaries of Blackness: AIDS and the Breakdown of Black Politics* (Chicago: University of Chicago Press, 1997), 153.

33. John Leland, "Twilight of a Difficult Man," *New York Times,* 19 May 2017.

34. *HIV and AIDS 1981–2000,* Center for Disease Control, 1 January 2001.

35. "Listen to Reagan's Press Secretary Laugh About Gay People Dying of AIDS," *Slate,* 1 December 2015.

36. Nina Biddle, Lisa Conte, and Edwin Diamond, "AIDS in the Media: Entertainment or Infotainment," in *Effective Health Communication for the 90s,* ed. Scott C. Ratzan (London: Routledge, 1993), 143.

37. Randy Shilts, *And the Band Played On: Politics, People and the AIDS Epidemic* (New York: St. Martin's Press, 1987), 573–82; Bernard J. Turnock, *Public Health: What It Is and How It Works* (Burlington, MA: Jones and Bartlett, 2012), 205.

38. Michael Schaller, *Ronald Reagan: America and Its President in the 1980s* (New York: Oxford University Press, 1992), 94.

39. Bill Press, *How the Republicans Stole Religion: Why the Religious Right Is Wrong About Faith & Politics and What We Can Do To Make It Right* (New York: Three Leaves Press, 2005), 155; Hartman, *A War for the Soul of America,* 156.

40. Gillian Frank, "Phyllis Schlafly's Legacy of Anti-Gay Activism," *Slate,* 6 September 2016.

41. Cynthia Carr, *Fire in the Belly: The Life and Times of David Wojnarowicz* (New York: Bloomsbury, 2012), 350–53.

42. "Silence=Death," Primary Source Sets: ACT UP and the AIDS Crisis, Digital Public Library of America.

43. "Today in Gay History," Back2Stonewall.com.

44. Gerald Boyd, "Reagan Urges Abstinence for Young to Avoid AIDS," *New York Times,* 2 April 1987.

45. *The AIDS Research Program of the National Institutes of Health* (Washington, DC: National Academies Press, 1991).

46. *Understanding AIDS,* 1988, US National Library of Medicine.
47. "Before Occupy: How AIDS Activists Seized Control of the FDA in 1988," *The Atlantic,* 6 December 2011.
48. US Food and Drug Administration, *Expanded Access and Expedited Approval of New Therapies Related to HIV/AIDS,* Washington, DC, online material.

Chapter 9: NEW WORLD ORDERS

1. Tom Bethell, "Can GOP Handle Its Iowa Surprise?: Conservatives Fear a Bork-Type Battle While Democrats Need Secret Ballot," *Los Angeles Times,* 10 February 1988.
2. John Corry, "Fireworks, Not Issues, in the News," *New York Times,* 18 February 1988.
3. Jon Margolis, "Bush Rolls in New Hampshire," *Chicago Tribune,* 18 February 1988; Adam Clymer, "Democrats Use Humor and Scorn in Mounting Attack Against Bush," *New York Times,* 20 July 1988; Jack Nelson, "Bush Promises New Policies to Build on Reagan's Record," *Los Angeles Times,* 19 August 1988; Lou Cannon, "Conservatives Laud Choice," *Washington Post,* 17 August 1988.
4. William Schneider, "Democrats: Nobody Here But Us Moderates," *Los Angeles Times,* 24 July 1988; Kevin Phillips, "Dukakis: Election Prospects and Post-Election Caveats," *Christian Science Monitor,* 2 August 1988.
5. Ed Rollins, *Bare Knuckles and Back Rooms: My Life in American Politics* (New York: Broadway Books, 1997), 125–28; Sidney Blumenthal, *Pledging Allegiance: The Last Campaign of the Cold War* (New York: HarperCollins, 1990), 257–60.
6. John Taylor, "Pawing the Dirt," *New York Magazine,* 17 August 1992, 16; John Robert Greene, *The Presidency of George Bush* (Lawrence: University Press of Kansas, 2000), 33–34.
7. "Boogie Man: The Lee Atwater Story," PBS Documentary, http://www.pbs.org/wgbh/pages/frontline/atwater/etc/script.html; John Brady, *Bad Boy: The Life and Politics of Lee Atwater* (Reading, MA: Addison-Wesley, 1996), 19.
8. Brady, *Bad Boy,* 182; Timothy McNulty, "'Outrageous' Debate Question Angers Kitty Dukakis," *Chicago Tribune,* 15 October 1988.
9. Henry Allen, "To the Polls, Grudgingly," *Washington Post,* 9 November 1988; Richard L. Berke, "50.16 Percent Voter Turnout Was Lowest Since 1924," *New York Times,* 18 December 1988.
10. Owen Ullmann, "Bush's Policy Towards Iraq Invited Exaggerations," *Philadelphia Inquirer,* 20 October 1992; Robert S. Greenberger, "U.N. Security Council Clears Use of Force to Oust Iraq From Kuwait After Jan. 15," *Wall Street Journal,* 30 November 1990; Tom Kenworthy and Helen Dewar, "Divided Congress Grants President Authority to Wage War Against Iraq," *Washington Post,* 13 January 1991.
11. Rick Atkison, "U.S. Victory Is Absolute," *Washington Post,* 1 March 1991.
12. "Transcript of President's State of the Union Message to Nation," *New York Times,* 30 January 1991; Jeffrey A. Engel, *When the World Seemed New: George* H. W. *Bush and the End of the Cold War* (Boston: Houghton Mifflin, 2017), 415–39.
13. Chester Pach, "Lyndon Johnson's Living Room War," *New York Times,* 30 March 2017.
14. Philip Seib, "Introduction," in Seib, ed., *Media and Conflict in the Twenty-First Century* (New York: Palgrave-McMillan, 2005), 11; Rick Atkison, *Crusade: The Untold Story of the Persian Gulf War* (New York: Houghton Mifflin, 1993), 416; Martha Brannigan, "CNN Is Raising Its Advertising Rates As Gulf War Sends Ratings Soaring," *Wall Street Journal,* 1 February 1991.
15. Editorial, "The President's Popularity," *New York Times,* 5 March 1991; Maureen

Dowd, "Unable to Out-Hero Bush, Democrats Just Join Him," *New York Times*, 8 March 1991.

16. Editorial, "The President's Popularity," *New York Times*, 5 March 1991; Michael R. Kagay, "History Suggests Bush's Popularity Will Ebb," *New York Times*, 22 May 1991.

17. Geraldine Fabrikant, "The Deal for MCA," *New York Times*, 27 November 1990.

18. John M. Berry, "Jobless Rate Hit 7.8 Pct. In June," *Washington Post*, 3 July 1992; Patrice Apodaca, "Facing 'Edge of a Cliff' at GM," *Los Angeles Times*, 9 April 1991; Agis Salpukas, "Its Cash Depleted, Pan Am Shuts Down," *New York Times*, 5 December 1991; Clyde H. Farnsworth, "U.S. Hardens Trade Stance with Japan," *New York Times*, 7 January 1991; James Risen, "Slow Growth Seen Plaguing Economy for Years to Come," *Los Angeles Times*, 25 November 1991.

19. James M. Poterba, "Federal Budget Policy in the 1980s," in *American Economic Policy in the 1980s*, ed. Martin Feldstein (Chicago: University of Chicago Press, 1995), 235; Congressional Budget Office, *Budget, 1990–1994*.

20. Bob Woodward, "In His Debut in Washington Power Struggles, Gingrich Threw a Bomb," *Washington Post*, 24 December 2011.

21. Judith A. Layzer, "Environmental Policy from 1980 to 2008: The Politics of Prevention," in *Conservatism and American Political Development*, ed. Brian J. Glenn and Steven M. Teles (New York: Oxford University Press, 2009), 234.

22. Richard Conniff, "The Political History of Cap and Trade," *Smithsonian*, August 2009; James Morton Turner and Andrew C. Isenberg, *The Republican Reversal: Conservatives and the Environment from Nixon to Trump* (Cambridge, MA: Harvard University Press, 2018), 115–21.

23. Don Shannon, "Spirits Soar as Bush Signs Disabled Rights Act Into Law," *Los Angeles Times*, 27 July 1990.

24. Al Kamen, "5–4 Ruling Stops Short of Overturning 'Roe,'" *Washington Post*, 4 July 1989.

25. David G. Savage, "Souter Wins Confirmation to High Court," *Los Angeles Times*, 3 October 1990; Douglas Frantz, "Thomas Seems Sure to Face Criticism on EEOC Policies," *Los Angeles Times*, 3 July 1991.

26. Hartman, *A War for the Soul of America*, 154; Edward Lazarus, *Closed Chambers: The Rise, Fall and Future of the Modern Supreme Court* (New York: Penguin Books, 2005), 451; Jane Mayer, *Strange Justice: The Selling of Clarence Thomas* (Boston: Houghton Mifflin, 1994), 30.

27. "Excerpts from Senate's Hearings on the Thomas Nomination," *New York Times*, 12 September 1991.

28. Sascha Cohen, "A Brief History of Sexual Harassment in America Before Anita Hill," *Time*, 15 April 2016.

29. Jane Mayer, *Strange Justice: The Selling of Clarence Thomas* (New York: Plume, 1994).

30. Brent Staples, "Lynching, as Surreal Slogan: Under Fire, the Judge Becomes the Victim," *New York Times*, 17 October 1991; Melissa Healy, "Thomas Confirmed, 52 to 48," *Los Angeles Times*, 16 October 1991.

31. Thomas B. Rosenstiel, "Television Leads Many Viewers to Second-Guess Jury," *Los Angeles Times*, 3 May 1992.

32. Hugh Hewitt, "When Television Throws a Riot," *Los Angeles Times*, 3 May 1992; Richard W. Stevenson, "Blacks Beat White Truck Driver as Cameras Record the Scene," *New York Times*, 1 May 1992; Howard Rosenberg, "TV's Own Domino Effect," *Los Angeles Times*, 15 May 1992.

33. Greg Krikorian and David Ferrell, "Impact of Beating Deals a Blow to Officers'

Image," *Los Angeles Times*, 9 March 1991; Seth Mydans, "Verdicts Set Off a Wave of Shock and Anger," *New York Times*, 30 April 1992; R. W. Apple Jr., "Riots and Ballots," *New York Times*, 2 May 1992.

34. E. J. Dionne Jr., "Buchanan Heaps Scorn on Democrats," *Washington Post*, 18 August 1992.

35. Patrick J. Buchanan, "Culture War Speech: Address to the Republican National Convention, 17 August 1992," http://voicesofdemocracy.umd.edu/buchanan-culture-war-speech-speech-text/, accessed 6 July 2015.

36. Walter Goodman, "The Republicans Play a Discordant Tune," *New York Times*, 19 August 1992.

37. Lloyd Grove, "Troublemaker: A Biography of Molly Ivins, an Unreconstructed Texas Liberal," *New York Times*, 27 December 2009.

38. "Approval Rating Drops in Survey: US Election," *South China Morning Post*, 10 June 1992; Andrew Rosenthal, "G.O.P. Plotting 2-Edged Effort to Bolster Bush," *New York Times*, 19 July 1992.

39. Sharon LaFraniere, "Governor's Camp Feels His Record on Crime Can Stand the Heat," *Washington Post*, 5 October 1992; Thomas B. Edsall, "Clinton Stuns Rainbow Coalition," *Washington Post*, 14 June 1992.

40. Howard Kurtz, "Campaign '92: 30-Second Politics," *Washington Post*, 8 October 1992; David E. Rosenbaum, "Skipping Ahead: On the Economy, Bush Tries to Keep Focus on the Future," *New York Times*, 13 September 1992.

41. Elizabeth Kolbert, "For Perot, What TV Gives It Can Also Take Away," *New York Times*, 9 May 1992; Cheryl Lavin, "Perot Talks: 'Deep Voodoo' and Other Topical Asides," *Chicago Tribune*, 24 May 1992; John Dillin, "Ross Perot Takes His Schoolmaster Campaign Nationwide in Lectures," *Christian Science Monitor*, 22 October 1992.

42. R. W. Apple Jr., "Clinton, Savoring Victory, Sizes Up Job Ahead," *New York Times*, 5 November 1992.

Chapter 10: THE ROARING 1990S

1. Erin Hatton, "The Rise of the Permanent Temp Economy," *New York Times*, 26 January 2013.

2. Lawrence Mishel and Jarod Bernstein, *The State of Working America, 1994–1995* (Washington, DC: M. E. Sharpe, 1994), 236.

3. Gwen Ifill, "Clinton's Blunt Reminder of the Mood That Elected Him," *New York Times*, 24 January 1993.

4. Dan Balz, "Can Clinton Bring Discipline to Economy?" *Washington Post*, 17 January 1993.

5. Richard L. Berke, "Clinton Aides Wondering, 'Where's Our Honeymoon?'" *New York Times*, 16 January 1993.

6. Thomas E. Ricks, "Clinton Reiterates He'll End Military's Ban on Homosexuals; Opposition Grows," *Wall Street Journal*, 26 January 1993.

7. Paul V. Horwitz, "'Don't Ask, Don't Tell, Don't Pursue'" Is White House's Compromise Solution," *New York Times*, 20 July 1993.

8. Ifill, "Clinton's Blunt Reminder"; Simon Tisdall, "Clinton Hit by Second Withdrawal," *Guardian*, 6 February 1993; Howard Kurtz, "Talk Radio's Early Word on Zoe Baird," *Washington Post*, 23 January 1993.

9. David Johnston, "U.S. Saw Waco Assault as Best Option," *New York Times*, 25 April 1993.

10. "Questions Arise Over FBI Role in 'Travelgate,'" *Christian Science Monitor*, 26 May 1993; Charles Donovan and Teresa Donovan, "Filegate: A Family Affair," *Wall Street Journal*, 2 July 1996.

11. Glenn Kessler, "History Lesson: More Republicans Than Democrats Supported NAFTA," *Washington Post*, 9 May 2016.

12. "Poll: Missile Attack Boosts Clinton Image," *Jerusalem Post*, 30 June 1993; Richard Morin, "President Perot? How the Impossible Could Happen," *Washington Post*, 30 May 1993; *Time*, 7 June 1993.

13. Karen Tumulty and William J. Eaton, "Clinton Budget Triumphs, 51–50," *Los Angeles Times*, 7 August 1993.

14. "Federal Net Outlays as Percent of Gross Domestic Product," Federal Reserve Bank of St. Louis Economic Research.

15. Maya Macguineas, "The Saving Grace of a Little Federal Debt," *Washington Post*, 7 January 2001.

16. Eric Pianin and David Hilzenrath, "House Passes Clinton Budget Plan by 2 Votes," *Washington Post*, 6 August 1993.

17. Garry Wills, "The Clinton Principle," *New York Times*, 19 January 1997.

18. Sidney Blumenthal, *The Clinton Wars* (New York: Farrar, Straus and Giroux, 2003), 115–22; Patterson, *Restless Giant*, 328–30.

19. Elizabeth Kolbert, "New Arena for Campaign Ads: Health Care," *New York Times*, 21 October 1993.

20. Garry Wills, "The Clinton Principle," *New York Times*, 19 January 1997.

21. Dan Balz and Ronald Brownstein, *Storming the Gates: Protest Politics and the Republic Revival* (Boston: Little, Brown, 1996), 118–19.

22. Balz and Brownstein, *Storming the Gates*, 120–21.

23. Julian E. Zelizer, *Pirate Politics: Newt Gingrich, Speaker Jim Wright, and the Rise of a New Republican Party* (New York: Penguin Press, forthcoming); Steven M. Gillon, *The Pact: Bill Clinton, Newt Gingrich, and the Rivalry That Defined a Generation* (New York: Oxford University Press, 2008), 59–61; Balz and Brownstein, *Storming the Gates*, 123–26; John M. Barry, *The Ambition and the Power: The Fall of Jim Wright: A True Story of Washington* (New York: Viking, 1989).

24. Balz and Brownstein, *Storming the Gates*, 125.

25. Gillon, *The Pact*, 115; Bob Baker, "What's the Rush?" *Los Angeles Times*, 20 January 1991.

26. Nicole Hemmer, *Messengers of the Right: Conservative Media and the Transformation of American Politics* (Philadelphia: University of Pennsylvania Press, 2016), 263; Jeffrey Yorke, "Limbaugh, Bush's House Guest," *Washington Post*, 9 June 1992; Gillon, *The Pact*, 125; Stacy D. Kramer, "The Gospel According to Rush," *Chicago Tribune*, 30 November 1992; David Remnick, "Day of the Dittohead," *Washington Post*, 20 February 1994.

27. Eric Morgenthaler, "A Common Touch: 'Dittoheads' All Over Make Rush Limbaugh Superstar of the Right," *Wall Street Journal*, 28 June 1993; Milton Beckerman, Letter to the Editor, "Limbaugh's Vitriol Is No Laughing Matter," *Wall Street Journal*, 22 July 1993; Molly Ivins, "It Ain't Funny, Rush," *Washington Post*, 14 October 1993; Richard Cohen, "President Limbaugh?" *Washington Post*, 7 September 1993; Howard Kurtz, "Radio Daze," *Washington Post*, 24 October 1994.

28. "Language: A Key Mechanism for Control," copy reproduced online at *New York Times*, 27 January 2012; Gillon, *The Pact*, 123–25; Theda Skocpol, *Boomerang: Health Care Reform and the Turn against Government* (New York: W. W. Norton, 1997).

29. Katherine Q. Seelye, "Republicans Get a Pep Talk from Rush Limbaugh," *New York Times*, 12 December 1994.

30. Dale Russakoff, "Gingrich Lobs a Few More Bombs," *Washington Post*, 10 November 1994.

31. "Dr. Fell's Election," *New York Times*, 10 November 1994; Lloyd Grove, "How to Triangulate an Oval Office," *Washington Post*, 28 November 1995.

32. Ann Devroy, "Clinton Proposes 'Middle-Class Bill of Rights,'" *Washington Post*, 16 December 1994.

33. "Simple Chip Could Mean Control Over TV Violence," *New York Times*, 11 July 1995.

34. John F. Harris, "Clinton Backs Measures to Block Offensive TV," *The Washington Post*, 11 July 1995.

35. Jerry Gray, "House Passes Bar to U.S. Sanction of Gay Marriage," *New York Times*, 13 July 1996; Peter Baker, "President Quietly Signs Law Aimed at Gay Marriage," *Washington Post*, 22 September 1996.

36. Alison Mitchell, "Appeal to Voters," *New York Times*, 24 January 1996; John F. Harris, "Clinton Avows Support for Affirmative Action," *Washington Post*, 20 July 1995; Robert Pear, "Overhauling Welfare: A Look at the Year Ahead," *New York Times*, 7 August 1996.

37. Elaine Woo, "Barbara Coe Dies at 79; foe of services for those in U.S. illegally," *Los Angeles Times*, 4 September 2013.

38. R. W. Apple Jr., "A Media-Wise Governor Runs a Smooth Race in California," *New York Times*, 24 October 1994; Anna Quindlen, "Bigots' Lament: 'They Keep Coming,'" *St. Louis Post-Dispatch*, 1 November 2004; "Polls Show Support for California Immigration Proposal," *New York Times*, 16 October 1994.

39. Southern Poverty Law Center, "The Second Wave," 31 July 2009.

40. Todd S. Purdum, "Terror in Oklahoma," *New York Times*, 6 May 1996; John F. Harris, "Clinton Rejects 'Patriot' Claim of Armed Groups," *Washington Post*, 6 May 1995.

41. Todd S. Purdum, "Desperately in Need of Winning Streak, Clinton Finds One," *New York Times*, 7 May 1995.

42. Garry Wills, "A Tale of Two Cities," *New York Review of Books*, 3 October 1996; Kevin Merida, "Gingrich Pledges to Find 'Common Ground' with Clinton," *Washington Post*, 7 November 1996.

Chapter 11: SCANDALIZED

1. Nicole Hemmer, *Messengers of the Right: Conservative Media and the Transformation of American Politics* (Philadelphia: University of Pennsylvania Press, 2016), 265–66.

2. Howard Kurtz, "Is Fox's News Channel Cable-Ready?" *Washington Post*, 14 October 1996.

3. Alyssa Rosenberg, "Before Roger Ailes Created Fox News, He Made Richard Nixon the Star of His Own Show," *Washington Post*, 18 May 2017; Joe McGinnis, *The Selling of the President* (New York: Simon & Schuster, 1969); Gabriel Sherman, *The Loudest Voice in the Room: How the Brilliant, Bombastic Roger Ailes Built Fox News—and Divided a Country* (New York: Random House, 2014), 34–98.

4. Lawrie Mifflin, "At the New Fox News Channel, the Buzzword is Fairness," *New York Times*, 7 October 1996; "Fox to Start a Channel for Cable Viewers in October," *New York Times*, 19 July 1996.

5. Kurtz, "Is Fox's News Channel Cable-Ready?"

6. Howard Kurtz, "Campaign Fund Hearings Barely Visible on Television," *Washington Post*, 15 July 1997.

7. Howard Kurtz, "The Dirt on Matt Drudge," *Washington Post*, 19 May 1997; Ethan Bronner, "Reports of Sexual Scandal Have Everybody Talking," *New York Times*, 23 January 1998.

8. Lisa de Moraes, "22.5 Million Watched Tape," *Washington Post*, 23 September 1998.

9. Eric Pianin, "Clinton Impeached," *Washington Post*, 20 December 1998; James N. Thurman, "The Media Prepares to Turn a Page," *Christian Science Monitor*, 1 February 1999; Bill Carter, "Viewers Tune in for Clinton Vote," *New York Times*, 23 December 1998. For more on the Clinton impeachment, see Peter Baker, *The Breach: Inside the Impeachment Trial of William Jefferson Clinton* (New York: Simon & Schuster, 2000); Richard A. Posner, *An Affair of State: The Investigation, Impeachment, and Trial of President Clinton* (Cambridge, MA: Harvard University Press, 1999).

10. Marjorie Williams, "Clinton and Women," *Vanity Fair* (May 1998): 194–97, 250–53.

11. Claudia Puig, "'Shock Jock' Howard Stern Readies His L.A. Offensive," *Los Angeles Times*, 27 June 1991.

12. Kevin Goldman, "Infinity Broadcasting Scores with Hands-Off Formula," *Wall Street Journal*, 16 March 1992.

13. Edmund L. Andrews, "Howard Stern Is the Object of FCC Fine," *New York Times*, 28 October 1992.

14. Paul Farhi, "Bad Taste, Good Business," *Washington Post*, 27 March 1994; David Hilzenrath and Cindy Skryzcki, "FCC Targets Employers of Radio 'Shock Jock,'" *Washington Post*, 1 January 1994.

15. Elizabeth Jensen, "Violence Floods Children's TV, New Study Says," *Wall Street Journal*, 20 September 1995.

16. James T. Patterson, *Restless Giant: The United States from Watergate to Bush v. Gore* (New York: Oxford University Press, 2005), 280.

17. Patterson, *Restless Giant*, 284.

18. Mireya Navarro, "Life of 22 Years Ends, but Not before Many Heard Message on AIDS," *New York Times*, 12 November 1994.

19. Stephanie Goldberg, "'The Real World' Turns 20," CNN.com, 23 May 2012.

20. John Paul Brammer, "'I'm Gay': It's Been Twenty Years Since Ellen Came Out on TV," *NBC News*, 27 April 2017; Tom Shales, "Will & Grace: Something Mild," *Washington Post*, 21 September 1998.

21. Caryn James, "In Pursuit of Love, Romantically or Not," *New York Times*, 5 June 1998; Nancy Hass, "'Sex' Sells, in the City and Elsewhere," *New York Times*, 11 July 1999; Tamara Ikenberg, "Life Imitating Art: Taking the 'Sex and the City' Tour in New York," *Jerusalem Post*, 7 April 2000.

22. Peter Bernstein, "Technological Change and First-Class Letter Mail," in *Diffusion to the Wire: Studies in Diffusion and Regulation of Telecommunications Technology*, ed. Allan Shampine (Hauppauge, NY: Nova, 2003), 94.

23. "Pornography," in *Contemporary American Politics and Society: Issues and Controversies*, ed. Robert Singh (London: Sage, 2003), 137.

24. Guy Gugliotta and Juliet Eilperin, "Gingrich Steps Down in Face of Rebellion," *Washington Post*, 7 November 1998; Martin Kettle, "Clinton's Poll Rating Soars," *Guardian*, 22 December 1998; Eric Schmitt, "In the End, Senate Passes No Harsh Judgment on Clinton," *New York Times*, 13 February 1999.

25. "Satisfaction with the United States," http://news.gallup.com/poll/1669/general-mood-country.aspx; "Economy," http://news.gallup.com/poll/1609/consumer-views-economy.aspx.

26. Transcript, "2000 State of the Union Address," *Washington Post*, 27 January 2000.

27. Illana DeBare, "Young, Rich, Now What?" *San Francisco Gate*, 4 June 1999.

28. Gary Rivlin, "If You Can Make It in Silicon Valley, You Can Make It . . . In Silicon Valley Again," *New York Times*, 5 June 2005.

29. Rivlin, "If You Can Make It in Silicon Valley."

30. Margaret Pugh O'Mara, *Cities of Knowledge: Cold War Science and the Search for the Next Silicon Valley* (Princeton, NJ: Princeton University Press, 2005), 71–75; Amy Harmon, "Stocks Drive a Rush to Riches in Manhattan's Silicon Alley," *New York Times*, 31 May 1999.

31. The Center for an Urban Future, *Why New York Needs a Jobs Policy*, December 1998.

32. Steven Greenhouse, "Janitors Struggle at the Edges of Silicon Valley's Success," *New York Times*, 18 April 2000.

33. Lawrence Mishel, "CEO-to-Worker Pay Imbalance Grows," *Economic Policy Institute*, 21 June 2006.

34. Jacob Hacker, *The Great Risk Shift: The New Economic Insecurity and the Decline of the American Dream* (New York: Oxford University Press, 2008).

35. Michael B. Katz, *The Price of Citizenship: Redefining the American Welfare State* (New York: Metropolitan, 2001), 33–58.

36. Greg J. Duncan and Jeanne Brooks-Gunn, "Urban Poverty, Welfare Reform, and Child Development," in *Locked in the Poorhouse: Cities, Race, and Poverty in the United States*, ed. Fred R. Harris and Lynn A. Curtis (Lanham, MD: Rowan & Littlefield, 2000), 15–17.

37. Julilly Kohler-Hausmann, *Getting Tough: Welfare and Imprisonment in 1970s America* (Princeton, NJ: Princeton University Press, 2017), 88–106; James Forman Jr., *Locking Up Our Own: Crime and Punishment in Black America* (New York: Farrar, Straus and Giroux, 2017), 151–84; Ann Devroy, "Crime Bill Is Signed With Flourish," *Washington Post*, 14 September 1994; Anthony Lewis, "Crime and Politics," *New York Times*, 16 September 1994.

38. Eric Schlosser, "The Prison-Industrial Complex," *The Atlantic*, December 1998, 51–77.

39. Manning Marable, "Along the Color Line: Racism, Prisons and the Future of Black America," *Los Angeles Sentinel*, 31 August and 7 September 2000.

40. Susan Pulliam and Terzah Ewing, "Fast-Forward Stocks Meet Rewind Button," *Wall Street Journal*, 22 March 2000.

41. Robert McMillan, "Turns out the Dot-Com Bust's Worst Flops Were Actually Fantastic Deals," *Wired*, 8 December 2014; Ernie Smith, "All Sock Puppets Go to Heaven," *Tedium*, 12 January 2017; Mike Tarsalasa, "Pets.com Killed by Sock Puppet," *Marketwatch*, 8 November 2000; "Pets.com Latest High-Profile Dot-Com Disaster," CNET, 2 January 2002; Johnny Ryan, *A History of the Internet and the Digital Future* (London: Reaktion Books, 2010), 129.

42. Ben Geier, "What Did We Learn from the DotCom Stock Bubble of 2000," *Time*, 2015.

43. Editorial, "The Dot-Com Bubble Bursts," *New York Times*, 24 December 2000.

44. Reed Abelson, "Pets.com, Sock Puppet's Home, Will Close," *New York Times*, 8 November 2000.

45. Abelson, "Pets.com, Sock Puppet's Home, Will Close."

46. "Satisfaction with the United States," http://news.gallup.com/poll/1669/general-mood-country.aspx; "Presidential Approval Ratings—Bill Clinton," http://news.gallup.com/poll/116584/presidential-approval-ratings-bill-clinton.aspx.

47. Frank Bruni, "House Republicans Stung By Bush's Criticism," *New York Times*, 2 October 1999; Richard L. Berke, "Triangulation: Politics' New Geometry Is Old Math," *New York Times*, 17 October 1999.

48. Paul Gigot, "So What Happened to Those Great Gore Issues?" *Wall Street Journal*, 20 October 2000; Jon Schwartz, "Gore Deserves Some Internet Credit, Some Say," *Washington Post*, 21 March 1999.

49. Evgenia Peretz, "Going After Gore," *Vanity Fair*, 4 September 2007.

50. "Trigger Happy Election Calls," *Christian Science Monitor*, 10 November 2000.

51. Chris Smith, *The Daily Show (The Book): An Oral History as Told by Jon Stewart, the Correspondents, Staff and Guests* (New York: Grand Central, 2016), 50.

52. Transcript, Ron Elving, "The Color of Politics: How Did Red States and Blue States Come to Be?" *All Things Considered*, National Public Radio, 13 November 2014; Tom Zeller, "One State, Two State, Red State, Blue State," *New York Times*, 8 February 2004.

53. Ford Fessenden, "Florida List for Purge of Voters Proves Flawed," *New York Times*, 10 July 2004; Gregory Palast, "Florida's Flawed 'Voter-Cleansing' Program," *Salon .com*, 4 December 2000.

54. Linda Greenhouse, "Bush Prevails: By Single Vote, Justices End Recount, Blocking Gore After 5-Week Struggle," *New York Times*, 13 December 2000.

Chapter 12: Compassion and Terror

1. Adam Clymer, "Filter Aid to Poor Through Churches, Bush Urges," *New York Times*, 23 July 1999; Richard L. Berke, "Bush Tests Presidential Run with a Flourish," *New York Times*, 8 March 1999; "Compassionate Conservatism," Press Release, Office of the Press Secretary, White House, 30 April 2002, http://georgewbush-whitehouse .archives.gov/news/releases/2002/04/text/20020430.html.

2. Lou Cannon and Carl M. Cannon, *Reagan's Disciple: George W. Bush's Troubled Quest for a Presidential Legacy* (New York: Public Affairs, 2008); Julian Borger, "Bush Kills Global Warming Treaty," *Guardian*, 29 March 2001; Meg Jacobs, "Wreaking Havoc from Within: George W. Bush's Energy Policy in Historical Perspective"; David Greenberg, "Creating Their Own Reality: The Bush Administration and Expertise in a Polarized Age," in *The Presidency of George W. Bush: A First Historical Assessment*, ed. Julian E. Zelizer (Princeton, NJ: Princeton University Press, 2010), 139–68, 213–14; Eric Planin, "Bush Plans to Shift Some EPA Enforcement to the States," *Washington Post*, 22 July 2001.

3. Scott Greenberg, "Looking Back at the Bush Tax Cuts, Fifteen Years Later," *Tax Foundation*, 7 June 2016; George W. Bush, Presidential Press Conference, 29 March 2001; Andrew Glass, "President Bush Signs Tax Cut into Law, June 7, 2001," *Politico*, 7 June 2016; Robin Toner, "Capitalist Tools: Cutting a Rightward Path," *New York Times*, 4 March 2001.

4. "Compassionate Conservatism," Press Release.

5. David Kuo, *Tempting Faith: An Inside Story of Political Seduction* (New York: Free Press, 2006), 126–28; Paul Kegor, *God and George W. Bush: A Spiritual Life* (New York: ReganBooks, 2004), 69; Clymer, "Filter Aid to Poor"; Terry M. Neal, "Bush Outlines Charity-Based Social Policies," *Washington Post*, 23 July 1999.

6. Kuo, *Tempting Faith*, 138–41.

7. Amy E. Black, Douglas L. Koopman, and David K. Ryden, *Of Little Faith: The Pol-*

itics of George W. Bush's Faith-Based Initiatives (Washington, DC: Georgetown University Press, 2004), 190.

8. Kuo, *Tempting Faith*, 166; Black, Koopman, and Ryden, *Of Little Faith*, 205, 125; Ron Suskind, "Why Are These Men Laughing?" *Esquire*, January 2003.

9. Black et al., *Of Little Faith*, 145, 164–65; Kevin M. Kruse, "Compassionate Conservatism: Religion in the Age of George W. Bush," in *The Presidency of George W. Bush*, 237–38.

10. "Congress Pushes for School Reforms," *New York Times*, 4 December 2001.

11. "No Child Left Behind Act," *Pittsburgh Courier*, 26 January 2002.

12. Kate Zernike, "School Dress Codes vs. a Sea of Bare Flesh," Jim Dwyer, "As Campaign Din Hits Peak, City Voters Have Heard It All," Bill Carter, "In A Nation of Early Risers, Morning TV is a Hot Market," C. J. Chivers, "Traced on Internet, Teacher Is Charged In '71 Jet Hijacking," Sheryl Gay Stolberg, "Scientists Urge Bigger Supply of Stem Cells," and Alison Mitchel and Richard Stevenson, "Key Leaders Talk of Possible Deals to Revive the Economy," *New York Times*, 11 September 2001.

13. Lisa Finnegan, *No Questions Asked: News Coverage Since 9/11* (Westport, CT: Praeger, 2007), 24.

14. Jane Fritsch, "Rescue Workers Rush In, But Many Do Not Return," *New York Times*, 12 September 2001; R. W. Apple Jr., "A Day of Terror," *New York Times*, 12 September 2001.

15. "Excerpts From President's Remarks on Investigation into Attacks," *New York Times*, 14 September 2001; Apple, "A Day of Terror"; Alison Mitchell and Katharine Q. Seelye, "A Day of Terror," *New York Times*, 12 September 2001.

16. Apple, "A Day of Terror."

17. Robert D. McFadden, "President, In New York, Offers Resolute Vows Atop the Rubble," *New York Times*, 15 November 2001.

18. Jonathan Alter, "Grits, Guts and Rudy Giuliani," *Newsweek*, 24 September 2001.

19. "Congress Approves Resolution Authorizing Force," *CNN.com*, 15 September 2001.

20. "Muslim Americans," *Pew Research Center*, 30 August 2011; Khalid Duran and Daniel Pipes, "Muslim Immigrants in the United States," *Center for Immigration Studies*, 1 August 2002.

21. Jodi Wilgoren, "A Nation Challenged: Arab Americans," *New York Times*, 4 November 2001.

22. Dana Milbank, "Bush Visits Mosque to Forestall Hate Crimes," *Washington Post*, 18 September 2001.

23. Milbank, "Bush Visits Mosque"; Samuel G. Freedman, "Six Days After 9/11, Another Anniversary Worth Honoring," *New York Times*, 7 September 2012.

24. "NYC Mayor to SNL: It's OK to Laugh," *ABC News*, 1 October 2001.

25. David E. Sanger and Steven Lee Myers, "President Says U.S. 'In Hot Pursuit' of Terror Group," *New York Times*, 29 September 2001.

26. "Use of Pinpoint Airpower Comes of Age in New War," *New York Times*, 24 December 2001.

27. "Brokaw May Have Been Exposed to Anthrax," *ABC News*, 15 October 2001.

28. Arthur Allen, "Anthrax Attack—or Panic Attack," *Salon*, 13 October 2001.

29. Robin Toner, "Bush Law-Enforcement Plan Troubles Both Right and Left," *New York Times*, 28 September 2001.

30. James Kuhnhenn, "House Passes Counterterrorism Bill," *Philadelphia Inquirer*, 25 October 2001.

31. "Idling on Airport Security," *New York Times*, 7 November 2001.

32. Lizette Alvarez, "Bush Seeking House Allies on Airport Security Plan," *New York*

Times, 1 November 2001; Robert Pear, "Congress Agrees to U.S. Takeover for Air Security," *New York Times*, 16 November 2001.

33. Barton Gellman, *Angler: The Cheney Vice Presidency* (New York: Penguin, 2009).

34. Gellman, *Angler*.

35. Tim Naftali, "George W. Bush and the War on Terror," in *The Presidency of George W. Bush*, 74.

36. Jane Mayer, *The Dark Side: The Inside Story of How the War on Terror Turned into a War on American Ideals* (New York: Doubleday, 2008); Tom Vanden Brook, "Waterboarding Didn't Work, Committee Report Finds," *USA Today*.

37. Jane Mayer, "Whatever It Takes," *The New Yorker*, 19 February 2007.

38. Dahlia Lithwick, "How Jack Bauer Shaped U.S. Torture Policy," *Newsweek*, 25 July 2008.

39. Nicholas Guyatt, *Another American Century?: The United States and the World Since 9/11* (London: Zed Books, 2003), 276–77.

40. "White House Scolds Maher Over Comments," *Ft. Wayne Journal-Gazette*, 27 September 2001; Bill Carter, "ABC to End 'Politically Incorrect,'" *New York Times*, 14 May 2002.

41. James Mann, *Rise of the Vulcans: The History of Bush's War Cabinet* (New York: Penguin, 2004).

42. Nicholas Lemann, "The Iraq Factor," *The New Yorker*, 22 January 2001; Spencer Ackerman and Franklin Foer, "The Radical," *New Republic*, 1 December 2003; Joel Roberts, "Plans for Iraq Attack Began on 9/11," *CBS News*, 4 September 2002.

43. Andy Barr, "Cleland Ad Causes Trouble for Chambliss," *Politico*, 12 November 2008; Julian E. Zelizer, *Arsenal of Democracy: The Politics of National Security from World War II to the War on Terrorism* (New York: Basic Books, 2010), 455.

44. John Schwartz, "U.S. to Drop Color-Coded Terror Alerts," *New York Times*, 24 November 2010; Jack Hitt, "The Business of Fear in This Era of Color-Coded Terror Alerts," *CNN.com*, 1 June 2003.

45. Kruse, "Compassionate Conservatism," 240–41.

46. Kruse, "Compassionate Conservatism," 241.

47. Kaplan, *With God on their Side*, 154.

48. Ron Suskind, "Faith, Certainty and the Presidency of George W. Bush," *New York Times Magazine*, 17 October 2004; Greenberg, "Creating their Own Reality."

49. Howard LaFranchi and Ann Scott Tyson, "Powell's 'Big Moment': Can He Sway a Skeptical World?" *Christian Science Monitor*, 5 February 2003.

50. Lynette Clemetson, "Protest Groups Using Updated Tactics to Spread Antiwar Message," *New York Times*, 15 January 2003; Robert D. McFadden, "From New York to Melbourne, Cries for Peace," *New York Times*, 16 February 2003.

51. Tom Shales, "A Media Role in Selling the War? No Question," *Washington Post*, 25 April 2007; "MSNBC Cancels Phil Donahue," *New York Times*, 26 February 2003.

52. Warren St. John, "Backlash Grows Against Celebrity Activists," *New York Times*, 23 March 2003.

53. Deglan de Breadun, "US Plans to Win Over Media and Public Opinion," *Irish Times*, 19 March 2003; Frank Rich, "Iraq Around the Clock," *New York Times*, 30 March 2003.

54. David Bauder, "Embedded War Reporters: Experiment Passes Muster," *Toronto Globe and Mail*, 23 April 2003; Matt Wells, "Embedded War Reporters 'Sanitised' Iraq War," *Guardian*, 6 November 2003.

55. Maureen Dowd, "The Iceman Cometh," *New York Times*, 4 May 2003; Frank Rich, *The Greatest Story Ever Sold: The Decline and Fall of Truth from 9/11 to Katrina*

(New York: Penguin, 2006), 73–91; "Mission Accomplished," *Media Matters for America*, 27 April 2006, https://www.mediamatters.org/research/2006/04/27 /mission-accomplished-a-look-back-at-the-medias/135513.

56. David Folkenflik, "Fox News Defends Its 'Patriotic' Coverage," *Baltimore Sun*, 2 April 2003.

57. Gail Russell Chaddock, "Congress Hits Warpath on Iraq Funding Issues," *Christian Science Monitor,* 7 October 2003.

58. Kurt Eichenwald, "The Deafness Before the Storm," *New York Times,* 10 September 2012.

59. Seymour M. Hersh, "Torture at Abu Ghraib," *The New Yorker,* 10 May 2004.

60. Transcript, *CNN,* Paula Zahn Show, 6 May 2004.

61. "Abu Guantanamo," *Der Spiegel,* 17 February 2006.

62. "Presidential Approval Ratings—George W. Bush," http://news.gallup.com/ poll/116500/presidential-approval-ratings-george-bush.aspx; Adam Nagourney and Janet Elder, "Bush's Approval Ratings Climb In Days After Hussein's Capture," *New York Times,* 17 December 2003.

Chapter 13: THE POLITICS OF MASS DESTRUCTION

1. Robin Toner, "The Abortion Issue: Opponents of Abortion Cheer New Administration," *New York Times,* 23 January 2001.

2. Paul Kengor, *God and George W. Bush: A Spiritual Life* (New York: ReganBooks, 2004), 94; Esther Kaplan, *With God on Their Side: How Christian Fundamentalists Trumped Science, Policy, and Democracy in George W. Bush's White House* (New York: Free Press, 2004), 146–47; Kevin M. Kruse, "Compassionate Conservatism: Religion in the Age of George W. Bush," in *The Presidency of George W. Bush: A First Historical Assessment*, ed. Julian E. Zelizer (Princeton, NJ: Princeton University Press, 2010), 240.

3. Lydia Saad, "Gay Rights Attitudes," *Gallup News,* 20 May 2005; Kruse, "Compassionate Conservatism," 243; John Ritter, "Gay Marriage Backers Seize Opportunity," *USA Today,* 22 March 2004; Rick Klein, "Vote Ties Civil Unions to Gay Marriage," *Boston Globe,* 30 March 2004.

4. Kaplan, *With God on their Side,* 156–61.

5. Jacques Steinberg, "Liberal Voices (Some Sharp) Get a New Home on the Radio Dial," *New York Times,* 31 March 2004; Alessandra Stanley, "Talk Network Makes Debut, With Rage a No-Show," *New York Times,* 1 April 2004; Jacques Steinberg, "Office Politics Give Liberal Radio a Rocky Start," *New York Times,* 31 May 2004; Jeff Leeds, "Air America, Home of Liberal Talk, Files for Bankruptcy Protection," *New York Times,* 14 October 2006.

6. Bruce Weber, "Strategy and Spin Are Cool, But Voters Like to Laugh," *New York Times,* 8 March 2004; Frazier Moore, "Jon Stewart Takes on Four More Years of Satire," *Toronto Globe and Mail,* 19 March 2004; Warren St. John, "The Week That Wasn't: Fake News Is More Trusted, and More Popular, Than Ever," *New York Times,* 3 October 2004; Matthew Baum, *Soft News Goes to War: Public Opinion an American Foreign Policy in the New Media Age* (Princeton, NJ: Princeton University Press, 2003).

7. Transcript, "Jon Stewart's America," *Crossfire,* CNN.com, 15 October 2004; Alessandra Stanley, "No Jokes or Spin. It's Time (Gasp) to Talk," *New York Times,* 20 October 2004.

8. Steve Friess, "The Father of All Web Campaigns," *Politico,* 30 September 2012; Jennifer Stromer-Galley, *Presidential Campaigning in the Internet Age* (New York:

Oxford University Press, 2004), 1; "How the Internet Invented Howard Dean," *Wired*, 1 January 2004.

9. Matthew Klam, "Fear and Laptops on the Campaign Trail," *New York Times Magazine*, 26 September 2004.

10. Kruse, "Compassionate Conservatism," 245; Michelle Goldberg, *Kingdom Coming: The Rise of Christian Nationalism* (New York: Norton, 2007), 50–52; Mark J. Rozell, "Bush and the Christian Right: The Triumph of Pragmatism," in *Religion and the Bush Presidency*, ed. Mark J. Rozell and Gleaves Whitney (New York: Palgrave, 2007), 22–23.

11. Kruse, "Compassionate Conservatism," 246; Goldberg, *Kingdom Coming*, 56.

12. William A. Galston, "Why the 2005 Social Security Initiative Failed, and What It Means for the Future," Brookings Institution, 21 September 2007; Kruse, "Compassionate Conservatism," 246.

13. Kruse, "Compassionate Conservatism," 246–47.

14. Adam Nagourney, "GOP Right is Splintered on Schiavo Intervention," *New York Times*, 23 March 2005; Janet Cook, "Some in GOP Fear Effort May Alienate Voters," *Los Angeles Times*, 22 March 2005; John-Thor Dahlburg, "Judge Raises Doubts About Schiavo Case," *Los Angeles Times*, 22 March 2005.

15. Felicia Lee, "After the Flood, the Reckoning," *New York Times*, 3 August 2006; "Hurricane Katrina Statistics," *CNN.com*, 28 August 2017; Chris Weller, "These Two Photos Show the Amazing Resilience of One Hurricane," *Business Insider*, 27 August 2015.

16. Frank Rich, *The Greatest Story Ever Sold: The Decline and Fall of Truth from 9/11 to Katrina* (New York: Penguin, 2006), 199–205.

17. "Breakdowns Marked Path from Hurricane to Anarchy," *New York Times*, 11 September 2005; Douglas Brinkley, *The Great Deluge: Hurricane Katrina, New Orleans and the Mississippi Coast* (New York: Morrow, 2006).

18. Harris Gardiner, "Police in Suburbs Blocked Evacuees, Witnesses Report," *New York Times*, 10 September 2005; David Carr, "More Horrible Than Truth," *New York Times*, 19 September 2005.

19. Alessandra Stanley, "Reporters Turn From Deference to Outrage," *New York Times*, 5 September 2005.

20. David Sanger, "Hard New Test for President," *New York Times*, 1 September 2005.

21. Elisabeth Bumiller, "Casualty of a Firestorm: Outrage, Bush and FEMA's Chief," *New York Times*; Mark Leibovich, "The Punch Line Who Refuses to Fade Away," *New York Times*, 26 August 2006; Arthur Spiegelman, "Dubya's 'Brownie' Quote Takes the Cake," *Times of India*, 31 December 2005.

22. Megan Thee Brenan, "Poll Finds Disapproval of Bush Unwavering," *New York Times*, 17 January 2009; "Presidential Approval Ratings: George W. Bush," *Gallup News*, 2005; Jeffrey M. Jones, "Despite Recent Lows, Bush Approval Average is Midrange," *Gallup News*, 5 January 2005.

23. Jacques Steinberg, "'Daily Show' Personality Gets His Own Platform," *New York Times*, 4 May 2005; Jacques Steinberg, "Truthiness: Not Quite Fact, Not Quite Fiction," *New York Times*, 25 December 2005.

24. Russell Smith, "Dictionary Indulges in a Little Truthiness of Its Own," *Toronto Globe and Mail*, 14 December 2006; Jacques Steinberg, "After Press Dinner, the Blogs Are Alive With the Sound of Colbert Chatter," *New York Times*, 3 May 2006.

25. Stephen Rodrick, "Limbaugh for Lefties," *New York Magazine*, 24 October 2007.

26. Linda Greenhouse, "Supreme Court Blocks Guantanamo Tribunals," *New York Times*, 29 June 2006.

27. Rick Atkinson, "The IED Problem Is Getting Out of Control. We've Got to Stop the Bleeding," *Washington Post,* 30 September 2007.

28. Adam Nagourney and Jim Rutenburg, "Tables Turned on the G.O.P. over the Iraq Issue," *New York Times,* 19 October 2006.

29. Paul Koring, "Rumsfeld Pays the Price," *Toronto Globe and Mail,* 9 November 2006.

30. Gary Gerstle, "Minorities, Multiculturalism and the Presidency of George W. Bush," in *The Presidency of George W. Bush,* 262; Robert Pear and Carl Hulse, "Immigrant Bill Dies in Senate; Defeat for Bush," *New York Times,* 29 June 2007.

31. Paul Koring, "Rumsfeld Pays the Price," *Toronto Globe and Mail,* 9 November 2006; Charles Krauthammer, "The Surge: First Fruits," *Washington Post,* 13 April 2007.

32. "Program is a Top Source of Data," *Toronto Globe and Mail,* 7 June 2013.

Chapter 14: POLARIZED POLITICS

1. David Bernstein, "The Speech," *Chicago Magazine,* 29 May 2007.

2. Transcript, "Exclusive: Palin on Foreign Policy," *CBS News,* 25 September 2008.

3. "Number of Foreclosures Soared in 2007," *NBC News,* 29 January 2008; Buck Wargo, "Nevada Remains First in Foreclosures in 2008," *Las Vegas Sun,* 23 January 2009; Robin Urevich, "At Ground Zero of a National Housing Crisis," *Las Vegas Sun,* 13 August 2008.

4. Matthew Frankel, "The Biggest Mergers and Acquisitions in Banking," *The Motley Fool,* 22 April 2015.

5. Andrew Ross Sorkin, *Too Big to Fail: The Inside Story of How Wall Street and Washington Fought to Save the Financial System—And Themselves* (New York: Penguin, 2009), 357–66; Jacob S. Hacker and Paul Pierson, *Winner-Take-All Politics: How Washington Made the Rich Richer—And Turned Its Back on the Middle Class* (New York: Simon & Schuster, 2010), 197.

6. Andrew Ross Sorkin, "Lehman Files for Bankruptcy; Merrill Is Sold," *New York Times,* 14 September 2008.

7. Edmund L. Andrews, "Bush Officials Urge Swift Action on Broad Rescue Powers," *New York Times,* 20 September 2008; Peter Baker, "Labeled as a Bailout, Plan Was Hard to Sell to a Skeptical Public," *New York Times,* 1 October 2008; "World Leaders Urge US Action Amid Market Panic," *Korea Times,* 1 October 2008; Thomas Friedman, "Rescue the Rescue," *New York Times,* 1 October 2008.

8. Henry M. Paulson, *On the Brink: Inside the Race to Stop the Collapse of the Global Financial System* (New York: Business Plus, 2010), 290–91.

9. Liz Halloran, "McCain Suspends Campaign, Shocks Republicans," *US News and World Report,* 24 September 2008; Alan S. Blinder, *After the Music Stopped: The Financial Crisis, the Response and the Work Ahead* (New York: Penguin, 2013), 187–93.

10. Siri Agrell, "Comfortable Cushion for Obama: Democrats Make Gains in House, Senate," *Globe and Mail,* 5 November 2008; Michael Grunwald, *The New New Deal: The Hidden Story of Change in the Obama Era* (New York: Simon & Schuster, 2013), 140; Eric Rauchway, "Neither a Depression nor a New Deal: Bailout, Stimulus, and the Economy," and Paul Starr, "Achievement without Credit: The Obama Presidency and Inequality," in *The Presidency of Barack Obama,* ed. Julian E. Zelizer (Princeton, NJ: Princeton University Press, 2018), 30–44, 45–61.

11. Adam Nagourney, "OBAMA: Racial Barrier Falls in Decisive Victory," *New York Times,* 5 November 2008.

12. Frank Newport, "Americans See Obama Election as Race Relations Milestone," *Gallup News,* 7 November 2008.

13. Jeff Zeleny, "Gregg Ends Bid for Commerce Job," *New York Times*, 12 February 2009; John Harwood, "'Partisan' Seeks a Prefix: Bi- or Post-," *New York Times*, 7 December 2008.

14. Jonathan Weisman, "GOP Doubts, Fears 'Post-Partisan' Obama," *Washington Post*, 7 January 2008.

15. Paul Krugman, "The Obama Gap," *New York Times*, 8 January 2009.

16. Grunwald, *The New New Deal*, 141.

17. Grunwald, *The New New Deal*, 141–43.

18. Grunwald, *The New New Deal*, 145–46.

19. "Senate Republicans Square Off Against Stimulus Bill," *Los Angeles Times*, 2 February 2009.

20. Carl Hulse, "Specter Switches Parties," *New York Times*, 28 April 2009; Susan Davis, "Maine GOP Senator Olympia Snowe Won't Seek Re-Election," *USA Today*, 12 Feburary 2012.

21. "Obama Signs Stimulus Plan into Law," *CBS News*, 17 February 2009; Farhana Hossain, Amanda Cox, John McGrath, and Stephan Weitberg, "The Stimulus Plan: How to Spend $787 Billion," *New York Times*, 5 January 2017.

22. E. J. Dionne Jr., *Our Divided Political Heart: The Battle for the American Idea in an Age of Discontent* (New York: Bloomsbury, 2012), 29–31; David Brooks, "Money for Idiots," *New York Times*, 20 February 2009; Sheryl Gay Stolberg, "Critique of Housing Plan Draws Quick White House Offensive," *New York Times*, 21 February 2009; Brian Stelter, "CNBC Replays Its Reporter's Tirade," *New York Times*, 23 February 2009; David Carr, "Cable Wars Are Killing Objectivity," *New York Times*, 19 April 2009.

23. Paul Krugman, "Tea Parties Forever," *New York Times*, 13 April 2009; Liz Robbins, "Protesters Air Views on Government Spending at Tax Day Tea Parties Across U.S.," *New York Times*, 16 April 2009; Carr, "Cable Wars Are Killing Objectivity," *New York Times*, 19 April 2009; Chris Ariens, "CNN Reporter at Chicago Tea Party," *Ad Week*, 15 September 2009; Theda Skocpol and Vanessa Williamson, *The Tea Party and the Remaking of Republican Conservatism* (New York: Oxford University Press, 2012), 130–34; Christopher S. Parker and Matt A. Barreto, *Change They Can't Believe In: The Tea Party and Reactionary Politics in America* (Princeton, NJ: Princeton University Press, 2013), 290, 301; Julian E. Zelizer, "Tea-Partied: President Obama's Encounters with the Conservative-Industrial Complex," in *The Presidency of Barack Obama*, 11–29.

24. "Paul Volcker: The Lion Lets Loose," *Bloomberg Businessweek*, 30 December 2009; Meg Jacobs, "Obama's Fight against Global Warming," in *The Presidency of Barack Obama*, 62–77.

25. Sarah Binder and Steven S. Smith, *Politics or Principle: Filibustering in the United States Senate* (Washington, DC: Brookings, 2001).

26. Thomas E. Mann and Norman Ornstein, *It's Even Worse Than It Looks: How the American Constitutional System Collided with the New Politics of Extremism* (New York: Basic Books, 2012), 92.

27. Reid Pillifant, "Architect of Obama's Health Care Plan Fears a 'Political' Decision by the Supreme Court, says Romney's Lying," *Politico*, 16 November 2011; Pam Belluck, "Massachusetts Legislation on Insurance Becomes Law," *New York Times*, 13 April 2006.

28. Avik Roy, "The Tortuous History of Conservatives and the Individual Mandate," *Forbes*, 7 February 2012.

29. Mitt Romney, "Mr. President, What's the Rush?" *USA Today*, 30 July 2009.

30. O. Kay Henderson, "Grassley, Conlin Quarrel Over Health Care Mandate," *Radio Iowa*, 10 September 2010.

31. Carl Hulse and Adam Nagourney, "McConnell Strategy Shuns Bipartisanship," *New York Times*, 16 March 2010.

32. Timothy Jost, "Examining the House Republican ACA Repeal and Replace Legislation," *Health Affairs*, 7 March 2017.

33. Joan Walsh, "GOP's Latest Shutdown Delusion," *Salon.com*, 7 October 2013.

34. Peter Grier, "Three Reasons Why Sarah Palin Joined Fox News," *Christian Science Monitor*, 12 January 2010.

35. Angie Drobnic Holan, "Joe Wilson of South Carolina Said Obama Lied, But He Didn't," *Politifact*, 9 September 2009; Ben Smith, "Wilson Breaks $1 Million," *Politico*, 12 September 2009.

36. Carl Hulse and Robert Pear, "Sweeping Health Care Overhaul Passes the House," *New York Times*, 8 November 2009; Robert Pear, "Senate Approves Health Care Bill in Party-Line Vote," *New York Times*, 25 December 2009.

37. Peter Baker and Carl Hulse, "Off Script, Obama and the G.O.P. Vent Politely," *New York Times*, 29 January 2010.

38. Sheryl Gay Stolberg and Robert Pear, "Obama Signs Health Care Overhaul into Law, With a Flourish," *New York Times*, 23 March 2010.

39. Brady Dennis, "Congress Passes Financial Reform Bill," *Washington Post*, 16 July 2010.

40. Arthur S. Brisbane, "Who Is Occupy Wall Street?" *New York Times*, 13 November 2011; Paul Sweeney, "Economist Who Inspired Occupy Movement Seeks to Tackle Inequality," *Irish Times*, 28 March 2014; Jaime Lalinde, Rebecca Sacks, Mark Guidacci, Elizabeth Nichols, and Max Chafin, "Revolution Number 99," *Vanity Fair*, 10 January 2012; Christopher Hayes, *Twilight of the Elites: America After Meritocracy* (New York: Crown, 2012), 230–32.

41. Andrew Ross Sorkin, "Occupy Wall Street: A Frenzy That Fizzled," *New York Times*, 18 September 2012; "What They Don't Want to Talk About," *New York Times*, 15 January 2012.

42. Thomas Piketty, *Capital in the Twenty-First Century* (Cambridge, MA: Belknap, 2014); Jeet Heer, "How to Succeed in Business Without Really Trying," *Toronto Globe and Mail*, 3 May 2014.

43. Jonathan Weisman and Laura Meckler, "Obama Concedes Shellacking," *Wall Street Journal*, 4 November 2010.

44. Tim Alberta, "John Boehner Unchained," *Politico Magazine* (November/December 2017); Markus Prior, *Post-Broadcast Democracy: How Media Choice Increases Inequality in Political Involvement and Polarizes Elections* (New York: Cambridge University Press, 2007).

45. Alberta, "John Boehner Unchained."

46. William Branigin, "Obama Reflects on 'Shellacking' in Midterm Elections," *Washington Post*, 3 November 2010; Dan Balz and William Branigin, "After Midterm Wins, GOP Vows to Block Obama's Agenda," *Washington Post*, 3 November 2010.

47. Mann and Ornstein, *It's Even Worse Than It Looks*, 8–10; Eric Cantor, Paul Ryan, and Kevin McCarthy, *Young Guns: A New Generation of Conservative Leaders* (New York: Simon & Schuster, 2010).

48. Mann and Ornstein, *It's Even Worse Than It Looks*, 5.

49. Brady Dennis, Alec MacGillis, and Lori Montgomery, "Origins of the Debt Showdown," *Washington Post*, 6 August 2011; Steve Benen, "Boehner Wants Congress to Tackle Debt Limit As 'Adults,'" *Washington Monthly*, 19 November 2010.

50. Cited in Craig Harrington and Alex Morash, "Will Fox News Finally Take the Debt Ceiling Seriously?" *Media Matters*, 20 March 2017.

51. Cited in Thomas M. DeFrank, "GOP Will Nix Bipartisan 'Gang of Six' Debt Proposal Because Obama Took Credit for It, Source Says," *New York Daily News*, 20 July 2011; Michael Kinsley, "When the Speaker Wouldn't Speak," *Los Angeles Times*, 29 July 2011; Alan Silverleib and Tom Cohen, "Obama Signs Debt Ceiling Bill, Ends Crisis," CNN.com, 2 August 2011; Zelizer, "Tea-Partied."

52. Thomas Byrne Edsall, *The Age of Austerity: How Scarcity Will Remake American Politics* (New York: Doubleday, 2012), 5; Mann and Ornstein, *It's Even Worse Than It Looks*, 4; Brad Plumer, "GAO: Debt Ceiling Fight Cost Taxpayers At Least $1.3 Billion," *Washington Post*, 23 July 2012; Brady Dennis, Alec MacGillis, and Lori Montgomery, "Origins of the Debt Showdown," *Washington Post*, 6 August 2011.

53. Konrad Yakabuski, "For Romney, A Delicate Piece of Political Surgery," *Toronto Globe and Mail*, 13 May 2011.

54. Jeff Zeleny, "Justices, By 5–4, Uphold Health Care Law," *New York Times*, 29 June 2012.

55. Peter Lattman and Annie Lowrey, "As Romney Campaign Advances, Private Equity Becomes Part of the Debate," *New York Times*, 11 January 2012; Michael Barbaro, "Obama Ad Focuses on Workers Who Lost Jobs When a Mill Acquired By Bain Capital Closed," *New York Times*, 15 May 2012; Michael D. Shear and Michael Barbaro, "In Video Clip, Romney Calls 47 percent 'Dependent' and Feeling Entitled," *New York Times*, 18 September 2012; Maureen Dowd, "Let Them Eat Crab Cake," *New York Times*, 19 September 2012; E. J. Dionne Jr., *Why The Right Went Wrong: Conservatism—From Goldwater to Trump and Beyond* (New York: Simon & Shuster, 2016), 374–76.

56. Paul Krugman, "Truth About Jobs," *New York Times*, 8 October 2012; Eric Benson, "Unskewed Polls Founder Takes Stock of Obama's Win," *New York Magazine*, 9 November 2012.

57. Will Oremus, "The Five Stages of Fox News Grief," *Slate*, 7 November 2012; Chris Ariens, "Here's What Time the Networks Called the 2012 Election," *TV Newser*, 5 November 2016; Elspeth Reeve, "The Whole Romney Ticket Believed in Unskewed Polls?" *The Atlantic*, 8 November 2012.

58 "The Success of the Voter Fraud Myth," *New York Times*, 19 September 2016; Aaron Blake, "Republicans Keep Admitting That Voter ID Helps Them Win, For Some Reason," *Washington Post*, 7 April 2016.

59 David Stout, "House Votes to Renew Voting Rights Act," *New York Times*, 13 July 2006; Carl Hulse, "By a Vote of 98–0, Senate Approves 25 Year Extension of Voting Rights Act," *New York Times*, 21 July 2006; Ari Berman, *Give Us the Ballot: The Modern Struggle for Voting Rights in America* (New York: Farrar, Straus and Giroux, 2015), 273–88; Michael Waldman, *The Fight to Vote* (New York: Simon & Schuster, 2017): 230–33; Ed Kilgore, "Throwing Away the Umbrella," *Washington Monthly*, 25 June 2013; Ari Berman, "Welcome to the First Presidential Election Since Voting Rights Act Gutted," *Rolling Stone*, 23 June 2016.

Chapter 15: THE TRUMP EFFECT

1. Alessandra Stanley, "In Debate's Dance, Romney Has More Missteps," *New York Times*, 17 October 2012.

2. Gail Collins, "Counting Benghazi Blessings," *New York Times*, 27 November 2014.

3. Jennifer Steinhauer and Michael S. Schmidt, "Benghazi Panel's Leader Under Fire As He Prepares to Face Hillary Clinton," *New York Times*, 21 October 2015.

4. Peter Baker, "After Leaks, Obama Leads Wide Effort at Damage Control," *New York Times*, 29 June 2013.

5. Patrick Graham, "Islamic State: Disease or Cure?" *Toronto Globe and Mail*, 13 December 2014.

6. Tom LoBianco, "Obama: ISIS Is Not Growing, But Not 'Decapitated,'" *CNN.com*, 13 November 2015; Maura Judkis and Griff White, "String of Paris Terrorist Attacks Leaves Over 120 Dead," *Washington Post*, 13 November 2015.

7. "Why Immigration Reform Died in Congress," *NBC News*, 1 July 2014; Eduardo Porter, "Perils in Philosophy of Austerity in the U.S.," *New York Times*, 31 October 2013; Jonathan Weisman and Ashley Parker, "Shutdown Is Over," *New York Times*, 17 October 2013; "Political Polarization in the American Public," *Pew Research Center*, 12 June 2014.

8. Libby Nelson, "Republicans Now Have Historic Majorities in State Legislatures. That's a Really Big Deal," *Vox*, 6 November 2014; David Byler, "The Other GOP Wave: State Legislatures," *RealClearPolitics*, 11 November 2014; Reid Wilson, "Republican Sweep Extends to State Level," *Washington Post*, 5 November 2014; Philip Bump, "David Brat Just Beat Eric Cantor. Who Is He?" *Washington Post*, 10 June 2014.

9. "Clinton Prepares for Benghazi Showdown with Republicans," *Time*, 21 October 2015.

10. Peter Baker and Michael D. Shear, "Obama to Put 'Everything I've Got' into Gun Control," *New York Times*, 16 January 2013.

11. Transcript, *Washington Post*, 21 December 2012; "States Lead the Way in Extending Open Carry Laws," *Guardian*, 15 January 2016; Emily Swanson, "Gun Control Laws: After Sandy Hook, Poll Finds Bump in Support for Greater Restrictions," *Huffington Post*, 16 December 2012.

12. "Zimmerman Is Acquitted in Trayvon Martin Shooting," *New York Times*, 13 July 2013; Maggie Clark, "Zimmerman Verdict Renews Focus on 'Stand Your Ground' Laws," *USA Today*, 15 July 2013.

13. Al Baker, J. David Goodman, and Benjamin Mueller, "Beyond the Chokehold: The Path to Eric Martin's Death," *New York Times*, 14 June 2015; Emily Brown, "Timeline: Michael Brown Shooting," *USA Today*, 14 August 2014.

14. Keeanga-Yamahtta Taylor, *From #BlackLivesMatter to Black Liberation* (New York: Haymarket Books, 2016); "Ferguson: Burned Buildings, 61 Arrests," *Los Angeles Times*, 25 November 2014; Amanda Terkel, "Police Officer Caught on Video Calling Michael Brown Protesters 'F***ing Animals,'" *Huffington Post*, 13 August 2014; Justine Hofherr, "Cop Who Told Protesters 'I will F***ing Kill You' 'Suspended Indefinitely,'" *Boston Globe*, 20 August 2014.

15. Emma G. Fitzsimmons, "12-Year-Old Boy Dies After Police in Cleveland Shoot Him," *New York Times*, 23 November 2014; Timothy Williams and Mitch Smith, "Cleveland Officer Will Not Face Charges in Tamir Rice Shooting Death," *New York Times*, 28 December 2015; Mitch Smith, "Tamir Rice's Family to Receive $6 Million from Cleveland," *New York Times*, 25 April 2016.

16. "Oklahoma Man Eric Harris Fatally Shot by Deputy Who Meant to Fire Taser," *NBC News*, 12 April 2015.

17. Michael S. Schmidt and Matt Apuzzo, "South Carolina Officer Is Charged with Murder of Walter Scott," *New York Times*, 7 April 2015.

18. Alex Sundby, "Video Shows Key Part of Freddie Gray Ride," *CBS News*, 20 May 2015.

19. Scott Daugherty, "Police Fatally Shot Man in Portsmouth, Handcuffed Him," *Virginian-Pilot*, 25 August 2015.

20. Kevin Rector, "Charges Dropped, Freddie Gray Case Concludes with Zero Convic-

tions Against Officers," *Baltimore Sun*, 27 July 2016; Ralph Ellis, Christopher Lett, and Sara Sidner, "Ex-Oklahoma Deputy Robert Bates Guilty of Killing Unarmed Suspect," *CNN*, 28 April 2016; Alex Johnson, "Cop Fired After Indictment in Killing of Virginia Teen William Chapman," *NBC News*, 3 September 2015; Alan Blinder, "Ex-Officer Who Shot Walter Scott Pleads Guilty in Charleston," *New York Times*, 2 May 2017.

21. Jay Caspian Kang, "Our Demand Is Simple: Stop Killing Us," *New York Times Magazine*, 4 May 2015.

22. Jessica Hersher, "What Happened When Dylann Roof Asked Google for Information About Race?" *NPR*, 10 January 2007; Aaron Morrison, "The Google Search That Launched Dylann Roof's Journey from Casual Racist to Mass Murderer," *Mic*, https://mic.com/articles/164193/dylann-roof-how-to-make-a-racist-radicalization-white-nationalism#.36zJnHI0k; Anti-Defamation League, "With Hate in Their Hearts: The State of White Supremacy in the United States," July 2015.

23. David A. Graham, "What Does the Planned Parenthood Video Show?" *The Atlantic*, 15 July 2015; "Activist Behind Anti–Planned Parenthood Videos Turns Himself In," *Washington Post*, 4 February 2016.

24. Alan Rappeport, "Questions on Speeches to Goldman Sachs Vex Hillary Clinton," *New York Times*, 4 February 2016; Charles M. Blow, "Clinton's Specter of Illegitimacy," *New York Times*, 24 October 2016.

25. David Weigel, "Why So Many Sanders Supporters Don't Want to Be Democrats," *Washington Post*, 25 May 2016.

26. Tessa Stuart, "Donald Trump's 13 Biggest Business Failures," *Rolling Stone*, 14 March 2016.

27. Michael Kranish and Marc Fisher, "The Inside Story of How 'The Apprentice' Rescued Donald Trump," *Fortune*, 8 September 2016; Michael Kranish, "A Fierce Will to Win Pushed Donald Trump to the Top," *Washington Post*, 19 January 2017.

28. Ashley Parker and Steve Eder, "Inside the Six Weeks Donald Trump was a Nonstop 'Birther,'" *New York Times*, 2 July 2016; Michael D. Shear, "Obama Releases Long-Form Birth Certificate," *New York Times*, 27 April 2011.

29. http://www.trumptwitterarchive.com/.

30. Michael Barbaro, "Donald Trump Clung to 'Birther' Lie for Years, and Still Isn't Apologetic," *New York Times*, 16 September 2016; Gregory Krieg, "14 of Trump's Most Outrageous 'Birther' Claims—Half From After 2011," *CNN*, 16 September 2016.

31. "Donald Trump's Announcement Speech," *Time*, 16 July 2015.

32. David A. Graham, "What the Press Got Right About Trump's Candidacy," *The Atlantic*, 16 June 2016.

33. Ben Schreckinger, "Trump Rallies Get Rough," *Politico*, 24 November 2015; Ben Mathis-Lilley, "A Continually Growing List of Violent Incidents at Trump Events," *Slate*, 25 April 2016.

34. Eric Alterman, "How False Equivalence Is Distorting the 2016 Election Coverage," *The Nation*, 20 June 2016; Derek Thompson, "The 'Trump Effect' on Cable News," *The Atlantic*, 17 June 2016.

35. Eric Bradner, "Trump Returns to 'Lyin' Ted' Moniker," *CNN*, 20 April 2016; Paul Solotaroff, "Trump Seriously: On the Trail With the GOP's Tough Guy," *Rolling Stone*, 9 September 2015; Gregory Krieg, "Trump Likens Carson's 'Pathology' to That of a Child Molester," *CNN*, 12 November 2015; Alexandra Jaffe, "Donald Trump Has 'Small Hands,' Marco Rubio Says," *NBC News*, 29 February 2016; Eliza Collins, "Les Moonves: Trump's Run is 'Damn Good for CBS," *Politico*, 29 February 2016; E. J. Dionne Jr., *Why The Right Went Wrong: Conservatism—From Goldwater to Trump and Beyond* (New York: Simon & Shuster, 2016), 434–39.

36. Ben Schreckinger, "Trump Taunts Rivals and Predicts a Quick End to GOP Race," *Politico*, 24 February 2016.

37. J. C. Derrick, "Trump Improves in New World Survey," *World*, 25 August 2016; Justin McCarthy, "Record High 60 percent of Americans Support Same Sex Marriage," *Gallup News*, 19 May 2015. More generally, see John Fea, *Believe Me: The Evangelical Road to Donald Trump* (Grand Rapids, MI: Eerdmans, 2017).

38. Shushannah Walshe and Alexander Mallin, "All But One Former GOP Nominee to Skip Republican National Convention," *ABC News*, 5 May 2016; Tessa Stuart, "27 Best Republican Excuses for Skipping Trump's RNC," *Rolling Stone*, 18 July 2016.

39. Stephen Stromberg, "The GOP's Despicable First Night of the Republican National Convention," *Washington Post*, 19 July 2016; Sam Frizell, "Chris Christie Fills New Convention Role: Donald Trump's Attack Dog," *Politico*, 19 July 2016.

40. "Full Text: Donald Trump 2016 RNC Draft Speech Transcript," *Politico*, 21 July 2016.

41. Michael M. Grymbaum, "Television Networks Struggle to Provide Equal Airtime in Era of Trump," *New York Times*, 30 May 2016.

42. Philip Bump, "Assessing a Clinton Argument that the Media Helped Elect Trump," *Washington Post*, 12 September 2017; Michael Crowley, "Trump Urges Russia to Hack Clinton's Email," *Politico*, 27 July 2016.

43. Margaret Sullivan, "Facebook's Role in Trump's Win is Clear. No Matter What Mark Zuckerburg Says," *Washington Post*, 7 September 2017; Natasha Bertrand, "Shuttered Facebook Group That Organized Anti-Clinton, Anti-Immigrant Rallies Across Texas Was Linked to Russia," *Business Insider*, 13 September 2017; Maya Kosoff, "Mark Zuckerburg's Russia Problem is Bigger Than Facebook," *Vanity Fair*, 14 September 2017.

44. Jennifer Agiesta, "Post-Convention Poll: Clinton Retakes Lead Over Trump," *CNN*, 2 August 2016; Shannon Stapleton, "Hillary Clinton Leads by a Dozen in Latest August Poll," *Newsweek*, 23 August 2016; Stephen Shepard, "Pollsters: Trump Approaching Zero Hour," *Politico*, 17 August 2016; Nick Bryant, "US Election: Has Trump Already Blown It?" *BBC News*, 19 August 2016; Jim Rutenburg and James Poniewozik, "Can the Media Recover From This Election?" *New York Times*, 8 November 2016.

45. Jonathan Martin, Jim Rutenberg, and Maggie Haberman, "Donald Trump Appoints Media Firebrand to Run Campaign," *New York Times*, 17 August 2016.

46. Joseph Bernstein, "Alt-White: How the Breitbart Machine Laundered Racist Hate," *Buzzfeed*, 5 October 2017; Sarah Posner, "How Donald Trump's New Campaign Chief Created an Online Haven for White Supremacists," *Mother Jones*, 22 August 2016; Martin, Rutenberg, and Haberman, "Donald Trump Appoints Media Firebrand."

47. Chris Kahn, "Clinton Leads Trump By 5 in Reuters/Ipsos Poll," *Reuters*, 26 August 2016; "Hillary Clinton's Alt-Right Speech, Annotated," *Washington Post*, 25 August 2016; Alan Rappeport, "Hillary Clinton Denounces the 'Alt-Right,' and the Alt-Right is Thrilled," *New York Times*, 26 August 2016.

48. Amy Chozick, "Hillary Clinton Calls Many Trump Backers 'Deplorables,' and G.O.P. Pounces," *New York Times*, 10 September 2016. On the problems in the Clinton campaign, see Jonathan Allen and Amie Parnes, *Shattered: Inside Hillary Clinton's Doomed Campaign* (New York: Crown, 2017); Amy Chozick, *Chasing Hillary: Ten Years, Two Presidential Campaigns, and One Intact Glass Ceiling* (New York: Harper, 2018).

49. Hannah Hartig, John Lapinski, and Stephanie Psyllos, "Clinton Holds Steady Against Trump as Campaign Enters Final Weeks: Poll," *NBC News*, 6 September 2016; "Transcript: Donald Trump's Taped Comments About Women," *New York Times*, 8 October 2016.

50. Ellen Nakashima, "U.S. Government Officially Accuses Russia of Hacking Campaign to Interfere with Elections," *Washington Post*, 7 October 2016.

51. David A. Fahrenthold, "Trump Recorded Having Extremely Lewd Conversation About Women in 2005," *Washington Post*, 8 October 2016; Tina Nguyen, "Report: Reince Preibus Urged Trump to Drop Out Over *Access Hollywood* Tape," *Vanity Fair*, 8 December 2016; Sarah Pulliam Bailey, "'Still the Best Candidate': Some Evangelicals Still Back Trump Despite Lewd Video," *Washington Post*, 8 October 2016; Jennifer Ageista, "Clinton Leads By 5 Heading Into Final Two Weeks," *CNN*, 25 October 2016.

52. Alex Lubben, "This One Insane Day Changed the Course of U.S. Politics Forever," *Vice News*, 23 June 2017; Nate Silver, "The Comey Letter Probably Cost Clinton the Election," *FiveThirtyEight*, 3 May 2017.

53. "Election Night Live: Media's Campaignpalooza Comes Down to a Wild End," *Advertising Age*, 8 November 2016.

54. Marisa Guthrie, "Inside Fox News' Studio as an 'Unreal, Surreal' Election Night Played Out," *Hollywood Reporter*, 9 November 2016; John McCormick, "The Election Came Down to 77,744 Votes in Pennsylvania, Wisconsin and Michigan," *Weekly Standard*, 10 November 2016.

55. Transcript, Donald Trump's Victory Speech, *CNN*, 9 November 2016.

Epilogue

1. David Jackson and Doug Stanglin, "Trump Is Now President: 'The Forgotten . . . Will Be Forgotten No Longer,'" *USA Today*, 20 January 2017; Peter Baker, "Trump Abandons Trans-Pacific Partnership, Obama's Signature Trade Deal," *New York Times*, 23 January 2017; Russell Berman, "What's In—And Out—of the Final Republican Tax Bill," *The Atlantic*, 17 December 2017; Dylan Scott and Alvin Ching, "The Republican Tax Bill Will Exacerbate Economic Inequality in America," *Vox*, 4 December 2017.

2. Shawn Musgrave and Patrick Nussbaum, "Trump Thrives in Areas That Lack Traditional News Outlets," *Politico*, 4 April 2018.

3. Sarah Frostenson, "The Women's Marches May Have Been the Largest Demonstration in US History," *Vox*, 31 January 2017; Seema Mehta, "Here's Where All Those Pink Hats at the Women's March Originated," *Los Angeles Times*, 21 January 2017; Christen A. Johnson and KT Hawbaker, "#MeToo: A Timeline of Events," *Chicago Tribune*, 19 March 2018; "The Silence Breakers," *Time*, 7 December 2017.

4. Steve Almasy and Darran Simon, "A Timeline of President Trump's Travel Bans," *CNN*, 30 March 2017; Andy Newman, "Highlights: Reaction to Trump's Travel Ban," *New York Times*, 29 January 2017; Amy B. Wang, "Trump Lashes Out at 'So-Called Judge' Who Temporarily Blocked Travel Ban," *Washington Post*, 4 February 2017; Rebecca Savransky, "Appeals Court Cites Trump Tweets in Ruling Against Travel Ban," *The Hill*, 12 June 2017.

5. Gregory Krieg, "How Donald Trump's Rhetoric Translates to Government Paper," *CNN*, 25 January 2017; Jill Colvin, "Trump Suggests Paying for US Border Wall with Pentagon Funds," *Stars and Stripes*, 27 March 2018.

6. Yeganeh Torbati, "U.S. Deportations Down in 2017 but Immigration Arrests Up," *Reuters*, 5 December 2017; Adam Edelman, "Trump Ends DACA Program, No New Applications Accepted," *NBC News*, 5 September 2017.

7. Joe Heim, "Recounting a Day of Rage, Hate, Violence and Death," *Washington Post*, 14 August 2017; Rosie Gray, "Trump Defends White-Nationalist Protesters: 'Some Very Fine People on Both Sides,'" *The Atlantic*, 15 August 2017.

8. Greg Toppo, "2017 is the Deadliest Year for Mass Killings in at Least a Decade," *USA Today*, 6 November 2017; Saeed Ahmed, "2 of the 5 Deadliest Mass Shoot-

ings in Modern US History Happened in the Last 35 Days," *CNN*, 6 November 2017; Elizabeth Chuck, Alex Johnson, and Corky Siemaszko, "17 Killed in Mass Shooting at High School in Parkland, Florida," *NBC News*, 14 February 2018; Emily Witt, "How the Survivors of Parkland Began the Never Again Movement," *The New Yorker*, 19 February 2018; Dana R. Fisher, "Here's Who Actually Attended the March for Our Lives," *Washington Post*, 28 March 2018.

9. Michael D. Shear and Matt Apuzzo, "F.B.I. Director James Comey Is Fired by Trump," *New York Times*, 9 May 2017; James Griffiths, "Trump Said He Considered 'This Russia Thing' Before Firing FBI Director Comey," *CNN*, 12 May 2017; Andrew Prokop, "All of Robert Mueller's Indictments and Plea Deals in the Russia Investigation So Far," *Vox*, 1 March 2018; Matt Apuzzo and Adam Goldman, "Andrew McCabe, a Target of Trump's F.B.I. Scorn, Is Fired Over Candor Questions," *New York Times*, 16 March 2018.

10. Kyle Cheney, "'Off the Rails': House Russia Probe Hits New Low," *Politico*, 3 March 2018; Erin Kelly, "Russia Probe: House Intel Republicans End Investigation, Find 'No Evidence' of Collusion," *USA Today*, 12 March 2018.

11. Jennifer Epstein, "Trump's Approval Nudges Higher Despite Turmoil, Two Polls Find," *Bloomberg*, 27 March 2018; Andrew Marantz, "How 'Fox and Friends' Rewrites Trump's Reality," *The New Yorker*, 15 January 2018; Callum Borchers, "Sean Hannity Personifies Trump's TV Presidency," *Washington Post*, 2 February 2018; Maxwell Tani and Asawin Suebsaeng, "Trump 'Cherishes' Lou Dobbs So Much He Puts Him on Speakerphone for Oval Office Meetings," *Daily Beast*, 2 April 2018; Kevin Liptak and Dan Merica, "Kudlow to Become Trump's Next Top Economic Adviser," *CNN*, 15 March 2018; Joe Concha, "Report: Fox News Anchor Heather Nauert to Join State Department," *The Hill*, 4 March 2017; Margaret Harding McGill and John Hendel, "How Trump's FCC Aided Sinclair's Expansion," *Mother Jones*, 6 August 2017; Brian Stelter, "Sinclair's New Media-Bashing Promos Rankle Local Anchors," *CNN*, 7 March 2018; Hadas Gold, "Sinclair Increases 'Must-Run' Boris Epshteyn Segments," *Politico*, 11 July 2017; Timothy Burke, "How America's Largest Local TV Owner Turned Its News Anchors Into Soldiers in Trump's War on the Media," *Deadspin*, 31 March 2018.

INDEX